高等院校立体化创新系列教材·外国语言文学及文化系列

美国文学史
及作品选读

A History of American Literature with Selected Readings

主　编　杜丽霞
副 主 编　石艳蕊
英语审校　Kenneth DeShane

西安交通大学出版社
XI'AN JIAOTONG UNIVERSITY PRESS

图书在版编目(ＣＩＰ)数据

美国文学史及作品选读：英文／杜丽霞主编.一
西安：西安交通大学出版社，2020.12(2023.8 重印)
ISBN 978－7－5693－1714－5

Ⅰ.①美… Ⅱ.①杜… Ⅲ.①英语-阅读教学-研究
生-教材②文学史-美国 Ⅳ.①H319.4：Ⅰ

中国版本图书馆 CIP 数据核字(2020)第 058615 号

书　　名	美国文学史及作品选读	
主　　编	杜丽霞	
责任编辑	李　蕊	

出版发行	西安交通大学出版社	
	(西安市兴庆南路 1 号　邮政编码 710048)	
网　　址	http://www.xjtupress.com	
电　　话	(029)82668357　82667874(市场营销中心)	
	(029)82668315(总编办)	
传　　真	(029)82668280	
印　　刷	西安五星印刷有限公司	

开　　本	710mm×1000mm　1/16	印张 23.375	字数 610 千字
版次印次	2020 年 12 月第 1 版　2023 年 8 月第 3 次印刷		
书　　号	ISBN 978－7－5693－1714－5		
定　　价	68.50 元		

如发现印装质量问题,请与本社市场营销中心联系。
订购热线:(029)82665248　(029)82667874
投稿热线:(029)82668531
读者信箱:rw_xjtu@126.com

版权所有　侵权必究

序 言

目前,国内市场上美国文学的教材资源已经比较丰富了。我们编写的这本教材,主要特点有以下几个方面:

第一,关切"追根溯源",从源头上审视美国文学。本教材第一章关于殖民地时代的文学介绍,不仅包含美国土著的诗歌作品,还有北方清教徒的作品及南方殖民先驱的作品。了解这些作品及其创作的时代背景,有利于学生从根源上认识美国的南北差异,了解南北冲突产生的原因。

第二,注重"文化土壤",帮助读者了解培育美国文学之"苗"的"土壤"。本教材对每一章涉及的历史背景和文学运动的介绍都比较细致,在必要的章节还对重要的哲学家和哲学思想予以介绍,有助于学生理解文学与哲学、文学与政治、美国文学与世界文学等多维度的关联关系。

第三,体现"作家作品多元性",帮助读者从更宽广的视角了解美国文学。本教材收录的作品大多来自美国主流作家,也有少数来自族裔作家,如非洲裔作家、犹太族作家、华裔作家等;收录的作品有反映北部风貌的,也有代表南部传统的;收录的作品体裁有小说、诗歌、散文,还有被其他教材忽视的戏剧,甚至有超越惯常意义上纯文学类型的作品,如托马斯·潘恩呼吁美国独立的《常识》、托马斯·杰斐逊的《独立宣言》和索尔·贝娄的诺贝尔文学奖获奖致辞。

第四,展示"不拘一格性",注重作家、作品的自身内部呼应。为了能让作品

1

更好地替作家"发言",有些作家的名目下收录了多部作品,或从一个作品里节选了多章内容。

第五,强调"生活启发性",让文学阅读成为学生获取生活智慧的有效途径。有些人认为,文学属于阳春白雪,距离现实生活较远。其实,无论中外古今,文学杰作探讨的内容无外乎人与人、人与自然、人与社会、人与自身的关系。作为源于生活又高于生活的思想结晶,文学能给人以生活的启迪和智慧,这才是文学最伟大、最恒久的魅力。

本教材适用于高校英语专业美国文学课程,同时也适合具有大学英语四级以上水平的英语文学爱好者阅读。

由于编者水平有限,时间也比较仓促,本教材难免存在不足,敬请批评指正,不胜感激。

编 者

2020 年 5 月 19 日

致 谢

本教材从最初构思到最后成书,得到了许多同仁的帮助。

首先,我要感谢西安交通大学外国语学院教材专项资金的鼎力支持,让我在总结了多年美国文学教学经验的基础上,实现了按照自己的教学规划编写和出版教材的夙愿。

其次,我要感谢与我们先后合作授课的美国外教们,尤其是贾森·巴里(Jason Barry)、肯尼思·德沙恩(Kenneth DeShane)、温蒂·巴尚特(Wendy Bashant)和克里斯滕·米伦(Kristen Mullen)。他们深厚的文学素养和独到的视角不仅令西安交通大学英语系的学子们受益匪浅,也给我们留下了永久的、无价的精神食粮和财富。谢谢上述几位外教给予的专家级的建议和无私的帮助。

我还要感谢同事和亲友的勉励和支持,感谢西安交通大学出版社的各位编辑及校对人员耐心细致的工作。你们的奉献令我怀有无限的感激。

而最为重要的感谢,要献给本教材内收录节选其作品的作家们和在编写此教材过程中我所使用的参考书目的作者们。没有这些作家们的卓越杰作,没有这些作者的前期成果资料,这本教材是不可能顺利出版的。由于无法联系到所有作者,我无法单独表示感谢。如果原作者看到此教材,请联系我,容我深表谢忱。

以下是本教材在编写过程中主要参考的一些图书：

Baym, Nina, et al. *The Norton Anthology of American Literature*. 5th ed. W. W. Norton & Company, Inc., 1998.

Gilbert, Sandra M., and Susan Gubar. *The Norton Anthology of Literature by Women: The Tradition in English*. W. W. Norton & Company, Inc., 1985.

Kearns, George, et al. *Macmillan Literature Series: American Literature*. Macmillan Publishing Company, 1984.

Glencoe Literature—The Reader's Choice: American Literature. Florida Edition, The McGraw-Hill Companies, 2003.

Bohner, Charles H. *Classic Short Fiction*. Prentice-Hall, 1986.

New, W. H. *Modern Stories in English*. 3rd ed. Copp Clark Pitman Ltd., 1991.

Allison, Alexander W., et al. *The Norton Anthology of Poetry*. 3rd ed. W. W. Norton & Company, Inc., 1983.

Guerin, Wilfred L., et al. *A Handbook of Critical Approaches to Literature*. 5th ed. Oxford University Press, 2005.

Toming, A History of American Literature. Yilin Press, 2002.

Baldick, Chris. *Oxford Concise Dictionary of Literary Terms*. Shanghai Foreign Language Education Press, 2000.

Hu, Yintong, et al. *American Literature*. Foreign Language Teaching and Research Press, 2017.

杜丽霞

2020 年 5 月 20 日

Contents

Part I

From the Beginning to the Revolution

(1492 – 1783)

Part Ⅱ

From the Revolution to the Civil War

(1783 – 1861)

Part Ⅲ

From the Civil War to World War Ⅰ

(1861 – 1914)

Part Ⅳ
From World War Ⅰ to World War Ⅱ
(1914 – 1945)

Part Ⅴ

American Literature since World War Ⅱ

(1945 –)

Part I

From the Beginning to the Revolution

(1492–1783)

Chapter 1

American Colonialism

Historical Background

American Literature begins with American experiences. Before we look at early American literature, it is necessary for us to examine the roots of American history.

The American continent used to be called the New World, because it was not discovered until the late 15th century, when in 1492, Christopher Columbus and his fleet sponsored by the Spanish Crown arrived at the island of San Salvador, in the modern day Bahamas, on October 12 (now celebrated as Columbus Day[①]). Because Columbus and his associates thought they had landed in the "Indies," or the Far East, they called the natives Indians. About 1502, the Italian explorer Amerigo Vespucci demonstrated to Europeans that the New World was not Asia's eastern outskirts as initially thought from Columbus' voyages, but instead a separate continent. Thus the New World has been named after him as "America."

Columbus's discovery of the American continent marked the start of the era of European exploration and settlement in the Americas. From the beginning of the 16th century, European settlers gradually came to North America. They were Spanish, French, Dutch, Swedish, German, Italian, Portuguese, and English. In the 17th century, the majority of colonists were English.

The first English colony established in today's United States was Jamestown, Virginia in 1607. In 1620, the ship *Mayflower* carried about one hundred Puritan Pilgrims to Plymouth, Massachusetts. A highly noteworthy thing is that these two colonies were established and inhabited by colonists who had come with their distinct

---

① Columbus Day: Currently, some Americans choose NOT to call it Columbus Day. Instead, they call it Indigenous People's Day, or Native's Day, or Native Americans' Day.

aspirations in mind. This, to a considerable degree, foreshadowed and contributed to the subsequent sharp differences, even conflicts, between the Northern and the Southern parts of the United States.

Experience is the key to early American Literature. American Indians, European explorers, frontier wives, Puritan Pilgrims and ministers in the North, and plantation owners in the South — were all the creators of the first American Literature.

▶ Questions for Consideration and Discussion

1. What do you think "American literature" means? In this sense, what does a national literature mean? To put it in another way, what do you think defines a nation's national literature?
2. Besides geographical names, what do the American North and the American South suggest in your mind? Exchange your ideas with your discussion partner.

American Indians

Before Columbus discovered the New World, the American Indians had been native to the land for thousands of years. According to modern archaeology and anthropology, they were descendants of Asians who crossed the land-bridge, today's Bering Strait, to America some 25,000 years ago. Columbus called the indigenous people Indians. However, no one name would adequately describe the variety of cultures that flourished from one end of the continent to the other. Today, ethnographers call them "Native Americans," and a lot of people call them "American Indians." Some native peoples refer to themselves as "American Indians," too.

Generation after generation these Native Americans had told stories, sung songs, and recited tales that embodied their past and told of their close relationship with the natural world. Many stories were about their life experiences such as planting, fishing, hunting, birth and death. Their mythologies, songs, and ritual chants were not written down. Most of these works of literature survived through oral tradition, each generation transmitting its literature to its young people by word of mouth. The result is a literature that is timeless, a literature created by no one author. It is a literature made by its people.

American Indian stories consist of origin stories, trickster tales, and historical narratives. Origin stories are about the origin of the earth. In one popular origin story, a turtle holds up the world. In another Cheyenne version, the creator Maheo has four chances to fashion the world from a watery universe. He sends four water birds diving to try to bring up earth from the bottom. Trickster tales are humorous tales with trickster characters who are in the form of animals, such as Coyote, Raven, Blue Jay, Mink, or Rabbit. These characters are clever and can change their appearance from human to animals — they are often called "shape-shifters." They can be heroes on one occasion or buffoons on another. Historical narratives are tribal records of historical events or legendary figures. Many stories describe European colonization from Native Americans' perspectives. One example is the Yuchi tale "Creation of the Whites," which recounts the emergence of Europeans from the ocean.

    The following are a traditional Navaho song and a traditional Ojibwa song. The Navaho, an agricultural people, are a large and varied group who settled in the American Southwest, where their culture still flourishes. The Ojibwa are a group of people who lived around the Great Lakes and throughout the Great Plains.

Navaho Traditional

Listen ! Rain Approaches !

Truly in the East
The white bean
And the great corn plant
Are tied with the white lightning.
5   Listen! It approaches!
The voice of the bluebird is heard.

Truly in the East
The white bean
And the great squash
10 Are tied with the rainbow.
Listen! It approaches!
The voice of the bluebird is heard.

Ojibwa Traditional

Calling One's Own

Awake! Flower of the forest, sky-treading bird of the prairie.
Awake! Awake! Wonderful fawn-eyed One.

When you look upon me I am satisfied; as flowers that drink dew.

The breath of your mouth is the fragrance of flowers in the morning,

5   Your breath is their fragrance at evening in the moon of fading-leaf.

Do not the red streams of my veins run toward you

As forest-streams to the sun in the moon of bright nights?

When you are beside me my heart sings; a branch it is, dancing,

Dancing before the Wind spirit in the moon of strawberries.

10   When you frown upon me, beloved, my heart grows dark —

A shining river the shadows of clouds darken,

Then with your smiles comes the sun and makes to look like gold

Furrows the cold wind drew in the water's face.

Myself! Behold me! Blood of my beating heart.

15   Earth smiles — the waters smile — even the sky of clouds smiles — but I,

I lose the way of smiling when you are not near,

Awake! Awake! My beloved.

▶ Questions for Consideration and Discussion

1. Use your imagination. Suppose you live in a community that has only oral language but no written form of it. What challenges and advantages do you think there are with regard to the people's communication and the cultural transmission and inheritance?

2. What view of nature is reflected in "Listen! Rain Approaches!" and "Calling One's Own"?

3. What are American Indian trickster stories? What European trickster stories and Chinese trickster stories have you ever heard of or read? In your view, why do people like trickster stories?

The Northern Puritans

In 1620, the ship *Mayflower* that carried about one hundred pilgrims sailing from Southampton, England, dropped anchor at Plymouth, Massachusetts. They were known as "Separatists," because unlike the majority of Puritans, they saw no hope of reforming the Church of England from within. They wished to follow Calvin's model and set up "particular" churches, each one founded on a formal covenant, entered into by those who professed their faith and swore to the covenant. They wanted to purify their lives and their church of what they saw as the corruptions of English society and its state religion, the Church of England. They chose to withdraw from the Church of England and even from England itself in order to worship as they saw fit. Actually, prior to voyaging to the New World, these Separatists had settled in Holland for years. Fearing that they would eventually lose their identity as a religious community living as strangers in a foreign land, they applied to settle in the New World. Their original grant was for land in the Virginia territory, but when storms prevented them from reaching Virginia, they settled instead at Plymouth, Massachusetts. Among this group, the leading figure was William Bradford (1590 – 1657).

In 1630, another group of Puritans arrived at the Massachusetts Bay Colony under the leadership of John Winthrop (1588 – 1649). Compared with the Pilgrims, their attitude toward the Church of England was less radical: they were dissenting but non-separating. In this group were many urban people, particularly of the rising middle class. Economically, many of them were men of substance. Some had been representatives in the House of Commons, and a very few were even among the nobility. They had had all sorts of vested interests in England and no desire to leave home, its comforts, and its privileges. Yet, with the accession of Charles I in 1625 and his dissolution of Parliament in 1629, it seemed that a civil war could possibly happen. Thus, they joined the Massachusetts Bay Colony.

With regard to these two groups of Puritans, no matter what differences they might have in their attitude toward the Church of England, their basic beliefs were identical: both held with Martin Luther that no pope or bishop had a right to impose any law on a Christian soul without consent, and with John Calvin that God chose freely those He would save and those He would damn eternally. Plymouth was eventually absorbed into the Massachusetts Bay Colony in 1691.

These Puritans compared themselves to the Israelites of old, who had been given the promise of a new land. John Winthrop was said to be the Puritan Moses whose education had prepared him to fulfill the "noble design of carrying a colony of chosen people into an American wilderness." When John Winthrop addressed the immigrants to the Massachusetts Bay Colony aboard the flagship *Arbella* in 1630, he told them that the eyes of the world were on them and that they would be an example for all, a "city upon a hill."

For the Puritans, everything aimed at personal salvation and the building of a new, God-centered society; they had a passionate desire to establish a New Jerusalem life; they worked long and hard so that their farms and trading enterprises would prosper; they believed that prosperity was a sign of God's special favor. They also kept reminding themselves that their souls were the constant battlegrounds between God and Satan and that every act and thought had to be judged according to whether it truly glorified God. In America, Puritan moralism and its sense of an elect people in a covenant with God deeply shaped the national character, one way or another.

Writing was an important part of Puritan life: it was often an extension of religion. The first book published in America was the *Bay Psalm Book* (1640), a translation of the Biblical Psalms. Many Puritans kept journals to help them carefully examine their spiritual lives. They also wrote spiritual autobiographies.

Puritan writing, in other words, was practical. They wrote no fiction, nor did they even approve of reading fiction, and they wrote no plays because they disapproved of the theater. They preferred to write in plain style. Writing was not a way of showing off cleverness or learning, but a way of serving God and the community. Their writings consisted largely of journals, sermons, hymns, histories, and poems. The most well-known titles include William Bradford's *Of Plymouth Plantation* (1856), Anne Bradstreet's poetic book *The Tenth Muse Lately Sprung up in America* (1650), and Jonathan Edwards's *Sinners in the Hands of an Angry God* (1741).

William Bradford (1590 – 1657)

William Bradford is best remembered as the Governor of the Plymouth Colony and the author of *Of Plymouth Plantation*. He epitomizes the spirit of determination and self-sacrifice that is characteristic of the first "Pilgrims," a word that Bradford himself was the first to use to describe the community of believers who navigated on the *Mayflower* and settled in Plymouth, Massachusetts in 1620.

Bradford was born in Yorkshire of parents who were modestly well off. His father died when he was an infant. After his mother remarried in 1593, he was brought up by his paternal grandparents and uncles. He did not receive a university education; instead he was taught the arts of farming. When he was twelve or thirteen, he heard the sermons that changed his life. Later, despite the oppositions of uncles and grandparents, he left home and joined the small community of believers known as "Separatists."

When the Separatists took up residence in the Netherlands, Bradford joined them in 1609 and there he learned to be a weaver. Later he went into business for himself.

Before the pilgrims disembarked from the *Mayflower* to settle in Plymouth, Massachusetts, they signed the *Mayflower Compact* and decided to form a government and follow an elected leader. When the first governor died in 1621, the people chose Bradford to take his place. He was so successful that he was re-elected thirty times. In 1630 he began writing *Of Plymouth Plantation*, his history of these early Americans and their long geographical and spiritual pilgrimage.

Of Plymouth Plantation
(Excerpt)

Chapter 9　Of Their Voyage, and How They Passed the Sea; and of Their Safe Arrival at Cape Cod

September 6, 1620. These troubles being blown over, and now all being compact together in one ship, they put to sea again with a prosperous wind, which continued divers days together, which was some encouragement unto them; yet, according to the usual manner, many were afflicted with seasickness. And I may not omit here a special work of God's providence. There was a proud and very profane young man, one of the seamen, of a lusty, able body, which made him the more haughty; he would always be contemning① the poor people in their sickness and cursing them daily with grievous execrations; and did not let② to tell them that he hoped to help to cast half of them overboard before they came to their journey's end, and to make merry with what they had; and if he were by any gently reproved, he would curse and swear most bitterly. But it pleased God before they came half seas over, to smite this young man with a grievous disease, of which he died in a desperate manner, and so was himself the first that was thrown overboard. Thus his curses lighted on his own head, and it was an astonishment to all his fellows, for they noted it to be the just hand of God upon him.

　　…

Being thus arrived in a good harbor, and brought safe to land, they fell upon their knees and blessed the God of Heaven who had brought them over the vast and furious ocean, and delivered them from all the perils and miseries thereof, again to set their feet on the firm and stable earth, their proper element…

But here I cannot but stay and make a pause, and stand half amazed at this poor people's present condition; and so I think will the reader, too, when he well considers the same. Being thus passed the vast ocean, and a sea of troubles before in their preparation (as may be remembered by that which went before), they had now no friends to welcome them, nor inns to entertain or refresh their weatherbeaten bodies; no houses or much less towns to repair to,

----

① contemning: condemning.

② let: hesitate.

to seek for succor①. It is recorded in Scripture as a mercy to the Apostle and his shipwrecked company, that the barbarians showed them no small kindness in refreshing them, but these savage barbarians, when they met with them (as after will appear) were readier to fill their sides full of arrows than otherwise. And for the season it was winter, and they that know the winters of that country know them to be sharp and violent, and subject to cruel and fierce storms, dangerous to travel to known places, much more to search an unknown coast. Besides, what could they see but a hideous and desolate wilderness, full of wild beasts and wild men? And what multitudes there might be of them they knew not. Neither could they, as it were, go up to the top of Pisgah② to view from this wilderness a more goodly country to feed their hopes; for which way soever they turned their eyes (save upward to the heavens) they could have little solace or content in respect of any outward objects. For summer being done, all things stand upon them with a weather-beaten face, and the whole country, full of woods and thickets, represented a wild and savage hue. If they looked behind them, there was the mighty ocean which they had passed and was now as a main bar and gulf to separate them from all the civil parts of the world. If it be said they had a ship to succor them, it is true; but what heard they daily from the master and company? But that with speed they should look out a place (with their shallop③) where they would be, at some near distance; for the season was such as he would not stir from thence till a safe harbor was discovered by them where they would be, and he might go without danger; and that victuals consumed apace, but he must and would keep sufficient for themselves and their return. Yea, it was muttered by some that if they got not a place in time, they would turn them and their goods ashore and leave them. Let it also be considered what weak hopes of supply and succor they left behind them, that might bear up their minds in this sad condition and trials they were under; and they could not but be very small. It is true, indeed, the affections and love of their brethren at Leyden was cordial and entire towards them, but they had little power to help them or themselves; and how the case stood between them and the merchants at their coming away hath already been declared.

What could now sustain them but the Spirit of God and His grace? May not and ought not the children of these fathers rightly say: "Our fathers were Englishmen which came over this great ocean, and were ready to perish in this wilderness; but they cried unto the Lord, and He heard their voice and looked on their adversity," etc. "Let them therefore praise the Lord, because He is good; and His mercies endure forever." "Yea, let them which have been redeemed of the Lord, show how He hath delivered them from the hand of the oppressor. When they wandered in the desert wilderness out of the way, and found no city to dwell in,

---

① succor: help or aid.
② Pisgah: According to the Bible, in Deuteronomy 34: 1, from the summit of Mount Pisgah Moses viewed the Promised Land.
③ shallop: small boat.

both hungry and thirsty, their soul was overwhelmed in them. Let them confess before the Lord His loving kindness and His wonderful works before the sons of men. "

Anne Bradstreet (1612 – 1672)

Anne Bradstreet was born and educated in England. Her father was the estate manager of the Earl of Lincoln. She voyaged with her family to Massachusetts when she was 16. Her husband was later elected governor of the Massachusetts Bay Colony. In addition to caring for eight children, she composed poems on subjects from daily life which expressed her personal feeling for family life and the new world. Some of her poems were taken by her sister's husband to England and published in 1650, which was the first published poetry book by an American. Her book *The Tenth Muse Lately Sprung Up in America* (1650) shows she was influenced by English writers. Her best works explore her love for her hushand, her sadness at the death of her parents and other family members, and her straggle to accept as God's will the losses she suffered.

To My Dear and Loving Husband

If ever two were one, then surely we.
If ever man were loved by wife, then thee;
If ever wife was happy in a man,
Compare with me, ye women, if you can.
5   I prize thy love more than whole mines of gold
Or all the riches thatthe East doth hold.
My love is such that rivers cannot quench,
Norought but love from thee give recompense.
Thy love is such I can no way repay,
10   The heavens reward thee manifold, I pray.
Then while we live, in love let's sopersevere
That when we live no more, we may live ever.

Upon the Burning of Our House

In silent night when rest I took,
For sorrow near I did not look,
I waken'd was with thund'ring noise
And piteous shrieks of dreadful voice.
5   That fearful sound of "fire!" and "fire!"

Let no man know is mydesire.

I, starting up, the light did spy,
And to my God my heart did cry
To straighten me in my Distress
10   And not to leave me succourless.
Then, coming out, beheld a space
The flame consume my dwelling place.

And when I could no longer look,
I blest His name that gave and took,
15   That laid my goods now in the dust.
Yea, so it was, and so'twas just.
It was His own; it was not mine.
Far be it that I should repine.

He might of all justly bereft,
20   But yet sufficient for us left.
When by the ruins oft I past,
My sorrowing eyes aside did cast,
And here and there the places spy
Where oft I sat and long did lie:

25   Here stood that trunk, and there that chest,
There lay that store I counted best,
My pleasant things in ashes lie,
And them behold no more shall I.
Under the roof no guest shall sit,
30   Nor at thy table eat a bit.

No pleasant tale shall e'er be told,
Nor things recounted done of old.
No candle e'er shall shine in thee,
Nor bridegroom's voice e'er heard shall be.
35   In silence ever shalt thou lie.
Adieu, Adieu, all's vanity.

Then straight I 'gin my heart to chide:
And did thy wealth on earth abide?

Didst fix thy hope on mould'ring dust?
40   The arm of flesh didst make thy trust?
Raise up thy thoughts above the sky
That dunghill mists away may fly.

Thou hast a house on high erect
Fram'd by that mighty Architect,
45   With glory richly furnished
Stands permanent, though this be fled.
It's purchased and paid for too
By Him who hath enough to do.

A price so vast as is unknown
50   Yet by His gift is made thine own.
There's wealth enough; I need no more.
Farewell, my pelf; farewell, my store.
The world no longer let me love;
My hope and treasure lies above.

Jonathan Edwards (1703 – 1758)

Jonathan Edwards is one of the most important theologians and preachers in early America.

Edwards was born in Connecticut and died in New Jersey. In 1729, he succeeded his grandfather as minister in Northampton, Massachusetts. He is best known, even notorious, for his sermon *Sinners in the Hands of an Angry God*, which he preached in 1741. As a preacher, he made his people fear the power of God. Actually, in 1750 some of Northampton Puritans began to disagree with their famous minister and removed him from his post. However, it is unfair to accuse him. After all, sermons such as this had been traditional for hundreds of years. Also it is unfair to allow *Sinners in the Hands of an Angry God* totally to represent him. For instance, his "The Beauty of the World" shows him in a softer light. In "The Beauty of the World" he makes the following remarks:

There are beauties that are more palpable and explicable, and there are hidden and secret beauties. The former pleases, and we can tell why; we can explain the particular point for the agreement that renders the thing pleasing. Such are all artificial regularities; we can tell wherein the regularity lies that affects us. [The] latter sort are those beauties that delight us and we cannot tell why. Thus, we find ourselves pleased in beholding the colour of the violets, but we know not what secret regularity or harmony it is that creates that pleasure in our minds. These hidden beauties are commonly by far the greatest, because the more complex a beauty is, the more hidden is it. In this latter fact consists principally the beauty of the world, and very much in light and colours. ...Those beauties, how lovely is the green of the face of the earth in all manner of colours, in flowers, the colour of the skies, and lovely tinctures of the morning and evening.

Hence the reason why almost all men, and those that seem to be very miserable, love life, because they cannot bear to lose sight of such a beautiful and lovely world. The ideas, that every moment whilst we live have a beauty that we take no distinct notice of, brings a pleasure that, when we come to the trial, we had rather live in such pain and misery than lose.

Sinners in the Hands of an Angry God
(Excerpt)

...

Your wickedness makes you as it were heavy as lead, and to tend downwards with great weight and pressure towards hell; and if God should let you go, you would immediately sink and swiftly descend and plunge into the bottomless gulf, and your healthy constitution, and your own care and prudence, and best contrivance, and all your righteousness, would have no more influence to uphold you and keep you out of hell, than a spider's web would have to stop a falling rock.... There are the black clouds of God's wrath now hanging directly over your heads, full of the dreadful storm, and big with thunder; and were it not for the restraining hand of God, it would immediately burst forth upon you. The sovereign pleasure of God, for the present, stays His rough wind; otherwise it would come with fury, and your destruction would come like a whirlwind, and you would be like the chaff of the summer threshing floor.

The wrath of God is like great waters that are dammed for the present; they increase more and more, and rise higher and higher, till an outlet is given; and the longer the stream is stopped, the more rapid and mighty is its course, when once it is let loose. It is true, that judgment against your evil works has not been executed hitherto; the floods of God's vengeance have been withheld; but your guilt in the mean time is constantly increasing, and you are every day treasuring up more wrath; the waters are constantly rising, and waxing more and more mighty; and there is nothing but the mere pleasure of God, that holds the waters back, that are unwilling to be stopped, and press hard to go forward. If God should only withdraw His hand from the flood-gate, it would immediately fly open, and the fiery floods of the fierceness and wrath of God, would rush forth with inconceivable fury, and would come upon you with omnipotent power; and if your strength were ten thousand times greater than it is, yea, ten thousand times greater than the strength of the stoutest, sturdiest devil in hell, it would be nothing to withstand or endure it.

The bow of God's wrath is bent, and the arrow made ready on the string, and justice bends the arrow at your heart, and strains the bow, and it is nothing but the mere pleasure of God, and that of an angry God, without any promise or obligation at all, that keeps the arrow one moment from being made drunk with your blood....

The God that holds you over the pit of hell, much as one holds a spider, or some loathsome insect over the fire, abhors you, and is dreadfully provoked: His wrath towards you burns like fire; He looks upon you as worthy of nothing else, but to be cast into the fire; He is of purer eyes than to bear to have you in His sight; you are ten thousand times more abominable in His eyes, than the most hateful venomous serpent is in ours....

O sinner! Consider the fearful danger you are in: it is a great furnace of wrath, a wide and bottomless pit, full of the fire of wrath, that you are held over in the hand of that God, whose wrath is provoked and incensed as much against you, as against many of the damned in hell. You hang by a slender thread, with the flames of divine wrath flashing about it, and ready every moment to singe it, and burn it asunder; and you have no interest in any Mediator, and nothing to lay hold of to save yourself, nothing to keep off the flames of wrath, nothing of your own, nothing that you ever have done, nothing that you can do, to induce God to spare you one moment. ...

▶▶ Questions for Consideration and Discussion

1. Puritan theology is a version of Calvinism. It asserts the basic sinfulness of humankind. Do you think human beings are inherently evil or good? What's your comment on the Puritans' values and way of living?

2. What is the picture of the New World based on William Bradford's description in *Of Plymouth Plantation*?

3. In "Upon the Burning of Our House," how did the speaker feel at first about the loss of her house and possessions in the fire? How did she later change her views? How do people today deal emotionally with losing their homes in a natural disaster?

4. Jonathan Edwards' sermon *Sinners in the Hands of an Angry God* does its utmost to arouse people's fear. What do you think is the unwholesome effect of fear? Do you think a sense of fear has positive effect too? Why or why not?

The Southern Colonists

The southern colonies began in 1607 with Jamestown, Virginia. Different from the northern colonies in New England that featured Puritan culture, the southern colonies were culturally, and religiously diverse. The southern English settlers came to pursue economic opportunities instead of religious freedom. There were also French, Dutch, Swiss, German, and Irish settlers. Much of the southern population lived on farms or plantations that were distant from one another. Often these plantations were largely self-sufficient. For the most part, southern gentlemen and ladies carried on correspondence with friends who often lived at great distances from them, as well as with family and friends back in England. Many of the southern colonists belonged to the Church of England, which the Puritans had attempted to reform. Therefore, the southern colonies' ties with the Old World were stronger. In contrast to the Puritan's dream of building the "city upon a hill," the southern people dreamed to find a "vale of plenty," which was proposed by Captain John Smith. They pursued material wealth and some of them lived an aristocratic life with large plantations.

The southern literature was secular and characterized by a sense of satire and humor. In their letters, journals, and public reports, southern writers recorded the details of their way of life, for instance William Byrd's *The History of the Dividing Line* and *A Progress to the Mines* (1732). Of course, not all the residents of the southern colonies were the prosperous owners of plantations. Most were hard working tradespeople, artisans, small farmers, indentured servants, and slaves. Yet the sophisticated gentleman and lady dominated our sense of the early southern colonies as we meet them in literature.

John Smith (1580 – 1631)

As an English adventurer and explorer, the twenty-seven-year-old Captain John Smith led one hundred men and four boys to found, in 1607, the first permanent English settlement, Jamestown, Virginia. After two years in Jamestown, he returned to England. In 1614, he returned to New England and explored the coast from Maine to Cape Cod, made maps, traded with Indians, and went back to England, never to return to America. In 1616, his *A Description of New England* was published.

A Description of New England

(Excerpt)

...

Who can desire more content, that has small means or but only his merit to advance his fortune, than to tread and plant that ground he has purchased by the hazard① of his life? If he have but the taste of virtue and magnanimity, what to such a mind can be more pleasant than planting and building a foundation for his posterity, got from the rude earth by God's blessing and his own industry, without prejudice to any? If he have any grain of faith or zeal in religion, what can he do less hurtful to any or more agreeable to God than to seek to convert those poor savages to know Christ and humanity? …What so truly suits with honor and honesty as the discovering things unknown, erecting towns peopling countries, informing the ignorant, reforming things unjust, teaching virtue, and gain to our native mother-country a kingdom to attend her, find employment for those that are idle because they know not what to do? [This is] so far from wronging any as to cause posterity to remembering thee…

Here nature and liberty afford us that freely which in England we want②, or it costs us dearly. What pleasure can be more than (being tired with any occasion ashore, in planting vines, fruits, or herbs, in contriving their own grounds, to the pleasure of their own minds, their fields, gardens, orchards, buildings, ships, and other works, etc.) to recreate themselves before their own doors, in their own boats upon the sea, where man, woman, and child, with a small hook and line, by angling may take divers sorts of excellent fish at their pleasures? And is it not pretty sport to pull up two pence, six pence, and twelve pence as fast as you can haul and veer③ a line? He is a very bad fisher [who] cannot kill in one day with his hook and line, one, two, or three hundred cods…If a man work but three days in seven he may get more than he can spend, unless he will be excessive….

For hunting also, the woods, lakes, and rivers afford not only chase sufficient for any that delight in that kind of toil or pleasure, but such beasts to hunt that besides the delicacy of their bodies for food, their skins are so rich as may well recompense thy daily labor with a captain's pay.

...

My purpose is not to persuade children from their parents, men from their wives, nor servants from their masters, only such as with free consent may be spared. But [if] each parish or village, in city or country, that will but apparel their fatherless children of thirteen or fourteen years of age, or young married people that have small wealth to live on, here by their

---

①   hazard:risk.

②   want:lack.

③   haul and veer:pull in and let out.

labor [they] may live exceeding well, provided always that first there be a sufficient power to command them, houses to receive them, means to defend them, and meet① provisions for them, for any place may be overlain② and it is most necessary to have a fortress and sufficient masters (as, carpenters, masons, fishers, fowlers, gardeners, husbandmen③, sawyers, smiths, spinners, tailors, weavers, and such like) to take ten, twelve, or twenty, or as there is occasion, for apprentices. The masters by this may quickly grow rich; these [apprentices] may learn [by] their trades themselves to do the like, to a general and an incredible benefit for king and country, master and servant.

William Byrd (1674 –1744)

William Byrd was one of the most brilliant of the southern landowning aristocracy. These southern gentry modeled themselves on the English upper classes, taking pride in stately homes furnished with fine china, paintings, and books. Though hard-working and religious, they were not afraid of some of the worldly pleasures that the Puritans shunned.

Byrd was born in Jamestown, which John Smith had helped establish sixty-seven years earlier. When he was seven years old, his rich father sent him to England for his education. There he met high class people including men of letters. He was fifty-two before he returned to Virginia. There he read his Greek and Latin classics every day; owned the second largest library in America, numbering 3,600 books; entertained and visited his neighbors; and managed his huge 180,000-acre estate, upon which he founded the city of Richmond.

Byrd's writings include diaries, travel books, and poems. One of his best-known works, *The History of the Dividing Line*, recounts his experiences on a surveying trip that defined the Virginia-North Carolina border. His other well-known work, *A Progress to the Mines* (1732), is Byrd's account of a trip to the iron-mining territory of western Virginia, where he visited the estate of former governor Spotswood. His writings showed how the southerners loved the material world of land, animals, plants and the local Indians.

---

① meet: sufficient.

② overlain: overwhelmed by an enemy.

③ husbandmen: farmers.

A Progress to the Mines
(Excerpt)

September 30, 1732.   The sun rose clear this morning and so did I, and finished all my little affairs by breakfast. It was then resolved to wait on the ladies on horseback, since the bright sun, the fine air, and the wholesome exercise all invited us to it. We forded the river a little above the ferry and rode six miles up the neck to a fine level piece of rich land, where we found about twenty plants of ginseng, with the scarlet berries growing on the top of the middle stalk. The root of this is of wonderful virtue in many cases, particularly to raise the spirits and promote perspiration, which makes it a specific in colds and coughs. The colonel complimented me with all we found in return for my telling him the virtues of it. We were all pleased to find so much of this king of plants so near the colonel's habitation and growing, too, upon his own land, but were, however, surprised to find it upon level ground, after we had been told it grew only upon the north side of stony mountains. I carried home this treasure with as much joy as if every root had been a graft of the tree of life, and washed and dried it carefully.

This airing made us as hungry as so many hawks, so that, between appetite and a very good dinner, 'twas difficult to eat like a philosopher.

▶▶ Questions for Consideration and Discussion

1. What is the picture of the New World based on John Smith's narrative in *A Description of New England*? How is it different from William Bradford's description in *Of Plymouth Plantation*? In your opinion, why does this difference exist?

2. What aspect of southern life does William Byrd's description show? How does it differ from the northern Puritans' life?

Chapter 2

American Revolution and Enlightenment

Historical Background

The American Revolution — also called the American Revolutionary War, or the American War of Independence — took place between 1775 and 1783, more than one and a half centuries after the first English colonists settled in Jamestown Colony and Plymouth Colony.

By the 1770s, the number of English colonies in America had risen to thirteen. And during the half-century before the Revolution, these colonies had begun to prosper. They looked less and less like perilous settlements on the edge of a wilderness. They communicated more with one another and grew aware of their mutual problems and feelings. They shared their anger over the oppressive political and economic policies imposed by the British government. However, at first, no one was thinking of revolution.

What infuriated the colonies were a series of intolerable laws and taxes. The Stamp Act of 1765 required that the colonists buy special stamps for newspapers, licenses, pamphlets, and many other documents. The Quartering Act of the same year forced colonists to feed and house British soldiers in their own homes. The Townshend Acts of 1767 taxed tea, glass, lead, and paper. When some of the colonial assemblies refused to abide by the new laws, the British government declared those assemblies "dissolved." Violence soon followed. In 1773, the British Parliament insisted again on its right and power to tax Americans. Soon afterward, the famous Boston Tea Party happened. Adopting the dress of Native Americans, protesters boarded a ship and dumped its load of British tea into Boston Harbor. The tax on tea became a symbol, and the famous Boston Tea Party became a symbol too — a symbol of American resistance.

Americans protested and petitioned King George III for "no taxation without representation." They said they wanted only what was reasonable; they wanted to share in their own government. Britain replied with the Intolerable Acts of 1774, designed to punish Massachusetts for the Boston Tea Party. Many more rights that had been granted to the colonists in their charters were revoked. Then on April 19, 1775, when a group of American Minutemen faced British redcoats on their way to seize American arms at the village of Concord, Massachusetts, Americans responded with force. However, it was not until January 1776 that a widely heard public voice demanded a complete break with England. The voice came from Thomas Paine, whose pamphlet *Common Sense* generated the growing demand for separation and pointed the way toward the Declaration of Independence (July 4th, 1776), which officially announced the Thirteen States' independence from the English rule.

As a matter of fact, a fundamental driving force behind the American Revolution was the intellectual revolution called the Enlightenment.

American Enlightenment

The American Enlightenment was inspired and influenced by the European Enlightenment, which was the movement of intellectual liberation developing in Western Europe from the late 17th century to the late 18th century. This period is often called the "Age of Reason," for Enlightenment thinkers re-examined all aspects of society (such as religion, government, justice, women's rights) through the application of reason, and they believed that reason is main source of all knowledge. With its forerunners in science and philosophy being Bacon, Descartes, Newton, and Locke, the European Enlightenment culminated with the writings of Rousseau, Diderot and Kant. Its central idea was the need for, and the capacity of, human reason to clear away ancient superstition, prejudice, dogma, and injustice. In *Discourse on Method* (1637) by Descartes (who is the father of modern rationalism, whose best known motto is "I think, therefore I am"), he stated that he would only accept those things his reason said were true. Enlightenment thinking emphasized rationality and scientific research rather than tradition and religious dogma. These new scientists and philosophers were called Deists; they deduced the existence of God from the construction of the universe itself rather than from the Bible. They were not interested in theology. Rather they were fascinated with humankind's own nature. The famous couplet by Alexander Pope (1688 – 1744), the English poet of the European Enlightenment period, well conveys the Enlightenment thinking: "Know then thyself, presume not God to scan; The proper study of mankind is man."

Enlightenment thinking also championed the idea of universal human rights. John Locke said that all people possessed the natural rights to life, liberty and property. He believed in the equality and independence of people. In his opinion, the governed should consent to be governed, and government should represent the interests of the people. Rousseau thought that people had the ultimate power in government; that if necessary, they could withdraw their support of their government. He held that the least amount of government was the best.

The Enlightenment ideas spread to the New Continent and influenced the reading public. The Americans began to break through the limitations of traditional Puritanism and accept the progressive ideas of justice, equality, liberty, and democracy. They believed that education could propel personal growth and social progress. Accordingly, members of the American enlightenment composed writings to educate the public and defend their revolutionary cause.

It is true that in this period of time America produced no professional writers. Yet, a great number of Americans expressed themselves on the subjects of liberty, government, law, reason, as well as on individual and national freedom. Most of the writings were public and utilitarian. The major forms were essays, pamphlets, political documents for purposes of social reform, revolutionary agitation, and philosophical declaration. Although such writings were not exactly belles letters, their stylistic and ideological influences on future American culture and literature cannot be underestimated. This was the period when American nationhood began to emerge. If Columbus "discovered" America, then the founding fathers like Thomas Jefferson and Benjamin Franklin "invented" it.

The prose of the great philosopher-statesmen made up a prominent part of the 18th century American Literature, with the best-known titles being Thomas Paine's *Common Sense*, Thomas Jefferson's The Declaration of Independence, and Benjamin Franklin's *The Autobiography*. Like in England, this was the great age of the newspaper and the moral essay; Benjamin Franklin said that he modeled his own style after the English essayists Joseph Addison and Richard Steele.

▶▶ Questions for Consideration and Discussion

1. Discuss with your partner what the Enlightenment is, and how it differs from Puritanism.
2. Select one philosopher from Descartes, Locke, Rousseau, Diderot and Kant and research his major philosophical ideas. Then find students who research other philosophers and find out about other philosophers' ideas.

Thomas Paine (1737 – 1809)

Thomas Paine was born in 1737 in England, the son of a Quaker. After a short, basic education, he started to work, at first for his father and later as an officer of the excise. His duties were to hunt for smugglers and collect the excise taxes on liquor and tobacco. In 1774, he met Benjamin Franklin in London, who advised him to emigrate to America, giving him letters of recommendation.

Paine landed at Philadelphia on November 30, 1774. Starting over as a publicist, he first published his *African Slavery in America* in the spring of 1775, criticizing the practice in America as being unjust and inhumane.

Paine is best remembered as the author of two of the most popular writings in the 18th century America: *Common Sense* (the first pamphlet published in America to urge immediate independence from Britain) and *Rights of Man*, which he wrote in England.

Common Sense

(Excerpt)

III. Thoughts on the Present State of American Affairs

In the following pages I offer nothing more than simple facts, plain arguments, and common sense; and have no other preliminaries to settle with the reader, than that he will divest himself of prejudice and prepossession, and suffer① his reason and his feelings to determine for themselves; that he will put on, or rather that he will not put off, the true character of a man, and generously enlarge his views beyond the present day.

Volumes have been written on the subject of the struggle between England and America. Men of all ranks have embarked in the controversy, from different motives, and with various designs; but all have been ineffectual, and the period of debate is closed. Arms, as the last resource, decide the contest; the appeal was the choice of the king, and the continent hath accepted the challenge.

...

As much hath been said of the advantages of reconciliation, which, like an agreeable dream, hath passed away and left us as we were, it is but right, that we should examine the contrary side of the argument, and inquire into some of the many material injuries which these colonies sustain, and always will sustain, by being connected with, and dependent on Great Britain. To examine that connection and dependence, on the principles of nature and common sense, to see what we have to trust to, if separated, and what we are to expect, if

—————————————

① suffer: allow.

dependent.

I have heard it asserted by some, that as America has flourished under her former connection with Great Britain, the same connection is necessary towards her future happiness, and will always have the same effect. Nothing can be more fallacious than this kind of argument. We may as well assert that because a child has thrived upon milk, that it is never to have meat, or that the first twenty years of our lives is to become a precedent for the next twenty. But even this is admitting more than is true; for I answer roundly that America would have flourished as much, and probably much more, had no European power taken any notice of her. The commerce by which she hath enriched herself are the necessaries of life, and will always have a market while eating is the custom of Europe.

...

It hath lately been asserted in Parliament, that the Colonies have no relation to each other but through the Parent Country, i. e. that Pennsylvania and the Jerseys and so on for the rest, are sister Colonies by the way of England; this is certainly a very roundabout way of proving relationship, but it is the nearest and only true way of proving enmity (or enemyship, if I may so call it.) France and Spain never were, nor perhaps ever will be, our enemies as AMERICANS, but as our being the SUBJECTS OF GREAT BRITAIN.

But Britain is the parent country, say some. Then the more shame upon her conduct. Even brutes do not devour their young, nor savages make war upon their families... Europe, and not England, is the parent country of America. This new World hath been the asylum for the persecuted lovers of civil and religious liberty from EVERY PART of Europe. Hither have they fled, not from the tender embraces of the mother, but from the cruelty of the monster; and it is so far true of England, that the same tyranny which drove the first emigrants from home, pursues their descendants still.

...

But, admitting that we were all of English descent, what does it amount to? Nothing. Britain, being now an open enemy, extinguishes every other name and title: and to say that reconciliation is our duty, is truly farcical. The first king of England, of the present line (William the Conqueror) was a Frenchman, and half the peers of England are descendants from the same country; wherefore, by the same method of reasoning, England ought to be governed by France.

...

Europe is too thickly planted with Kingdoms to be long at peace, and whenever a war breaks out between England and any foreign power, the trade of America goes to ruin, BECAUSE OF HER CONNECTION WITH BRITAIN. The next war may not turn out like the last, and should it not, the advocates for reconciliation now will be wishing for separation then, because neutrality in that case would be a safer convoy than a man of war. Everything that is right or reasonable pleads for separation. The blood of the slain, the weeping voice of nature cries, 'TIS TIME TO PART. Even the distance at which the Almighty hath placed England and America is a strong and natural proof that the authority of the one over the other, was never the design of Heaven... The Reformation was preceded by the discovery of America: As if the Almighty graciously meant to open a sanctuary to the persecuted in future years, when home should afford neither friendship nor safety.

The authority of Great Britain over this continent, is a form of government, which sooner or later must have an end: And a serious mind can draw no true pleasure by looking forward, under the painful and positive conviction that what he calls "the present constitution" is merely temporary. As parents, we can have no joy, knowing that this government is not sufficiently lasting to ensure anything which we may bequeath to posterity: And by a plain method of argument, as we are running the next generation into debt, we ought to do the work of it, otherwise we use them meanly and pitifully. In order to discover the line of our duty rightly, we should take our children in our hand, and fix our station a few years farther into life; that eminence will present a prospect which a few present fears and prejudices conceal from our sight.

...

It is repugnant to reason, to the universal order of things, to all examples from former ages, to suppose that this continent can longer remain subject to any external power. The most sanguine in Britain does not think so. The utmost stretch of human wisdom cannot, at this time, compass a plan short of separation, which can promise the continent even a year's security. Reconciliation is now a fallacious dream. Nature hath deserted the connection, and Art cannot supply her place. For, as Milton wisely expresses, "never can true reconcilement grow where wounds of deadly hate have pierced so deep."

...

A government of our own is our natural right: and when a man seriously reflects on the precariousness of human affairs, he will become convinced that it is infinitely wiser and safer to form a constitution of our own in a cool deliberate manner, while we have it in our power, than to trust such an interesting event to time and chance.

...

▷▷ Questions for Consideration and Discussion

1. What are some of the main reasons why some Americans want to reconcile with the British instead of fighting? How does Paine refute them?
2. Of the many arguments that Thomas Paine gives for America to separate from the British, which is the most convincing to you? Try to be as specific as possible.
3. Compare Jonathan Edwards' sermon excerpt of "Sinners in the Hands of an Angry God" in the forgoing chapter with the extracted text from Thomas Paine's *Common Sense*. Which do you think is an example of reasoned argument for persuasion? Which is an emotional appeal? What are the advantages and the disadvantages of these two styles? Please use textual proofs to support your position.

Thomas Jefferson(1743 –1826)

Thomas Jefferson was a Virginian. His father, Peter Jefferson, died when Thomas was fourteen and left him 2,750 acres of land. Jefferson added to this acreage until he died, and at one time owned almost 10,000 acres.

By the time he entered the College of William & Mary in Williamsburg in 1760, Jefferson had mastered Latin and Greek, played the violin respectably, and was a skilled horseman. In Williamsburg, he was fortunate enough to make the acquaintance of three men who strongly influenced his life: Governor Francis Fauquier, a fellow of the Royal Society; George Wythe, one of the best teachers of law in the country; and Dr. William Small, an immigrant from Scotland who taught mathematics and philosophy and also introduced Jefferson "to the invigorating realm of the Scottish Enlightenment."

Upon graduation from college, Jefferson practiced law for a short time. In 1775, he attended the Continental Congress, and in the following year, he was requested to draft the Declaration of Independence, which was edited by the Second Continental Congress and adopted in its final form on July 4, 1776.

During his lifetime, Jefferson played many roles: he was a philosopher, scientist, farmer, architect, inventor (he invented a plow that revolutionized farming), governor of Virginia, ambassador to France, Secretary of State, Vice President, and the third President of the United States. The books in his library of ten thousand volumes were ultimately the beginning of the Library of Congress. Even though Jefferson was a man of many talents and achievements, he once said that he wished to be remembered for only three things: drafting the Declaration of Independence, writing and supporting the Virginia Statute for Religious Freedom (1786), and founding the University of Virginia.

Jefferson remained an agrarian aristocrat all his life, and it is to the liberty of mind and the values of the land that he always returned.

The Declaration of Independence was announced on July 4, 1776, which was later proclaimed Independence Day. The writing is eloquent, clear, direct and forceful. It expressed the minds of the American people and served effectively for the American call for independence.

The Declaration of Independence

(Excerpt)

The Unanimous Declaration of the Thirteen United States of America

When in the Course of human events, it becomes necessary for one people to dissolve the political bands which have connected them with another, and to assume among the powers of the earth, the separate and equal station to which the Laws of Nature and of Nature's God entitle them, a decent respect to the opinions of mankind requires that they should declare the causes which impel them to the separation.

We hold these truths to be self-evident, that all men are created equal, that they are endowed by their Creator with certain unalienable Rights, that among these are Life, Liberty and the pursuit of Happiness. — That to secure these rights, Governments are instituted among Men, deriving their just powers from the consent of the governed, — That whenever any Form of Government becomes destructive of these ends, it is the Right of the People to alter or to abolish it, and to institute new Government, laying its foundation on such principles and organizing its powers in such form, as to them shall seem most likely to effect their Safety and Happiness. Prudence, indeed, will dictate that Governments long established should not be changed for light and transient causes; and accordingly all experience hath shown, that mankind are more disposed to suffer, while evils are sufferable, than to right themselves by abolishing the forms to which they are accustomed. But when a long train of abuses and usurpations, pursuing invariably the same Object evinces a design to reduce them under absolute Despotism, it is their right, it is their duty, to throw off such Government, and to provide new Guards for their future security. — Such has been the patient sufferance of these Colonies; and such is now the necessity which constrains them to alter their former Systems of Government. The history of the present King of Great Britain is a history of repeated injuries and usurpations, all having in direct object the establishment of an absolute Tyranny over these States. To prove this, let Facts be submitted to a candid world.

He has refused his Assent to Laws the most wholesome and necessary for the public good.

He has forbidden his Governors to pass Laws of immediate and pressing importance, unless suspended in their operation till his Assent should be obtained; and when so suspended, he has utterly neglected to attend to them.

He has refused to pass other Laws for the accommodation of large districts of people, unless those people would relinquish the right of Representation in the Legislature, a right inestimable to them and formidable to tyrants only.

He has called together legislative bodies at places unusual, uncomfortable, and distant from the depository of their public Records, for the sole purpose of fatiguing them into compliance with his measures.

He has dissolved Representative Houses repeatedly, for opposing with manly firmness his invasions on the rights of the people.

He has refused for a long time, after such dissolutions, to cause others to be elected; whereby the Legislative powers, incapable of Annihilation, have returned to the People at large for their exercise; the State remaining in the mean time exposed to all the dangers of invasion from without, and convulsions within.

He has endeavoured to prevent the population of these States; for that purpose obstructing the Laws for Naturalization of Foreigners; refusing to pass others to encourage their migrations hither, and raising the conditions of new Appropriations of Lands.

He has obstructed the Administration of Justice, by refusing his Assent to Laws for establishing Judiciary powers.

He has made Judges dependent on his Will alone, for the tenure of their offices, and the amount and payment of their salaries.

He has erected a multitude of New Offices, and sent hither swarms of Officers to harass our people, and eat out their substance.

He has kept among us, in times of peace, Standing Armies without the Consent of our legislatures.

He has affected to render the Military independent of, and superior to, the Civil power.

He has combined with others to subject us to a jurisdiction foreign to our constitution, and unacknowledged by our laws; giving his Assent to their Acts of pretended Legislation:

For Quartering large bodies of armed troops among us;

For protecting them, by a mock Trial, from punishment for any Murders which they should commit on the Inhabitants of these States;

For cutting off our Trade with all parts of the world;

For imposing Taxes on us without our Consent;

For depriving us in many cases, of the benefits of Trial by Jury;

For transporting us beyond Seas to be tried for pretended offences;

...

He has excited domestic insurrections amongst us, and has endeavoured to bring on the inhabitants of our frontiers the merciless Indian Savages whose known rule of warfare is an undistinguished destruction of all ages, sexes and conditions.

In every stage of these Oppressions We have Petitioned for Redress in the most humble terms. Our repeated Petitions have been answered only by repeated injury. A Prince whose character is thus marked by every act which may define a Tyrant is unfit to be the ruler of a free people.

Nor have We been wanting in attentions to our British brethren. We have warned them from time to time of attempts by their legislature to extend an unwarrantable jurisdiction over us. We have reminded them of the circumstances of our emigration and settlement here. We have appealed to their native justice and magnanimity, and we have conjured them by the ties of our common kindred to disavow these usurpations, which would inevitably interrupt our connections and correspondence. They too have been deaf to the voice of justice and of consanguinity①. We must, therefore, acquiesce in the necessity which denounces our Separation and hold them, as we hold the rest of mankind, Enemies in War, in Peace Friends.

We, therefore, the Representatives of the United States of America in General Congress Assembled, appealing to the Supreme Judge of the world for the rectitude of our intentions,

---

① consanguinity: blood relationship.

do in the Name and by Authority of the good People of these Colonies, solemnly publish and declare that these United Colonies are, and of Right ought to be Free and Independent States; that they are Absolved from all Allegiance to the British Crown, and that all political connection between them and the State of Great Britain is and ought to be totally dissolved; and that as Free and Independent States, they have full Power to levy War, conclude Peace, contract Alliances, establish Commerce, and to do all other Acts and Things which Independent States may of right do. And for the support of this Declaration, with a firm reliance on the protection of divine Providence, we mutually pledge to each other our Lives, our Fortunes and our sacred Honor.

Questions for Consideration and Discussion

1. According to Jefferson, what human rights are unalienable? How do you interpret the phrase "pursuit of happiness"?
2. What accusations does Jefferson make against the British King? In a statement, summarize the complaints against the King.
3. In the final sentence of the Declaration, what do the signers pledge? What do you think their fate would have been if Britain had been the victor of the Revolution?
4. How is the faith in reason reflected in the Declaration?
5. It has long been noticed that the Declaration of Independence is ironic and hypocritical because it claims that "all men are created equal" and denounces the political tyranny and economic oppression imposed by Great Britain; however, a blatant fact was that blacks and women were not treated as equals. Furthermore, Thomas Jefferson, the author, like many other signers of the political document, was a slave owner. What do you make of this terrible contradiction?

Benjamin Franklin (1706 – 1790)

Benjamin Franklin was born in a candle maker's home in Boston and lived there in his early years. He quit school at twelve on account of financial problems and became an apprentice to his elder brother who was a printer. Leaving Boston at the age of seventeen and arriving penniless in Philadelphia, he soon established himself as a printer and a civic leader. He became rich and retired from business at the age of forty-two.

After retiring, Franklin devoted lots of time to his deepest interest — science. His work on lightning rods, earthquakes, bifocal lenses, and electricity made him world famous, and the Franklin stove is still used in some American homes.

However, public affairs dominated the last half of his life. He was the only person who signed all four of the Declaration of Independence, the Treaty of Alliance with

France, the Treaty of Paris, and the Constitution.

At the time of his death, no other American was better known or more respected. His energy, curiosity, tact, charm, and practicality brought him many successes in business, literature, science, and government. His rags-to-riches experience became the archetype of many Americans' dreams of success, thus inspired numerous ordinary Americans.

Franklin won his reputation as a great man of letters mainly through his two masterpieces: *Poor Richard's Almanack* and *The Autobiography of Benjamin Franklin*. He published *Poor Richard's Almanack* every year for twenty-five years (1733 – 1758). The unusual thing with it was that he enlivened his almanac with Poor Richard's proverbs and aphorisms.

Franklin began writing his autobiography at the age 65, when he was already internationally famous. He told his story in the form of a letter to his son. He never completed his autobiography, not even reaching the time when he drafted the Declaration of Independence.

The Autobiography of Benjamin Franklin was a typical embodiment of Puritanism and the Enlightenment. We find in it the Puritan's emphasis on self-improvement, self-analysis, and moral and ethical values, along with the Enlightenment's emphasis on rationalism, order, and education.

The Autobiography of Benjamin Franklin
(Excerpt)

It was about this time I conceived the bold and arduous project of arriving at moral perfection. I wished to live without committing any fault at any time; I would conquer all that either natural inclination, custom, or company might lead me into. As I knew, or thought I knew, what was right and wrong, I did not see why I might not always do the one and avoid the other. But I soon found I had undertaken a task of more difficulty than I had imagined. While my care was employed in guarding against one fault, I was often surprised by another; habit took the advantage of inattention; inclination was sometimes too strong for reason. I concluded, at length, that the mere speculative conviction that it was our interest to be completely virtuous was not sufficient to prevent our slipping, and that the contrary habits must be broken, and good ones acquired and established, before we can have any dependence on a steady, uniform rectitude of conduct. For this purpose I therefore contrived the following method.

In the various enumerations of the moral virtues I met in my reading, I found the catalogue more or less numerous, as different writers included more or fewer ideas under the same name. Temperance, for example, was by some confined to eating and drinking, while by others it was extended to mean the moderating every other pleasure, appetite, inclination, or passion, bodily or mental, even to our avarice and ambition. I proposed to myself, for the sake of clearness, to use rather more names, with fewer ideas annexed to each, than a few names with more ideas; and I included under thirteen names of virtues all that at that time occurred to me as necessary or desirable, and annexed to each a short precept, which fully expressed the extent I gave to its meaning.

These names of virtues, with their precepts were:

1. Temperance

   Eat not to dullness; drink not to elevation.

2. Silence

   Speak not but what may benefit others or yourself; avoid trifling conversation.

3. Order

   Let all your things have their places; let each part of your business have its time.

4. Resolution

   Resolve to perform what you ought; perform without fail what you resolve.

5. Frugality

   Make no expense but to do good to others or yourself, i. e. , waste nothing.

6. Industry

   Lose no time; be always employed in something useful; cut off all unnecessary actions.

7. Sincerity

   Use no hurtful deceit; think innocently and justly, and, if you speak, speak accordingly.

8. Justice

   Wrong none by doing injuries or omitting the benefits that are your duty.

9. Moderation

   Avoid extremes; forbear resenting injuries so much as you think they deserve.

10. Cleanliness

   Tolerate no uncleanness in body, clothes, or habitation.

11. Tranquility

   Be not disturbed at trifles, or at accidents common or unavoidable.

12. Chastity

   Rarely use venery but for health or offspring, never to dullness, weakness, or the injury of your own or another's peace or reputation.

13. Humility

   Imitate Jesus and Socrates.

My intention being to acquire the habitude of all these virtues, I judged it would be well not to distract my attention by attempting the whole at once, but to fix it on one of them at a time, and, when I should be master of that, then to proceed to another, and so on, till I should have gone thro' the thirteen; and, as the previous acquisition of some might facilitate the acquisition of certain others, I arranged them with that view, as they stand above.

Temperance first, as it tends to procure that coolness and clearness of head which is so necessary where constant vigilance was to be kept up, and guard maintained against the unremitting attraction of ancient habits and the force of perpetual temptations. This being acquired and established, *Silence* would be more easy; ... I gave *Silence* the second place. This and the next, *Order*, I expected would allow me more time for attending to my project and my studies. *Resolution*, once becoming habitual, would keep me firm in my endeavors to obtain all the subsequent virtues; *Frugality* and *Industry*, freeing me from my remaining debt, and producing affluence and independence, would make more easy the practice of *Sincerity* and *Justice*, etc. Conceiving, then, that, agreeably to the advice of Pythagoras in his Garden Verses, daily examination would be necessary, I contrived the following method for conducting that examination.

I made a little book, in which I allotted a page for each of the virtues. I ruled each page with red ink, so as to have seven columns, one for each day of the week, marking each column with a letter for the day. I crossed these columns with thirteen red lines, marking the beginning of each line with the first letter of one of the virtues, on which line, and in its proper column, I might mark, by a little black spot, every fault I found upon examination to have been committed respecting that virtue upon that day.

TEMPERANCE.							
Eat Not to Dullness; *Drink Not to Elevation.*							
	S	M	T	W	T	F	S
T							
S	* *	*		*		*	
O	*	*	*		*	*	*
R			*			*	
F		*			*		
I			*				
S							
J							
M							
Cl.							
T							
Ch.							
H							

I determined to give a week's strict attention to each of the virtues successively. Thus, in the first week, my great guard was to avoid *every the least offense against Temperance*, leaving the other virtues to their ordinary chance, only marking every evening the faults of the day. Thus, if in the first week I could keep my first line, marked T, clear of spots, I supposed the habit of that virtue so much strengthened, and its opposite weakened, that I might venture extending my attention to include the next, and for the following week keep both lines clear of spots. Proceeding thus to the last, I could go thro' a course complete in thirteen weeks, and four courses in a year. And like him who, having a garden to weed, does not attempt to eradicate all the bad herbs at once, which would exceed his reach and his strength, but works on one of the beds at a time, and, having accomplished the first, proceeds to a second, so I should have, I hoped, the encouraging pleasure of seeing on my pages the progress I made in virtue, by clearing successively my lines of their spots, till in the end, by a number of courses, I should be happy in viewing a clean book, after a thirteen weeks' daily examination.

...

The precept of *Order* requiring that *every part of my business should have its allotted time*, one page in my little book contained the following scheme of employment for the twenty-four hours of a natural day.

	5	Rise, wash, and address powerful goodness; contrive day's business, and take the resolution of the day; prosecute the present Study, and breakfast
	6	
	7	
	8	Work
	9	
	10	
	11	
Morning Question: What good shall I do this day?	12	Read, or overlook my accounts, and dine
	1	
	2	Work
	3	
	4	
	5	
	6	Put things in their places, supper, music, or diversion, or conversation, examination of the day
	7	
	8	
	9	
	10	Sleep
	11	
Evening Question: What good have I done today?	12	
	1	
	2	
	3	
	4	

I entered upon the execution of this plan for self-examination, and continued it, with occasional intermissions, for some time. I was surprised to find myself so much fuller of faults than I had imagined; but I had the satisfaction of seeing them diminish...

My scheme of *Order* gave me the most trouble; and I found that, tho' it might be practicable where a man's business was such as to leave him the disposition of his time, that of a journeyman printer, for instance, it was not possible to be exactly observed by a master, who must mix with the world, and often receive people of business at their own hours. *Order*, too, with regard to places for things, papers, etc., I found extremely difficult to acquire. I had not been early accustomed to it, and, having an exceeding good memory, I was not so sensible of the inconvenience attending want of method. ...

In truth, I found myself incorrigible with respect to *Order*; and now I am grown old, and my memory bad, I feel very sensibly the want of it. But, on the whole, tho' I never arrived at the perfection I had been so ambitious of obtaining, but fell far short of it, yet I was, by the endeavor, a better and a happier man than I otherwise should have been if I had not attempted it; as those who aim at perfect writing by imitating the engraved copies, though they never reach the wished-for excellence of those copies, their hand is mended by the endeavor, and is tolerable while it continues fair and legible.

It may be well my posterity should be informed that to this little artifice, with the blessing of God, their ancestor owed the constant felicity of his life down to his seventy-ninth year, in which this is written. What reverses may attend the remainder is in the hand of Providence; but, if they arrive, the reflection on past happiness enjoyed ought to help his bearing them with more resignation. To *Temperance* he ascribes his long-continued health and what is still left to him of a good constitution; to *Industry* and *Frugality*, the early easiness of his circumstances and acquisition of his fortune, with all that knowledge that enabled him to be a useful citizen, and obtained for him some degree of reputation among the learned; to *Sincerity* and *Justice*, the confidence of his country, and the honorable employs it conferred upon him; and to the joint influence of the whole mass of the virtues, even in the imperfect state he was able to acquire them, all that evenness of temper, and that cheerfulness in conversation, which makes his company still sought for, and agreeable even to his younger acquaintance. I hope, therefore, that some of my descendants may follow the example and reap the benefit.

...

In this piece it was my design to explain and enforce this doctrine, that vicious actions are not hurtful because they are forbidden, but forbidden because they are hurtful, the nature of man alone considered; that it was, therefore, every one's interest to be virtuous who wished to be happy even in this world...

My list of virtues contained at first but twelve; but a Quaker friend having kindly informed me that I was generally thought proud, that my pride showed itself frequently in conversation, that I was not content with being in the right when discussing any point, but was overbearing and rather insolent, of which he convinced me by mentioning several instances, I determined endeavoring to cure myself, if I could, of this vice or folly among the rest, and I added *Humility* to my list, giving an extensive meaning to the word.

I cannot boast of much success in acquiring the reality of this virtue, but I had a good deal with regard to the appearance of it. I made it a rule to forbear all direct contradiction to the sentiments of others, and all positive assertion of my own. I even forbid myself, agreeably to the old laws of our Junto, the use of every word or expression in the language that imported a fixed opinion, such as *certainly*, *undoubtedly*, etc., and I adopted, instead of them, *I conceive*, *I apprehend*, or *I imagine* a thing to be so or so, or *it so appears to me at present*. When another asserted something that I thought an error, I denied myself the pleasure of contradicting him abruptly and of showing immediately some absurdity in his proposition; and in answering, I began by observing that in certain cases or circumstances his opinion would be right, but in the present case there appeared or seemed to me some difference, etc. I soon found the advantage of this change in my manner; the conversations I engaged in went on more pleasantly.

The modest way in which I proposed my opinions procured them a readier reception and less contradiction; I had less mortification when I was found to be in the wrong, and I more easily prevailed with others to give up their mistakes and join with me when I happened to be in the right.

Questions for Consideration and Discussion

1. What thirteen virtues did Benjamin Franklin list as essential for living a good life? As a young person living in the 21st century, do you think these virtues still work well in today's world or may some of them be outdated? Please elaborate on your argument with your discussion partner.

2. How many virtues did Franklin's list contain at first? Why did he modify it? What policy did he take to acquire the virtue he added? How does it illuminate your way of smooth communication?

3. Benjamin Franklin proposed to "imitate Jesus and Socrates" to acquire the virtue of humility. Do you agree that Jesus and Socrates were humble people? Use examples to argue for or against the point made by Benjamin Franklin.

Part Ⅱ

From the Revolution to the Civil War

(1783–1861)

Part II

From the Revolution to the Civil War

(1783-1861)

Chapter 3

American Romanticism and Transcendentalism

Historical Background

The American Revolution ended in 1783 with the Treaty of Paris. George Washington became the first president of the new, independent nation in 1789. Despite backward modes of transportation and communication, the newly formed United States of America developed and extended its territory rapidly towards the west. The purchase of Louisiana from France in 1803 under the third president, Thomas Jefferson, vastly enlarged American territory. In 1812, due to the commercial conflicts between the U. S. and Britain, a war was declared on Britain on the battlefield of Canada. Internal divisions occurred in the United States because the people in the West wanted to possess the land of Canada while the Southern plantation owners hoped to grab Florida from the hands of Spain. The war ended two years later with a U. S. victory, which greatly contributed to the new nation's pride and nationalism. By 1821, the total number of States had risen to twenty-three from the original thirteen.

Texas, which was originally part of the Mexican Republic, was annexed in 1844. Shortly afterward, the Mexican-American War (1846 – 1848) ended with the defeat of Mexico and the acquisition of California and New Mexico.

As the United States consolidated and grew, so did its sins, which included the near-genocide of the American Indians, the enslavement of blacks, and the staged "Executive's War" against Mexico. Along with the national sins were problems such as materialism, child labor, and political corruption. Yet, the territorial expansion enhanced Americans' confidence and ambition. Adventurous people went to the West, dreaming of making a fortune. They displayed courage and optimism when confronted by various hardships and dangers. Thanks to the westward movement, roads and waterways were improved, and a new network of trade and communication was created. Freshly-built factories gradually turned the country from an agricultural economy into an increasingly urban and industrialized one. The recently founded republic was growing into a prosperous and vital country.

American Romanticism and Transcendentalism

After the thirteen colonies gained independence from English control, Americans acknowledged, in spite of their political independence, much of the same literary canon as the British. Educated Americans in the new nation were more familiar with Greek, Roman and European history and literature than with the American writers of the Colonial and Revolutionary eras. Educated American children learned Greek and Latin literature in childhood. In 1820, nearly four decades after American independence, it was still possible for a British critic, Sydney Smith, to ask, "In the four quarters of the globe, who reads an American book?" Smith, like many other Europeans, mocked American literature as writings from an unformed, uncultured, and unsophisticated place.

But as Americans continued to build the nation, an increasing nationalism developed. Americans began to call for a literature that would celebrate the new country and express true Americanism. To the pleasure of Americans, in the same year that Smith asked his mocking question, Washington Irving's *The Sketch Book*, which contained his short story masterpieces "Rip Van Winkle" and "The Legend of Sleepy Hollow," was published in England. The next year William Cullen Bryant gained fame for his poem "Thanatopsis." In 1823, James Fenimore Cooper brought out the first of his Leather-stocking novels, *The Pioneers*. And in 1827, Edgar Allan Poe published his first volume of poetry. These writers began to draw international attention.

Why were these writers and their works so special? They were belletrists who began writing about American people in American places dealing with American problems, even though their characters and settings were not always American, and their forms were usually British. For instance, Irving's "Rip Van Winkle" resembles the German folktale "Peter Claus," and his "The Devil and Tom Walker" reminds a well-read reader of the German legend about Faust, who makes a pact with the Devil and exchanges his soul for unlimited knowledge and worldly pleasures. Another example, James Fenimore Cooper's *The Spy* (1821), shows a considerable degree of imitation of Sir Walter Scott's historical novels. Though these writers still relied on European models, they did take the first steps towards Americanism: they wrote about the American wilderness, the American Revolution, American pioneers, and American life; they praised American heroes and told American tales; their subjects were freedom and expansion, which definitely were not European subjects.

More remarkable was Ralph Waldo Emerson. He lengthened the first steps taken by Irving, Bryant, Cooper, and Poe. His stirring lecture *The American Scholar* (1937) has often been called America's "Intellectual Declaration of Independence." In the lecture, Emerson exclaims: "We will walk on our own feet; we will work with our own hands; we will speak our own minds." The nation listened and took the words to heart. Inspired directly or indirectly by Emerson, American writers began to free themselves from European models and created a distinctly American Romantic literature (also called New England Renaissance, or American Renaissance), which didn't end until the end of the Civil War.

American Romanticism was the first full-fledged literary movement developing in the United States. It was made up of a group of authors who wrote and published roughly between the 1820s and 1860s. It had its origins in European countries like Germany, France, and England.

Two phenomena facilitated the influence of European Romanticism on American Romanticism. First, by the second quarter of the 19th century, Americans had had quick access to contemporary British literature and criticism: after the wartime disruptions to trade was over, crossing the Atlantic on sailing ships or steamboats enabled any book or magazine to be republished in the larger coastal cities like Boston and New York a month or less after its appearance in London. Second, many of the leading American Romantics visited Europe and received first-hand influence from European Romanticism: Irving spent years in England and Spain, Cooper in France; Longfellow went to Europe a couple of times and stayed long to study European languages and literature; Emerson called on Walter Savage Landor in Italy, William Wordsworth in England, and Thomas Carlyle in Scotland.

Romanticism began in Europe in the late eighteenth century. It was a reaction to Classicism, the Age of Reason movement in the arts that attempted to duplicate the order and balance in the art of Greece and Rome. While Classicism stressed reason and social concerns, Romanticism stressed imagination, emotion, personal concerns, and individual experience. Romanticists often demonstrated a profound love of nature, a fascination with the supernatural, the mysterious and gothic, a yearning for the picturesque and exotic, a deep-rooted idealism, and a passionate nationalism. The British poet William Wordsworth and the German poet Johann Wolfgang von Goethe were among the earliest Romantic writers.

Transcendentalism, a unique contribution of American Romanticism, was represented by New England writers such as Emerson, Thoreau, and Margaret Fuller. Transcendentalism is based on the idea that the most fundamental truths about life and death can be reached only by going beyond the world of the senses. The transcendentalists believed that each and every man and woman could rise above the material world, and that each human mind could know something of the ultimate spiritual reality but could not know it through logic or the data of the senses. Rather, that knowledge came through a deep, free *intuition*, which they recognized as the "highest power of the soul."

Although American Romanticism had shared characteristics with European Romanticism, it had its own unique features. For instance, it didn't show the same political radicalism. American Romantic writers gave a distinct voice about the national culture in their works.

Early American Romanticists included Irving, Cooper, Bryant, and Poe. They were followed by the enduring names of Emerson, Thoreau, Hawthorne, Melville, Whitman, and Dickinson. Now let's take a moment to look at Cooper, Thoreau, and Melville, who are not anthologized in this book because of the limited space. Cooper was the first successful American novelist and was noted for his Leather-stocking series, which included five novels: *The Pioneers* (1823), *The Last of the Mohicans* (1826), *The Prairie* (1827), *The Pathfinder* (1840), and *The Deerslayer* (1841). In these books, Cooper gave a vital description of the life of a frontiersman named Natty Bumppo. He also wrote stories about the sea. He published his first — and best — sea-story *The Pilot* in 1823. It is a record of a group of American sailors' lives during the Revolutionary War. His works contributed to people's appreciation for American life. Thoreau was directly inspired by Emerson. He answered Emerson's appeal of going to nature with experiment and practice. His masterpiece *Walden; or, Life in the Woods* (1854) recounts the two years, two months, and two days he spent at Walden Pond. Another noteworthy thing about Thoreau was that he was jailed in the Concord jail for one night on account of refusing to pay a tax which might have been used to support the imperialistic Mexican War. In the wake of the event, he wrote his famous essay "Civil Disobedience" (1849). Melville is now best remembered for his whaling story, *Moby-Dick* (1851), which is regarded as one of the most vital stories available to the American imagination. The novel tells the story of Captain Ahab and his crew who are searching for a monstrous white whale on the dangerous ocean. The end of the story is the tragic death of everyone except Ishmael, who survived to tell the story to the world. Melville, like Hawthorne, set himself against the optimism of Emerson and the Transcendentalists. Hawthorne can be called the highest peak of

American Romanticism in fiction. He reflected on the Puritans' history and wrote his enduring masterpiece *The Scarlet Letter* (1850). Harriet Beecher Stowe, horrified by the evils of slavery, wrote the influential antislavery novel *Uncle Tom's Cabin* (1852). Like Thoreau, Whitman received direct inspiration from Emerson — Without Emerson, Whitman's great poetry, which he edited and reedited and published in *Leaves of Grass*, might never have been written. Dickinson also received profound influence from Emerson. She was little known in her lifetime. However, after her death, she became one of the greatest poets of the English language.

▶ Questions for Consideration and Discussion

1. What parts of Transcendentalism do you agree with and which do you disagree with? And why?
2. Enlighteners emphasized the power of reason and rationality, but Romanticists valued the power of emotion and imagination. What's your opinion? Should one prevail over the other or should they meet somewhere in between? Why?
3. "Let nature be your teacher," advised the English Romantic poet William Wordsworth. What lessons have you learned from nature?

Washington Irving (1783 – 1859)

Washington Irving was the first American storyteller to be recognized internationally as a man of letters.

Irving was born into a wealthy New York family at the end of the Revolutionary War and named after George Washington. Following his family's wish, he began to study law when he was sixteen, but he preferred reading literary works and listening to the folktales from the rural Hudson Valley. At nineteen he started to publish pieces of satire in a newspaper edited by his brother, and by the age of twenty-four, he was publishing a satirical magazine named *Salmagundi*. He liked to use pen names instead of his real name for his essays and sketches. In 1809, he used the pseudonym Diedrich Knickerbocker to publish *A History of New York from the Beginning of the World to the End of the Dutch Dynasty*. The book, written in a humorous and satirical tone, combined old tales and the history of old New York, showing the customs and lifestyles of the early Dutch settlers. Well received by the public, it established Irving as a humorous writer.

In 1815, Irving travelled to Europe and in the next seventeen years lived in Britain, Holland, France, Germany, Spain, and Italy. He studied local traditions, customs, and tales, and later adapted and used them in his writings. In 1820, he published his *The Sketch Book*, which included some local stories he had learned during his stay in these different countries. The most famous stories "Rip Van Winkle" and "The Legend of Sleepy Hollow" are borrowed from German folktales and retold by Knickerbocker. They have become classical American stories widely known in the world.

Irving returned to America in 1846 and lived at Sunnyside on the bank of the Hudson River until his death. His writings included travel books, tales, sketches, histories, and biographies featuring humor, satire, elegance and nostalgia.

Rip Van Winkle
(Excerpt)

...

Whoever has made a voyage up the Hudson must remember the Kaatskill mountains. They are a dismembered branch of the great Appalachian family, and are seen away to the west of the river, swelling up to a noble height, and lording it over the surrounding country. Every change of season, every change of weather, indeed, every hour of the day, produces some change in the magical hues and shapes of these mountains, and they are regarded by all the good wives, far and near, as perfect barometers. When the weather is fair and settled, they are clothed in blue and purple, and print their bold outlines on the clear evening sky; but sometimes, when the rest of the landscape is cloudless, they will gather a hood of gray vapors about their summits, which, in the last rays of the setting sun, will glow and light up like a crown of glory.

At the foot of these fairy mountains, the voyager may have descried the light smoke curling up from a village, whose shingle-roofs gleam among the trees, just where the blue tints of the upland melt away into the fresh green of the nearer landscape. It is a little village of great antiquity, having been founded by some of the Dutch colonists, in the early times of the province, just about the beginning of the government of the good Peter Stuyvesant[①], (may he rest in peace!) and there were some of the houses of the original settlers standing within a few years,with lattice windows, gable fronts surmounted with weathercocks, and built of small yellow bricks brought from Holland.

In that same village, and in one of these very houses (which, to tell the precise truth, was sadly time-worn and weather-beaten), there lived, many years since, while the country was yet a province of Great Britain, a simple, good-natured fellow, of the name of Rip Van

---

① Peter Stuyvesant (1592 – 1672): Dutch colonial governor who tried to resist the English seizure of New Yourk.

Winkle. He was a descendant of the Van Winkles who figured so gallantly in the chivalrous days of Peter Stuyvesant, and accompanied him to the siege of Fort Christina. He inherited, however, but little of the martial character of his ancestors. I have observed that he was a simple, good-natured man; he was, moreover, a kind neighbor, and an obedient henpecked husband. Indeed, to the latter circumstance might be owing that meekness of spirit which gained him such universal popularity; for those men are apt to be obsequious and conciliating abroad, who are under the discipline of shrews at home. Their tempers, doubtless, are rendered pliant and malleable in the fiery furnace of domestic tribulation, and a curtain-lecture is worth all the sermons in the world for teaching the virtues of patience and long-suffering. A termagant wife may, therefore, in some respects, be considered a tolerable blessing, and if so, Rip Van Winkle was thrice blessed.

Certain it is, that he was a great favorite among all the good wives of the village, who, as usual with the amiable sex, took his part in all family squabbles, and never failed, whenever they talked those matters over in their evening gossipings, to lay all the blame on Dame Van Winkle. The children of the village, too, would shout with joy whenever he approached. He assisted at their sports, made their playthings, taught them to fly kites and shoot marbles, and told them long stories of ghosts, witches, and Indians. Whenever he went dodging about the village, he was surrounded by a troop of them hanging on his skirts, clambering on his back, and playing a thousand tricks on him with impunity; and not a dog would bark at him throughout the neighborhood.

The great error in Rip's composition was an insuperable aversion to all kinds of profitable labor. It could not be for want of assiduity① or perseverance; for he would sit on a wet rock, with a rod as long and heavy as a Tartar's lance, and fish all day without a murmur, even though he should not be encouraged by a single nibble. He would carry a fowling-piece on his shoulder, for hours together, trudging through woods and swamps, and up hill and down dale, to shoot a few squirrels or wild pigeons. He would never refuse to assist a neighbor even in the roughest toil, and was a foremost man in all country frolics for husking Indian corn, or building stone fences; the women of the village, too, used to employ him to run their errands, and to do such little odd jobs as their less obliging husbands would not do for them. In a word, Rip was ready to attend to anybody's business but his own; but as to doing family duty, and keeping his farm in order, he found it impossible.

In fact, he declared it was of no use to work on his farm; it was the most pestilent little piece of ground in the whole country; everything about it went wrong, in spite of him. His fences were continually falling to pieces; his cow would either go astray, or get among the cabbages; weeds were sure to grow quicker in his fields than anywhere else; the rain always made a point of setting in just as he had some out-door work to do; so that though his patrimonial estate had dwindled away under his management, acre by acre, until there was

---

① assiduity: constant attention to what one is doing.

little more left than a mere patch of Indian corn and potatoes, yet it was the worst-conditioned farm in the neighborhood.

His children, too, were as ragged and wild as if they belonged to nobody. His son Rip, an urchin begotten in his own likeness, promised to inherit the habits, with the old clothes, of his father. He was generally seen trooping like a colt at his mother's heels, equipped in a pair of his father's cast-off galligaskins, which he had much ado to hold up with one hand, as a fine lady does her train in bad weather.

Rip Van Winkle, however, was one of those happy mortals, of foolish, well-oiled dispositions, who take the world easy, eat white bread or brown, whichever can be got with least thought or trouble, and would rather starve on a penny than work for a pound. If left to himself, he would have whistled life away, in perfect contentment; but his wife kept continually dinning in his ears about his idleness, his carelessness, and the ruin he was bringing on his family. Morning, noon, and night, her tongue was incessantly going, and every thing he said or did was sure to produce a torrent of household eloquence. Rip had but one way of replying to all lectures of the kind, and that, by frequent use, had grown into a habit. He shrugged his shoulders, shook his head, cast up his eyes, but said nothing. This, however, always provoked a fresh volley from his wife, so that he was fain to draw off his forces, and take to the outside of the house — the only side which, in truth, belongs to a henpecked husband.

Rip's sole domestic adherent was his dog Wolf, who was as much henpecked as his master; for Dame Van Winkle regarded them as companions in idleness, and even looked upon Wolf with an evil eye, as the cause of his master's going so often astray. True it is, in all points of spirit befitting in honorable dog, he was as courageous an animal as ever scoured the woods — but what courage can withstand the evil-doing and all-besetting terrors of a woman's tongue? The moment Wolf entered the house, his crest fell, his tail drooped to the ground, or curled between his legs, he sneaked about with a gallows air, casting many a sidelong glance at Dame Van Winkle, and at the least flourish of a broomstick or ladle, he would fly to the door with yelping precipitation.

Times grew worse and worse with Rip Van Winkle as years of matrimony① rolled on; a tart temper never mellows with age, and a sharp tongue is the only edged tool that grows keener with constant use. For a long while he used to console himself, when driven from home, by frequenting a kind of perpetual club of the sages, philosophers, and other idle personages of the village, which held its sessions on a bench before a small inn, designated by a rubicund portrait of his Majesty George the Third. Here they used to sit in the shade through a long, lazy summer's day, talking listlessly over village gossip, or telling endless, sleepy stories about nothing. But it would have been worth any statesman's money to have heard the profound discussions which sometimes took place, when by chance an old newspaper fell into their hands from some passing traveller. How solemnly they would listen to the contents, as

---

① matrimony: marriage.

drawled out by Derrick Van Bummel, the school-master, a dapper learned little man, who was not to be daunted by the most gigantic word in the dictionary; and how sagely they would deliberate upon public events some months after they had taken place.

The opinions of this junto were completely controlled by Nicholas Vedder, a patriarch of the village, and landlord of the inn, at the door of which he took his seat from morning till night, just moving sufficiently to avoid the sun, and keep in the shade of a large tree; so that the neighbors could tell the hour by his movements as accurately as by a sun-dial. It is true, he was rarely heard to speak, but smoked his pipe incessantly. His adherents, however (for every great man has his adherents), perfectly understood him, and knew how to gather his opinions. When any thing that was read or related displeased him, he was observed to smoke his pipe vehemently, and to send forth, frequent, and angry puffs; but when pleased, he would inhale the smoke slowly and tranquilly, and emit it in light and placid clouds, and sometimes, taking the pipe from his mouth, and letting the fragrant vapor curl about his nose, would gravely nod his head in token of perfect approbation.

From even this stronghold the unlucky Rip was at length routed by his termagant wife, who would suddenly break in upon the tranquility of the assemblage, and call the members all to nought; nor was that august personage, Nicholas Vedder himself, sacred from the daring tongue of this terrible virago, who charged him outright with encouraging her husband in habits of idleness.

Poor Rip was at last reduced almost to despair; and his only alternative, to escape from the labor of the farm and the clamor of his wife, was to take gun in hand, and stroll away into the woods. Here he would sometimes seat himself at the foot of a tree, and share the contents of his wallet with Wolf, with whom he sympathized as a fellow-sufferer in persecution. "Poor Wolf," he would say, "thy mistress leads thee a dog's life of it; but never mind, my lad, whilst I live thou shalt never want a friend to stand by thee!" Wolf would wag his tail, look wistfully in his master's face, and if dogs can feel pity, I verily believe he reciprocated the sentiment with all his heart.

In a long ramble of the kind, on a fine autumnal day, Rip had unconsciously scrambled to one of the highest parts of the Kaatskill mountains. He was after his favorite sport of squirrel shooting, and the still solitudes had echoed and re-echoed with the reports of his gun. Panting and fatigued, he threw himself, late in the afternoon, on a green knoll, covered with mountain herbage, that crowned the brow of a precipice. From an opening between the trees, he could overlook all the lower country for many a mile of rich woodland. He saw at a distance the lordly Hudson, far, far below him, moving on its silent but majestic course, with the reflection of a purple cloud, or the sail of a lagging bark, here and there sleeping on its glassy bosom and at last losing itself in the blue highlands.

On the other side he looked down into a deep mountain glen, wild, lonely, and shagged, the bottom filled with fragments from the impending cliffs, and scarcely lighted by the reflected rays of the setting sun. For some time Rip lay musing on this scene; evening was gradually advancing; the mountains began to throw their long blue shadows over the valleys; he saw that it would be dark long before he could reach the village; and he heaved a heavy sigh when he thought of encountering the terrors of Dame Van Winkle.

As he was about to descend, he heard a voice from a distance hallooing: "Rip Van Winkle! Rip Van Winkle!" He looked around, but could see nothing but a crow winging its solitary flight across the mountain. He thought his fancy must have deceived him, and turned again to descend, when he heard the same cry ring through the still evening air, "Rip Van Winkle! Rip Van Winkle!" — at the same time Wolf bristled up his back, and giving a low growl, skulked to his master's side, looking fearfully down into the glen. Rip now felt a vague apprehension① stealing over him; he looked anxiously in the same direction, and perceived a strange figure slowly toiling up the rocks, and bending under the weight of something he carried on his back. He was surprised to see any human being in this lonely and unfrequented place, but supposing it to be some one of the neighborhood in need of his assistance, he hastened down to yield it.

On nearer approach, he was still more surprised at the singularity of the stranger's appearance. He was a short, square-built old fellow, with thick bushy hair, and a grizzled beard. His dress was of the antique Dutch fashion — a cloth jerkin strapped round the waist — several pairs of breeches, the outer one of ample volume, decorated with rows of buttons down the sides, and bunches at the knees. He bore on his shoulders a stout keg, that seemed full of liquor, and made signs for Rip to approach and assist him with the load. Though rather shy and distrustful of this new acquaintance, Rip complied with his usual alacrity; and mutually relieving each other, they clambered up a narrow gully, apparently the dry bed of a mountain torrent. As they ascended, Rip every now and then heard long rolling peals, like distant thunder, that seemed to issue out of a deep ravine, or rather cleft between lofty rocks, toward which their rugged path conducted. He paused for an instant, but supposing it to be the muttering of one of those transient thunder-showers which often take place in the mountain heights, he proceeded. Passing through the ravine, they came to a hollow, like a small amphitheatre, surrounded by perpendicular precipices, over the brinks of which impending trees shot their branches, so that you only caught glimpses of the azure sky, and the bright evening cloud. During the whole time Rip and his companion had labored on in silence; for though the former marvelled greatly what could be the object of carrying a keg of liquor up this wild mountain, yet there was something strange and incomprehensible about the unknown, that inspired awe, and checked familiarity.

On entering the amphitheatre, new objects of wonder presented themselves. On a level spot in the centre was a company of odd-looking personages playing at ninepins. They were dressed in quaint outlandish fashion; some wore short doublets, others jerkins, with long knives in their belts, and most of them had enormous breeches, of similar style with that of the guide's. Their visages, too, were peculiar; one had a large head, broad face, and small

---

① apprehension: anxiety or fear that something bad or unpleasant will happen.

piggish eyes; the face of another seemed to consist entirely of nose, and was surmounted by a white sugar-loaf hat, set off with a little red cock's tail. They all had beards, of various shapes and colors. There was one who seemed to be the commander. He was a stout old gentleman, with a weather-beaten countenance; he wore a laced doublet, broad belt and hanger, high-crowned hat and feather, red stockings, and high-heeled shoes, with roses in them. The whole group reminded Rip of the figures in an old Flemish painting, in the parlor of Dominie Van Schaick, the village parson, and which had been brought over from Holland at the time of the settlement.

What seemed particularly odd to Rip was, that though these folks were evidently amusing themselves, yet they maintained the gravest faces, the most mysterious silence, and were, withal, the most melancholy party of pleasure he had ever witnessed. Nothing interrupted the stillness of the scene but the noise of the balls, which, whenever they were rolled, echoed along the mountains like rumbling peals of thunder.

As Rip and his companion approached them, they suddenly desisted from their play, and stared at him with such a fixed statue-like gaze, and such strange uncouth, lack-lustre countenances, that his heart turned within him, and his knees smote together. His companion now emptied the contents of the keg into large flagons, and made signs to him to wait upon the company. He obeyed with fear and trembling; they quaffed the liquor in profound silence, and then returned to their game.

By degrees, Rip's awe and apprehension subsided. He even ventured, when no eye was fixed upon him, to taste the beverage which he found had much of the flavor of excellent Hollands. He was naturally a thirsty soul, and was soon tempted to repeat the draught. One taste provoked another; and he reiterated his visits to the flagon so often, that at length his senses were overpowered, his eyes swam in his head, his head gradually declined, and he fell into a deep sleep.

On waking, he found himself on the green knoll whence he had first seen the old man of the glen. He rubbed his eyes — it was a bright sunny morning. The birds were hopping and twittering among the bushes, and the eagle was wheeling aloft, and breasting the pure mountain breeze. "Surely," thought Rip, "I have not slept here all night." He recalled the occurrences before he fell asleep. The strange man with the keg of liquor — the mountain ravine — the wild retreat among the rocks — the woe-begone party at ninepins — the flagon — "Oh! that flagon! that wicked flagon!" thought Rip — "what excuse shall I make to Dame Van Winkle?"

He looked round for his gun, but in place of the clean well-oiled fowling-piece, he found an old firelock lying by him, the barrel encrusted with rust, the lock falling off, and the stock worm-eaten. He now suspected that the grave roysterers of the mountains had put a trick upon him, and, having dosed him with liquor, had robbed him of his gun. Wolf, too, had disappeared, but he might have strayed away after a squirrel or partridge. He whistled after him and shouted his name, but all in vain; the echoes repeated his whistle and shout, but no dog was to be seen.

He determined to revisit the scene of the last evening's gambol, and if he met with any of the party, to demand his dog and gun. As he rose to walk, he found himself stiff in the joints, and wanting in his usual activity. "These mountain beds do not agree with me," thought Rip, "and if this frolic, should lay me up with a fit of the rheumatism, I shall have a blessed time with Dame Van Winkle." With some difficulty he got down into the glen: he found the gully up which he and his companion had ascended the preceding evening; but to his astonishment a mountain stream was now foaming down it, leaping from rock to rock, and filling the glen with babbling murmurs. He, however, made shift to scramble up its sides, working his toilsome way through thickets of birch, sassafras, and witch-hazel; and sometimes tripped up or entangled by the wild grape vines that twisted their coils and tendrils from tree to tree, and spread a kind of network in his path.

At length he reached to where the ravine had opened through the cliffs to the amphitheatre; but no traces of such opening remained. The rocks presented a high impenetrable wall, over which the torrent came tumbling in a sheet of feathery foam, and fell into a broad deep basin, black from the shadows of the surrounding forest. Here, then, poor Rip was brought to a stand. He again called and whistled after his dog; he was only answered by the cawing of a flock of idle crows, sporting high in the air about a dry tree that overhung a sunny precipice; and who, secure in their elevation, seemed to look down and scoff at the poor man's perplexities. What was to be done? The morning was passing away, and Rip felt famished for want of his breakfast. He grieved to give up his dog and gun; he dreaded to meet his wife; but it would not do to starve among the mountains. He shook his head, shouldered the rusty firelock, and, with a heart full of trouble and anxiety, turned his steps homeward.

As he approached the village, he met a number of people, but none that he knew, which somewhat surprised him, for he had thought himself acquainted with every one in the country round. Their dress, too, was of a different fashion from that to which he was accustomed. They all stared at him with equal marks of surprise, and whenever they cast eyes upon him, invariably stroked their chins. The constant recurrence of this gesture, induced Rip, involuntarily, to do the same, when, to his astonishment, he found his beard had grown a foot long!

He had now entered the skirts of the village. A troop of strange children ran at his heels, hooting after him, and pointing at his gray beard. The dogs, too, not one of which he recognized for an old acquaintance, barked at him as he passed. The very village was altered: it was larger and more populous. There were rows of houses which he had never seen before, and those which had been his familiar haunts had disappeared. Strange names were over the doors — strange faces at the windows — everything was strange. His mind now misgave him; he began to doubt whether both he and the world around him were not bewitched. Surely this was his native village, which he had left but a day before. There stood the Kaatskill mountains — there ran the silver Hudson at a distance — there was every hill and dale precisely as it had always been — Rip was sorely perplexed — "That flagon last night," thought he, "has addled my poor head sadly!"

It was with some difficulty that he found the way to his own house, which he approached with silent awe, expecting every moment to hear the shrill voice of Dame Van Winkle. He found the house gone to decay — the roof had fallen in, the windows shattered, and the doors off the hinges. A half-starved dog, that looked like Wolf, was skulking about it. Rip called him by name, but the cur snarled, showed his teeth, and passed on. This was an unkind cut indeed — "My very dog," sighed poor Rip, "has forgotten me!"

He entered the house, which, to tell the truth, Dame Van Winkle had always kept in neat order. It was empty, forlorn, and apparently abandoned. This desolateness overcame all his connubial fears — he called loudly for his wife and children — the lonely chambers rang for a moment with his voice, and then all again was silence.

He now hurried forth, and hastened to his old resort, the village inn — but it too was gone. A large rickety wooden building stood in its place, with great gaping windows, some of them broken, and mended with old hats and petticoats, and over the door was painted, "The Union Hotel, by Jonathan Doolittle." Instead of the great tree that used to shelter the quiet little Dutch inn of yore, there now was reared a tall naked pole, with something on the top that looked like a red nightcap, and from it was fluttering a flag, on which was a singular assemblage of stars and stripes — all this was strange and incomprehensible. He recognized on the sign, however, the ruby face of King George, under which he had smoked so many a peaceful pipe, but even this was singularly metamorphosed. The red coat was changed for one of blue and buff, a sword was held in the hand instead of a sceptre, the head was decorated with a cocked hat, and underneath was painted in large characters, "GENERAL WASHINGTON."

There was, as usual, a crowd of folk about the door, but none that Rip recollected. The very character of the people seemed changed. There was a busy, bustling, disputatious tone about it, instead of the accustomed phlegm and drowsy tranquility. He looked in vain for the sage Nicholas Vedder, with his broad face, double chin, and fair long pipe, uttering clouds of tobacco-smoke, instead of idle speeches; or Van Bummel, the schoolmaster, doling forth the contents of an ancient newspaper. In place of these, a lean, bilious-looking fellow, with his pockets full of handbills, was haranguing, vehemently about rights of citizens — elections — members of Congress — liberty — Bunker's hill — heroes of seventy-six — and other words, which were a perfect Babylonish jargon to the bewildered Van Winkle.

The appearance of Rip, with his long, grizzled beard, his rusty fowling-piece, his uncouth dress, and the army of women and children at his heels, soon attracted the attention of the tavern politicians. They crowded round him, eying him from head to foot, with great curiosity. The orator bustled up to him, and drawing him partly aside, inquired "which side he voted?" Rip stared in vacant stupidity. Another short but busy little fellow pulled him by the arm, and rising on tiptoe, inquired in his ear, whether he was Federal or Democrat. Rip was equally at a loss to comprehend the question; when a knowing, self-important old gentleman, in a sharp cocked hat, made his way through the crowd, putting them to the right and left with his elbows as he passed, and planting himself before Van Winkle, with one arm akimbo, the other resting on his cane, his keen eyes and sharp hat penetrating, as it were, into his very soul, demanded in an austere tone, "What brought him to the election with a gun on his shoulder, and a mob at his heels, and whether he meant to breed a riot in the village?"

"Alas! gentlemen," cried Rip, somewhat dismayed, "I am a poor quiet man, a native of the place, and a loyal subject of the King, God bless him!"

Here a general shout burst from the bystanders — "a tory! a tory! a spy! a refugee! hustle him! away with him!" It was with great difficulty that the self-important man in the cocked hat restored order; and having assumed a tenfold austerity of brow, demanded again of the unknown culprit, what he came there for, and whom he was seeking. The poor man humbly assured him that he meant no harm, but merely came there in search of some of his neighbors, who used to keep about the tavern.

"Well — who are they? — name them."

Rip bethought himself a moment, and inquired, "Where's Nicholas Vedder?"

There was a silence for a little while, when an old man replied, in a thin piping voice, "Nicholas Vedder? why, he is dead and gone these eighteen years! There was a wooden tombstone in the churchyard that used to tell all about him, but that's rotten and gone too."

"Where's Brom Dutcher?"

"Oh, he went off to the army in the beginning of the war; some say he was killed at the storming of Stony-Point — others say he was drowned in a squall at the foot of Antony's Nose. I don't know — he never came back again."

"Where's Van Bummel, the schoolmaster?"

"He went off to the wars, too; was a great militia general, and is now in Congress."

Rip's heart died away, at hearing of these sad changes in his home and friends, and finding himself thus alone in the world. Every answer puzzled him too, by treating of such enormous lapses of time, and of matters which he could not understand: war — Congress — Stony-Point; — he had no courage to ask after any more friends, but cried out in despair, "Does nobody here know Rip Van Winkle?"

"Oh, Rip Van Winkle!" exclaimed two or three. "Oh, to be sure! that's Rip Van Winkle yonder, leaning against the tree."

Rip looked, and beheld a precise counterpart of himself as he went up the mountain; apparently as lazy, and certainly as ragged. The poor fellow was now completely confounded. He doubted his own identity, and whether he was himself or another man. In the midst of his bewilderment, the man in the cocked hat demanded who he was, and what was his name?

"God knows!" exclaimed he at his wit's end; "I'm not myself — I'm somebody else — that's me yonder — no — that's somebody else, got into my shoes — I was myself last night, but I fell asleep on the mountain, and they've changed my gun, and everything's changed, and I'm changed, and I can't tell what's my name, or who I am!"

The by-standers began now to look at each other, nod, wink significantly, and tap their fingers against their foreheads. There was a whisper, also, about securing the gun, and keeping the old fellow from doing mischief. At the very suggestion of which, the self-important man with the cocked hat retired with some precipitation. At this critical moment a fresh, comely woman pressed through the throng to get a peep at the gray-bearded man. She had a chubby child in her arms, which, frightened at his looks, began to cry. "Hush, Rip," cried she, "hush, you little fool; the old man won't hurt you." The name of the child, the air of the mother, the tone of her voice, all awakened a train of recollections in his mind.

"What is your name, my good woman?" asked he.

"Judith Cardenier."

"And your father's name?"

"Ah, poor man, Rip Van Winkle was his name, but it's twenty years since he went away from home with his gun, and never has been heard of since — his dog came home without him; but whether he shot himself, or was carried away by the Indians, nobody can tell. I was then but a little girl."

Rip had but one more question to ask; but he put it with a faltering voice:

"Where's your mother?"

"Oh, she too had died but a short time since; she broke a blood-vessel in a fit of passion at a New-England peddler."

There was a drop of comfort, at least, in this intelligence. The honest man could contain himself no longer. He caught his daughter and her child in his arms. "I am your father!" cried he — "Young Rip Van Winkle once — old Rip Van Winkle now — Does nobody know poor Rip Van Winkle!"

All stood amazed, until an old woman, tottering out from among the crowd, put her hand to her brow, and peering under it in his face for a moment, exclaimed, "Sure enough! it is Rip Van Winkle — it is himself. Welcome home again, old neighbor. Why, where have you been these twenty long years?"

Rip's story was soon told, for the whole twenty years had been to him but as one night. The neighbors stared when they heard it; some were seen to wink at each other, and put their tongues in their cheeks; and the self-important man in the cocked hat, who, when the alarm was over, had returned to the field, screwed down the corners of his mouth, and shook his head — upon which there was a general shaking of the head throughout the assemblage.

It was determined, however, to take the opinion of old Peter Vanderdonk, who was seen slowly advancing up the road. He was a descendant of the historian of that name, who wrote one of the earliest accounts of the province. Peter was the most ancient inhabitant of the village, and well versed in all the wonderful events and traditions of the neighborhood. He recollected Rip at once, and corroborated his story in the most satisfactory manner. He assured the company that it was a fact, handed down from his ancestor the historian, that the Kaatskill mountains had always been haunted by strange beings. That it was affirmed that the great Hendrick Hudson, the first discoverer of the river and country, kept a kind of vigil there every twenty years, with his crew of the Half-moon; being permitted in this way to revisit the scenes of his enterprise, and keep a guardian eye upon the river and the great city called by his name. That his father had once seen them in their old Dutch dresses playing at ninepins in the hollow of the mountain; and that he himself had heard, one summer afternoon, the sound of their balls, like distant peals of thunder.

To make a long story short, the company broke up, and returned to the more important concerns of the election. Rip's daughter took him home to live with her; she had a snug, well-furnished house, and a stout cheery farmer for a husband, whom Rip recollected for one of the urchins that used to climb upon his back. As to Rip's son and heir, who was the ditto of himself, seen leaning against the tree, he was employed to work on the farm; but evinced an hereditary disposition to attend to any thing else but his business.

Rip now resumed his old walks and habits; he soon found many of his former cronies, though all rather the worse for the wear and tear of time; and preferred making friends among the rising generation, with whom he soon grew into great favor.

Having nothing to do at home, and being arrived at that happy age when a man can be idle with impunity, he took his place once more on the bench, at the inn door, and was reverenced as one of the patriarchs of the village, and a chronicle of the old times "before the war." It was some time before he could get into the regular track of gossip, or could be made to comprehend the strange events that had taken place during his torpor. How that there had been a revolutionary war — that the country had thrown off the yoke of old England — and that, instead of being a subject to his Majesty George the Third, he was now a free citizen of the United States. Rip, in fact, was no politician; the changes of states and empires made but little impression on him; but there was one species of despotism under which he had long groaned, and that was — petticoat government. Happily, that was at an end; he had got his neck out of the yoke of matrimony, and could go in and out whenever he pleased, without dreading the tyranny of Dame Van Winkle. Whenever her name was mentioned, however, he shook his head, shrugged his shoulders, and cast up his eyes; which might pass either for an expression of resignation to his fate, or joy at his deliverance.

He used to tell his story to every stranger that arrived at Mr. Doolittle's hotel. He was observed, at first, to vary on some points every time he told it, which was, doubtless, owing to his having so recently awaked. It at last settled down precisely to the tale I have related, and not a man, woman, or child in the neighborhood, but knew it by heart. Some always pretended to doubt the reality of it, and insisted that Rip had been out of his head, and that this was one point on which he always remained flighty. The old Dutch inhabitants, however, almost universally gave it full credit. Even to this day, they never hear a thunder-storm of a summer afternoon about the Kaatskill, but they say Hendrick Hudson and his crew are at their game of ninepins; and it is a common wish of all henpecked husbands in the neighborhood, when life hangs heavy on their hands, that they might have a quieting draught out of Rip van Winkle's flagon.

...

⟫ Questions for Consideration and Discussion

1. Do you agree that Rip is an irresponsible man for his family? Would you view him as a comic figure or a tragic figure? Why?

2. What ideas of Romanticism do you find in this story?

3. Why do you think this story is so popular with the Americans? Do you like the story? Why or why not?

William Cullen Bryant(1794 –1878)

William Cullen Bryant, the "father of American poetry," is the first American lyric poet of distinction.

Bryant grew up in a small village in western Massachusetts. As a boy he spent much time exploring the mysteries of the forests and hills in the countryside. Encouraged by his father, who loved poetry, he took a great interest in reading and writing poems from an early age. When he was thirteen, one of his religious poems was published. At the age of thirteen, he composed his thought-provoking poem "Thanatopsis." The title of the poem is a Greek word meaning "view of death." When the poem was sent by his father to the *North American Review*, a major literary magazine, the editors found the poem so impressive that some doubted its true origins and thought Bryant's father had actually written it. "No one on this side of the Atlantic is capable of writing such verse," said one editor.

Although Bryant's father encouraged him to write poems, the father recommended that his son become a lawyer in order to make a living. Bryant received legal training and practiced law for a short time. Then he began a career as a journalist. He became the editor-in-chief of *New York Evening Post* and worked with it for half a century. As an influential editor, he supported the early labor movement, freedom of speech, women's rights, and the abolition of slavery. Bryant played a significant role in Lincoln's election to the presidency. When Lincoln came to New York City in 1860 to make his speech, he was introduced by Bryant to the voters.

Apart from his work with newspapers, Bryant continued to compose poems. His noble and romantic verses, often replete with themes of nature and solitude, established his reputation of the "father of American poetry." Bryant will be remembered longest as the poet of his native Berkshire hills and streams in such poems as "Thanatopsis" and "To a Waterfowl."

Thanatopsis

To him who in the love of Nature holds
Communion with her visible forms, she speaks

A various language; for his gayer hours
She has a voice of gladness, and a smile
5 And eloquence of beauty, and she glides
Into his darker musings, with a mild
And healing sympathy, that steals away
Their sharpness, ere he is aware. When thoughts
Of the last bitter hour come like a blight
10 Over thy spirit, and sad images
Of the stern agony, and shroud, and pall,
And breathless darkness, and the narrow house,
Make thee to shudder, and grow sick at heart; —
Go forth under the open sky, and list
15 To Nature's teachings, while from all around —
Earth and her waters, and the depths of air —
Comes a still voice.

Yet a few days, and thee
The all-beholding sun shall see no more
In all his course; nor yet in the cold ground,
20 Where thy pale form was laid, with many tears,
Nor in the embrace of ocean, shall exist
Thy image. Earth, that nourished thee, shall claim
Thy growth, to be resolved to earth again,
And, lost each human trace, surrendering up
25 Thine individual being, shalt thou go
To mix forever with the elements;
To be a brother to the insensible rock,
And to the sluggish clod, which the rude swain
Turns with his share, and treads upon. The oak
30 Shall send his roots abroad, and pierce thy mould.

Yet not to thine eternal resting-place
Shalt thou retire alone, nor couldst thou wish
Couch more magnificent. Thou shalt lie down
With patriarchs of the infant world — with kings,
35 The powerful of the earth — the wise, the good,
Fair forms, and hoary seers of ages past,
All in one mighty sepulcher. The hills
Rock-ribbed and ancient as the sun — the vales
Stretching in pensive quietness between;

40   The venerable woods — rivers that move
        In majesty, and the complaining brooks
        That make the meadows green; and, poured round all,
        Old Ocean's gray and melancholy waste —
        Are but the solemn decorations all
45   Of the great tomb of man! The golden sun,
        The planets, all the infinite host of heaven,
        Are shining on the sad abodes of death,
        Through the still lapse of ages. All that tread
        The globe are but a handful to the tribes
50   That slumber in its bosom. — Take the wings
        Of morning, pierce the Barcan wilderness,
        Or lose thyself in the continuous woods
        Where rolls the Oregon, and hears no sound,
        Save his own dashings — yet the dead are there:
55   And millions in those solitudes, since first
        The flight of years began, have laid them down
        In their last sleep — the dead reign there alone.
        So shalt thou rest; and what if thou withdraw
        In silence from the living, and no friend
60   Take note of thy departure? All that breathe
        Will share thy destiny. The gay will laugh
        When thou art gone, the solemn brood of care
        Plod on, and each one as before will chase
        His favorite phantom; yet all these shall leave
65   Their mirth and their employments, and shall come
        And make their bed with thee. As the long train
        Of ages glide away, the sons of men,
        The youth in life's green spring, and he who goes
        In the full strength of years, matron and maid,
70   The speechless babe, and the gray-headed man —
        Shall one by one be gathered to thy side
        By those, who in their turn shall follow them.

        So live, that when thy summons comes to join
        The innumerable caravan which moves
75   To that mysterious realm, where each shall take
        His chamber in the silent halls of death,
        Thou go not, like the quarry-slave at night,
        Scourged to his dungeon, but, sustained and soothed

By an unfaltering trust, approach thy grave
80   Like one who wraps the drapery of his couch
About him, and lies down to pleasant dreams.

To a Waterfowl

Whither, 'midst falling dew,
While glow the heavens with the last steps of day,
Far, through their rosy depths, dost thou pursue
Thy solitary way?

5   Vainly the fowler's eye
Might mark thy distant flight, to do thee wrong,
As, darkly seen against the crimson sky,
Thy figure floats along.

Seek'st thou the plashy brink
10   Of weedy lake, or marge of river wide,
Or where the rocking billows rise and sink
On the chafed ocean side?

There is a Power, whose care
Teaches thy way along that pathless coast, —
15   The desert and illimitable air
Lone wandering, but not lost.

All day thy wings have fanned,
At that far height, the cold thin atmosphere;
Yet stoop not, weary, to the welcome land,
20   Though the dark night is near.

And soon that toil shall end,
Soon shalt thou find a summer home, and rest,
And scream among thy fellows; reeds shall bend,
Soon, o'er thy sheltered nest.

25   Thou'rt gone, the abyss of heaven
      Hath swallowed up thy form, yet, on my heart
      Deeply hath sunk the lesson thou hast given,
      And shall not soon depart.

      He, who, from zone to zone,
30   Guides through the boundless sky thy certain flight,
      In the long way that I must trace alone,
      Will lead my steps aright.

▶▶ Questions for Consideration and Discussion

1. Are you afraid of death? What's your view of death? How is the view of death expressed in "Thanatopsis" the same or different from others that you know about?
2. What lesson about death does the poet expect us to learn from closely observing nature? According to the poet, what is the overall relationship between human beings and nature? What power does the poet think nature has?
3. What comforting observation about death does the poet make? With what emotion does Bryant advise people to face death?
4. How many possible destinations does the poet think the waterfowl might be flying to? Why does the waterfowl not stop its flight?
5. The sight of a flying waterfowl makes the speaker reflect upon his own life. What comparison does the speaker make between the bird's flight and his own life? What "lesson" does the speaker receive, and why might the lesson "not soon depart"? Explain.
6. Waterfowls ordinarily travel in groups, or at least in pairs. Why is it important and meaningful that this bird is alone? What do you think the poet feels about his own life?

▎ Edgar Allan Poe(1809 – 1849)

Edgar Allan Poe led a short, unhappy, melodramatic life marked by poverty, restlessness, and feverishly creative activity. He was always struggling, and sometimes he was overwhelmingly lonely. Nevertheless, after his death, he became one of the most widely read and influential American writers. He has been regarded as a master of the horror tale, a patron saint of the detective story, and a renowned literary critic.

Poe was born in a traveling actors' family in Boston. When he was still a little boy, he lost both of his parents and was adopted by a wealthy Virginia couple, the Allans. He received a good education and seemed to be heading to the life of a gentleman when he entered the University of Virginia. However, heavy gambling debts and a wild life forced him to drop out. Later, the Allans helped him win an appointment to the United States Military Academy at West Point. However, Poe liked writing poems, which conflicted with the rigid life in the military academy (he published his first book of poetry at the age of eighteen, and his second book two years later in 1829). He deliberately broke rules and was expelled after less than a year's stay there. His third book of poems was published soon after his expulsion and was dedicated to "the U.S. Corps of Cadets."

Knowing that he was not going to inherit the Allans' fortune, Poe had to make his own way in the world. He moved from job to job (usually as an editor or journalist), from city to city; he spent much of his remaining years in four literary centers: Baltimore, Richmond, Philadelphia, and New York. He continued to write poems, short stories, and reviews. In 1838, he published his only novel, *The Narrative of Arthur Gordon Pym*, a sea adventure. His *Tales of the Grotesque and Arabesque* came out in 1840.

In 1835, he secretly married his cousin Virginia, who was then only 13 years old.

Poe contributed stories and poems to an assortment of journals. But he was unable to escape his spirit-breaking poverty. Even "The Raven," his most popular work, brought him little money. When his beloved wife Virginia died in 1847, the deep sorrow was more than he could bear. He died soon afterward in 1849. When he died, he was completely "alone."

A few writers have found Poe's writing unpolished and juvenile: Emerson called him "the jingle man," and Mark Twain said he would read Poe only if someone paid him. Yet many writers and critics, especially Europeans, have admired Poe more than any other American writer. The Irish poet W. B. Yeats considered Poe as "the greatest of American Poets."

Poe is still praised for his extraordinary ability to create unforgettable images, musical language, fearful moods and atmosphere. Poe's most abiding ambition was to become a powerful critic. He thought poetry should appeal only to the sense of beauty, not truth; informational poetry, poetry of ideas, or any sort of didactic poetry was illegitimate. He set himself against realistic details in poetry. He also held that both poems and tales should be short enough to be read in one sitting; otherwise, the unity of effect would be dissipated.

Poe populated his short stories and poetry with a myriad deviant types of characters, including aristocratic madmen, self-tormented murderers and neurasthenic necrophiliacs, so as to produce the greatest possible horrific effects on the reader. Poe created detective stories when he was thirty-two. In his detective stories, the heroes are brilliant preternatural logicians.

To Helen

Helen, thy beauty is to me
Like those Nicean barks① of yore,
That gently, o'er a perfumed sea,
The weary, way-worn wanderer bore
5   To his own native shore.

On desperate seas long wont to roam,
Thy hyacinth hair, thy classic face,
Thy Naiad airs have brought me home
To the glory that was Greece.
10   And the grandeur that was Rome.

Lo! in yon brilliant window-niche
How statue-like I see thee stand!
The agate lamp within thy hand,
Ah! Psyche from the regions which
15   Are Holy Land!

The Raven

Once upon a midnight dreary, while I pondered, weak and weary,
Over many a quaint and curious volume of forgotten lore —
While I nodded, nearly napping, suddenly there came a tapping,
As of some one gently rapping, rapping at my chamber door.
5   "'Tis some visitor," I muttered, "tapping at my chamber door —
Only this and nothing more."

---

①   Nicean barks: Poe may be referring to boats from the shipbuilding city of Nicea in Asia Minor. It is likely, however, that he created the phrase for its melodious sound.

Ah, distinctly I remember it was in the bleak December;
And each separate dying ember wrought its ghost upon the floor.
Eagerly I wished the morrow; — vainly I had sought to borrow
10 From my books surcease of sorrow — sorrow for the lost Lenore —
For the rare and radiant maiden whom the angels name Lenore —
　　　　Nameless *here* for evermore.

And the silken, sad, uncertain rustling of each purple curtain
Thrilled me — filled me with fantastic terrors never felt before;
15 So that now, to still the beating of my heart, I stood repeating
"'Tis some visitor entreating entrance at my chamber door —
Some late visitor entreating entrance at my chamber door; —
　　　　This it is and nothing more."

Presently my soul grew stronger; hesitating then no longer,
20 "Sir," said I, "or Madam, truly your forgiveness I implore;
But the fact is I was napping, and so gently you came rapping,
And so faintly you came tapping, tapping at my chamber door,
That I scarce was sure I heard you" — here I opened wide the door; —
　　　　Darkness there and nothing more.

25 Deep into that darkness peering, long I stood there wondering, fearing,
Doubting, dreaming dreams no mortal ever dared to dream before;
But the silence was unbroken, and the stillness gave no token,
And the only word there spoken was the whispered word, "Lenore?"
This I whispered, and an echo murmured back the word, "Lenore!" —
30 　　　　Merely this and nothing more.

Back into the chamber turning, all my soul within me burning,
Soon again I heard a tapping somewhat louder than before.
"Surely," said I, "surely that is something at my window lattice;
Let me see, then, what thereat is, and this mystery explore —
35 Let my heart be still a moment and this mystery explore; —
　　　　'Tis the wind and nothing more!"

Open here I flung the shutter, when, with many a flirt and flutter,
In there stepped a stately Raven of the saintly days of yore;
Not the least obeisance made he; not a minute stopped or stayed he;
40 But, with mien of lord or lady, perched above my chamber door —
Perched upon a bust of Pallas just above my chamber door —

Perched, and sat, and nothing more.

Then this ebony bird beguiling my sad fancy into smiling,
By the grave and stern decorum of the countenance it wore,
45 "Though thy crest be shorn and shaven, thou," I said, "art sure no craven,
Ghastly grim and ancient Raven wandering from the Nightly shore —
Tell me what thy lordly name is on the Night's Plutonian shore!"
        Quoth the Raven "Nevermore."

Much I marvelled this ungainly fowl to hear discourse so plainly,
50 Though its answer little meaning — little relevancy bore;
For we cannot help agreeing that no living human being
Ever yet was blessed with seeing bird above his chamber door —
Bird or beast upon the sculptured bust above his chamber door,
        With such name as "Nevermore."

55 But the Raven, sitting lonely on the placid bust, spoke only
That one word, as if his soul in that one word he did outpour.
Nothing farther then he uttered — not a feather then he fluttered —
Till I scarcely more than muttered "Other friends have flown before —
On the morrow *he* will leave me, as my Hopes have flown before."
60   Then the bird said "Nevermore."

Startled at the stillness broken by reply so aptly spoken,
"Doubtless," said I, "what it utters is its only stock and store
Caught from some unhappy master whom unmerciful Disaster
Followed fast and followed faster till his songs one burden bore —
65 Till the dirges of his Hope that melancholy burden bore
        Of 'Never — nevermore.'"

But the Raven still beguiling all my fancy into smiling,
Straight I wheeled a cushioned seat in front of bird, and bust and door;
Then, upon the velvet sinking, I betook myself to linking
70 Fancy unto fancy, thinking what this ominous bird of yore —
What this grim, ungainly, ghastly, gaunt, and ominous bird of yore
        Meant in croaking "Nevermore."

This I sat engaged in guessing, but no syllable expressing
To the fowl whose fiery eyes now burned into my bosom's core;

75 This and more I sat divining, with my head at ease reclining
On the cushion's velvet lining that the lamp-light gloated o'er,
But whose velvet-violet lining with the lamp-light gloating o'er,
  She shall press, ah, nevermore!

Then, methought, the air grew denser, perfumed from an unseen censer
80 Swung by Seraphim whose foot-falls tinkled on the tufted floor.
"Wretch," I cried, "thy God hath lent thee — by these angels he hath sent thee
Respite — respite and nepenthe from thy memories of Lenore;
Quaff, oh quaff this kind nepenthe and forget this lost Lenore!"
  Quoth the Raven "Nevermore."

85 "Prophet!" said I, "thing of evil! — prophet still, if bird or devil! —
Whether Tempter sent, or whether tempest tossed thee here ashore,
Desolate yet all undaunted, on this desert land enchanted —
On this home by Horror haunted — tell me truly, I implore —
Is there — is there balm in Gilead? — tell me — tell me, I implore!"
90   Quoth the Raven "Nevermore."

"Prophet!" said I, "thing of evil! — prophet still, if bird or devil!
By that Heaven that bends above us — by that God we both adore —
Tell this soul with sorrow laden if, within the distant Aidenn,
It shall clasp a sainted maiden whom the angels name Lenore —
95 Clasp a rare and radiant maiden whom the angels name Lenore."
  Quoth the Raven "Nevermore."

"Be that word our sign of parting, bird or fiend!" I shrieked, upstarting —
"Get thee back into the tempest and the Night's Plutonian shore!
Leave no black plume as a token of that lie thy soul hath spoken!
100 Leave my loneliness unbroken! — quit the bust above my door!
Take thy beak from out my heart, and take thy form from off my door!"
  Quoth the Raven "Nevermore."

And the Raven, never flitting, still is sitting, still is sitting
On the pallid bust of Pallas just above my chamber door;
105 And his eyes have all the seeming of a demon's that is dreaming,
And the lamp-light o'er him streaming throws his shadow on the floor;
And my soul from out that shadow that lies floating on the floor
  Shall be lifted — nevermore!

▶ Questions for Consideration and Discussion

1. What condition was the speaker in before encountering Helen?

2. It's common for a beautiful woman to be compared to flowers or birds, but it's uncommon that a pretty woman is compared to boats, as Helen is in the poem. What is the point of Helen's being compared to boats? Considering the places to which Helen brings the speaker and the place from which she comes, name the three kinds of joys or comforts she seems to provide.

3. What characteristics of Romanticism does "To Hellen" display?

4. Evaluate the speaker's emotional state at the beginning of "The Raven," in the next-to-the-last stanza, and in the last stanza. What does the future probably hold for the speaker?

5. As a critic, Poe asserted that a work of literature must arrange all of its elements so that they combine to achieve a single effect. In fact, Poe believed that a poet or a short story writer must begin with an idea of a single effect and then create the characters and incidents to produce that effect. What is the single effect of "The Raven"? How does each element of it contribute to the single effect?

Ralph Waldo Emerson (1803 – 1882)

Ralph Waldo Emerson is a philosopher, poet, essayist, lecturer, and leading transcendentalist. His famous address, *The American Scholar*, delivered in 1837, expresses a strong desire to create a new national identity, i.e., an American identity. Inspiring American writers to write about the American landscape and the American people's life, the speech has been praised as America's "intellectual Declaration of Independence."

Emerson was born in Boston into a Unitarian minister's home. Though his father died when he was only eight, he received good schooling. He attended Harvard, studied theology, and became a Unitarian minister himself in 1829. In the same year, he was married, but his beloved wife died only sixteen months later.

Though working as a minister, Emerson had a crisis of faith himself. His skepticism toward Christianity was strengthened by his exposure to the German "higher criticism." In 1832, for reasons of conscience, Emerson resigned his ministry and sailed for Europe, where he met Wordsworth, Carlyle, Coleridge, and some other English writers. After returning from Europe, he married again and settled in the village of Concord, Massachusetts. He began his lifelong career as lecturer and writer.

His first book *Nature* was self-published in 1836; it has been a major document in American Romanticism and Transcendentalism. In 1841 he published *Essays*, and his "Self-Reliance" in this book made Emerson internationally famous. The year 1844 saw the publication of his *Essays: Second Series*, which contained his famous essay, "The Poet." In 1849 his *Representative Men* came out; in this book of biographies of a number of great men including Plato, Shakespeare, and Napoleon, Emerson explored the "uses of great men." In 1860, he published his *The Conduct of Life*.

Emerson's writings show his optimism in the progress of man and society, his belief in individualism, independence, and self-reliance. His essays and his speeches influenced many American writers as well as American people throughout the nineteenth century and well into the twentieth century.

At Concord, Emerson and other important writers of his time, including Henry David Thoreau, Bronson Alcott, and Margaret Fuller, established the Transcendental Club. *The Dial* magazine was edited and published to promote their transcendentalist ideas.

Nature
(Excerpt)
Introduction

Our age is retrospective. It builds the sepulchers of the fathers. It writes biographies, histories, and criticism. The foregoing generations beheld God and nature face to face; we, through their eyes. Why should not we also enjoy an original relation to the universe? Why should not we have a poetry and philosophy of insight and not of tradition, and a religion by revelation to us, and not the history of theirs? Embosomed for a season in nature, whose floods of life stream around and through us, and invite us by the powers they supply, to action proportioned to nature, why should we grope among the dry bones of the past, or put the living generation into masquerade out of its faded wardrobe? The sun shines to-day also. There is more wool and flax in the fields. There are new lands, new men, new thoughts. Let us demand our own works and laws and worship.

...

Chapter I Nature

To go into solitude, a man needs to retire as much from his chamber as from society. I am not solitary whilst I read and write, though nobody is with me. But if a man would be alone, let him look at the stars. The rays that come from those heavenly worlds, will separate between him and what he touches. One might think the atmosphere was made transparent with this design, to give man, in the heavenly bodies, the perpetual presence of the sublime.

Seen in the streets of cities, how great they are! If the stars should appear one night in a thousand years, how would men believe and adore; and preserve for many generations the remembrance of the city of God which had been shown! But every night come out these envoys of beauty, and light the universe with their admonishing smile.

The stars awaken a certain reverence, because though always present, they are inaccessible; but all natural objects make a kindred impression, when the mind is open to their influence. Nature never wears a mean appearance. Neither does the wisest man extort her secret, and lose his curiosity by finding out all her perfection. Nature never became a toy to a wise spirit. The flowers, the animals, the mountains, reflected the wisdom of his best hour, as much as they had delighted the simplicity of his childhood.

When we speak of nature in this manner, we have a distinct but most poetical sense in the mind. We mean the integrity of impression made by manifold natural objects. It is this which distinguishes the stick of timber of the wood-cutter, from the tree of the poet. The charming landscape which I saw this morning, is indubitably made up of some twenty or thirty farms. Miller owns this field, Locke that, and Manning the woodland beyond. But none of them owns the landscape. There is a property in the horizon which no man has but he whose eye can integrate all the parts, that is, the poet. This is the best part of these men's farms, yet to this their warranty-deeds give no title.

To speak truly, few adult persons can see nature. Most persons do not see the sun. At least they have a very superficial seeing. The sun illuminates only the eye of the man, but shines into the eye and the heart of the child. The lover of nature is he whose inward and outward senses are still truly adjusted to each other; who has retained the spirit of infancy even into the era of manhood. His intercourse with heaven and earth, becomes part of his daily food. In the presence of nature, a wild delight runs through the man, in spite of real sorrows. Nature says, — he is my creature, and maugre① all his impertinent griefs, he shall be glad with me. Not the sun or the summer alone, but every hour and season yields its tribute of delight; for every hour and change corresponds to and authorizes a different state of the mind, from breathless noon to grimmest midnight. Nature is a setting that fits equally well a comic or a mourning piece. In good health, the air is a cordial of incredible virtue. Crossing a bare common, in snow puddles, at twilight, under a clouded sky, without having in my thoughts any occurrence of special good fortune, I have enjoyed a perfect exhilaration. I am glad to the brink of fear. In the woods too, a man casts off his years, as the snake his slough, and at what period soever of life, is always a child. In the woods, is perpetual youth. Within these plantations of God, a decorum and sanctity reign, a perennial festival is dressed, and the guest sees not how he should tire of them in a thousand years. In the woods, we return to reason and faith. There I feel that nothing can befall me in life, — no disgrace, no calamity, (leaving me my eyes,) which nature cannot repair. Standing on the bare ground, — my head bathed

---

① maugre: (old-fashioned English) in spite of

by the blithe air, and uplifted into infinite space, — all mean egotism vanishes. I become a transparent eye-ball; I am nothing; I see all; the currents of the Universal Being circulate through me; I am part or particle of God. The name of the nearest friend sounds then foreign and accidental: to be brothers, to be acquaintances, — master or servant, is then a trifle and a disturbance. I am the lover of uncontained and immortal beauty. In the wilderness, I find something more dear and connate than in streets or villages. In the tranquil landscape, and especially in the distant line of the horizon, man beholds somewhat as beautiful as his own nature.

The greatest delight which the fields and woods minister, is the suggestion of an occult relation between man and the vegetable. I am not alone and unacknowledged. They nod to me, and I to them. The waving of the boughs in the storm, is new to me and old. It takes me by surprise, and yet is not unknown. Its effect is like that of a higher thought or a better emotion coming over me, when I deemed I was thinking justly or doing right.

Yet it is certain that the power to produce this delight, does not reside in nature, but in man, or in a harmony of both. It is necessary to use these pleasures with great temperance. For, nature is not always tricked in holiday attire, but the same scene which yesterday breathed perfume and glittered as for the frolic of the nymphs, is overspread with melancholy today. Nature always wears the colors of the spirit. To a man laboring under calamity, the heat of his own fire hath sadness in it. Then, there is a kind of contempt of the landscape felt by him who has just lost by death a dear friend. The sky is less grand as it shuts down over less worth in the population.

Chapter Ⅳ Language

Language is a third use which Nature subserves to man. Nature is the vehicle of thought, and in a simple, double, and threefold degree.

1. Words are signs of natural facts.

2. Particular natural facts are symbols of particular spiritual facts.

3. Nature is the symbol of spirit.

1. Words are signs of natural facts. The use of natural history is to give us aid in supernatural history. The use of the outer creation is to give us language for the beings and changes of the inward creation. Every word which is used to express a moral or intellectual fact, if traced to its root, is found to be borrowed from some material appearance. *Right* means straight; *wrong* means twisted. Spirit primarily means *wind*; *transgression*, the crossing of a *line*; *supercilious*, the *raising* of *the eyebrow*. We say the *heart* to express *emotion*, the *head* to denote thought; and *thought* and *emotion* are, in their turn, words borrowed from sensible things, and now appropriated to spiritual nature. Most of the process by which this transformation is made, is hidden from us in the remote time when language was framed; but the same tendency may be daily observed in children. Children and savages use only nouns or names of things, which they continually convert into verbs, and apply to analogous mental acts.

2. But this origin of all words that convey a spiritual import, — so conspicuous a fact in

the history of language, — is our least debt to nature. It is not words only that are emblematic; it is things which are emblematic. Every natural fact is a symbol of some spiritual fact. Every appearance in nature corresponds to some state of the mind, and that state of the mind can only be described by presenting that natural appearance as its picture. An enraged man is a lion, a cunning man is a fox, a firm man is a rock, a learned man is a torch. A lamb is innocence; a snake is subtle spite; flowers express to us the delicate affections. Light and darkness are our familiar expression for knowledge and ignorance; and heat for love. Visible distance behind and before us, is respectively our image of memory and hope.

Who looks upon a river in a meditative hour, and is not reminded of the flux of all things? Throw a stone into the stream, and the circles that propagate themselves are the beautiful type of all influence. ...

The American Scholar
(Excerpt)

...

The first in time and the first in importance of the influence upon the mind is that of nature. Every day, the sun; and, after sunset, night and her stars. Ever the winds blow; ever the grass grows. Every day, men and women, conversing, beholding and beholden. The scholars must needs stand wistful and admiring before this great spectacle. He must settle its value in his mind. What is nature to him? There is never a beginning, there is never an end to the inexplicable continuity of this web of God, but always circular power returning to itself. Therein it resembles his own spirit, whose beginning, whose ending he never can find — so entire, so boundless. Far, too, as her splendors shine, system on system shooting like rays, upward, downward, without center, without circumference, — in the mass and in the particle, nature hastens to render account of herself to the mind.

Classification begins. To young mind, every thing is individual, stands by itself. By and by, it finds how to join two things, and see in them one nature; then three, then three thousand; and so, tyrannized over by its own unifying instinct, it goes on tying things together, diminishing anomalies, discovering roots running under ground, whereby contrary and remote things cohere, and flower out from one stem. It presently learns, that, since the dawn of history, there has been a constant accumulation and classifying of facts. But what is classification but the perceiving that these objects are not chaotic, and are not foreign, but have a law which is also a law of the human mind? The astronomer discovers that geometry, a pure abstraction of the human mind, is the measure of planetary motion. The chemist finds proportions and intelligible method throughout matter; and science is nothing but the finding of analogy, identity, in the most remote parts. The ambitious soul sits down before each refractory fact; one after another, reduces all strange constitutions, all new powers, to their class and their law, and goes on for ever to animate the last fibre of organization, the outskirts of nature, by insight.

...

The next great influence into the spirit of the scholar is the mind of the Past, — in whatever form, whether of literature, of art, of institutions, that mind is inscribed. Books are the best type of the influence of the past, and perhaps we shall get at the truth, — learn the amount of this influence more conveniently, — by considering their value alone.

The theory of books is noble. The scholar of the first age received into him the world around; brooded thereon; gave it the new arrangement of his own mind, and uttered it again. It came into him life; it went out from him truth. It came to him short-lived actions; it went out from him immortal thoughts. It came to him business; it went from him poetry. It was dead fact; now, it is quick thought. It can stand, and it can go. It now endures, it now flies, it now inspires. Precisely in proportion to the depth of mind from which it issued, so high does it soar, so long does it sing.

Or, I might say, it depends on how far the process had gone, of transmuting life into truth. In proportion to the completeness of the distillation, so will the purity and imperishableness of the product be. But none is quite perfect. As no air-pump can by any means make a perfect vacuum, so neither can any artist entirely exclude the conventional, the local, the perishable from his book, or write a book of pure thought, that shall be as efficient, in all respects, to a remote posterity, as to contemporaries, or rather to the second age. Each age, it is found, must write its own books; or rather, each generation for the next succeeding. The books of an older period will not fit this.

Yet hence arises a grave mischief. The sacredness which attaches to the act of creation, the act of thought, is instantly transferred to the record. The poet chanting was felt to be a divine man. Henceforth the chant is divine also. The writer was a just and wise spirit. Henceforward it is settled the book is perfect; as love of the hero corrupts into worship of his statue. Instantly the book becomes noxious. The guide is a tyrant. We sought a brother, and lo, a governor. The sluggish and perverted mind of the multitude, always slow to open to the incursions of Reason, having once so opened, having once received this book, stands upon it, and makes an outcry if it is disparaged. Colleges are built on it. Books are written on it by thinkers, not by Man Thinking, by men of talent, that is, who start wrong, who set out from accepted dogmas, not from their own sight of principles. Meek young men grow up in libraries, believing it their duty to accept the views which Cicero, which Locke, which Bacon, have given; forgetful that Cicero, Locke and Bacon were only young men in libraries when they wrote these books.

Hence, instead of Man Thinking, we have the bookworm. Hence the book-learned class, who value books, as such; not as related to nature and the human constitution, but as making a sort of Third Estate with the world and soul. Hence the restorers of readings, the emendators, the bibliomaniacs of all degrees. This is bad; this is worse than it seems.

Books are the best of things, well used; abused, among the worst. What is the right use? What is the one end which all means go to effect? They are for nothing but to inspire. I had better never see a book than to be warped by its attraction clean out of my own orbit, and made a satellite instead of a system. The one thing in the world of value is the active soul, — the soul, free, sovereign, active. This every man is entitled to; this every man contains within him, although in almost all men obstructed, and as yet unborn. The soul active sees absolute truth and utters truth, or creates. In this action it is genius; not the privilege of here and there a favorite, but the sound estate of every man. In its essence it is progressive. The book, the college, the school of art, the institution of any kind, stop with some past utterance of genius. This is good, say they, — let us hold by this. They pin me down. They look backward and not forward. But genius always looks forward. The eyes of man are set in his forehead, not in his hindhead. Man hopes. Genius creates. To create, — to create, — is the proof of a divine presence. Whatever talents may be, if the man create not, the pure efflux of the Deity is not his; — cinders and smoke there may be, but not yet flame. There are creative manners, there are creative actions, and creative words; manners, actions, words, that is, indicative of no custom or authority, but springing spontaneous from the mind's own sense of good and fair.

On the other part, instead of being its own seer, let it receive always from another mind its truth, though it were in torrents of light, without periods of solitude, inquest, and self-recovery; and a fatal disservice is done. Genius is always sufficiently the enemy of genius by over-influence. The literature of every nation bear me witness. The English dramatic poets have Shakespearized now for two hundred years.

Undoubtedly there is a right way of reading, so it be sternly subordinated. Man Thinking must not be subdued by his instruments. Books are for the scholar's idle times. When he can read God directly, the hour is too precious to be wasted in other men's transcripts of their readings. But when the intervals of darkness come, as come they must, — when the sun is hid, and the stars withdraw their shining, — we repair to the lamps which were kindled by their ray, to guide our steps to the East again, where the dawn is. We hear, that we may speak. The Arabian proverb says, "A fig tree, looking on a fig tree, becometh fruitful."

...

Of course, there is a portion of reading quite indispensable to a wise man. History and exact science he must learn by laborious reading. Colleges, in like manner, have their indispensable office, — to teach elements. But they can only highly serve us when they aim not to drill, but to create; when they gather from far every ray of various genius to their hospitable halls, and by the concentrated fires set the hearts of their youth on flame. Thought and knowledge are natures in which apparatus and pretension avail nothing. Gowns and pecuniary foundations, though of towns of gold, can never countervail the least sentence or syllable of wit. Forget this, and our American colleges will recede in their public importance, whilst they grow richer every year.

▶▶ Questions for Consideration and Discussion

1. According to the excerpt from the introduction to *Nature*, what's Emerson's tone toward the age he lived in, critical or praising? Please explain.

2. What does Emerson mean when he describes himself as a "transparent eyeball" when in the woods? What does this state of mind have to do with his concept of the "Over-soul"?

3. What do you think is the difference between the kind of meaning Emerson finds in nature and the meaning a botanist, a geographer, or an astrophysicist finds in nature?

4. In Emerson's view, what's the right use of books? Do you agree with Emerson with regard to reading? Why or why not?

5. Emerson claims that "Gowns and pecuniary foundations, though of towns of gold, can never countervail the least sentence or syllable of wit. Forget this, and our American colleges will recede in their public importance, whilst they grow richer every year." Do you agree or disagree? Why?

Nathaniel Hawthorne (1804 – 1864)

Nathaniel Hawthorne is best known today for his short stories and his romance novels that explore issues of moral and social responsibilities in Puritan New England.

Descended from Puritans, Hawthorne was born in 1804 in the port town Salem, Massachusetts. His father was a sea captain who died when he was four years old. Supported by his maternal uncle, a wealthy man, Hawthorne received a good education; he attended Bowdoin College in 1821, with his college friends including Longfellow, a future poet, and Franklin Pierce, a future president.

One of Hawthorne's ancestors was a judge playing a part in the notorious witch trials of Salem in 1692. Hawthorne felt that the traits of his Puritan ancestors had "intertwined themselves" with his own character; he was concerned with human conscience, feeling of guilt, and ethical issues. After graduating from Bowdoin College he was drawn back to Salem. Yet Hawthorne was no Puritan. He looked back with distaste upon "the whole dismal severity of the Puritanic code of law." For twelve years he lived in semi-seclusion in his mother's house, studying the American past and writing short stories for various periodicals. In 1837, his first collection of short stories *Twice-Told Tales* was published; it turned out to be a modest success.

In Hawthorne's day, the Transcendentalist movement was a dominant force in New England intellectual circles. In 1841, Hawthorne was drawn to live at Brook Farm, the experimental utopian community set up by the Transcendental reformers. However, feeling disillusioned, he left within a year — this experience was later reflected in his *The Blithedale Romance* (1852). In 1842, he married and moved to the Old Manse, the house in Concord, where Emerson had lived. In 1846, he published the second collection of stories, *Mosses from an Old Manse*.

Unable to support his family as a writer, in and out from 1839 to 1849, Hawthorne earned his living in the custom houses in Boston and Salem. In 1849, he lost his Salem custom house job when the political administration changed. After losing his job, he started to work on his long fiction *The Scarlet Letter*, a sensational story set in Puritanic Boston about adultery between Puritan priest Arthur Dimsdale and a young lady Hester Prynne, who had been married to an estranged physician, Roger Chillingworth. *The Scarlet Letter*, coming out in 1850, was a great success. In a critical essay entitled "Out of the Very Heart of New England" by Henry James (originally published in 1879), James praised the romance, saying "The publication of *The Scarlet Letter* was in the United States a literary event of the first importance. The book was the finest piece of imaginative writing yet put forth in the country ... Something might at last be sent to Europe as exquisite in quality as anything that had been received, and the best of it was that the thing was absolutely American; it belonged to the soil, to the air, it came out of the very heart of New England. "

The Scarlet Letter was followed in 1851 by *The House of the Seven Gables*, another successful novel. After his college friend Franklin Pierce was elected president in 1853, Hawthorne was appointed consul at Liverpool, England. He held the position for four years, and after his retirement he traveled extensively in Europe and continued to write.

Hawthorne returned from Europe to the United States in 1860, lived in Concord, and devoted his remaining years to literature before he died a sudden death in 1864.

Hawthorne explores human limitations, like sin, guilt, egotism, pride, and isolation. He called the tales that explore these issues "allegories of the heart. " Human souls and social evils are the main subjects of Hawthorne's works.

The Scarlet Letter

(Excerpt)

Chapter 14   Hester and the Physician

Hester bade little Pearl run down to the margin of the water, and play with the shells and tangled seaweed, until she should have talked awhile with yonder gatherer of herbs. So the child flew away like a bird, and, making bare her small white feet, went pattering along the moist margin of the sea. Here and there she came to a full stop, and peeped curiously into a pool, left by the retiring tide as a mirror for Pearl to see her face in. Forth peeped at her, out of the pool, with dark, glistening curls around her head, and an elf-smile in her eyes, the image of a little maid, whom Pearl, having no other playmate, invited to take her hand, and run a race with her. But the visionary little maid, on her part, beckoned likewise, as if to say, "This is a better place! Come thou into the pool!" And Pearl, stepping in, mid-leg deep, beheld her own white feet at the bottom; while, out of a still lower depth, came the gleam of a kind of fragmentary smile, floating to and fro in the agitated water.

Meanwhile, her mother had accosted the physician.

"I would speak a word with you," said she — "a word that concerns us much."

"Aha! and is it Mistress Hester that has a word for old Roger Chillingworth?" answered he, raising himself from his stooping posture. "With all my heart! Why, mistress, I hear good tidings of you, on all hands! No longer ago than yester-eve, a magistrate, a wise and godly man, was discoursing of your affairs, Mistress Hester, and whispered me that there had been question concerning you in the council. It was debated whether or no, with safety to the common weal, yonder scarlet letter might be taken off your bosom. On my life, Hester, I made my entreaty to the worshipful magistrate that it might be done forthwith!"

"It lies not in the pleasure of the magistrates to take off this badge," calmly replied Hester. "Were I worthy to be quit of it, it would fall away of its own nature, or be transformed into something that should speak a different purport."

"Nay, then, wear it, if it suit you better," rejoined he. "A woman must needs follow her own fancy, touching the adornment of her person. The letter is gaily embroidered, and shows right bravely on your bosom!"

All this while, Hester had been looking steadily at the old man, and was shocked, as well as wonder-smitten, to discern what a change had been wrought upon him within the past seven years. It was not so much that he had grown older; for though the traces of advancing life were visible, he bore his age well, and seemed to retain a wiry vigour and alertness. But the former aspect of an intellectual and studious man, calm and quiet, which was what she best remembered in him, had altogether vanished, and been succeeded by an eager, searching, almost fierce, yet carefully guarded look. It seemed to be his wish and purpose to mask this expression with a smile; but the latter played him false, and flickered over his visage so derisively, that the spectator could see his blackness all the better for it. Ever and anon, too, there came a glare of red light out of his eyes; as if the old man's soul were on fire, and kept on smouldering duskily within his breast, until, by some casual puff of passion, it was blown into a momentary flame. This he repressed, as speedily as possible, and strove to look as if nothing of the kind had happened.

In a word, old Roger Chillingworth was a striking evidence of man's faculty of transforming himself into a devil, if he will only, for a reasonable space of time, undertake a devil's office. This unhappy person had effected such a transformation, by devoting himself, for seven years, to the constant analysis of a heart full of torture, and deriving his enjoyment thence, and adding fuel to those fiery tortures which he analysed and gloated over.

The scarlet letter burned on Hester Prynne's bosom. Here was another ruin, the responsibility of which came partly home to her.

"What see you in my face," asked the physician, "that you look at it so earnestly?"

"Something that would make me weep, if there were any tears bitter enough for it," answered she. "But let it pass! It is of yonder miserable man that I would speak."

"And what of him?" cried Roger Chillingworth eagerly, as if he loved the topic, and were glad of an opportunity to discuss it with the only person of whom he could make a confidant. "Not to hide the truth, Mistress Hester, my thoughts happen just now to be busy with the gentleman. So speak freely; and I will make answer."

"When we last spake together," said Hester, "now seven years ago, it was your pleasure to extort a promise of secrecy, as touching the former relation betwixt yourself and me. As the life and good fame of yonder man were in your hands, there seemed no choice to me, save to be silent, in accordance with your behest. Yet it was not without heavy misgivings that I thus bound myself; for, having cast off all duty towards other human beings, there remained a duty towards him; and something whispered me that I was betraying it, in pledging myself to keep your counsel. Since that day, no man is so near to him as you. You tread behind his every footstep. You are beside him, sleeping and waking. You search his thoughts. You burrow and rankle in his heart! Your clutch is on his life, and you cause him to die daily a living death; and still he knows you not. In permitting this, I have surely acted a false part by the only man to whom the power was left me to be true!"

"What choice had you?" asked Roger Chillingworth. "My finger, pointed at this man, would have hurled him from his pulpit into a dungeon — thence, peradventure, to the gallows!"

"It had been better so!" said Hester Prynne.

"What evil have I done the man?" asked Roger Chillingworth again. "I tell thee, Hester Prynne, the richest fee that ever physician earned from monarch could not have bought such care as I have wasted on this miserable priest! But for my aid, his life would have burned away in torments, within the first two years after the perpetration of his crime and thine. For, Hester, his spirit lacked the strength that could have borne up, as thine has, beneath a burden like thy scarlet letter. Oh, I could reveal a goodly secret! But enough! What art can do, I have exhausted on him. That he now breathes, and creeps upon earth, is owing all to me!"

"Better he had died at once!" said Hester Prynne.

"Yea, woman, thou sayest truly!" cried old Roger Chillingworth, letting the lurid fire of his heart blaze out before her eyes. "Better had he died at once! Never did mortal suffer what this man has suffered. And all, all, in the sight of his worst enemy! He has been conscious of me. He has felt an influence dwelling always upon him like a curse. He knew, by some spiritual sense — for the Creator never made another being so sensitive as this — he knew that no friendly hand was pulling at his heart-strings, and that an eye was looking curiously into him, which sought only evil, and found it. But he knew not that the eye and hand were mine! With the superstition common to his brotherhood, he fancied himself given over to a fiend, to be tortured with frightful dreams, and desperate thoughts, the sting of remorse, and despair of pardon; as a foretaste of what awaits him beyond the grave. But it was the constant shadow of my presence! — the closest propinquity of the man whom he had most vilely wronged! — and who had grown to exist only by this perpetual poison of the direst revenge! Yea, indeed! — he did not err! — there was a fiend at his elbow! A mortal man, with once a human heart, has become a fiend for his especial torment!"

The unfortunate physician, while uttering these words, lifted his hands with a look of horror, as if he had beheld some frightful shape, which he could not recognise, usurping the place of his own image in a glass. It was one of those moments — which sometimes occur only at the interval of years — when a man's moral aspect is faithfully revealed to his mind's eye. Not improbably, he had never before viewed himself as he did now.

"Hast thou not tortured him enough?" said Hester, noticing the old man's look. "Has he not paid thee all?"

"No! — no! — he has but increased the debt!" answered the physician; and as he proceeded, his manner lost its fiercer characteristics, and subsided into gloom. "Dost thou remember me, Hester, as I was nine years agone? Even then, I was in the autumn of my days, nor was it the early autumn. But all my life had been made up of earnest, studious, thoughtful, quiet years, bestowed faithfully for the increase of mine own knowledge, and faithfully, too, though this latter object was but casual to the other — faithfully for the advancement of human welfare. No life had been more peaceful and innocent than mine; few lives so rich with benefits conferred. Dost thou remember me? Was I not, though you might deem me cold, nevertheless a man thoughtful for others, craving little for himself — kind, true, just, and of constant, if not warm affections? Was I not all this?"

"All this, and more," said Hester.

"And what am I now?" demanded he, looking into her face, and permitting the whole evil within him to be written on his features. "I have already told thee what I am! A fiend! Who made me so?"

"It was myself!" cried Hester, shuddering. "It was I, not less than he. Why hast thou not avenged thyself on me?"

"I have left thee to the scarlet letter," replied Roger Chillingworth. "If that have not avenged me, I can do no more!"

He laid his finger on it, with a smile.

"It has avenged thee!" answered Hester Prynne.

"I judged no less," said the physician. "And now, what wouldst thou with me touching this man?"

"I must reveal the secret," answered Hester firmly. "He must discern thee in thy true character. What may be the result, I know not. But this long debt of confidence, due from me to him, whose bane and ruin I have been, shall at length be paid. So far as concerns the overthrow or preservation of his fair fame and his earthly state, and perchance his life, he is in thy hands. Nor do I — whom the scarlet letter has disciplined to truth, though it be the truth of red-hot iron, entering into the soul — nor do I perceive such advantage in his living any longer a life of ghastly emptiness, that I shall stoop to implore thy mercy. Do with him as thou wilt!

There is no good for him — no good for me — no good for thee! There is no good for little Pearl! There is no path to guide us out of this dismal maze. "

"Woman, I could well-nigh pity thee!" said Roger Chillingworth, unable to restrain a thrill of admiration too; for there was a quality almost majestic in the despair which she expressed. "Thou hadst great elements. Peradventure, hadst thou met earlier with a better love than mine, this evil had not been. I pity thee, for the good that has been wasted in thy nature!"

"And I thee," answered Hester Prynne, "for the hatred that has transformed a wise and just man to a fiend! Wilt thou yet purge it out of thee, and be once more human? If not for his sake, then doubly for thine own! Forgive, and leave his further retribution to the Power that claims it! I said, but now, that there could be no good event for him, or thee, or me, who are here wandering together in this gloomy maze of evil, and stumbling, at every step, over the guilt wherewith we have strewn our path. It is not so! There might be good for thee, and thee alone, since thou hast been deeply wronged, and hast it at thy will to pardon. Wilt thou give up that only privilege? Wilt thou reject that priceless benefit?"

"Peace, Hester, peace!" replied the old man, with gloomy sternness. "It is not granted me to pardon. I have no such power as thou tellest me of. My old faith, long forgotten, comes back to me, and explains all that we do, and all we suffer. By thy first step awry, thou didst plant the germ of evil; but since that moment, it has all been a dark necessity. Ye that have wronged me are not sinful, save in a kind of typical illusion; neither am I fiend-like, who have snatched a fiend's office from his hands. It is our fate. Let the black flower blossom as it may! Now go thy ways, and deal as thou wilt with yonder man. "

He waved his hand and betook himself again to his employment of gathering herbs.

Chapter 18   A Flood of Sunshine

Arthur Dimmesdale gazed into Hester's face with a look in which hope and joy shone out, indeed, but with fear betwixt them, and a kind of horror at her boldness, who had spoken what he vaguely hinted at but dared not speak.

But Hester Prynne, with a mind of native courage and activity, and for so long a period not merely estranged, but outlawed, from society, had habituated herself to such latitude of speculation as was altogether foreign to the clergyman. She had wandered, without rule or guidance, in a moral wilderness; as vast, as intricate and shadowy, as the untamed forest, amid the gloom of which they were now holding a colloquy that was to decide their fate. Her intellect and heart had their home, as it were, in desert places, where she roamed as freely as the wild Indian in his woods. For years past she had looked from this estranged point of view at human institutions, and whatever priests or legislators had established; criticising all with hardly more reverence than the Indian would feel for the clerical band, the judicial robe, the pillory, the gallows, the fireside, or the church. The tendency of her fate and fortunes had been to set her free. The scarlet letter was her passport into regions where other women dared not tread. Shame, Despair, Solitude! These had been her teachers — stern and wild ones —

and they had made her strong, but taught her much amiss.

The minister, on the other hand, had never gone through an experience calculated to lead him beyond the scope of generally received laws; although, in a single instance, he had so fearfully transgressed one of the most sacred of them. But this had been a sin of passion, not of principle, nor even purpose. Since that wretched epoch, he had watched, with morbid zeal and minuteness, not his acts — for those it was easy to arrange — but each breath of emotion, and his every thought. At the head of the social system, as the clergyman of that day stood, he was only the more trammelled by its regulations, its principles, and even its prejudices. As a priest, the framework of his order inevitably hemmed him in. As a man who had once sinned, but who kept his conscience all alive and painfully sensitive by the fretting of an unhealed wound, he might have been supposed safer within the line of virtue than if he had never sinned at all.

Thus, we seem to see that, as regarded Hester Prynne, the whole seven years of outlaw and ignominy had been little other than a preparation for this very hour. But Arthur Dimmesdale! Were such a man once more to fall, what plea could be urged in extenuation of his crime? None; unless it avail him somewhat, that he was broken down by long and exquisite suffering; that his mind was darkened and confused by the very remorse which harrowed it; that, between fleeing as an avowed criminal, and remaining as a hypocrite, conscience might find it hard to strike the balance; that it was human to avoid the peril of death and infamy, and the inscrutable machinations of an enemy; that, finally, to this poor pilgrim, on his dreary and desert path, faint, sick, miserable, there appeared a glimpse of human affection and sympathy, a new life, and a true one, in exchange for the heavy doom which he was now expiating. And be the stern and sad truth spoken, that the breach which guilt has once made into the human soul is never, in this mortal state, repaired. It may be watched and guarded; so that the enemy shall not force his way again into the citadel, and might even, in his subsequent assaults, select some other avenue, in preference to that where he had formerly succeeded. But there is still the ruined wall, and, near it, the stealthy tread of the foe that would win over again his unforgotten triumph.

The struggle, if there were one, need not be described. Let it suffice, that the clergyman resolved to flee, and not alone.

"If, in all these past seven years," thought he, "I could recall one instant of peace or hope, I would yet endure, for the sake of that earnest of Heaven's mercy. But now, — since I am irrevocably doomed, — wherefore should I not snatch the solace allowed to the condemned culprit before his execution? Or, if this be the path to a better life, as Hester would persuade me, I surely give up no fairer prospect by pursuing it! Neither can I any longer live without her companionship; so powerful is she to sustain — so tender to soothe! O Thou to whom I dare not lift mine eyes, wilt Thou yet pardon me!"

"Thou wilt go!" said Hester calmly, as he met her glance.

The decision once made, a glow of strange enjoyment threw its flickering brightness over the trouble of his breast. It was the exhilarating effect — upon a prisoner just escaped from the dungeon of his own heart — of breathing the wild, free atmosphere of an unredeemed, unchristianised, lawless region. His spirit rose, as it were, with a bound, and attained a nearer prospect of the sky, than throughout all the misery which had kept him grovelling on the earth. Of a deeply religious temperament, there was inevitably a tinge of the devotional in his mind.

"Do I feel joy again?" cried he, wondering at himself. "Methought the germ of it was dead in me! O Hester, thou art my better angel! I seem to have flung myself — sick, sin-stained, and sorrow-blackened-down upon these forest-leaves, and to have risen up all made anew, and with new powers to glorify Him that hath been merciful! This is already the better life! Why did we not find it sooner?"

"Let us not look back," answered Hester Prynne. "the past is gone! Wherefore should we linger upon it now? See! With this symbol, I undo it all, and make it as it had never been!"

So speaking, she undid the clasp that fastened the scarlet letter, and, taking it from her bosom, threw it to a distance among the withered leaves. The mystic token alighted on the hither verge of the stream. With a hand's breadth farther flight it would have fallen into the water, and have given the little brook another woe to carry onward, besides the unintelligible tale which it still kept murmuring about. But there lay the embroidered letter, glittering like a lost jewel, which some ill-fated wanderer might pick up, and thenceforth be haunted by strange phantoms of guilt, sinkings of the heart, and unaccountable misfortune.

The stigma gone, Hester heaved a long, deep sigh, in which the burden of shame and anguish departed from her spirit. Oh, exquisite relief! She had not known the weight, until she felt the freedom! By another impulse, she took off the formal cap that confined her hair; and down it fell upon her shoulders, dark and rich, with at once a shadow and a light in its abundance, and imparting the charm of softness to her features. There played around her mouth, and beamed out of her eyes, a radiant and tender smile, that seemed gushing from the very heart of womanhood. A crimson flush was glowing on her cheek, that had been long so pale. Her sex, her youth, and the whole richness of the beauty, came back from what men call the irrevocable past, and clustered themselves, with her maiden hope, and a happiness before unknown, within the magic circle of this hour. And, as if the gloom of the earth and sky had been but the effluence of these two mortal hearts, it vanished with their sorrow. All at once, as with a sudden smile of heaven, forth burst the sunshine, pouring a very flood into the obscure forest, gladdening each green leaf, transmuting the yellow fallen ones to gold, and gleaming adown the grey trunks of the solemn trees. The objects that had made a shadow hitherto, embodied the brightness now. The course of the little brook might be traced by its merry gleam afar into the wood's heart of mystery, which had become a mystery of joy.

Such was the sympathy of Nature — that wild, heathen Nature of the forest, never subjugated by human law, nor illumined by higher truth — with the bliss of these two spirits! Love, whether newly born, or aroused from a death-like slumber, must always create a sunshine, filling the heart so full of radiance, that it overflows upon the outward world. Had the forest still kept its gloom, it would have been bright in Hester's eyes, and bright in Arthur

Dimmesdale's!

Hester looked at him with the thrill of another joy.

"Thou must know Pearl!" said she. "Our little Pearl! Thou hast seen her — yes, I know it! — but thou wilt see her now with other eyes. She is a strange child! I hardly comprehend her! But thou wilt love her dearly, as I do, and wilt advise me how to deal with her."

"Dost thou think the child will be glad to know me?" asked the minister, somewhat uneasily. "I have long shrunk from children, because they often show a distrust — a backwardness to be familiar with me. I have even been afraid of little Pearl!"

"Ah, that was sad!" answered the mother. "But she will love thee dearly, and thou her. She is not far off. I will call her! Pearl! Pearl!"

"I see the child," observed the minister. "Yonder she is, standing in a streak of sunshine, a good way off, on the other side of the brook, so thou thinkest the child will love me?"

Hester smiled, and again called to Pearl, who was visible, at some distance, as the minister had described her, like a bright-apparelled vision, in a sunbeam, which fell down upon her through an arch of boughs. The ray quivered to and fro, making her figure dim or distinct — now like a real child, now like a child's spirit — as the splendour went and came again. She heard her mother's voice, and approached slowly through the forest.

Pearl had not found the hour pass wearisomely, while her mother sat talking with the clergyman. The great black forest — stern as it showed itself to those who brought the guilt and troubles of the world into its bosom — became the playmate of the lonely infant, as well as it knew how. Sombre as it was, it put on the kindest of its moods to welcome her. It offered her the partridge-berries, the growth of the preceding autumn, but ripening only in the spring, and now red as drops of blood upon the withered leaves. These Pearl gathered, and was pleased with their wild flavour. The small denizens of the wilderness hardly took pains to move out of her path. A partridge, indeed, with a brood of ten behind her, ran forward threatingly, but soon repented of her fierceness, and clucked to her young ones not to be afraid. A pigeon, alone on a low branch, allowed Pearl to come beneath, and uttered a sound as much of greeting as alarm. A squirrel, from the lofty depths of his domestic tree, chattered either in anger or merriment — for a squirrel is such a choleric and humorous little personage, that it is hard to distinguish between his moods — so he chattered at the child, and flung down a nut upon her head. It was a last year's nut, and already gnawed by his sharp tooth. A fox, startled from his sleep by her light footstep on the leaves, looked inquisitively at Pearl, as doubting whether it were better to steal off, or renew his nap on the same spot. A wolf, it is said — but here the tale has surely lapsed into the improbable — came up, and smelt of Pearl's robe, and offered his savage head to be patted by her hand. The truth seems to be, however, that the mother-forest, and these wild things which it nourished, all recognised a kindred wildness in the human child.

And she was gentler here than in the grassy-margined streets of the settlement, or in her mother's cottage. The flowers appeared to know it; and one and another whispered as she passed, "Adorn thyself with me, thou beautiful child, adorn thyself with me!" — and, to please them, Pearl gathered the violets, and anemones, and columbines, and some twigs of the freshest green, which the old trees held down before her eyes. With these she decorated her hair, and her young waist, and became a nymph-child, or an infant dryad, or whatever else was in closest sympathy with the antique wood. In such guise had Pearl adorned herself, when she heard her mother's voice, and came slowly back.

Slowly; for she saw the clergyman!

>> Questions for Consideration and Discussion

1. In Chapter 14, what changes had come over Chillingworth in the past seven years? What effected the changes?
2. According to Chapter 14, why didn't Chillingworth avenge him on Hester? Did his revenge on Dimmesdale produce an effective result?
3. In Chapter 18, what words are used to describe the will of nature? In what way is nature and community contrasted?
4. Nathaniel Hawthorne is concerned with moral and ethical problems in *The Scarlet Letter*. What moral lesson can we readers learn through the reading of the fiction?

Henry Wadsworth Longfellow (1807 – 1882)

Like Washington Irving, Longfellow was strongly influenced by European Romanticism. He had great success in making poetry popular in America. As the best-known and the most beloved American poet of his day, when Longfellow turned seventy-five, the American people celebrated his birthday as if it were a national holiday. When he died, statues were dedicated in his honor across the country, and a memorial bust was placed in the Poet's Corner of Westminster Abbey in London — he is the only American so honored.

Longfellow was born into a well-to-do family in Maine. Educated at Bowdoin College, he showed great talent in English language and literature. He went to Europe a couple of times and stayed there long enough to study European languages and literature. He made a living mainly by teaching a variety of European languages and literatures at Bowdoin and then at Harvard. In 1845 he published the anthology *The Poets and Poetry of Europe*, which brought European poems to American readers.

Longfellow's poems are on a wide range of subjects, contemporary, and historical. His extraordinary technical skill is shown in various verse forms and meters. He domesticates Greek meters to write long narrative poems including *Evangeline* (1847), *The Courtship of Miles Standish* (1858), and *The Song of Hiawatha* (1855), which were American Indian legends from the past.

Besides being a poet, Longfellow also translated *The Divine Comedy*, the 14th century epic by the Italian poet Dante. He published textbooks on modern languages and a travel book, *Outre-Mer*, which retold foreign legends and was patterned after Washington Irving's *The Sketch Book*.

Longfellow's short lyrics are pleasant to a large number of readers. The most popular ones are "A Psalm of Life" and "The Tide Rises, the Tide Falls."

A Psalm of Life

What the Heart of the Young Man Said to the Psalmist

Tell me not, in mournful numbers,
    "Life is but an empty dream!"
For the soul is dead that slumbers,
    And things are not what they seem.

5   Life is real! Life is earnest!
    And the grave is not its goal;
"Dust thou art, to dust returnest,"
    Was not spoken of the soul.

Not enjoyment, and not sorrow,
10   Is our destined end or way;
But to act, that each to-morrow
    Finds us farther than to-day.

Art is long, and Time is fleeting,
    And our hearts, though stout and brave,
15   Still, like muffled drums, are beating
    Funeral marches to the grave.

In the world's broad field of battle,
    In the bivouac of Life,
Be not like dumb, driven cattle!
20   Be a hero in the strife!

Trust no Future, howe'er pleasant!

Let the dead Past bury its dead!
Act, — act in the living Present!
    Heart within, and God o'erhead!

25 Lives of great men all remind us
        We can make our lives sublime,
    And, departing, leave behind us
        Footprints on the sands of time;

    Footprints, that perhaps another,
30   Sailing o'er life's solemn main,
    A forlorn and shipwrecked brother,
        Seeing, shall take heart again.

    Let us, then, be up and doing,
        With a heart for any fate;
35 Still achieving, still pursuing,
        Learn to labor and to wait.

The Tide Rises, the Tide Falls

    The tide rises, the tide falls,
    The twilight darkens, the curlew calls;
    Along the sea-sands damp and brown
    The traveller hastens toward the town,
5   And the tide rises, the tide falls.

    Darkness settles on roofs and walls,
    But the sea, the sea in the darkness calls;
    The little waves, with their soft, white hands,
    Efface the footprints in the sands,
10   And the tide rises, the tide falls.

    The morning breaks; the steeds in their stalls
    Stamp and neigh, as the hostler calls;
    The day returns, but nevermore
    Returns the traveller to the shore,
15   And the tide rises, the tide falls.

▶▶ Questions for Consideration and Discussion

1. In "A Psalm of Life," to whom does the narrator speak? What demand does the speaker make in stanza 1?

2. In the Bible, Psalm 103 includes such lines as "The life of mortals is like grass, / they flourish like a flower of the field; / the wind blows over it and it is gone, / and its place remembers it no more." In the Bible's *Ecclesiastes*, the opening verses go as " 'Meaningless! Meaningless! ' / says the Teacher. / 'Utterly meaningless! / Everything is meaningless! '" And the *Book of Job* in the Bible contains such lines as "Man born of woman / is of few days and full of trouble. / He springs up like a flower and withers away; / Like a fleeting shadow, he does not endure." After reading the above verses, would you react like the speaker of "A Psalm of Life" or would you react differently? Please explain.

3. The most basic device of poetry — the one that gives poetry most of its musical quality — is repetition, which includes not only the repetition of sounds and rhythms but also of words and lines. Generally speaking, repetition is used for emphasis. In "The Tide Rises, the Tide Falls" which line is repeated the most times? What does it suggest?

4. In both "A Psalm of Life" and "The Tide Rises, the Tide Falls", the image of "footprints" is used. What can footprints do in the first poem? What happens to the footprints in the latter poem?

5. Both "A Psalm of Life" (1838) and "The Tide Rises, the Tide Falls" (1879) offer large views of life. But how is the tone, or poet's attitude, different in the two poems? Which poem do you like better? Please explain.

▌ Walt Whitman (1819 – 1892)

Walt Whitman, one of the few greatest poets America has yet produced, is now best remembered for his collection of poems called *Leaves of Grass*. He influenced modern American poetry greatly, possibly more than anyone before him.

Whitman was born into a farmer's home in New York City's Long Island, then a place of rolling hills and lush green fields. His father became a farmer-turned carpenter who moved the family into Brooklyn in 1823 during a building boom. Whitman lived almost his entire life in Long Island, Manhattan, and Brooklyn. He left school at 11 years old and began to work as an office boy, doctor's helper, printer's assistant, journalist, country schoolmaster, editor, house builder, and nurse. He travelled briefly down the Mississippi, absorbing the variety of American life.

Largely self-taught, Whitman read voraciously, becoming acquainted with the works of Homer, Dante, and Shakespeare, as well as the Bible.

In 1855, at his own cost Whitman published his first edition of *Leaves of Grass*, which contained 12 poems. In free verse, Whitman celebrated the diversity, energy, and turbulence of 19th century American life. For him, no subject was too commonplace. Many people were shocked by the poems' unconventional style and content. But, upon receiving a copy of the book sent by Whitman, an unknown poet, Emerson was very excited. Emerson wrote to Whitman: "I greet you at the beginning of a great career." Emerson thought the book was "the most extraordinary piece of wit and wisdom that America has yet contributed." Here was the new American voice Emerson had been calling for.

Through the years, Whitman revised, rearranged, and added new poems to *Leaves of Grass*. He imagined all his poems as one vast poem that expressed his all-embracing view of world. In all, he published nine editions of *Leaves of Grass*, with the first five editions at his own expense, and the final one in 1892 including 383 titled poems.

Whitman was nurtured by the transcendentalists. But he was no country-dwelling person. He did not contemplate the quiet joys of nature. His poetry extends the transcendentalists' joy in nature to a love for humanity in all its manifestations. Among his poems, "Song of Myself," "When Lilacs Last in the Dooryard Bloom'd," "Crossing Brooklyn Ferry," and "I Hear America Singing" are among the most widely read ones. "Song of Myself," in particular, is well-known. It is his celebration of individuality as well as his celebration of his oneness with the world; it is a celebration of life itself; he celebrates democracy, equality between men and women, and equality between men of different skin colors and social status.

Song of Myself
(Excerpt)

1

I celebrate myself, and sing myself,
And what I assume you shall assume,
For every atom belonging to me as good belongs to you.

I loafe and invite my soul,
5   I lean and loafe at my ease observing a spear of summer grass.

My tongue, every atom of my blood, form'd from this soil, this air,
Born here of parents born here from parents the same, and their
　　parents the same,
I, now thirty-seven years old in perfect health begin,
　　Hoping to cease not till death.

10　Creeds and schools in abeyance,
Retiring back a while sufficed at what they are, but never forgotten,
I harbor for good or bad, I permit to speak at every hazard,
　　Nature without check with original energy.

6

A child said *What is the grass*? fetching it to me with full hands;
How could I answer the child? I do not know what it is any more than he.

I guess it must be the flag of my disposition, out of hopeful green stuff woven.

Or I guess it is the handkerchief of the Lord,
5　A scented gift and remembrancer① designedly dropt,
Bearing the owner's name someway in the corners, that we may see and remark, and
Say *whose*?

Or I guess the grass is itself a child, the produced babe of the vegetation.

Or I guess it is a uniform hieroglyphic,
And it means,Sprouting alike in broad zones and narrow zones,
10　Growing among black folks as among white,
Kanuck②, Tuckahoe③, Congressman, Cuff④, I give them the same, I receive them
　　the same.

And now it seems to me the beautiful uncut hair of graves.
Tenderly will I use you curling grass,
It may be you transpire from the breasts of young men,

---

①　remembrancer:reminder.
②　Kanuck:A French Canadian.
③　Tuckahoe:A Virginian, eater of the American Indian food plant tuckahoe.
④　Cuff:A black.

15   It may be you are from old people, or from offspring taken soon out of their mothers'
        laps,
    And here you are the mothers' laps.

    This grass is very dark to be from the white heads of old mothers,
    Darker than the colorless beards of old men,
    Dark to come from under the faint red roofs of mouths.

20   O I perceive after all so many uttering tongues,
    And I perceive they do not come from the roofs of mouths for nothing.

    I wish I could translate the hints about the dead young men and women,
    And the hints about old men and mothers, and the offspring taken soon out of their
        laps.

    What do you think has become of the young and old men?
25   And what do you think has become of the women and children?

    They are alive and well somewhere,
    The smallest sprout shows there is really no death,
    And if ever there was it led forward life, and does not wait at the end to arrest it,
    And ceas'd the moment life appear'd.

30   All goes onward and outward, nothing collapses,
    And to die is different from what any one supposed, and luckier.

16

    I am of old and young, of the foolish as much as the wise,
    Regardless of others, ever regardful of others,
    Maternal as well as paternal, a child as well as a man,
    Stuff'd with the stuff that is coarse and stuff'd with the stuff that is fine,
5   One of the Nation of many nations, the smallest the same and the largest the same,
    A Southerner soon as a Northerner, a planter nonchalant and hospitable...
    ...
    A learner with the simplest, a teacher of the thoughtfullest,
    A novice beginning yet experiment of myriads of seasons,
    Of every hue and caste am I, of every rank and religion,
10   A farmer, mechanic, artist, gentleman, sailor, quaker,
    Prisoner, fancy-man, rowdy, lawyer, physician, priest.

I resist any thing better than my own diversity,
Breathe the air but leave plenty after me,
And am not stuck up, and am in my place.

15   (The moth and the fish-eggs are in their place,
The bright suns I see and the dark suns I cannot see are in their place,
The palpable is in its place and the impalpable is in its place.)

21

I am the poet of the Body and I am the poet of the Soul,
The pleasures of heaven are with me and the pains of hell are with me,
The first I graft and increase upon myself, the latter I translate into new tongue.

I am the poet of the woman the same as the man,
15   And I say it is as great to be a woman as to be a man,
And I say there is nothing greater than the mother of men.

I chant the chant of dilation or pride,
We have had ducking and deprecating about enough,
I show that size is only development.

10   Have you outstript the rest? are you the President?
It is a trifle, they will more than arrive there every one, and still pass on.
…

24

Walt Whitman, a kosmos, of Manhattan the son,
Turbulent, fleshy, sensual, eating, drinking and breeding,
No sentimentalist, no stander above men and women or apart from them,
No more modest than immodest.

5   Unscrew the locks from the doors!
Unscrew the doors themselves from their jambs!

Whoever degrades another degrades me,
And whatever is done or said returns at last to me.

Through me the afflatus surging and surging, through me the current and index.

10   I speak the pass-word primeval, I give the sign of democracy,

By God! I will accept nothing which all cannot have their counterpart of on the same
    terms.

Through me many long dumb voices,

Voices of the interminable generations of prisoners and slaves,

Voices of the diseas'd and despairing and of thieves and dwarfs,

15   Voices of cycles of preparation and accretion,

And of the threads that connect the stars, and of wombs and of the father-stuff,

And of the rights of them the others are down upon,

Of the deform'd, trivial, flat, foolish, despised,

Fog in the air, beetles rolling balls of dung.

20   Through me forbidden voices,

Voices of sexes and lusts, voices veil'd and I remove the veil,

Voices indecent by me clarified and transfigur'd.

I do not press my fingers across my mouth,

I keep as delicate around the bowels as around the head and heart,

25   Copulation is no more rank to me than death is.

I believe in the flesh and the appetites,

Seeing, hearing, feeling, are miracles, and each part and tag of me is a miracle.

Divine am I inside and out, and I make holy whatever I touch or am touch'd from,

The scent of these arm-pits aroma finer than prayer,

30   This head more than churches, bibles, and all the creeds.

    ...

52

The spotted hawk swoops by and accuses me, he complains of my gab and my
    loitering.

I too am not a bit tamed, I too am untranslatable,

I sound my barbaric yawp over the roofs of the world.

The last scud of day holds back for me,

5   It flings my likeness after the rest and true as any on the shadow'd wilds,

It coaxes me to the vapor and the dusk.

I depart as air, I shake my white locks at the runaway sun,

I effuse my flesh in eddies, and drift it in lacy jags.

I bequeath myself to the dirt to grow from the grass I love,

10   If you want me again look for me under your boot soles.

You will hardly know who I am or what I mean,

But I shall be good health to you nevertheless,

And filter and fiber your blood.

Failing to fetch me at first keep encouraged,

15   Missing me one place search another,

I stop somewhere waiting for you.

I Hear America Singing

I hear America singing, the varied carols I hear.

Those of mechanics, each one singing his as it should be blithe and strong,

The carpenter singing his as he measures his plank or beam,

The mason singing his as he makes ready for work, or leaves off work,

5   The boatman singing what belongs to him in his boat, the deckhand singing on the steamboat deck,

The shoemaker singing as he sits on his bench, the hatter singing as he stands,

The wood-cutter's song, the ploughboy's on his way in the morning, or at noon intermission or at sundown,

The delicious singing of the mother, or of the young wife at work, or of the girl sewing or washing,

Each singing what belongs to him or her and to none else,

10   The day what belongs to the day — at night the party of young fellows, robust, friendly,

Singing with open mouths their strong melodious songs.

▶▶ Questions for Consideration and Discussion

1. Name as many characteristics of Whitman's "self" as you can, based upon "Song of Myself." Which characteristics seem the most prominent?

2. Consider the image of the grass in sections 6 and 52 of "Song of Myself." What does the grass have to do with life and death?

3. By associating himself with the grass, what does the poet suggest about himself? Summarize Whitman's attitude toward nature.

4. What occupations does the speaker of "I Hear America Sing" say represent America? What do these occupations tell you about Whitman's view of his country?

5. What song do you hear China sing? Compose a short poem and share your composition with your desk-mate to see if you hear similar sounds.

6. Whitman's poems were introduced into China during the May Fourth Movement. Why did his poems well suit the Chinese society of that era?

Harriet Beecher Stowe (1811 –1896)

Harriet Beecher Stowe is best remembered as the little *woman* who wrote *Uncle Tom's Cabin* that made the great American Civil War, as president Lincoln said to her when she was invited to the White House in 1863.

Harriet Beecher Stowe was born into a religious family in Connecticut; her father was an eminent Evangelical Calvinist minister. In 1824, she went to Hartford Female Seminary, which had been established by her elder sister Catherine. In 1832, when her father was appointed president of Lane Theological Seminary in Cincinnati, Ohio, the family moved to Ohio. In 1836, she married Calvin Ellis Stowe who was a professor at the seminary. In the 1830s and the 1840s, she wrote short stories; her first book — a collection of stories titled *The Mayflower* — appeared in 1843. In 1850, Stowe returned to New England when her husband became a professor at Bowdoin College in Maine.

Stowe's eighteen years of living in Ohio gave her opportunities to observe slavery at close hand. The miserable lives of the oppressed slaves aroused in her great sympathy. Outraged by the Fugitive Slave Act of 1850, which made it criminal for anybody to aid an escaping slave, Stowe started to write *Uncle Tom's Cabin*. The novel first appeared in the abolitionist magazine *The National Era* as a serial publication during 1851, and appeared in book form in 1852. It turned out to be an immediate success; in this setting, it was well received. Between 1852 and 1860 it was reprinted in twenty-two languages; and in the United States during the last half of the 19th century, it was outsold only by the Bible. It evoked the public to think about the evil institution of slavery. Thus, it helped push abolitionism from the margins to the mainstream, moving the nation closer to the Civil War.

Uncle Tom's Cabin is the first well-known sociological novel in American literature. It has been called the "cornerstone of American protest literature."

Uncle Tom's Cabin

(Excerpt)

Chapter 33 Cassy

"And behold, the tears of such as were oppressed, and they had no comforter; and on the side of their oppressors there was power, but they had no comforter."

— ECCL. 4: 1

It took but a short time to familiarize Tom with all that was to be hoped or feared in his new way of life. He was an expert and efficient workman in whatever he undertook; and was, both from habit and principle, prompt and faithful. Quiet and peaceable in his disposition, he hoped, by unremitting diligence, to avert from himself at least a portion of the evils of his condition. He saw enough of abuse and misery to make him sick and weary; but he determined to toil on, with religious patience, committing himself to Him that judgeth righteously, not without hope that some way of escape might yet be opened to him.

Legree took a silent note of Tom's availability. He rated him as a first-class hand; and yet he felt a secret dislike to him, — the native antipathy of bad to good. He saw, plainly, that when, as was often the case, his violence and brutality fell on the helpless, Tom took notice of it; for, so subtle is the atmosphere of opinion, that it will make itself felt, without words; and the opinion even of a slave may annoy a master. Tom in various ways manifested a tenderness of feeling, a commiseration for his fellow-sufferers, strange and new to them, which was watched with a jealous eye by Legree. He had purchased Tom with a view of eventually making him a sort of overseer, with whom he might, at times, intrust his affairs, in short absences; and, in his view, the first, second, and third requisite for that place, was *hardness*. Legree made up his mind, that, as Tom was not hard to his hand, he would harden him forthwith; and some few weeks after Tom had been on the place, he determined to commence the process.

One morning, when the hands were mustered for the field, Tom noticed, with surprise, a new comer among them, whose appearance excited his attention. It was a woman, tall and slenderly formed, with remarkably delicate hands and feet, and dressed in neat and respectable garments. By the appearance of her face, she might have been between thirty-five and forty; and it was a face that, once seen, could never be forgotten, — one of those that, at a glance, seem to convey to us an idea of a wild, painful, and romantic history. Her forehead was high, and her eyebrows marked with beautiful clearness. Her straight, well-formed nose, her finely-cut mouth, and the graceful contour of her head and neck, showed that she must once have been beautiful; but her face was deeply wrinkled with lines of pain, and of proud and bitter endurance. Her complexion was sallow and unhealthy, her cheeks thin, her features sharp, and her whole form emaciated. But her eye was the most remarkable feature, — so large, so heavily black, overshadowed by long lashes of equal darkness, and so wildly, mournfully despairing. There was a fierce pride and defiance in every line of her face, in every curve of the flexible lip, in every motion of her body; but in her eye was a deep, settled night of anguish, — an expression so hopeless and unchanging as to contrast fearfully with the scorn and pride expressed by her whole demeanor.

Where she came from, or who she was, Tom did not know. The first he did know, she was walking by his side, erect and proud, in the dim gray of the dawn. To the gang, however, she was known; for there was much looking and turning of heads, and a smothered yet apparent exultation among the miserable, ragged, half-starved creatures by whom she was surrounded.

"Got to come to it, at last, — glad of it!" said one.

"He! he! he!" said another; "you'll know how good it is, Misse!"

"We'll see her work!"

"Wonder if she'll get a cutting up, at night, like the rest of us!"

"I'd be glad to see her down for a flogging, I'll bound!" said another.

The woman took no notice of these taunts, but walked on, with the same expression of angry scorn, as if she heard nothing. Tom had always lived among refined, and cultivated people, and he felt intuitively, from her air and bearing, that she belonged to that class; but how or why she could be fallen to those degrading circumstances, he could not tell. The woman neither looked at him nor spoke to him, though, all the way to the field, she kept close at his side.

Tom was soon busy at his work; but, as the woman was at no great distance from him, he often glanced an eye to her, at her work. He saw, at a glance, that a native adroitness and handiness made the task to her an easier one than it proved to many. She picked very fast and very clean, and with an air of scorn, as if she despised both the work and the disgrace and humiliation of the circumstances in which she was placed.

In the course of the day, Tom was working near the mulatto woman who had been bought in the same lot with himself. She was evidently in a condition of great suffering, and Tom often heard her praying, as she wavered and trembled, and seemed about to fall down. Tom silently, as he came near to her, transferred several handfuls of cotton from his own sack to hers.

"O, don't, don't!" said the woman, looking surprised; "it'll get you into trouble."

Just then Sambo came up. He seemed to have a special spite against this woman; and, flourishing his whip, said, in brutal, guttural tones, "What dis yer, Luce, — foolin a'?" and, with the word, kicking the woman with his heavy cow-hide shoe, he struck Tom across the face with his whip.

Tom silently resumed his task; but the woman, before at the last point of exhaustion, fainted.

"I'll bring her to!" said the driver, with a brutal grin. "I'll give her something better than camphire!" and, taking a pin from his coat-sleeve, he buried it to the head in her flesh. The woman groaned, and half rose. "Get up, you beast, and work, will yer, or I'll show yer a trick more!"

The woman seemed stimulated, for a few moments, to an unnatural strength, and worked with desperate eagerness.

"See that you keep to dat ar," said the man, "or yer'll wish yer's dead to-night, I reckin!"

"That I do now!" Tom heard her say; and again he heard her say, "O, Lord, how long! O, Lord, why don't you help us?"

At the risk of all that he might suffer, Tom came forward again, and put all the cotton in his sack into the woman's.

"O, you mustn't! you donno what they'll do to ye!" said the woman.

"I can bar it!" said Tom, "better'n you;" and he was at his place again. It passed in a moment.

Suddenly, the stranger woman whom we have described, and who had, in the course of her work, come near enough to hear Tom's last words, raised her heavy black eyes, and fixed them, for a second, on him; then, taking a quantity of cotton from her basket, she placed it in his.

"You know nothing about this place," she said, "or you wouldn't have done that. When you've been here a month, you'll be done helping anybody; you'll find it hard enough to take care of your own skin!"

"The Lord forbid, Missis!" said Tom, using instinctively to his field companion the respectful form proper to the high bred with whom he had lived.

"The Lord never visits these parts," said the woman, bitterly, as she went nimbly forward with her work; and again the scornful smile curled her lips.

But the action of the woman had been seen by the driver, across the field; and, flourishing his whip, he came up to her.

"What! what!" he said to the woman, with an air of triumph, "YOU a foolin'? Go along! yer under me now, — mind yourself, or yer'll cotch it!"

A glance like sheet-lightning suddenly flashed from those black eyes; and, facing about, with quivering lip and dilated nostrils, she drew herself up, and fixed a glance, blazing with rage and scorn, on the driver.

"Dog!" she said, "touch me, if you dare! I've power enough, yet, to have you torn by the dogs, burnt alive, cut to inches! I've only to say the word!"

"What de devil you here for, den?" said the man, evidently cowed, and sullenly retreating a step or two. "Didn't mean no harm, Misse Cassy!"

"Keep your distance, then!" said the woman. And, in truth, the man seemed greatly inclined to attend to something at the other end of the field, and started off in quick time.

The woman suddenly turned to her work, and labored with a despatch that was perfectly astonishing to Tom. She seemed to work by magic. Before the day was through, her basket was filled, crowded down, and piled, and she had several times put largely into Tom's. Long after dusk, the whole weary train, with their baskets on their heads, defiled up to the building appropriated to the storing and weighing the cotton. Legree was there, busily conversing with the two drivers.

"Dat ar Tom's gwine to make a powerful deal o' trouble; kept a puttin' into Lucy's basket. — One o' these yer dat will get all der niggers to feelin' 'bused, if Mas'r don't watch him!" said Sambo.

"Hey-dey! The black cuss!" said Legree. "He'll have to get a breakin' in, won't he, boys?"

Both negroes grinned a horrid grin, at this intimation.

"Ay, ay! Let Mas'r Legree alone, for breakin' in! De debil heself couldn't beat Mas'r at dat!" said Quimbo.

"Wal, boys, the best way is to give him the flogging to do, till he gets over his notions. Break him in!"

"Lord, Mas'r'll have hard work to get dat out o' him!"

"It'll have to come out of him, though!" said Legree, as he rolled his tobacco in his mouth.

"Now, dar's Lucy, — de aggravatinest, ugliest wench on de place!" pursued Sambo.

"Take care, Sam; I shall begin to think what's the reason for your spite agin Lucy."

"Well, Mas'r knows she sot herself up agin Mas'r, and wouldn't have me, when he telled her to."

"I'd a flogged her into 't," said Legree, spitting, "only there's such a press o' work, it don't seem wuth a while to upset her jist now. She's slender; but these yer slender gals will bear half killin' to get their own way!"

"Wal, Lucy was real aggravatin' and lazy, sulkin' round; wouldn't do nothin', — and Tom he tuck up for her."

"He did, eh! Wal, then, Tom shall have the pleasure of flogging her. It'll be a good practice for him, and he won't put it on to the gal like you devils, neither."

"Ho, ho! haw! haw! haw!" laughed both the sooty wretches; and the diabolical sounds seemed, in truth, a not unapt expression of the fiendish character which Legree gave them.

"Wal, but, Mas'r, Tom and Misse Cassy, and dey among 'em, filled Lucy's basket. I ruther guess der weight 's in it, Mas'r!"

"*I do the weighing*!" said Legree, emphatically.

Both the drivers again laughed their diabolical laugh.

"So!" he added, "Misse Cassy did her day's work."

"She picks like de debil and all his angels!"

"She's got 'em all in her, I believe!" said Legree; and, growling a brutal oath, he proceeded to the weighing-room.

Slowly the weary, dispirited creatures, wound their way into the room, and, with crouching reluctance, presented their baskets to be weighed.

Legree noted on a slate, on the side of which was pasted a list of names, the amount.

Tom's basket was weighed and approved; and he looked, with an anxious glance, for the success of the woman he had befriended.

Tottering with weakness, she came forward, and delivered her basket. It was of full weight, as Legree well perceived; but, affecting anger, he said,

"What, you lazy beast! short again! stand aside, you'll catch it, pretty soon!"

The woman gave a groan of utter despair, and sat down on a board.

The person who had been called Misse Cassy now came forward, and, with a haughty, negligent air, delivered her basket. As she delivered it, Legree looked in her eyes with a sneering yet inquiring glance.

She fixed her black eyes steadily on him, her lips moved slightly, and she said something in French. What it was, no one knew; but Legree's face became perfectly demoniacal in its expression, as she spoke; he half raised his hand, as if to strike, — a gesture which she regarded with fierce disdain, as she turned and walked away.

"And now," said Legree, "come here, you Tom. You see, I telled ye I didn't buy ye jest for the common work; I mean to promote ye, and make a driver of ye; and to-night ye may jest as well begin to get yer hand in. Now, ye jest take this yer gal and flog her; ye've seen enough on't to know how."

"I beg Mas'r's pardon," said Tom; "hopes Mas'r won't set me at that. It's what I an't used to, — never did, — and can't do, no way possible."

"Ye'll larn a pretty smart chance of things ye never did know, before I've done with ye!" said Legree, taking up a cow-hide, and striking Tom a heavy blow across the cheek, and following up the infliction by a shower of blows.

"There!" he said, as he stopped to rest; "now, will ye tell me ye can't do it?"

"Yes, Mas'r," said Tom, putting up his hand, to wipe the blood that trickled down his face. "I'm willin' to work, night and day, and work while there's life and breath in me; but this yer thing I can't feel it right to do; — and, Mas'r, I *never* shall do it, — *never!*"

Tom had a remarkably smooth, soft voice, and a habitually respectful manner, that had given Legree an idea that he would be cowardly, and easily subdued. When he spoke these last words, a thrill of amazement went through every one; the poor woman clasped her hands, and said, "O Lord!" and every one involuntarily looked at each other and drew in their breath, as if to prepare for the storm that was about to burst.

Legree looked stupefied and confounded; but at last burst forth, —

"What! ye blasted black beast! tell *me* ye don't think it *right* to do what I tell ye! What have any of you cussed cattle to do with thinking what's right? I'll put a stop to it! Why, what do ye think ye are? May be ye think ye'r a gentleman master, Tom, to be a telling your master what's right, and what an't! So you pretend it's wrong to flog the gal!"

"I think so, Mas'r," said Tom; "the poor crittur's sick and feeble; 't would be downright cruel, and it's what I never will do, nor begin to. Mas'r, if you mean to kill me, kill me; but, as to my raising my hand agin any one here, I never shall, — I'll die first!"

Tom spoke in a mild voice, but with a decision that could not be mistaken. Legree shook with anger; his greenish eyes glared fiercely, and his very whiskers seemed to curl with passion; but, like some ferocious beast, that plays with its victim before he devours it, he kept back his strong impulse to proceed to immediate violence, and broke out into bitter raillery.

"Well, here's a pious dog, at last, let down among us sinners! — a saint, a gentleman, and no less, to talk to us sinners about our sins! Powerful holy critter, he must be! Here, you rascal, you make believe to be so pious, — didn't you never hear, out of yer Bible, 'Servants, obey yer masters'? Ain't I yer master? Didn't I pay down twelve hundred dollars, cash, for all there is inside yer old cussed black shell? An't yer mine, now, body and soul?" he said, giving Tom a violent kick with his heavy boot; "tell me!"

In the very depth of physical suffering, bowed by brutal oppression, this question shot a gleam of joy and triumph through Tom's soul. He suddenly stretched himself up, and, looking earnestly to heaven, while the tears and blood that flowed down his face mingled, he exclaimed,

"No! no! no! my soul an't yours, Mas'r! You haven't bought it, — ye can't buy it! It's been bought and paid for, by one that is able to keep it; — no matter, no matter, you can't harm me!"

"I can't!" said Legree, with a sneer; "we'll see, — we'll see! Here, Sambo, Quimbo, give this dog such a breakin' in as he won't get over, this month!"

The two gigantic negroes that now laid hold of Tom, with fiendish exultation in their faces, might have formed no unapt personification of powers of darkness. The poor woman screamed with apprehension, and all rose, as by a general impulse, while they dragged him unresisting from the place.

Questions for Consideration and Discussion

1. How many main characters are there in this chapter? Who are they?
2. What words are used to describe Tom, Gassy, the slaves, Legree and his two slave-drivers?
3. How does Christianity contribute to Uncle Tom's personality?
4. *Uncle Tom's Cabin* moved the United States closer to the Civil War. But this outcome was what Stowe had hoped to avert. By demonstrating the evil and unchristian nature of slavery, her aim had been to inspire voluntary emancipation of slaves. Think about the relationship between an author and his/her work, to what extent do you think a novelist could dictate the purpose of his/her work?
5. Do you know any other literary works, contemporary or historical, created in Chinese or any other languages, that have brought about social reforms? Exchange your thoughts with your desk-mate.

Frederick Douglass (1817 – 1895)

Frederick Douglass, born a slave on a Maryland plantation as Frederick Bailey, is now best remembered for his autobiography *Narrative of the Life of Frederick Douglass* (1845), which was later revised, expanded and republished as *My Bondage and My Freedom* (1855) and *Life and Times of Fredrick Douglass* (1882).

Douglass's father was a white man who was never known to him. Soon after his birth, Douglass was forcibly separated from his slave mother. When he was eight, he was sent to Baltimore and lived with the Auld family. He learned to read in the Auld household, at first with the support of Mrs. Auld but later against her orders. When Mr. Auld discovered that Douglass received reading lessons from Mrs. Auld, he forbade it, saying that learning "would forever unfit him to be a slave." Furthermore, teaching slaves reading and writing was against the law throughout the South.

What Douglass read made him long for freedom. At the age of twenty, Frederick escaped to freedom in Massachusetts. Later, he attended an antislavery society there. He changed his name to Douglass in order to avoid being found and returned to his master. In 1841, he was invited to speak at an antislavery meeting. His moving speech won him a reputation as a great orator. He wrote his autobiography in 1845, *Narrative of the Life of Frederick Douglass*. Because the book contained information that might have led to his capture, Douglass fled to England where abolitionist groups welcomed him and purchased his freedom in 1847. After he returned to the United States, he published the antislavery magazine, *The North Star*, which urged political solutions to slavery. He updated his autobiography in 1855 and 1882. His writing style was simple and plain.

Narrative of the Life of Frederick Douglass
(Excerpt)
Chapter VII

I lived in Master Hugh's family about seven years. During this time, I succeeded in learning to read and write. In accomplishing this, I was compelled to resort to various stratagems. I had no regular teacher. My mistress, who had kindly commenced to instruct me, had, in compliance with the advice and direction of her husband, not only ceased to instruct, but had set her face against my being instructed by any one else. It is due, however, to my mistress to say of her, that she did not adopt this course of treatment immediately. She at first lacked the depravity indispensable to shutting me up in mental darkness. It was at least necessary for her to have some training in the exercise of irresponsible power, to make her equal to the task of treating me as though I were a brute.

My mistress was, as I have said, a kind and tender-hearted woman; and in the simplicity of her soul she commenced, when I first went to live with her, to treat me as she supposed one human being ought to treat another. In entering upon the duties of a slaveholder, she did not seem to perceive that I sustained to her the relation of a mere chattel, and that for her to treat me as a human being was not only wrong, but dangerously so. Slavery proved as injurious to her as it did to me. When I went there, she was a pious, warm, and tender-hearted woman. There was no sorrow or suffering for which she had not a tear. She had bread for the hungry, clothes for the naked, and comfort for every mourner that came within her reach. Slavery soon proved its ability to divest her of these heavenly qualities. Under its influence, the tender heart became stone, and the lamblike disposition gave way to one of tiger-like fierceness. The first step in her downward course was in her ceasing to instruct me. She now commenced to practise her husband's precepts. She finally became even more violent in her opposition than her husband himself. She was not satisfied with simply doing as well as he had commanded; she seemed anxious to do better. Nothing seemed to make her more angry than to see me with a newspaper. She seemed to think that here lay the danger. I have had her rush at me with a face made all up of fury, and snatch from me a newspaper, in a manner that fully revealed her apprehension. She was an apt woman; and a little experience soon demonstrated, to her satisfaction, that education and slavery were incompatible with each other.

From this time I was most narrowly watched. If I was in a separate room any considerable length of time, I was sure to be suspected of having a book, and was at once called to give an account of myself. All this, however, was too late. The first step had been taken. Mistress, in teaching me the alphabet, had given me the inch, and no precaution could prevent me from taking the ell.

The plan which I adopted, and the one by which I was most successful, was that of making friends of all the little white boys whom I met in the street. As many of these as I could, I converted into teachers. With their kindly aid, obtained at different times and in different places, I finally succeeded in learning to read. When I was sent of errands, I always took my book with me, and by going one part of my errand quickly, I found time to get a lesson before my return. I used also to carry bread with me, enough of which was always in the house, and to which I was always welcome; for I was much better off in this regard than many of the poor white children in our neighborhood. This bread I used to bestow upon the hungry little urchins, who, in return, would give me that more valuable bread of knowledge. I am strongly tempted to give the names of two or three of those little boys, as a testimonial of the gratitude and affection I bear them; but prudence forbids; — not that it would injure me, but it might embarrass them; for it is almost an unpardonable offence to teach slaves to read in this Christian country. It is enough to say of the dear little fellows, that they lived on Philpot Street, very near Durgin and Bailey's ship-yard. I used to talk this matter of slavery over with them. I would sometimes say to them, I wished I could be as free as they would be when they got to be men. "You will be free as soon as you are twenty-one, but I am a slave for life! Have not I as good a right to be free as you have?" These words used to trouble them; they would express for me the liveliest sympathy, and console me with the hope that something would occur by which I might be free.

I was now about twelve years old, and the thought of being a slave for life began to bear heavily upon my heart. Just about this time, I got hold of a book entitled "The Columbian

Orator. " Every opportunity I got, I used to read this book. Among much of other interesting matter, I found in it a dialogue between a master and his slave. The slave was represented as having run away from his master three times. The dialogue represented the conversation which took place between them, when the slave was retaken the third time. In this dialogue, the whole argument in behalf of slavery was brought forward by the master, all of which was disposed of by the slave. The slave was made to say some very smart as well as impressive things in reply to his master — things which had the desired though unexpected effect; for the conversation resulted in the voluntary emancipation of the slave on the part of the master.

In the same book, I met with one of Sheridan's① mighty speeches on and in behalf of Catholic emancipation. These were choice documents to me. I read them over and over again with unabated interest. They gave tongue to interesting thoughts of my own soul, which had frequently flashed through my mind, and died away for want of utterance. The moral which I gained from the dialogue was the power of truth over the conscience of even a slaveholder. What I got from Sheridan was a bold denunciation of slavery, and a powerful vindication of human rights. The reading of these documents enabled me to utter my thoughts, and to meet the arguments brought forward to sustain slavery; but while they relieved me of one difficulty, they brought on another even more painful than the one of which I was relieved. The more I read, the more I was led to abhor and detest my enslavers. I could regard them in no other light than a band of successful robbers, who had left their homes, and gone to Africa, and stolen us from our homes, and in a strange land reduced us to slavery. I loathed them as being the meanest as well as the most wicked of men. As I read and contemplated the subject, behold! that very discontentment which Master Hugh had predicted would follow my learning to read had already come, to torment and sting my soul to unutterable anguish. As I writhed under it, I would at times feel that learning to read had been a curse rather than a blessing. It had given me a view of my wretched condition, without the remedy. It opened my eyes to the horrible pit, but to no ladder upon which to get out. In moments of agony, I envied my fellow-slaves for their stupidity. I have often wished myself a beast. I preferred the condition of the meanest reptile to my own. Any thing, no matter what, to get rid of thinking! It was this everlasting thinking of my condition that tormented me. There was no getting rid of it. It was pressed upon me by every object within sight or hearing, animate or inanimate. The silver trump of freedom had roused my soul to eternal wakefulness. Freedom now appeared, to disappear no more forever. It was heard in every sound, and seen in every thing. It was ever present to torment me with a sense of my wretched condition. I saw nothing without seeing it, I heard nothing without hearing it, and felt nothing without feeling it. It looked from every star, it smiled in every calm, breathed in every wind, and moved in every storm.

I often found myself regretting my own existence, and wishing myself dead; and but for the hope of being free, I have no doubt but that I should have killed myself, or done something

---

① Sheridan's: Richard Brinsley Sheridan (1751 – 1816), Irish dramatist and political leader.

for which I should have been killed. While in this state of mind, I was eager to hear any one speak of slavery. I was a ready listener. Every little while, I could hear something about the abolitionists. It was some time before I found what the word meant. It was always used in such connections as to make it an interesting word to me. If a slave ran away and succeeded in getting clear, or if a slave killed his master, set fire to a barn, or did any thing very wrong in the mind of a slaveholder, it was spoken of as the fruit of abolition. Hearing the word in this connection very often, I set about learning what it meant. The dictionary afforded me little or no help. I found it was "the act of abolishing;" but then I did not know what was to be abolished. Here I was perplexed. I did not dare to ask any one about its meaning, for I was satisfied that it was something they wanted me to know very little about. After a patient waiting, I got one of our city papers, containing an account of the number of petitions from the north, praying for the abolition of slavery in the District of Columbia, and of the slave trade between the States. From this time I understood the words abolition and abolitionist, and always drew near when that word was spoken, expecting to bear something of importance to myself and fellow-slaves. The light broke in upon me by degrees. I went one day down on the wharf of Mr. Waters; and seeing two Irishmen unloading a scow of stone, I went, unasked, and helped them. When we had finished, one of them came to me and asked me if I were a slave. I told him I was. He asked, "Are ye a slave for life?" I told him that I was. The good Irishman seemed to be deeply affected by the statement. He said to the other that it was a pity so fine a little fellow as myself should be a slave for life. He said it was a shame to hold me. They both advised me to run away to the north; that I should find friends there, and that I should be free. I pretended not to be interested in what they said, and treated them as if I did not understand them; for I feared they might be treacherous. White men have been known to encourage slaves to escape, and then, to get the reward, catch them and return them to their masters. I was afraid that these seemingly good men might use me so; but I nevertheless remembered their advice, and from that time I resolved to run away. I looked forward to a time at which it would be safe for me to escape. I was too young to think of doing so immediately; besides, I wished to learn how to write, as I might have occasion to write my own pass. I consoled myself with the hope that I should one day find a good chance. Meanwhile, I would learn to write.

The idea as to how I might learn to write was suggested to me by being in Durgin and Bailey's ship-yard, and frequently seeing the ship carpenters, after hewing, and getting a piece of timber ready for use, write on the timber the name of that part of the ship for which it was intended. When a piece of timber was intended for the larboard side, it would be marked thus — "L." When a piece was for the starboard side, it would be marked thus — "S." A piece for the larboard side forward, would be marked thus — "L. F." When a piece was for starboard side forward, it would be marked thus — "S. F." For larboard aft, it would be marked thus — "L. A." For starboard aft, it would be marked thus — "S. A." I soon learned the names of these letters, and for what they were intended when placed upon a piece of timber in the ship-yard. I immediately commenced copying them, and in a short time was able to make the four letters named. After that, when I met with any boy who I knew could write, I would tell him I could write as well as he. The next word would be, "I don't believe you. Let me see you try it." I would then make the letters which I had been so fortunate as to learn, and ask him to beat that. In this way I got a good many lessons in writing, which it is quite possible I should never have gotten in any other way. During this time, my copy-book was the board fence, brick wall, and pavement; my pen and ink was a lump of chalk. With these, I learned mainly how to write. I then commenced and continued copying the Italics in *Webster's Spelling Book*, until I could make them all without looking on the book. By this time, my little Master Thomas had gone to school, and learned how to write, and had written over a number of copy-books. These had been brought home, and shown to some of our near neighbors, and then laid aside. My mistress used to go to class meeting at the Wilk Street meeting house every Monday afternoon, and leave me to take care of the house. When left thus, I used to spend the time in writing in the spaces left in Master Thomas's copy-book, copying what he had written. I continued to do this until I could write a hand very similar to that of Master Thomas. Thus, after a long, tedious effort for years, I finally succeeded in learning how to write.

▶▶ Questions for Consideration and Discussion

1. How did slavery injure Douglass' Mistress? Do you agree that slavery is evil not only for the black but also for the white? Please explain.
2. Why was learning to read and write so important to Douglass? What can you learn from Douglass' desire for knowledge?

Emily Dickinson (1830 – 1886)

Emily Dickinson is now regarded as one of the greatest poets of the English language. However, she was unknown to the public during her lifetime. After her death, her younger sister Lavinia found her poems and helped get them to print. Without titles, the poems were numbered roughly according to the time they were written. In all, approximately eighteen hundred poems were found. Now, the first sentence of a poem is taken as its title.

Dickinson was born in Amherst, Massachusetts, into a family that was economically, politically, and intellectually prominent. Her father, serving in powerful positions as a state representative and a state senator, helped found Amherst College and was its treasurer for 36 years. Emily was the second child of the family, with an older brother Austin and a younger sister Lavinia. Her brother became a successful lawyer, serving as a justice of the peace and then following his father as treasurer of Amherst College. She enjoyed a close relationship with both of her siblings but felt distant from her mother and her authoritative father. Neither Emily nor her sister married.

Emily had the benefit of a good education. In 1840, she attended Amherst Academy and studied there for six years. This period was described as "a blossoming period in her life, full and joyous" by her biographer Richard B. Sewall. At seventeen she attended Mount Holyoke Female Seminary, which was 10 miles away, but severe homesickness made her return home after one year.

In Emily's entire life, she only took very occasional trips to Boston, Philadelphia and Washington; other than those rare ventures, Emily had no extended exposure to the world outside her hometown. She led an adult life of seclusion. As she grew older, she communicated with fewer and fewer people.

Emily was well-read. She was familiar with the works of the contemporary American writers such as Emerson (who was her enduring favorite), Longfellow, and Thoreau. Her deepest literary debts were to the Bible and to British writers, including Shakespeare, Milton, Keats, Charles Dickens, the Brownings, Tennyson, and the Brontë sisters. But no influence overshadowed her own spirit. Her life of solitude enabled her to focus on her world more sharply. Though the subjects of her poetry are conventional ones — life, love, nature, death, and eternity — her perspective was exceptionally original. More remarkably, the style of her poems is dazzlingly distinctive. She used capitalization and dashes frequently, experimented with grammar, rhyme, and meter, which sometimes appeared confusing to readers and critics. Early editors of Dickinson's works deemed her style "not correct." They rewrote what Dickinson had written in order to make it "proper." But eventually, people came to see her creative genius.

Success is counted sweetest

Success is counted sweetest
By those who ne'er succeed.
To comprehend a nectar
Requires sorest need.

5   Not one of all the Purple Host
Who took the Flag today

Can tell the definition
So clear of Victory

As he defeated — dying —
10   On whose forbidden ear
The distant strains of triumph
Burst agonized and clear!

I died for Beauty — but was scarce

I died for Beauty — but was scarce
Adjusted in the tomb
When One who died for Truth, was lain
In an adjoining Room —

5   He questioned softly "Why I failed"?
"For Beauty", I replied —
"And I — for Truth — Themself are One —
We Brethren, are", He said —

And so, as Kinsmen, met a Night —
10   We talked between the Rooms —
Until the Moss had reached our lips —
and covered up — our names.

Tell all the Truth but tell it slant—

Tell all the Truth but tell it slant —
Success in Circuit lies
Too bright for our infirm Delight
The Truth's superb surprise

5   As Lightning to the Children eased
With explanation kind
The Truth must dazzle gradually
Or every man be blind —

The Brain — is wider than the Sky —

The Brain — is wider than the Sky —
For — put them side by side —
The one the other will contain
With ease — and You — beside —

5　The Brain is deeper than the sea —
For — hold them — Blue to Blue —
The one the other will absorb —
As Sponges — Bucklets — do —

The Brain is just the weight of God —
10　For — Heft them — Pound for Pound —
And they will differ — if they do —
As Syllable from Sound —

Because I could not stop for Death—

Because I could not stop for Death—
He kindly stopped for me —
The Carriage held but just Ourselves —
And Immortality.

5　We slowly drove — He knew no haste
And I had put away
My labor and my leisure too,
For His Civility —

We passed the School, where Children strove
10　At Recess — in the Ring —
We passed the Fields of Gazing Grain —
We passed the Setting Sun —

Or rather — He passed Us —
The Dews drew quivering and chill —
15　For only Gossamer, my Gown —

My Tippet — only Tulle —

We paused before a House that seemed
A Swelling of the Ground —
The Roof was scarcely visible —
20   The Cornice — in the Ground —

Since then — 'tis Centuries — and yet
Feels shorter than the Day
I first surmised the Horses' Heads
Were toward Eternity —

The Soul selects her own Society —

The Soul selects her own Society —
Then — shuts the Door —
To her divine Majority —
Present no more —

5   Unmoved — she notes the Chariots — pausing —
At her low Gate —
Unmoved — an Emperor be kneeling
Upon her Mat —

I've known her — from an ample nation —
10   Choose One —
Then — close the Valves of her attention —
Like Stone —

Elysium is as far as to

Elysium is as far as to
The very next Room,
If in that room a Friend await
Felicity or Doom —

5   What fortitude the Soul contains,
That it can so endure

The accent of a coming Foot —
The opening of a Door —

"Nature" is what we see —

"Nature" is what we see —
The Hill — the Afternoon —
Squirrel — Eclipse — the Bumble-bee —
Nay — Nature is Heaven.

5 "Nature" is what we hear —
The Bobolink — the Sea —
Thunder — the Cricket —
Nay — Nature is Harmony.

"Nature" is what we know —
10 Yet have no art to say —
So impotent our wisdom is
To Her simplicity.

Questions for Consideration and Discussion

1. Do you think that Dickinson's statement "Success is counted sweetest by those who ne'er succeed" sounds contradictory? What psychological truth do you find in this poem?

2. In "I died for Beauty — but was scarce", what view does Dickinson have toward death, toward afterlife? Is death something thoroughly fearful? How does death progress?

3. In "Tell all the Truth but tell it slant", Dickinson advises us not to tell things in a straight-forward way. Do you also think that the way people tell the truth makes a difference? Please explain.

4. Do you agree with the observation expressed in "The Brain — is wider than the Sky — "? Why or why not?

5. In "Because I could not stop for Death", what three things did the speaker pass? What might these three things represent?

6. In "The Soul selects her own Society", what two things leave the soul unmoved?

7. According to "Elysium is as far as to", on what condition is paradise as near as the next room?

8. In " 'Nature' is what we see—", how would you interpret the twice-used "Nay"?

9. Among the above eight poems, which one do you like best? Which one do you like least? Why?

10. On the one hand, some authors were very popular in their lifetime but declined in popularity afterward. On the other hand, some writers were little known in their lifetime but would, in time, be viewed as great writers. What, in your view, causes these phenomena? What elements do you think determine the value of a literary work and the place of a writer in the short term and in the long term?

11. It is said that the dashes in Dickinson's poems not only serve as pauses, but also call attention to shifts in meaning or action; that in reading the poems aloud, the dashes can also create moments of silence; that the capitalization of common nouns can draw readers' attention and emphasize their importance. Do you share the same opinion? Why or why not?

Part III

From the Civil War to World War I

(1861–1914)

Part III

From the Civil War to World War I

(1861–1914)

Chapter 4

American Realism and Naturalism

Historical Background

Regional economic differences helped bring about the outbreak of the Civil War in 1861. In the South, enslaved African Americans provided the labor needed for an agricultural economy based on growing and selling cotton. In the North, free people, both white and black, worked for wages in the mines, factories, and trading companies of a growing industrial economy.

As the nation expanded westward, many Southerners wanted slavery to expand with it, but most Northerners did not. As each new western state entered the Union, a decision had to be made: would the state be slave or free? Compromise after compromise was reached until the tension became too great. In November 1860, Abraham Lincoln, who opposed the expansion of slavery, won the presidential election. In response, South Carolina and other Southern states — together known as the Confederacy — began to secede from the United States. Lincoln and his Republican Party treated this secession as a rebellion, and he vowed to preserve the Union. When Confederate cannons fired at Fort Sumter, South Carolina, the Civil War began.

Most of the Civil War was fought in the South. It was fought on a scale that America had never before seen. During the first year of fighting, the Southern eleven states were triumphant. By the end of 1862, however, the North's naval blockades and larger armies began to bring it victories. Then, on January 1, 1863, the events took a dramatic turn. Lincoln issued the Emancipation Proclamation, which declared that all enslaved people in the rebellious states were free. The North's fight to save the Union became a war to end slavery.

Eventually, in April of 1865, after a long and bitter war with more than 600,000 deaths, the Confederate Armies surrendered to the Union troops: the war ended in a victory for the North. The slave economy was destroyed.

For the new nation, the Civil War was a tragedy of the greatest magnitude. The loss of life and ruin of property, especially in the South, were astonishing. Nevertheless, the country prospered materially while the South went through a period known as Reconstruction. The westward movement continued. The isolated frontier was becoming only a memory when railroads continued to crisscross the continent: The first trans-continental railroad was completed in 1869, and by 1885 four transcontinental railroad lines were built. The great cities expanded rapidly: The population of Philadelphia tripled between 1870 and 1910; that of New York City quadrupled. As the new capital of the Midwest, Chicago's population multiplied an astounding twenty times.

The discovery and extraction of coal, oil, iron, gold, silver, and other kinds of mineral wealth produced large numbers of vast, individual fortunes. For the first time, the nation as a whole was rich enough to capitalize its own further development. By the 1890s, there were over four thousand American millionaires. Some millionaires' wealth greatly exceeded one million dollars, for instance Andrew Carnegie, who made his fortune in iron and steel, J. P. Morgan, the great financier, John Rockefeller, founder of the Standard Oil Company, and Cornelius Vanderbilt, the magnate in railroads.

As wealth grew more conspicuous, poverty became more visible. In the countryside, increasing numbers of farmers, dependent for transportation of their crops on the monopolistic railroads, were squeezed off the land by the owners of the railroads that crisscrossed the continent — in his fiction *The Octopus* (1901), Frank Norris characterized the railroads as the giant "octopus." Everywhere independent farmers were placed "under the lion's paw" of the land speculators and absentee landlords, as Hamlin Garland's short story "Under the Lion's Paw" describes. Large-scale farming also squeezed family farmers, though it was true that such practices increased gross agricultural yields.

In the big cities, an oversupply of labor kept wages down. It allowed industrialists to maintain inhumane and dangerous working conditions for men, women, and children who competed for jobs.

In brief, between the end of the Civil War and the beginning of World War I, the United States of America was wholly transformed. The main shifts in population were from country to city, from farm to factory, from foreign nations (mostly European nations) to America. Even though Chinese immigrants had made great contributions to the building of railroads, in 1882 the Chinese Exclusion Act prohibited Chinese workers from immigrating to the United States.

This period was an age when America became urbanized and industrialized. It changed from a nation of distinct regions into a nation expanding from the Atlantic to the Pacific as a result of railroad construction. This period was also an age of extremes:

moral decline versus rapid economic growth, the shocking poverty of the poor versus the dazzling wealth of the rich, gloom versus hope. That was why later historians called this period the Gilded Age — this term was derived from Mark Twain's 1873 novel, *The Gilded Age: A Tale of Today*, which satirized an era of serious social problems masked by a thin gold gilding.

American Realism

The Civil War challenged the nation's self-confidence; it thus put an end to the optimism of the mid-nineteenth century. Responding to the brutality of the Civil War and the new conditions of American life, the literature of the decades following the Civil War turned from Romanticism and Transcendental optimism toward a franker portrayal of society and human nature. Consequently, American literature entered the age of Realism.

In part, Realism was a reaction against Romanticism. Realism turned from an emphasis on the strange toward a faithful treatment of the ordinary. As the American novelist Frank Norris said, "Realism is the kind of fiction that confines itself to the type of normal life." William Dean Howells, one of the earliest exponents of Realism, claimed that realism "is nothing more and nothing less than the truthful treatment of materials." Howells also said, "Let fictions cease to lie about life; let it portray men and women as they are."

American writers began studying everyday life and crafting it in realistic and detailed ways. Some writers found inspiration for colorful portrayals of their own local regions — they set their literature in the regions they knew best. In an age when transportation and communication were not what they are like today, regional literature was especially popular. In doing so, they fed Americans' curiosity about distinctive language, landforms, and customs in other parts of the country. For instance, Mark Twain illustrated for the whole nation the life on the Mississippi. Kate Chopin's stories portrayed the colorful mixture of languages and cultures in Louisiana. The aim of most regional fiction was to capture the special atmosphere, the "local color." Some other writers, called naturalists, were influenced by European scientists, philosophers, and writers such as Charles Darwin, Herbert Spencer, and Émile Zola. They focused on the powerful biological and socioeconomic forces that shape the lives of individuals.

Thus, it can be said that American realism, as a broader term, is inclusive of American regionalism, American local color writing, and American naturalism. Given that American naturalism forms a very important part of American realism and deserves to appear under its own title, American naturalist writers will be discussed in next section.

This period witnessed a more rapid increase in the number and importance of newspapers and literary periodicals across the nation. Many "writers" who went on to become "authors" got their start as newspaper journalists: for instance Mark Twain, William Dean Howells, Frank Norris, Stephen Crane, and Theodore Dreiser. Magazines and periodicals provided sources and audiences for many writers.

The three figures who dominated American prose fiction in the last quarter of the 19th century were Mark Twain, William Dean Howells, and Henry James. For half a century, Howells was friend, editor, correspondent, and champion of both Twain and James. The most outstanding poet of the age was Edwin Arlington Robinson.

▶▶ Questions for Consideration and Discussion

1. Before American realism, America had gone through Puritanism, Enlightenment, and Romanticism and Transcendentalism. Please summarize the dominant characteristics of each literary period and compare them with the traits of American realism.

2. In what way are local colorism, regionalism, and naturalism suitable to be identified as realism?

3. Do you think big wars usually become turning points in a nation's political, economical, cultural, and intellectual lives? Why or why not?

Mark Twain (1835 –1910)

Mark Twain can be regarded as the greatest humorist of the 19th century. He is a writer of top degree importance in American literature.

Mark Twain's real name was Samuel Langhorne Clemens. He was born in Florida, Missouri, and grew up in Hannibal, Missouri, on the west bank of the Mississippi River. After his father's death when he was 12, he became a journeyman printer and later a riverboat pilot. He loved the life on the Mississippi River so much that he later chose a pen name that would link him with the river forever: "Mark twain!" was a river call meaning "two fathoms" (about 3. 6 meters), indicating that the water was deep enough for the steamboats' safe passage.

When the outbreak of the Civil War closed the Mississippi River, Twain headed for the American West, dreaming of striking it rich. Failing to become rich, he supported himself by newspaper reporting, specializing in humorous feature stories. Soon the pseudonym "Mark Twain" was well-known in California and Nevada.

In 1865, he published his short story "The Celebrated Jumping Frog of Calaveras County", which made him well-known in the East as well. In 1867, as a correspondent for the *Alta California*, Twain set out for Europe and the Middle East. This journey provided the material for *Innocents Abroad* (1869), which recounts both American and European prejudices and manners. In 1870, he married Olivia Langdon, a wealthy eastern lady, and the family moved to Connecticut, where Twain met Charles Warner and William Dean Howells. With Warner, Twain collaborated on *The Gilded Age* (1874), a satire that gave its name to the era of corrupt materialism that followed the Civil War. In Howells' *Atlantic Monthly*, Twain recounted his experiences as a riverboat pilot in a series, "Old Times on the Mississippi," later called *Life on the Mississippi* (1883).

The Adventures of Tom Sawyer (1876), which recounts the escapades of a boy growing up in a Mississippi river town in the 1830s, established Twain as a master of fiction. Its sequel, *The Adventures of Huckleberry Finn* (1883), confirmed him as one of the greatest novelists America has ever produced.

Twain's later years were darkened by financial misfortunes and the deaths of his loved ones. As a result, he produced works of dark satire and philosophic brooding — *A Connecticut Yankee in King Arthur's Court* (1889) is satirical fantasy about an inventor who finds himself transported back to medieval times, *Pudd'nhead Wilson* (1894) is an attack on racial discrimination, and *The Man That Corrupted Hadleyburg* (1900) is probably the best of his powerful pessimistic tales.

Mark Twain did not write a story; he told it. His mastery of American speech — the native vernacular — and his ability "to spin a yarn" are unrivaled. Whether his yarn spinning is aimed at pure entertainment or at social satire, his humor is irresistible. His realism and detail influenced many later American fiction writers. This was what Ernest Hemingway meant when he said "All modern American literature comes from one book by Mark Twain called *Huckleberry Finn.*"

Twain died on April 21, 1910.

Life on the Mississippi
(Excerpt)
Chapter 4 The Boys' Ambition

When I was a boy, there was but one permanent ambition among my comrades in our village on the west bank of the Mississippi River. That was, to be a steamboatman. We had transient ambitions of other sorts, but they were only transient. When a circus came and went, it left us all burning to become clowns; the first negro minstrel show that came to our section left us all suffering to try that kind of life; now and then we had a hope that if we lived and were good, God would permit us to be pirates. These ambitions faded out, each in its turn; but the ambition to be a steamboatman always remained.

Once a day a cheap, gaudy packet① arrived upward from St. Louis, and another downward from Keokuk. Before these events, the day was glorious with expectancy; after them, the day was a dead and empty thing. Not only the boys, but the whole village, felt this. After all these years I can picture that old time to myself now, just as it was then: the white town drowsing in the sunshine of a summer's morning; the streets empty, or pretty nearly so; one or two clerks sitting in front of the Water Street stores, with their splint-bottomed chairs tilted back against the wall, chins on breasts, hats slouched over their faces, asleep — with shingle-shavings enough around to show what broke them down; a sow and a litter of pigs loafing along the sidewalk, doing a good business in watermelon rinds and seeds; two or three lonely little freight piles scattered about the levee②; a pile of skids on the slope of the stone-paved wharf, and the fragrant town drunkard asleep in the shadow of them; two or three wood flats at the head of the wharf, but nobody to listen to the peaceful lapping of the wavelets against them; the great Mississippi, the majestic, the magnificent Mississippi, rolling its mile-wide tide along, shining in the sun; the dense forest away on the other side; the "point" above the town, and the "point" below, bounding the river-glimpse and turning it into a sort of sea, and withal a very still and brilliant and lonely one. Presently a film of dark smoke appears above one of those remote "points"; instantly a negro drayman, famous for his quick eye and prodigious voice, lifts up the cry, "S-t-e-a-m-boat a-comin'!" and the scene changes! The town drunkard stirs, the clerks wake up, a furious clatter of drays follows, every house and store pours out a human contribution, and all in a twinkling the dead town is alive and moving. Drays, carts, men, boys, all go hurrying from many quarters to a common center, the wharf. Assembled there, the people fasten their eyes upon the coming boat as upon a wonder they are seeing for the first time.

And the boat is rather a handsome sight, too. She is long and sharp and trim and pretty; she has two tall, fancy-topped chimneys, with a gilded device of some kind swung between them; a fanciful pilot-house, all glass and "gingerbread", perched on top of the texas deck behind them; the paddle-boxes are gorgeous with a picture or with gilded rays above the boat's name; the boiler deck, the hurricane deck, and the texas deck are fenced and ornamented with clean white railings; there is a flag gallantly flying from the jack-staff; the furnace doors are open and the fires glaring bravely; the upper decks are black with passengers; the captain stands by the big bell, calm, imposing, the envy of all; great volumes of the blackest smoke are rolling and tumbling out of the chimneys — a husbanded grandeur created with a bit of pitch pine just before arriving at a town; the crew are grouped on the forecastle; the broad stage is run far out over the port bow, and an envied deckhand stands picturesquely on the end of it with a coil of rope in his hand; the pent steam is screaming through the gauge-cocks, the captain lifts his hand, a bell rings, the wheels stop; then they turn back, churning the water to

---

① packet: boat that carries mail, passengers, and freight at fixed times over a fixed route.

② levee: landing place along the river.

foam, and the steamer is at rest. Then such a scramble as there is to get aboard, and to get ashore, and to take in freight and to discharge freight, all at one and the same time; and such a yelling and cursing as the mates facilitate it all with! Ten minutes later the steamer is under way again, with no flag on the jack-staff and no black smoke issuing from the chimneys. After ten more minutes the town is dead again, and the town drunkard asleep by the skids once more.

My father was a justice of the peace, and I supposed he possessed the power of life and death over all men and could hang anybody that offended him. This was distinction enough for me as a general thing; but the desire to be a steamboatman kept intruding, nevertheless.

I first wanted to be a cabin-boy, so that I could come out with a white apron on and shake a tablecloth over the side, where all my old comrades could see me; later I thought I would rather be the deckhand who stood on the end of the stage-plank with the coil of rope in his hand, because he was particularly conspicuous. But these were only day-dreams, — they were too heavenly to be contemplated as real possibilities.

By and by one of our boys went away. He was not heard of for a long time.

At last he turned up as apprentice engineer or "striker" on a steamboat.

This thing shook the bottom out of all my Sunday-school teachings.

That boy had been notoriously worldly, and I just the reverse; yet he was exalted to this eminence, and I left in obscurity and misery. There was nothing generous about this fellow in his greatness. He would always manage to have a rusty bolt to scrub while his boat tarried at our town, and he would sit on the inside guard and scrub it, where we could all see him and envy him and loathe him. And whenever his boat was laid up he would come home and swell around the town in his blackest and greasiest clothes, so that nobody could help remembering that he was a steamboatman; and he used all sorts of steamboat technicalities in his talk, as if he were so used to them that he forgot common people could not understand them. He would speak of the "labboard" side of a horse in an easy, natural way that would make one wish he was dead. And he was always talking about ' St. Looy' like an old citizen; he would refer casually to occasions when he "was coming down Fourth Street," or when he was "passing by the Planter's House," or when there was a fire and he took a turn on the brakes of "the old Big Missouri;" and then he would go on and lie about how many towns the size of ours were burned down there that day.

Two or three of the boys had long been persons of consideration among us because they had been to St. Louis once and had a vague general knowledge of its wonders, but the day of their glory was over now. They lapsed into a humble silence, and learned to disappear when the ruthless "cub"-engineer approached. This fellow had money, too, and hair oil. Also an ignorant silver watch and a showy brass watch chain. He wore a leather belt and used no suspenders. If ever a youth was cordially admired and hated by his comrades, this one was.

No girl could withstand his charms. He "cut out" every boy in the village. When his boat blew up at last, it diffused a tranquil contentment among us such as we had not known for months. But when he came home the next week, alive, renowned, and appeared in church all battered up and bandaged, a shining hero, stared at and wondered over by everybody, it seemed to us that the partiality of Providence for an undeserving reptile had reached a point where it was open to criticism.

This creature's career could produce but one result, and it speedily followed. Boy after boy managed to get on the river. The minister's son became an engineer. The doctor's and the post-master's sons became "mud clerks;" the wholesale liquor dealer's son became a barkeeper on a boat; four sons of the chief merchant, and two sons of the county judge, became pilots.

Pilot was the grandest position of all. The pilot, even in those days of trivial wages, had a princely salary — from a hundred and fifty to two hundred and fifty dollars a month, and no board to pay. Two months of his wages would pay a preacher's salary for a year.

Now some of us were left disconsolate. We could not get on the river — at least our parents would not let us.

So by and by I ran away. I said I never would come home again till I was a pilot and could come in glory. But somehow I could not manage it. I went meekly aboard a few of the boats that lay packed together like sardines at the long St. Louis wharf, and very humbly inquired for the pilots, but got only a cold shoulder and short words from mates and clerks. I had to make the best of this sort of treatment for the time being, but I had comforting daydreams of a future when I should be a great and honored pilot, with plenty of money, and could kill some of these mates and clerks and pay for them.

The Adventures of Huckleberry Finn
(Excerpt)
Chapter XIX

Two or three days and nights went by; I reckon I might say they swum by, they slid along so quiet and smooth and lovely. Here is the way we put in the time. It was a monstrous big river down there — sometimes a mile and a half wide; we run nights, and laid up and hid day-times; soon as night was most gone, we stopped navigating and tied up — nearly always in the dead water under a tow-head; and then cut young cottonwoods and willows and hid the raft with them. Then we set out the lines. Next we slid into the river and had a swim, so as to freshen up and cool off; then we set down on the sandy bottom where the water was about knee deep, and watched the daylight come. Not a sound, anywheres — perfectly still — just like the whole world was asleep, only sometimes the bull-frogs a-cluttering, maybe. The first thing to see, looking away over the water, was a kind of dull line — that was the woods on t'other side — you couldn't make nothing else out; then a pale place in the sky; then more paleness, spreading around; then the river softened up, away off, and warn't black any more, but gray; you could see little dark spots drifting along, ever so far away — trading scows, and such things; and long black streaks — rafts; sometimes you could hear a sweep screaking; or jumbled up voices, it was so still, and sounds come so far; and by-and-by you could see a streak on the water which you know by the look of the streak that there's a snag there in a swift current which breaks on it and makes that streak look that way; and you see the mist curl up off of the water, and the east reddens up, and the river, and you make out a log cabin in the edge of the woods, away on the bank on t'other side of the river, being a wood-yard, likely, and piled by them cheats so you can throw a dog through it anywheres; then the nice breeze blows up, and comes fanning you from over there, so cool and fresh, and sweet to smell, on account of the woods and the flowers; but sometimes not that way, because they've left dead fish laying around, gars, and such, and they do get pretty rank; and next you've got the full day, and everything smiling in the sun, and the song-birds just going it!

A little smoke couldn't be noticed, now, so we would take some fish off of the lines, and cook up a hot breakfast. And afterwards we would watch the lonesomeness of the river, and kind of lazy along, and by-and-by lazy off to sleep. Wake up, by-and-by, and look to see what done it, and maybe see a steamboat, coughing along up stream, so far off towards the other side you couldn't tell nothing about her only whether she was stern-wheel or side-wheel; then for about an hour there wouldn't be nothing to hear nor nothing to see — just solid lonesomeness. Next you'd see a raft sliding by, away off yonder, and maybe a galoot on it chopping, because they're most always doing it on a raft; you'd see the ax flash, and come down — you don't hear nothing; you see that ax go up again, and by the time it's above the man's head, then you hear the *k'chunk*! — it had took all that time to come over the water. So we would put in the day, lazying around, listening to the stillness. Once there was a thick fog, and the rafts and things that went by was beating tin pans so the steamboats wouldn't run over them. A scow or a raft went by so close we could hear them talking and cussing and laughing — heard them plain; but we couldn't see no sign of them; it made you feel crawly, it was like spirits carrying on that way in the air. Jim said he believed it was spirits; but I says:

"No, spirits wouldn't say, 'dern the dern fog.'"

Soon as it was night, out we shoved; when we got her out to about the middle, we let her alone, and let her float wherever the current wanted her to; then we lit the pipes, and dangled our legs in the water and talked about all — kinds of things — we was always naked, day and night, whenever the mosquitoes would let us — the new clothes Buck's folks made for me was too good to be comfortable, and besides I didn't go much on clothes, nohow.

Sometimes we'd have that whole river all to ourselves for the longest time. Yonder was the banks and the islands, across the water; and maybe a spark — which was a candle in a cabin window — and sometimes on the water you could see a spark or two — on a raft or a scow, you know; and maybe you could hear a fiddle or a song coming over from one of them crafts. It's lovely to live on a raft. We had the sky, up there, all speckled with stars, and we used to lay on our backs and look up at them, and discuss about whether they was made, or only just happened — Jim he allowed they was made, but I allowed they happened; I judged it would have took too long to *make* so many. Jim said the moon could a *laid* them; well, that looked kind of reasonable, so I didn't say nothing against it, because I've seen a frog lay most as many, so of course it could be done. We used to watch the stars that fell, too, and see them streak down. Jim allowed they'd got spoiled and was hove out of the nest.

Once or twice of a night we would see a steamboat slipping along in the dark, and now and then she would belch a whole world of sparks up out of her chimbleys, and they would rain down in the river and look awful pretty; then she would turn a corner and her lights would wink out and her pow-wow shut off and leave the river still again; and by-and-by her waves would get to us, a long time after she was gone, and joggle the raft a bit, and after that you wouldn't hear nothing for you couldn't tell how long, except maybe frogs or something.

After midnight the people on shore went to bed, and then for two or three hours the shores was black — no more sparks in the cabin windows. These sparks was our clock — the first one that showed again meant morning was coming, so we hunted a place to hide and tie up, right away.

One morning about day-break, I found a canoe and crossed over a chute to the main shore — it was only two hundred yards — and paddled about a mile up a crick amongst the cypress woods, to see if I couldn't get some berries. Just as I was passing a place where a kind of a cow-path crossed the crick, here comes a couple of men tearing up the path as tight as they could foot it. I thought I was a goner, for whenever anybody was after anybody I judged it was *me* — or maybe Jim. I was about to dig out from there in a hurry, but they was pretty close to me then, and sung out and begged me to save their lives — said they hadn't been doing nothing, and was being chased for it — said there was men and dogs a-coming. They wanted to jump right in, but I says —

"Don't you do it. I don't hear the dogs and horses yet; you've got time to crowd through the brush and get up the crick a little ways; then you take to the water and wade down to me and get in — that'll throw the dogs off the scent."

They done it, and as soon as they was aboard I lit out for our tow-head, and in about five or ten minutes we heard the dogs and the men away off, shouting. We heard them come along towards the crick, but couldn't see them; they seemed to stop and fool around a while; then, as we got further and further away all the time, we couldn't hardly hear them at all; by the time we had left a mile of woods behind us and struck the river, everything was quiet, and we paddled over to the tow-head and hid in the cottonwoods and was safe.

One of these fellows was about seventy, or upwards, and had a bald head and very gray whiskers. He had an old battered-up slouch hat on, and a greasy blue woolen shirt, and ragged old blue jeans britches stuffed into his boot tops, and home-knit galluses①— no, he only had one. He had an old longtailed blue jeans coat *with* slick brass buttons, flung over his arm, and both of them had big fat ratty-looking carpet-bags.

The other fellow was about thirty and dressed about as ornery. After breakfast we all laid off and talked, and the first thing that come out was that these chaps didn't know one another.

"What got you into trouble?" says the baldhead to t'other chap.

"Well, I'd been selling an article to take the tartar off the teeth — and it does take it off, too, and generly the enamel with it — but I staid about one night longer than I ought to, and was just in the act of sliding out when I ran across you on the trail this side of town, and you told me they were coming, and begged me to help you to get off. So I told you I was

---

① galluses: suspenders.

expecting trouble myself and would scatter *with* you. That's the whole yarn — what's yourn?"

"Well, I'd been a-runnin' a little temperance revival thar 'bout a week, and was the pet of the women-folks, big and little, for I was makin' it mighty warm for the rummies, I *tell* you, and takin' as much as five or six dollars a night — ten cents a head, children and niggers free — and business a growin' all the time; when somehow or another a little report got around last night that I had a way of puttin' in my time with a private jug on the sly. A nigger rousted me out this mornin', and told me the people was getherin' on the quiet, with their dogs and horses, and they'd be along pretty soon and give me' bout half an hour's start, and then run me down, if they could; and if they got me they'd tar and feather me and ride me on a rail, sure. I didn't wait for no breakfast — I warn't hungry. "

"Old man," says the young one, "I reckon we might double-team it together; what do you think?"

"I ain't undisposed. What's your line — mainly?"

"Jour printer, by trade; do a little in patent medicines; theatre-actor — tragedy, you know; take a turn at mesmerism and phrenology when there's a chance; teach singing-geography school for a change; sling a lecture, sometimes — oh, I do lots of things — most anything that comes handy, so it ain't work. What's your lay?"

"I've done considerable in the doctoring way in my time. Layin' on o' hands is my best holt — for cancer, and paralysis, and sich things; and I k'n tell a fortune pretty good, when I've got somebody along to find out the facts for me. Preachin's my line, too; and workin' camp-meetin's; and missionaryin' around. "

Nobody never said anything for a while; then the young man hove a sigh and says —

"Alas!"

"What're you alassin' about?" says the baldhead.

"To think I should have lived to be leading such a life, and be degraded down into such company. " And he begun to wipe the corner of his eye with a rag.

"Dern your skin, ain't the company good enough for you?" says the baldhead, pretty pert and uppish.

"Yes, it *is* good enough for me; it's as good as I deserve; for who fetched me so low, when I was so high? I did myself. I don't blame *you*, gentlemen — far from it; I don't blame anybody. I deserve it all. Let the cold world do its worst; one thing I know — there's a grave somewhere for me. The world may go on just as it's always done, and take everything from me — loved ones, property, everything — but it can't take that. Some day I'll lie down in it and forget it all, and my poor broken heart will be at rest. " He went on a-wiping.

"Drot your pore broken heart," says the baldhead; "what are you heaving your pore broken heart at *us* f'r? *We* hain't done nothing. "

"No, I know you haven't. I ain't blaming you, gentlemen. I brought myself down — yes, I did it myself. It's right I should suffer — perfectly right — I don't make any moan. "

"Brought you down from whar? Whar was you brought down from?"

"Ah, you would not believe me; the world never believes — let it pass — 'tis no matter. The secret of my birth — "

"The secret of your birth? Do you mean to say — "

"Gentlemen," says the young man, very solemn, "I will reveal it to you, for I feel I may have confidence in you. By rights I am a duke!"

Jim's eyes bugged out when he heard that; and I reckon mine did, too. Then the baldhead says: "No! you can't mean it?"

"Yes. My great-grandfather, eldest son of the Duke of Bridgewater, fled to this country about the end of the last century, to breathe the pure air of freedom; married here, and died, leaving a son, his own father dying about the same time. The second son of the late duke seized the title and estates — the infant real duke was ignored. I am the lineal descendant of that infant — I am the rightful Duke of Bridgewater; and here am I, forlorn, torn from my high estate, hunted of men, despised by the cold world, ragged, worn, heart-broken, and degraded to the companionship of felons on a raft!"

Jim pitied him ever so much, and so did I. We tried to comfort him, but he said it warn't much use, he couldn't be much comforted; said if we was a mind to acknowledge him, that would do him more good than most anything else; so we said we would, if he would tell us how. He said we ought to bow, when we spoke to him, and say "Your Grace," or "My Lord," or "Your Lordship" — and he wouldn't mind it if we called him plain "Bridgewater," which he said was a title, anyway, and not a name; and one of us ought to wait on him at dinner, and do any little thing for him he wanted done.

Well, that was all easy, so we done it. All through dinner Jim stood around and waited on him, and says, "Will yo' Grace have some o' dis, or some o' dat?" and so on, and a body could see it was mighty pleasing to him.

But the old man got pretty silent, by-and-by — didn't have much to say, and didn't look pretty comfortable over all that petting that was going on around that duke. He seemed to have something on his mind. So, along in the afternoon, he says:

"Looky here, Bilgewater," he says, "I'm nation sorry for you, but you ain't the only person that's had troubles like that."

"No?"

"No, you ain't. You ain't the only person that's ben snaked down wrongfully out'n a high place."

"Alas!"

"No, you ain't the only person that's had a secret of his birth." And by jings, he begins to cry.

"Hold! What do you mean?"

"Bilgewater, kin I trust you?" says the old man, still sort of sobbing.

"To the bitter death!" He took the old man by the hand and squeezed it, and says, "The secret of your being: speak!"

"Bilgewater, I am the late Dauphin!"

You bet you, Jim and me stared this time. Then the duke says:

"You are what?"

"Yes, my friend, it is too true — your eyes is lookin' at this very moment on the pore disappeared Dauphin, Looy the Seventeen, son of Looy the Sixteen and Marry Antonette. "

"You! At your age! No! You mean you're the late Charlemagne; you must be six or seven hundred years old, at the very least. "

"Trouble has done it, Bilgewater, trouble has done it; trouble has brung these gray hairs and this premature balditude. Yes, gentlemen, you see before you, in blue jeans and misery, the wanderin', exiled, trampled-on, and sufferin' rightful King of France. "

Well, he cried and took on so, that me and Jim didn't know hardly what to do, we was so sorry — and so glad and proud we'd got him with us, too. So we set in, like we done before with the duke, and tried to comfort him. But he said it warn't no use, nothing but to be dead and done with it all could do him any good; though he said it often made him feel easier and better for a while if people treated him according to his rights, and got down on one knee to speak to him, and always called him "Your Majesty," and waited on him first at meals, and didn't set down in his presence till he asked them. So Jim and me set to majestying him, and doing this and that and t'other for him, and standing up till he told us we might set down. This done him heaps of good, and so he got cheerful and comfortable. But the duke kind of soured on him, and didn't look a bit satisfied with the way things was going; still, the king acted real friendly towards him, and said the duke's great-grandfather and all the other Dukes of Bilgewater was a good deal thought of by *his* father and was allowed to come to the palace considerable; but the duke staid huffy a good while, till by-and-by the king says:

"Like as not we got to be together a blamed long time, on this h-yer raft, Bilgewater, and so what's the use o' your bein' sour? It'll only make things oncomfortable. It ain't my fault I warn't born a duke, it ain't your fault you warn't born a king — so what's the use to worry? Make the best o' things the way you find 'em, says I — that's my motto. This ain't no bad thing that we've struck here — plenty grub and an easy life — come, give us your hand, Duke, and le's all be friends. "

The duke done it, and Jim and me was pretty glad to see it. It took away all the uncomfortableness, and we felt mighty good over it, because it would a been a miserable business to have any unfriendliness on the raft; for what you want, above all things, on a raft, is for everybody to be satisfied, and feel right and kind towards the others.

It didn't take me long to make up my mind that these liars warn't no kings nor dukes at all, but just low-down humbugs and frauds. But I never said nothing, never let on; kept it to myself; it's the best way; then you don't have no quarrels, and don't get into no trouble. If they wanted us to call them kings and dukes, I hadn't no objections, 'long as it would keep peace in the family; and it warn't no use to tell Jim, so I didn't tell him. If I never learnt nothing else out of pap, I learnt that the best way to get along with his kind of people is to let them have their own way.

▷▷ Questions for Consideration and Discussion

1. What did the Mississippi River look like based on the description made by Mark Twain in the two selections? How did it influence the riverside town Hannibal and its

inhabitants?

2. Why did Twain and his boyhood friends crave to be steamboatmen? What do you think they could experience as a steamboatman? When you were small, did you want to leave your hometown to experience the outside world? What was your ideal job when you were in your early teenage years?

3. Explain why *The Adventures of Huckleberry Finn* is praised by Ernest Hemingway as the book "all modern American literature comes from"?

Henry James (1843 – 1916)

Henry James is now firmly established as one of America's major novelists and critics, as a subtle psychological realist and an unsurpassed literary stylist and craftsman.

Henry James was born in New York City. His father was an independently wealthy philosopher and religious visionary; his slightly older brother, William James, was the first notable American psychologist and perhaps America's most influential philosopher. He also had two younger brothers and a sister.

In his early youth, James and his siblings travelled back and forth between America and Europe (with stays mainly in England, Switzerland and France) and were taken to European galleries, libraries, museums, and theaters. James' formal schooling was unsystematic, but he mastered French well enough to begin a lifelong study of its literature, and from childhood on he was aware of the intricate network of institutions and traditions in Europe.

In his later teens, James' interest in literature and writing intensified, and by the time he was twenty-one, he was publishing reviews and stories in some of the leading American journals — *Atlantic Monthly*, *North American Review*, *Galaxy*, and *Nation*. He spent most of his adult life in Europe. In 1876, he decided to settle in England permanently. In 1915, he became a naturalized British subject out of impatience with America's reluctance to enter World War I.

James never married. He maintained close ties with his family, kept up a large correspondence, was extremely social and knew most of great contemporaries in the arts, many intimately — but he lived and worked alone.

Henry James was a publishing author for more than half a century. His published writings — including tales, novellas, novels, plays, autobiographies, criticism, travel pieces, letters, reviews, and biographies — altogether perhaps amount to as much as one hundred volumes. He is best remembered for his so-called "international theme" fiction, which tell of Americans in Europe and occasionally of Europeans in America, such as *The American* (1877), *The Europeans* (1878), *Daisy Miller* (1879), *The Portrait of a Lady* (1881), *The Wings of the Dove* (1902), *The Ambassador* (1903), and *The Golden Bowl* (1904). In his early international theme novels, which came out in the 1870s and 1880s, he wrote about naive young Americans — like Christopher Newman in *The American*, and Daisy Miller in *Daisy Miller* — in tension with the traditions, customs, and values of the Old World. *The Portrait of a Lady* has been regarded as his first masterpiece of the international theme. In this fiction, the complex inner lives of his American characters, especially the female protagonist Isabel Archer, are fully and realistically projected. In his last three international theme novels — *The Wings of the Dove*, *The Ambassador*, and *The Golden Bowl*, the world is like the very atmosphere of the mind. These dramas of the characters' perceptions and impressions of the world are widely considered to be James' most influential contribution to the craft of fiction.

Henry James is also a well-known literary critic. *The Art of Fiction* (1884) fairly represents his central aesthetic conceptions. He claims that "the deepest quality of a work of art will always be the quality of the mind of the producer" and that "no good novel will ever proceed from a superficial mind. " He advised novelists to "dramatize, dramatize, dramatize," emphasizing the necessity for novelists to "show" rather than "tell. " He followed his own advice and increasingly removed himself as controlling narrator. We know that the more the author withdraws, the more the reader is forced to enter the process of creating meaning. We are now accustomed to having our fiction thus "objectified"; it is James who is largely responsible for this development in narrative technique.

It is worthy of pointing out that even though James' intricate style and choice of highly cultivated characters in his fiction ran counter to the vernacular tradition popularized by Mark Twain, James attracted, in his own lifetime, a select company of admirers and made a good living from his writings. In the years between the two world wars, when American literary taste reached a new level of sophistication, his intrinsic importance as well as his wide influence received increasing recognition.

Daisy Miller was originally titled *Daisy Miller*: *A Study*. The titular character is a young American beauty from a rich family travelling in Europe with her mother and younger brother. In the eyes of her Europeanized American compatriots, her behavior is too unconventional and outrageous. She dies of malaria, and thus pays for her willful resistance to European social mores with her life. The original subtitle "study" manifests that James was a cosmopolitan who was concerned about exploring the American national character as it was tested by cultural displacement; he observed American culture by observing it in the contact zone of the two cultures.

Daisy Miller

(Excerpt)

Chapter Ⅲ

Winterbourne, who had returned to Geneva the day after his excursion to Chillon, went to Rome toward the end of January. His aunt had been established there for several weeks, and he had received a couple of letters from her. "Those people you were so devoted to last summer at Vevey have turned up here, courier and all," she wrote. "They seem to have made several acquaintances, but the courier continues to be the most *intime*. The young lady, however, is also very intimate with some third-rate Italians, with whom she rackets about in a way that makes much talk. Bring me that pretty novel of Cherbuliez's — 'Paule Méré' — and don't come later than the 23rd."

In the natural course of events, Winterbourne, on arriving in Rome, would presently have ascertained Mrs. Miller's address at the American banker's and have gone to pay his compliments to Miss Daisy. "After what happened at Vevey, I think I may certainly call upon them," he said to Mrs. Costello.

"If, after what happens — at Vevey and everywhere — you desire to keep up the acquaintance, you are very welcome. Of course a man may know every one. Men are welcome to the privilege!"

"Pray what is it that happens — here, for instance?" Winterbourne demanded.

"The girl goes about alone with her foreigners. As to what happens further, you must apply elsewhere for information. She has picked up half a dozen of the regular Roman fortune hunters, and she takes them about to people's houses. When she comes to a party she brings with her a gentleman with a good deal of manner and a wonderful mustache."

"And where is the mother?"

"I haven't the least idea. They are very dreadful people."

Winterbourne meditated a moment. "They are very ignorant — very innocent only. Depend upon it they are not bad."

"They are hopelessly vulgar," said Mrs. Costello. "Whether or no being hopelessly vulgar is being 'bad' is a question for the metaphysicians. They are bad enough to dislike, at any rate; and for this short life that is quite enough."

The news that Daisy Miller was surrounded by half a dozen wonderful mustaches checked Winterbourne's impulse to go straightway to see her. He had, perhaps, not definitely flattered himself that he had made an ineffaceable impression upon her heart, but he was annoyed at hearing of a state of affairs so little in harmony with an image that had lately flitted in and out of his own meditations; the image of a very pretty girl looking out of an old Roman window and asking herself urgently when Mr. Winterbourne would arrive. If, however, he determined to wait a little before reminding Miss Miller of his claims to her consideration, he went very soon to call upon two or three other friends. One of these friends was an American lady who had spent several winters at Geneva, where she had placed her children at school. She was a very accomplished woman, and she lived in the Via Gregoriana. Winterbourne found her in a little crimson drawing room on a third floor; the room was filled with southern sunshine. He had not been there ten minutes when the servant came in, announcing "Madame Mila!" This announcement was presently followed by the entrance of little Randolph Miller, who stopped in the middle of the room and stood staring at Winterbourne. An instant later his pretty sister crossed the threshold; and then, after a considerable interval, Mrs. Miller slowly advanced.

"I know you!" said Randolph.

"I'm sure you know a great many things," exclaimed Winterbourne, taking him by the hand. "How is your education coming on?"

Daisy was exchanging greetings very prettily with her hostess, but when she heard Winterbourne's voice she quickly turned her head. "Well, I declare!" she said.

"I told you I should come, you know," Winterbourne rejoined, smiling.

"Well — I didn't believe it," said Miss Daisy.

"I am much obliged to you," laughed the young man.

"You might have come to see me!" said Daisy.

"I arrived only yesterday."

"I don't believe that!" the young girl declared.

Winterbourne turned with a protesting smile to her mother, but this lady evaded his glance, and, seating herself, fixed her eyes upon her son. "We've got a bigger place than this," said Randolph. "It's all gold on the walls."

Mrs. Miller turned uneasily in her chair. "I told you if I were to bring you, you would say something!" she murmured.

"I told *you!*" Randolph exclaimed. "I tell *you*, sir!" he added jocosely, giving Winterbourne a thump on the knee. "It *is* bigger, too!"

Daisy had entered upon a lively conversation with her hostess; Winterbourne judged it becoming to address a few words to her mother. "I hope you have been well since we parted at Vevey," he said.

Mrs. Miller now certainly looked at him — at his chin. "Not very well, sir," she answered.

"She's got the dyspepsia," said Randolph. "I've got it too. Father's got it. I've got it most!"

This announcement, instead of embarrassing Mrs. Miller, seemed to relieve her. "I suffer from the liver," she said. "I think it's this climate; it's less bracing than Schenectady, especially in the winter season. I don't know whether you know we reside at Schenectady. I was saying to Daisy that I certainly hadn't found any one like Dr. Davis, and I didn't believe I should. Oh, at Schenectady he stands first; they think everything of him. He has so much to do, and yet there was nothing he wouldn't do for me. He said he never saw anything like my dyspepsia, but he was bound to cure it. I'm sure there was nothing he wouldn't try. He was just going to try something new when we came off. Mr. Miller wanted Daisy to see Europe for herself. But I wrote to Mr. Miller that it seems as if I couldn't get on without Dr. Davis. At Schenectady he stands at the very top; and there's a great deal of sickness there, too. It affects my sleep."

Winterbourne had a good deal of pathological gossip with Dr. Davis's patient, during which Daisy chattered unremittingly to her own companion. The young man asked Mrs. Miller how she was pleased with Rome. "Well, I must say I am disappointed," she answered. "We had heard so much about it; I suppose we had heard too much. But we couldn't help that. We had been led to expect something different."

"Ah, wait a little, and you will become very fond of it," said Winterbourne.

"I hate it worse and worse every day!" cried Randolph.

"You are like the infant Hannibal," said Winterbourne.

"No, I ain't!" Randolph declared, at a venture.

"You are not much like an infant," said his mother. "But we have seen places," she resumed, "that I should put a long way before Rome." And in reply to Winterbourne's interrogation, "There's Zürich," she concluded, "I think Zürich is lovely; and we hadn't heard half so much about it."

"The best place we've seen is the City of Richmond!" said Randolph.

"He means the ship," his mother explained. "We crossed in that ship. Randolph had a good time on the City of Richmond."

"It's the best place I've seen," the child repeated. "Only it was turned the wrong way."

"Well, we've got to turn the right way some time," said Mrs. Miller with a little laugh. Winterbourne expressed the hope that her daughter at least found some gratification in Rome, and she declared that Daisy was quite carried away. "It's on account of the society — the society's splendid. She goes round everywhere; she has made a great number of acquaintances. Of course she goes round more than I do. I must say they have been very sociable; they have taken her right in. And then she knows a great many gentlemen. Oh, she thinks there's nothing like Rome. Of course, it's a great deal pleasanter for a young lady if she knows plenty of gentlemen."

By this time Daisy had turned her attention again to Winterbourne. "I've been telling Mrs. Walker how mean you were!" the young girl announced.

"And what is the evidence you have offered?" asked Winterbourne, rather annoyed at Miss Miller's want of appreciation of the zeal of an admirer who on his way down to Rome had stopped neither at Bologna nor at Florence, simply because of a certain sentimental impatience. He remembered that a cynical compatriot had once told him that American women — the pretty ones, and this gave a largeness to the axiom — were at once the most exacting in the world and the least endowed with a sense of indebtedness.

"Why, you were awfully mean at Vevey," said Daisy. "You wouldn't do anything. You wouldn't stay there when I asked you."

"My dearest young lady," cried Winterbourne, with eloquence, "have I come all the way to Rome to encounter your reproaches?"

"Just hear him say that!" said Daisy to her hostess, giving a twist to a bow on this lady's dress. "Did you ever hear anything so quaint?"

"So quaint, my dear?" murmured Mrs. Walker in the tone of a partisan of

Winterbourne.

"Well, I don't know," said Daisy, fingering Mrs. Walker's ribbons. "Mrs. Walker, I want to tell you something."

"Mother-r," interposed Randolph, with his rough ends to his words, "I tell you you've got to go. Eugenio'll raise — something!"

"I'm not afraid of Eugenio," said Daisy with a toss of her head. "Look here, Mrs. Walker," she went on, "you know I'm coming to your party."

"I am delighted to hear it."

"I've got a lovely dress!"

"I am very sure of that."

"But I want to ask a favor — permission to bring a friend."

"I shall be happy to see any of your friends," said Mrs. Walker, turning with a smile to Mrs. Miller.

"Oh, they are not my friends," answered Daisy's mamma, smiling shyly in her own fashion. "I never spoke to them."

"It's an intimate friend of mine — Mr. Giovanelli," said Daisy without a tremor in her clear little voice or a shadow on her brilliant little face.

Mrs. Walker was silent a moment; she gave a rapid glance at Winterbourne. "I shall be glad to see Mr. Giovanelli," she then said.

"He's an Italian," Daisy pursued with the prettiest serenity. "He's a great friend of mine; he's the handsomest man in the world — except Mr. Winterbourne! He knows plenty of Italians, but he wants to know some Americans. He thinks ever so much of Americans. He's tremendously clever. He's perfectly lovely!"

It was settled that this brilliant personage should be brought to Mrs. Walker's party, and then Mrs. Miller prepared to take her leave. "I guess we'll go back to the hotel," she said.

"You may go back to the hotel, Mother, but I'm going to take a walk," said Daisy.

"She's going to walk with Mr. Giovanelli," Randolph proclaimed.

"I am going to the Pincio," said Daisy, smiling.

"Alone, my dear — at this hour?" Mrs. Walker asked. The afternoon was drawing to a close — it was the hour for the throng of carriages and of contemplative pedestrians. "I don't think it's safe, my dear," said Mrs. Walker.

"Neither do I," subjoined Mrs. Miller. "You'll get the fever, as sure as you live. Remember what Dr. Davis told you!"

"Give her some medicine before she goes," said Randolph.

The company had risen to its feet; Daisy, still showing her pretty teeth, bent over and kissed her hostess. "Mrs. Walker, you are too perfect," she said. "I'm not going alone; I am going to meet a friend."

"Your friend won't keep you from getting the fever," Mrs. Miller observed.

"Is it Mr. Giovanelli?" asked the hostess.

Winterbourne was watching the young girl; at this question his attention quickened. She stood there, smiling and smoothing her bonnet ribbons; she glanced at Winterbourne. Then, while she glanced and smiled, she answered, without a shade of hesitation, "Mr. Giovanelli—the beautiful Giovanelli."

"My dear young friend," said Mrs. Walker, taking her hand pleadingly, "don't walk off to the Pincio at this hour to meet a beautiful Italian."

"Well, he speaks English," said Mrs. Miller.

"Gracious me!" Daisy exclaimed, "I don't want to do anything improper. There's an easy way to settle it." She continued to glance at Winterbourne. "The Pincio is only a hundred yards distant; and if Mr. Winterbourne were as polite as he pretends, he would offer to walk with me!"

Winterbourne's politeness hastened to affirm itself, and the young girl gave him gracious leave to accompany her. They passed downstairs before her mother, and at the door Winterbourne perceived Mrs. Miller's carriage drawn up, with the ornamental courier whose acquaintance he had made at Vevey seated within. "Goodbye, Eugenio!" cried Daisy; "I'm going to take a walk." The distance from the Via Gregoriana to the beautiful garden at the other end of the Pincian Hill is, in fact, rapidly traversed. As the day was splendid, however, and the concourse of vehicles, walkers, and loungers numerous, the young Americans found their progress much delayed. This fact was highly agreeable to Winterbourne, in spite of his consciousness of his singular situation. The slow-moving, idly gazing Roman crowd bestowed much attention upon the extremely pretty young foreign lady who was passing through it upon his arm; and he wondered what on earth had been in Daisy's mind when she proposed to expose herself, unattended, to its appreciation. His own mission, to her sense, apparently, was to consign her to the hands of Mr. Giovanelli; but Winterbourne, at once annoyed and gratified, resolved that he would do no such thing.

"Why haven't you been to see me?" asked Daisy. "You can't get out of that."

"I have had the honour of telling you that I have only just stepped out of the train."

"You must have stayed in the train a good while after it stopped!" cried the young girl with her little laugh. "I suppose you were asleep. You have had time to go to see Mrs. Walker."

"I knew Mrs. Walker —" Winterbourne began to explain.

"I know where you knew her. You knew her at Geneva. She told me so. Well, you knew me at Vevey. That's just as good. So you ought to have come." She asked him no other question than this; she began to prattle about her own affairs. "We've got splendid rooms at the hotel; Eugenio says they're the best rooms in Rome. We are going to stay all winter, if we don't die of the fever; and I guess we'll stay then. It's a great deal nicer than I thought; I thought it would be fearfully quiet; I was sure it would be awfully poky. I was sure we should be going round all the time with one of those dreadful old men that explain about the pictures and things. But we only had about a week of that, and now I'm enjoying myself. I know ever so many people, and they are all so charming. The society's extremely select. There are all kinds — English, and Germans, and Italians. I think I like the English best. I like their style of conversation. But there are some lovely Americans. I never saw anything so hospitable. There's something or other every day. There's not much dancing; but I must say I never thought dancing was everything. I was always fond of conversation. I guess I shall have plenty at Mrs. Walker's, her rooms are so small. " When they had passed the gate of the Pincian Gardens, Miss Miller began to wonder where Mr. Giovanelli might be. "We had better go straight to that place in front," she said, "where you look at the view. "

"I certainly shall not help you to find him," Winterbourne declared.

"Then I shall find him without you," cried Miss Daisy.

"You certainly won't leave me!" cried Winterbourne.

She burst into her little laugh. "Are you afraid you'll get lost — or run over? But there's Giovanelli, leaning against that tree. He's staring at the women in the carriages; did you ever see anything so cool?"

Winterbourne perceived at some distance a little man standing with folded arms nursing his cane. He had a handsome face, an artfully poised hat, a glass in one eye, and a nosegay in his buttonhole. Winterbourne looked at him a moment and then said, "Do you mean to speak to that man?"

"Do I mean to speak to him? Why, you don't suppose I mean to communicate by signs?"

"Pray understand, then," said Winterbourne, "that I intend to remain with you. "

Daisy stopped and looked at him, without a sign of troubled consciousness in her face, with nothing but the presence of her charming eyes and her happy dimples. "Well, she's a cool one!" thought the young man.

"I don't like the way you say that," said Daisy. "It's too imperious. "

"I beg your pardon if I say it wrong. The main point is to give you an idea of my meaning. "

The young girl looked at him more gravely, but with eyes that were prettier than ever. "I have never allowed a gentleman to dictate to me, or to interfere with anything I do. "

"I think you have made a mistake," said Winterbourne. "You should sometimes listen to a gentleman — the right one. "

Daisy began to laugh again. "I do nothing but listen to gentlemen!" she exclaimed. "Tell me if Mr. Giovanelli is the right one?"

The gentleman with the nosegay in his bosom had now perceived our two friends, and was approaching the young girl with obsequious rapidity. He bowed to Winterbourne as well as to the latter's companion; he had a brilliant smile, an intelligent eye; Winterbourne thought him not a bad-looking fellow. But he nevertheless said to Daisy, "No, he's not the right one. "

Daisy evidently had a natural talent for performing introductions; she mentioned the name of each of her companions to the other. She strolled alone with one of them on each side of her; Mr. Giovanelli, who spoke English very cleverly — Winterbourne afterward learned that he had practiced the idiom upon a great many American heiresses — addressed her a great deal of very polite nonsense; he was extremely urbane, and the young American, who said nothing, reflected upon that profundity of Italian cleverness which enables people to appear more gracious in proportion as they are more acutely disappointed. Giovanelli, of course, had counted upon something more intimate; he had not bargained for a party of three. But he kept his temper in a manner which suggested far-stretching intentions. Winterbourne flattered himself that he had taken his measure. "He is not a gentleman," said the young American; "he is only a clever imitation of one. He is a music master, or a penny-a-liner, or a third-rate artist. Damn his good looks!" Mr. Giovanelli had certainly a very pretty face; but Winterbourne felt a superior indignation at his own lovely fellow countrywoman's not knowing the difference between a spurious gentleman and a real one. Giovanelli chattered and jested and made himself wonderfully agreeable. It was true that, if he was an imitation, the imitation was brilliant. "Nevertheless," Winterbourne said to himself, "a nice girl ought to know!" And then he came back to the question whether this was, in fact, a nice girl. Would a nice girl, even allowing for her being a little American flirt, make a rendezvous with a presumably low-lived foreigner? The rendezvous in this case, indeed, had been in broad daylight and in the most crowded corner of Rome, but was it not impossible to regard the choice of these circumstances as a proof of extreme cynicism? Singular though it may seem, Winterbourne was vexed that the young girl, in joining her amoroso①, should not appear more impatient of his own company, and he was vexed because of his inclination. It was impossible to regard her as a perfectly well-conducted young lady; she was wanting in a certain indispensable delicacy. It would therefore simplify matters greatly to be able to treat her as the object of one of those sentiments which are called by romancers "lawless passions." That she should seem to wish to get rid of him would help him to think more lightly of her, and to be able to think more lightly of her would make her much less perplexing. But Daisy, on this occasion, continued to present herself as an inscrutable combination of audacity and innocence.

She had been walking some quarter of an hour, attended by her two cavaliers, and responding in a tone of very childish gaiety, as it seemed to Winterbourne, to the pretty speeches of Mr. Giovanelli, when a carriage that had detached itself from the revolving train drew up beside the path. At the same moment Winterbourne perceived that his friend Mrs. Walker — the lady whose house he had lately left — was seated in the vehicle and was beckoning to him. Leaving Miss Miller's side, he hastened to obey her summons. Mrs. Walker was flushed; she wore an excited air. "It is really too dreadful," she said. "That girl must not do this sort of thing. She must not walk here with you two men. Fifty people have noticed her."

Winterbourne raised his eyebrows. "I think it's a pity to make too much fuss about it."

"It's a pity to let the girl ruin herself!"

"She is very innocent," said Winterbourne.

"She's very crazy!" cried Mrs. Walker. "Did you ever see anything so imbecile as her mother? After you had all left me just now, I could not sit still for thinking of it. It seemed too pitiful, not even to attempt to save her. I ordered the carriage and put on my bonnet, and came here as quickly as possible. Thank Heaven I have found you!"

"What do you propose to do with us?" asked Winterbourne, smiling.

"To ask her to get in, to drive her about here for half an hour, so that the world may see

---

① amoroso: lover (Italian).

she is not running absolutely wild, and then to take her safely home. "

"I don't think it's a very happy thought," said Winterbourne; "but you can try. "

Mrs. Walker tried. The young man went in pursuit of Miss Miller, who had simply nodded and smiled at his interlocutor in the carriage and had gone her way with her companion. Daisy, on learning that Mrs. Walker wished to speak to her, retraced her steps with a perfect good grace and with Mr. Giovanelli at her side. She declared that she was delighted to have a chance to present this gentleman to Mrs. Walker. She immediately achieved the introduction, and declared that she had never in her life seen anything so lovely as Mrs. Walker's carriage rug.

"I am glad you admire it," said this lady, smiling sweetly. "Will you get in and let me put it over you?"

"Oh, no, thank you," said Daisy. "I shall admire it much more as I see you driving round with it. "

"Do get in and drive with me!" said Mrs. Walker.

"That would be charming, but it's so enchanting just as I am!" and Daisy gave a brilliant glance at the gentlemen on either side of her.

"It may be enchanting, dear child, but it is not the custom here," urged Mrs. Walker, leaning forward in her victoria① with her hands devoutly clasped.

"Well, it ought to be, then!" said Daisy. "If I didn't walk I should expire. "

"You should walk with your mother, dear," cried the lady from Geneva, losing patience.

"With my mother, dear!" exclaimed the young girl. Winterbourne saw that she scented interference. "My mother never walked ten steps in her life. And then, you know," she added with a laugh, "I am more than five years old. "

"You are old enough to be more reasonable. You are old enough, dear Miss Miller, to be talked about. "

Daisy looked at Mrs. Walker, smiling intensely. "Talked about? What do you mean?"

"Come into my carriage, and I will tell you. "

Daisy turned her quickened glance again from one of the gentlemen beside her to the other. Mr. Giovanelli was bowing to and fro, rubbing down his gloves and laughing very agreeably; Winterbourne thought it a most unpleasant scene. "I don't think I want to know what you mean," said Daisy presently. "I don't think I should like it. "

Winterbourne wished that Mrs. Walker would tuck in her carriage rug and drive away, but this lady did not enjoy being defied, as she afterward told him. "Should you prefer being thought a very reckless girl?" she demanded.

"Gracious!" exclaimed Daisy. She looked again at Mr. Giovanelli, then she turned to Winterbourne. There was a little pink flush in her cheek; she was tremendously pretty. "Does Mr. Winterbourne think," she asked slowly, smiling, throwing back her head, and glancing at him from head to foot, "that, to save my reputation, I ought to get into the carriage?"

---

①   victoria:a horse-drawn carriage for two with a raised seat in front for the driver.

Winterbourne colored; for an instant he hesitated greatly. It seemed so strange to hear her speak that way of her "reputation." But he himself, in fact, must speak in accordance with gallantry. The finest gallantry, here, was simply to tell her the truth; and the truth, for Winterbourne, as the few indications I have been able to give have made him known to the reader, was that Daisy Miller should take Mrs. Walker's advice. He looked at her exquisite prettiness, and then he said, very gently, "I think you should get into the carriage."

Daisy gave a violent laugh. "I never heard anything so stiff! If this is improper, Mrs. Walker," she pursued, "then I am all improper, and you must give me up. Goodbye; I hope you'll have a lovely ride!" and, with Mr. Giovanelli, who made a triumphantly obsequious salute, she turned away.

Mrs. Walker sat looking after her, and there were tears in Mrs. Walker's eyes. "Get in here, sir," she said to Winterbourne, indicating the place beside her. The young man answered that he felt bound to accompany Miss Miller, whereupon Mrs. Walker declared that if he refused her this favour she would never speak to him again. She was evidently in earnest. Winterbourne overtook Daisy and her companion, and, offering the young girl his hand, told her that Mrs. Walker had made an imperious claim upon his society. He expected that in answer she would say something rather free, something to commit herself still further to that "recklessness" from which Mrs. Walker had so charitably endeavored to dissuade her. But she only shook his hand, hardly looking at him, while Mr. Giovanelli bade him farewell with a too emphatic flourish of the hat.

Winterbourne was not in the best possible humour as he took his seat in Mrs. Walker's victoria. "That was not clever of you," he said candidly, while the vehicle mingled again with the throng of carriages.

"In such a case," his companion answered, "I don't wish to be clever; I wish to be earnest!"

"Well, your earnestness has only offended her and put her off."

"It has happened very well," said Mrs. Walker. "If she is so perfectly determined to compromise herself, the sooner one knows it the better; one can act accordingly."

"I suspect she meant no harm," Winterbourne rejoined.

"So I thought a month ago. But she has been going too far."

"What has she been doing?"

"Everything that is not done here. Flirting with any man she could pick up; sitting in corners with mysterious Italians; dancing all the evening with the same partners; receiving visits at eleven o'clock at night. Her mother goes away when visitors come."

"But her brother," said Winterbourne, laughing, "sits up till midnight."

"He must be edified by what he sees. I'm told that at their hotel everyone is talking about her, and that a smile goes round among all the servants when a gentleman comes and asks for Miss Miller."

"The servants be hanged!" said Winterbourne angrily. "The poor girl's only fault," he presently added, "is that she is very uncultivated."

"She is naturally indelicate," Mrs. Walker declared.

"Take that example this morning. How long had you known her at Vevey?"

"A couple of days. "

"Fancy, then, her making it a personal matter that you should have left the place!"

Winterbourne was silent for some moments; then he said, "I suspect, Mrs. Walker, that you and I have lived too long at Geneva!" And he added a request that she should inform him with what particular design she had made him enter her carriage.

"I wished to beg you to cease your relations with Miss Miller — not to flirt with her — to give her no further opportunity to expose herself — to let her alone, in short. "

"I'm afraid I can't do that," said Winterbourne. "I like her extremely. "

"All the more reason that you shouldn't help her to make a scandal. "

"There shall be nothing scandalous in my attentions to her. "

"There certainly will be in the way she takes them. But I have said what I had on my conscience," Mrs. Walker pursued. "If you wish to rejoin the young lady I will put you down. Here, by the way, you have a chance. "

The carriage was traversing that part of the Pincian Garden that overhangs the wall of Rome and overlooks the beautiful Villa Borghese. It is bordered by a large parapet, near which there are several seats. One of the seats at a distance was occupied by a gentleman and a lady, toward whom Mrs. Walker gave a toss of her head. At the same moment these persons rose and walked toward the parapet. Winterbourne had asked the coachman to stop; he now descended from the carriage. His companion looked at him a moment in silence; then, while he raised his hat, she drove majestically away. Winterbourne stood there; he had turned his eyes toward Daisy and her cavalier. They evidently saw no one; they were too deeply occupied with each other. When they reached the low garden wall, they stood a moment looking off at the great flat-topped pine clusters of the Villa Borghese; then Giovanelli seated himself, familiarly, upon the broad ledge of the wall. The western sun in the opposite sky sent out a brilliant shaft through a couple of cloud bars, whereupon Daisy's companion took her parasol out of her hands and opened it. She came a little nearer, and he held the parasol over her; then, still holding it, he let it rest upon her shoulder, so that both of their heads were hidden from Winterbourne. This young man lingered a moment, then he began to walk. But he walked — not toward the couple with the parasol; toward the residence of his aunt, Mrs. Costello.

▶▶ Questions for Consideration and Discussion

1. In this chapter, how does Henry James reveal the conflict between Mrs. Walker and Daisy through the eyes of Winterbourne? What do you think Winterbourne, Mrs. Walker, Daisy, Mrs. Miller and Giovanelli represent respectively?

2. Some people say that compared with Europeans, Americans tend to be loud, more straightforward, less cultured and less sophisticated. Do you think such differences are more cultural or more individual, or a combination?

3. Do you like Daisy Miller? Do you think she is naive or flirtatious? If you were in Daisy's place, would you speak and behave differently? Please explain.

William Dean Howells (1837 – 1920)

William Dean Howells is best remembered for being, in his time, a leading, if not the most adamant, advocate to argue the cause for realism and the cause against romanticized fiction. He was particularly known for his tenure as editor of *The Atlantic Monthly* (the preeminent literary magazine of the day), in which he introduced and promoted the careers of a wide variety of writers, including Mark Twain and Henry James. He was nicknamed "The Dean of American Letters" because, by the time he died in 1920, he had served for thirty years as first president of the American Academy of Arts and Letters, the organization that seeks to identify and honor the most distinguished works in these fields. In the course of his lifelong career as literary arbiter, he was remarkably international in outlook and promoted in his diverse critical writings such non-American contemporaries as Leo Tolstoy, Henrik Ibsen, Émile Zola, George Eliot, and Thomas Hardy. He also championed many younger American writers and recognized many talented women writers early — among them Edith Wharton, Emily Dickinson, and Sarah Orne Jewett. He is even better known for actively promoting the careers of such emerging realists and naturalists as Stephen Crane, Hamlin Garland, and Frank Norris.

Howells was born one of eight children in Ohio in 1837, to a poor, respectable, proud, and culturally informed family. As a young boy, he started to set type for the series of unsuccessful newspapers his good-natured and somewhat impractical father owned. From his earliest years, Howells had both literary passions and literary ambitions. When he was not setting type or reading books, he was teaching himself several foreign languages.

In 1860, as a journalist he went to New England, where he was welcomed by such leading writers as James Russell Lowell, Ralph Waldo Emerson, and Nathaniel Hawthorne. That year he wrote Abraham Lincoln's campaign biography *Life of Abraham Lincoln*, which helped Lincoln become elected and which brought Howells recognition and an appointment as American Consul in Venice. After he returned to America in 1866, he worked as an editor for several well-known literary journals, culminating with *The Atlantic Monthly*.

Howells' most famous novel is *The Rise of Silas Lapham* (1885), which traces the moral rise of Silas Lapham and the collapse of the paint manufacturing company that he had built out of a combination of sheer luck, hard work, and shady business dealings. One of his most widely read short stories is "Editha" (1905), in which he characteristically explores the double moral failure of a society and of an individual who has been corrupted by its worst values.

Editha

The air was thick with the war feeling, like the electricity of a storm which had not yet burst. Editha sat looking out into the hot spring afternoon, with her lips parted, and panting with the intensity of the question whether she could let him go. She had decided that she could not let him stay, when she saw him at the end of the still leafless avenue, making slowly up towards the house, with his head down and his figure relaxed. She ran impatiently out on the veranda, to the edge of the steps, and imperatively demanded greater haste of him with her will before she called him aloud to him: "George!"

He had quickened his pace in mystical response to her mystical urgence, before he could have heard her; now he looked up and answered, "Well?"

"Oh, how united we are!" she exulted, and then she swooped down the steps to him, "What is it?" she cried.

"It's war," he said, and he pulled her up to him and kissed her.

She kissed him back intensely, but irrelevantly, as to their passion, and uttered from deep in her throat. "How glorious!"

"It's war," he repeated, without consenting to her sense of it; and she did not know just what to think at first. She never knew what to think of him; that made his mystery, his charm. All through their courtship, which was contemporaneous with the growth of the war feeling, she had been puzzled by his want of seriousness about it. He seemed to despise it even more than he abhorred it. She could have understood his abhorring any sort of bloodshed; that would have been a survival of his old life when he thought he would be a minister, and before he changed and took up the law. But making light of a cause so high and noble seemed to show a want of earnestness at the core of his being. Not but that she felt herself able to cope with a congenital① defect of that sort, and make his love for her save him from himself. Now perhaps the miracle was already wrought in him. In the presence of the tremendous fact that he announced, all triviality seemed to have gone out of him; she began to feel that. He sank down on the top step, and wiped his forehead with his handkerchief, while she poured out upon him her question of the origin and authenticity of his news.

All the while, in her duplex emotioning, she was aware that now at the very beginning she must put a guard upon herself against urging him, by any word or act, to take the part that her whole soul willed him to take, for the completion of her ideal of him. He was very nearly perfect as he was, and he must be allowed to perfect himself. But he was peculiar, and he might very well be reasoned out of his peculiarity. Before her reasoning went her emotioning: her nature pulling upon his nature, her womanhood upon his manhood, without her knowing the means she was using to the end she was willing. She had always supposed that the man who won her would have done something to win her; she did not know what,

---

① congenital: existing since or before birth.

but something. George Gearson had simply asked her for her love, on the way home from a concert, and she gave her love to him, without, as it were, thinking. But now, it flashed upon her, if he could do something worthy to have won her — be a hero, her hero — it would be even better than if he had done it before asking her; it would be grander. Besides, she had believed in the war from the beginning.

"But don't you see, dearest," she said, "that it wouldn't have come to this if it hadn't been in the order of Providence? And I call any war glorious that is for the liberation of people who have been struggling for years against the cruelest oppression. Don't you think so, too?"

"I suppose so," he returned, languidly. "But war! Is it glorious to break the peace of the world?"

"That ignoble peace! It was no peace at all, with that crime and shame at our very gates." She was conscious of parroting the current phrases of the newspapers, but it was no time to pick and choose her words. She must sacrifice anything to the high ideal she had for him, and after a good deal of rapid argument she ended with the climax: "But now it doesn't matter about the how or why. Since the war has come, all that is gone. There are no two sides any more. There is nothing now but our country."

He sat with his eyes closed and his head leant back against the veranda, and he remarked, with a vague smile, as if musing aloud, "Our country — right or wrong."

"Yes, right or wrong!" she returned, fervidly. "I'll go and get you some lemonade." She rose rustling, and whisked away; when she came back with two tall glasses of clouded liquid on a tray, and the ice clucking in them, he still sat as she had left him, and she said, as if there had been no interruption. "But there is no question of wrong in this case. I call it a sacred war. A war for liberty and humanity, if ever there was one. And I know you will see it just as I do, yet."

He took half the lemonade at a gulp, and he answered as he set the glass down: "I know you always have the highest ideal. When I differ from you I ought to doubt myself."

A generous sob rose in Editha's throat for the humility of a man, so very nearly perfect, who was willing to put himself below her.

Besides, she felt, more subliminally, that he was never so near slipping through her fingers as when he took that meek way.

"You shall not say that! Only, for once I happen to be right." She seized his hand in her two hands, and poured her soul from her eyes into his. "Don't you think so?" she entreated him.

He released his hand and drank the rest of his lemonade, and she added, "have mine, too," but he shook his head in answering, "I've no business to think so, unless I act so, too."

Her heart stopped a beat before it pulsed on with leaps that she felt in her neck. She had noticed that strange thing in men: they seemed to feel bound to do what they believed, and not think a thing was finished when they said it, as girls did. She knew what was in his mind, but she pretended not, and she said, "oh, I am not sure," and then faltered.

He went on as if to himself, without apparently heeding her: "there's only one way of proving one's faith in a thing like this. "

She could not say that she understood, but she did understand.

He went on again. "If I believed — if I felt as you do about this war — Do you wish me to feel as you do?"

Now she was really not sure; so she said: "George, I don't know what you mean. "

He seemed to muse away from her as before. "There is a sort of fascination in it. I suppose that at the bottom of his heart every man would like at times to have his courage tested, to see how he would act. "

"How can you talk in that ghastly way?"

"It is rather morbid. Still, that's what it comes to, unless you're swept away by ambition or driven by conviction. I haven't the conviction or the ambition, and the other thing is what it comes to with me. I ought to have been a preacher, after all; then I couldn't have asked it of myself, as I must, now I'm a lawyer. And you believe it's a holy war, Editha?" he suddenly addressed her. "Oh, I know you do! But you wish me to believe so, too?"

She hardly knew whether he was mocking or not, in the ironical way he always had with her plainer mind. But the only thing was to be outspoken with him.

"George, I wish you to believe whatever you think is true, at any and every cost. If I've tried to talk you into anything, I take it all back. "

"Oh, I know that, Editha. I know how sincere you are, and how — I wish I had your undoubting spirit! I'll think it over; I'd like to believe as you do. But I don't, now; I don't, indeed. It isn't this war alone; though this seems peculiarly wanton and needless; but it's every war — so stupid; it makes me sick. Why shouldn't this thing have been settled reasonably?"

"Because," she said, very throatily again, "God meant it to be war. "

"You think it was God? Yes, I suppose that is what people will say. "

"Do you suppose it would have been war if God hadn't meant it?"

"I don't know. Sometimes it seems as if God had put this world into men's keeping to work it as they pleased. "

"Now, George, that is blasphemy. "

"Well, I won't blaspheme. I'll try to believe in your pocket Providence," he said, and then he rose to go.

"Why don't you stay to dinner?" Dinner at Balcom's Works was at one o'clock.

"I'll come back to supper, if you'll let me. Perhaps I shall bring you a convert. "

"Well, you may come back, on that condition. "

"All right. If I don't come, you'll understand. "

He went away without kissing her, and she felt it a suspension of their engagement. It all interested her intensely; she was undergoing a tremendous experience, and she was being equal to it. While she stood looking after him, her mother came out through one of the long windows onto the veranda, with a catlike softness and vagueness.

"Why didn't he stay to dinner?"

"Because — because — war has been declared," Editha pronounced, without turning.

Her mother said, "Oh, my!" and then said nothing more until she had sat down in one of the large Shaker chairs and rocked herself for some time. Then she closed whatever tacit passage of thought there had been in her mind with the spoken words: "Well, I hope he won't go."

"And I hope he will," the girl said, and confronted her mother with a stormy exaltation that would have frightened any creature less unimpressionable than a cat.

Her mother rocked herself again for an interval of cogitation. What she arrived at in speech was: "Well, I guess you've done a wicked thing, Editha Balcom."

The girl said, as she passed indoors through the same window her mother had come out by: "I haven't done anything — yet."

In her room, she put together all her letters and gifts from Gearson, down to the withered petals of the first flower he had offered, with that timidity of his veiled in that irony of his. In the heart of the packet she enshrined her engagement ring which she had restored to the pretty box he had brought it her in. Then she sat down, if not calmly yet strongly, and wrote:

> "George: — I understood when you left me. But I think we had better emphasize your meaning that if we cannot be one in everything we had better be one in nothing. So I am sending these things for your keeping till you have made up your mind.
>
> "I shall always love you, and therefore I shall never marry any one else. But the man I marry must love his country first of all, and be able to say to me,
>
> > " 'I could not love thee, dear, so much,
> >
> > Loved I not honor more'. ①
>
> "There is no honor above America with me. In this great hour there is no other honor.
>
> "Your heart will make my words clear to you. I had never expected to say so much, but it has come upon me that I must say the utmost. Editha."

She thought she had worded her letter well, worded it in a way that could not be bettered; all had been implied and nothing expressed.

She had it ready to send with the packet she had tied with red, white, and blue ribbon, when it occurred to her that she was not just to him, that she was not giving him a fair chance. He had said he would go and think it over, and she was not waiting. She was pushing, threatening, compelling. That was not a woman's part. She must leave him free, free, free. She could not accept for her country or herself a forced sacrifice.

In writing her letter she had satisfied the impulse from which it sprang; she could well afford to wait till he had thought it over. She put the packet and the letter by, and rested

---

① Lines from Richard Lovelace's (1618 – 1658) poem "To Lucasta, Going to the Wars".

serene in the consciousness of having done what was laid upon her by her love itself to do, and yet used patience, mercy, justice.

She had her reward. Gearson did not come to tea, but she had given him till morning, when, late at night there came up from the village the sound of a fife and drum, with a tumult of voices, in shouting, singing, and laughing. The noise drew nearer and nearer; it reached the street end of the avenue; there it silenced itself, and one voice, the voice she knew best, rose over the silence. It fell; the air was filled with cheers; the fife and drum struck up, with the shouting, singing, and laughing again, but now retreating; and a single figure came hurrying up the avenue.

She ran down to meet her lover and clung to him. He was very gay, and he put his arm round her with a boisterous laugh. "Well, you must call me Captain now; or Cap, if you prefer; that's what the boys call me. Yes, we've had a meeting at the town-hall, and everybody has volunteered; and they selected me for captain, and I'm going to the war, the big war, the glorious war, the holy war ordained by the pocket Providence that blesses butchery. Come along; let's tell the whole family about it. Call them from their downy beds, father, mother, Aunt Hitty, and all the folks!"

But when they mounted the veranda steps he did not wait for a larger audience; he poured the story out upon Editha alone.

"There was a lot of speaking, and then some of the fools set up a shout for me. It was all going one way, and I thought it would be a good joke to sprinkle a little cold water on them. But you can't do that with a crowd that adores you. The first thing I knew I was sprinkling hell-fire on them. 'Cry havoc, and let slip the dogs of war.' That was the style. Now that it had come to the fight, there were no two parties; there was one country, and the thing was to fight to a finish as quick as possible. I suggested volunteering then and there, and I wrote my name first of all on the roster. Then they elected me — that's all. I wish I had some ice-water."

She left him walking up and down the veranda, while she ran for the ice-pitcher and a goblet, and when she came back he was still walking up and down, shouting the story he had told her to her father and mother, who had come out more sketchily dressed than they commonly were by day. He drank goblet after goblet of the ice-water without noticing who was giving it, and kept on talking, and laughing through his talk wildly. "It's astonishing," he said, "how well the worse reason looks when you try to make it appear the better. Why, I believe I was the first convert to the war in that crowd tonight! I never thought I should like to kill a man; but now I shouldn't care; and the smokeless powder lets you see the man drop that you kill. It's all for the country! What a thing it is to have a country that can't be wrong, but if it is, is right, anyway!"

Editha had a great, vital thought, an inspiration. She set down the ice-pitcher on the veranda floor, and ran up-stairs and got the letter she had written him. When at last he noisily bade her father and mother, "Well, good-night. I forgot I woke you up; I sha'n't want any sleep myself," she followed him down the avenue to the gate. There, after the whirling words that seemed to fly away from her thoughts and refuse to serve them, she made a last effort to solemnize the moment that seemed so crazy, and pressed the letter she had written upon him.

"What's this?" he said. "Want me to mail it?"

"No, no. It's for you. I wrote it after you went this morning. Keep it — keep it — and read it sometime — " She thought, and then her inspiration came: "Read it if ever you doubt what you've done, or fear that I regret your having done it. Read it after you've started."

They strained each other in embraces that seemed as ineffective as their words, and he kissed her face with quick, hot breaths that were so unlike him, that made her feel as if she had lost her old lover and found a stranger in his place. The stranger said: "What a gorgeous flower you are, with your red hair, and your blue eyes that look black now, and your face with the color painted out by the white moonshine! Let me hold you under the chin, to see whether I love blood, you tiger-lily!" Then he laughed Gearson's laugh, and released her, scared and giddy. Within her wilfulness she had been frightened by a sense of subtler force in him, and mystically mastered as she had never been before.

She ran all the way back to the house, and mounted the steps panting. Her mother and father were talking of the great affair. Her mother said: "Wa'n't Mr. Gearson in rather of an excited state of mind? Didn't you think he acted curious?"

"Well, not for a man who'd just been elected captain and had set 'em up for the whole of Company A," her father chuckled back.

"What in the world do you mean, Mr. Balcom? Oh! There's Editha!" She offered to follow the girl indoors.

"Don't come, mother!" Editha called, vanishing.

Mrs. Balcom remained to reproach her husband. "I don't see much of anything to laugh at."

"Well, it's catching. Caught it from Gearson. I guess it won't be much of a war, and I guess Gearson don't think so either. The other fellows will back down as soon as they see we mean it. I wouldn't lose any sleep over it. I'm going back to bed, myself."

Gearson came again next afternoon, looking pale and rather sick, but quite himself, even to his languid irony. "I guess I'd better tell you, Editha, that I consecrated myself to your god of battles last night by pouring too many libations to him down my own throat. But I'm all right now. One has to carry off the excitement, somehow."

"Promise me," she commanded, "that you'll never touch it again!"

"What! Not let the cannikin clink? Not let the soldier drink? Well, I promise."

"You don't belong to yourself now; you don't even belong to me. You belong to your country, and you have a sacred charge to keep yourself strong and well for your country's sake. I have been thinking, thinking all night and all day long."

"You look as if you had been crying a little, too," he said, with his queer smile.

"That's all past. I've been thinking, and worshipping you. Don't you suppose I know all that you've been through, to come to this? I've followed you every step from your old theories and opinions."

"Well, you've had a long row to hoe."

"And I know you've done this from the highest motives — "

"Oh, there won't be much pettifogging to do till this cruel war is — "

"And you haven't simply done it for my sake. I couldn't respect you if you had."

"Well, then we'll say I haven't. A man that hasn't got his own respect intact wants the respect of all the other people he can corner. But we won't go into that. I'm in for the thing now, and we've got to face our future. My idea is that this isn't going to be a very protracted struggle; we shall just scare the enemy to death before it comes to a fight at all. But we must provide for contingencies, Editha. If anything happens to me — "

"Oh, George!" She clung to him, sobbing.

"I don't want you to feel foolishly bound to my memory. I should hate that, wherever I happened to be."

"I am yours, for time and eternity — time and eternity." She liked the words; they satisfied her famine for phrases.

"Well, say eternity; that's all right; but time's another thing; and I'm talking about time. But there is something! My mother! If anything happens — "

She winced, and he laughed. "You're not the bold soldier-girl of yesterday!" Then he sobered. "If anything happens, I want you to help my mother out. She won't like my doing this thing. She brought me up to think war a fool thing as well as a bad thing. My father was in the Civil War; all through it; lost his arm in it." She thrilled with the sense of the arm round her; what if that should be lost? He laughed as if divining her: "Oh, it doesn't run in the family, as far as I know!" Then he added gravely: "He came home with misgivings about war, and they grew on him. I guess he and mother agreed between them that I was to be brought up in his final mind about it; but that was before my time. I only knew him from my mother's report of him and his opinions; I don't know whether they were hers first; but they were hers last. This will be a blow to her. I shall have to write and tell her — "

He stopped, and she asked: "Would you like me to write, too, George?"

"I don't believe that would do. No, I'll do the writing. She'll understand a little if I say that I thought the way to minimize it was to make war on the largest possible scale at once — that I felt I must have been helping on the war somehow if I hadn't helped keep it from coming, and I knew I hadn't; when it came, I had no right to stay out of it."

Whether his sophistries satisfied him or not, they satisfied her. She clung to his breast, and whispered, with closed eyes and quivering lips: "Yes, yes, yes!"

"But if anything should happen, you might go to her and see what you could do for her. You know? It's rather far off; she can't leave her chair — "

"Oh, I'll go, if it's the ends of the earth! But nothing will happen! Nothing can! I — "

She felt her lifted with his rising, and Gearson was saying, with his arm still round her, to her father: "Well, we're off at once, Mr. Balcom. We're to be formally accepted at the capital, and then bunched up with the rest somehow, and sent into camp somewhere, and got to the front as soon as possible. We all want to be in the van, of course; we're the first company to report to the Governor. I came to tell Editha, but I hadn't got round to it. "

She saw him again for a moment at the capital, in the station, just before the train started southward with his regiment. He looked well, in his uniform, and very soldierly, but somehow girlish, too, with his clean-shaven face and slim figure. The manly eyes and the strong voice satisfied her, and his preoccupation with some unexpected details of duty flattered her. Other girls were weeping and bemoaning themselves, but she felt a sort of noble distinction in the abstraction, the almost unconsciousness, with which they parted. Only at the last moment he said: "Don't forget my mother. It mayn't be such a walk-over as I supposed," and he laughed at the notion.

He waved his hand to her as the train moved off — she knew it among a score of hands that were waved to other girls from the platform of the car, for it held a letter which she knew was hers. Then he went inside the car to read it, doubtless, and she did not see him again. But she felt safe for him through the strength of what she called her love. What she called her God, always speaking the name in a deep voice and with the implication of a mutual understanding, would watch over him and keep him and bring him back to her. If with an empty sleeve, then he should have three arms instead of two, for both of hers should be his for life. She did not see, though, why she should always be thinking of the arm his father had lost.

There were not many letters from him, but they were such as she could have wished, and she put her whole strength into making hers such as she imagined he could have wished, glorifying and supporting him. She wrote to his mother glorifying him as their hero, but the brief answer she got was merely to the effect that Mrs. Gearson was not well enough to write herself, and thanking her for her letter by the hand of someone who called herself "Yours truly, Mrs. W. J. Andrews."

Editha determined not to be hurt, but to write again quite as if the answer had been all she expected. Before it seemed as if she could have written, there came news of the first skirmish, and in the list of the killed, which was telegraphed as a trifling loss on our side, was Gearson's name. There was a frantic time of trying to make out that it might be, must be, some other Gearson; but the name and the company and the regiment and the State were too definitely given.

Then there was a lapse into depths out of which it seemed as if she never could rise again; then a lift into clouds far above all grief, black clouds, that blotted out the sun, but where she soared with him, with George — George! She had the fever that she expected of herself, but she did not die in it; she was not even delirious, and it did not last long. When she was well enough to leave her bed, her one thought was of George's mother, of his strangely worded wish that she should go to her and see what she could do for her. In the exaltation of the duty laid upon her — it buoyed her up instead of burdening her — she rapidly recovered.

Her father went with her on the long railroad journey from northern New York to western Iowa; he had business out at Davenport, and he said he could just as well go then as any other time; and he went with her to the little country town where George's mother lived in a little house on the edge of the illimitable cornfields, under trees pushed to a top of the rolling prairie. George's father had settled there after the Civil War, as so many other old soldiers had done; but they were Eastern people, and Editha fancied touches of the East in the June rose overhanging the front door, and the garden with early summer flowers stretching from the gate of the paling fence.

It was very low inside the house, and so dim, with the closed blinds, that they could scarcely see one another: Editha tall and black in her crapes which filled the air with the smell of their dyes; her father standing decorously apart with his hat on his forearm, as at funerals; a woman rested in a deep arm-chair, and the woman who had let the strangers in stood behind the chair.

The seated woman turned her head round and up, and asked the woman behind her chair: "*Who* did you say?"

Editha, if she had done what she expected of herself, would have gone down on her knees at the feet of the seated figure and said, "I am George's Editha," for answer.

But instead of her own voice she heard that other woman's voice, saying: "Well, I don't know as I *did* get the name just right. I guess I'll have to make a little more light in here," and she went and pushed two of the shutters ajar.

Then Editha's father said, in his public will-now-address-a-few-remarks tone: "My name is Balcom, ma'am — Junius H. Balcom, of Balcom's Works, New York; my daughter — "

"Oh!" the seated woman broke in, with a powerful voice, the voice that always surprised Editha from Gearson's slender frame. "Let me see you. Stand round where the light can strike on your face," and Editha dumbly obeyed. "So, you're Editha Balcom," she sighed.

"Yes," Editha said, more like a culprit than a comforter.

"What did you come for?" Mrs. Gearson asked.

Editha's face quivered and her knees shook. "I came — because — because George — " She could go no further.

"Yes," the mother said, "he told me he had asked you to come if he got killed. You didn't expect that, I suppose, when you sent him."

"I would rather have died myself than done it!" Editha said, with more truth in her deep voice than she ordinarily found in it. "I tried to leave him free — "

"Yes, that letter of yours, that came back with his other things, left him free."

Editha saw now where George's irony came from.

"It was not to be read before — unless — until — I told him so," she faltered.

"Of course, he wouldn't read a letter of yours, under the circumstances, till he thought you wanted him to. Been sick?" the woman abruptly demanded.

"Very sick," Editha said, with self-pity.

"Daughter's life," her father interposed, "was almost despaired of, at one time."

Mrs. Gearson gave him no heed. "I suppose you would have been glad to die, such a brave person as you! I don't believe *he* was glad to die. He was always a timid boy, that way; he was afraid of a good many things; but if he was afraid he did what he made up his mind to.

I suppose he made up his mind to go, but I knew what it cost him by what it cost me when I heard of it. I had been through *one* war before. When you sent him you didn't expect he would get killed. "

The voice seemed to compassionate Editha, and it was time. " No, " she huskily murmured.

" No, girls don't; women don't, when they give their men up to their country. They think they'll come marching back, somehow, just as gay as they went, or if it's an empty sleeve, or even an empty pantaloon, it's all the more glory, and they're so much the prouder of them, poor things!"

The tears began to run down Editha's face; she had not wept till then; but it was now such a relief to be understood that the tears came.

"No, you didn't expect him to get killed, " Mrs. Gearson repeated, in a voice which was startlingly like George's again. " You just expected him to kill some one else, some of those foreigners, that weren't there because they had any say about it, but because they had to be there, poor wretches — conscripts, or whatever they call 'em. You thought it would be all right for my George, *your* George, to kill the sons of those miserable mothers and the husbands of those girls that you would never see the faces of. " The woman lifted her powerful voice in a psalm-like note. "I thank my God he didn't live to do it! I thank my God they killed him first, and that he ain't livin' with their blood on his hands!" She dropped her eyes, which she had raised with her voice, and glared at Editha. "What you got that black on for?" She lifted herself by her powerful arms so high that her helpless body seemed to hang limp its full length. "Take it off, take it off, before I tear it from your back!"

The lady who was passing the summer near Balcom's Works was sketching Editha's beauty, which lent itself wonderfully to the effects of a colorist. It had come to that confidence which is rather apt to grow between artist and sitter, and Editha had told her everything.

"To think of your having such a tragedy in your life!" the lady said. She added: "I suppose there are people who feel that way about war. But when you consider the good this war has done — how much it has done for the country! I can't understand such people, for my part. And when you had come all the way out there to console her — got up out of a sick-bed! Well!"

"I think, " Editha said, magnanimously, " she wasn't quite in her right mind; and so did papa. "

"Yes, " the lady said, looking at Editha's lips in nature and then at her lips in art, and giving an empirical touch to them in the picture. "But how dreadful of her! How perfectly — excuse me — how vulgar!"

A light broke upon Editha in the darkness which she felt had been without a gleam of brightness for weeks and months. The mystery that had bewildered her was solved by the word; and from that moment she rose from grovelling in shame and self-pity, and began to live again in the ideal.

> ## Questions for Consideration and Discussion

1. What different views of war and of God are held by Editha and George's parents? What's your comment on their views?
2. What does Editha think of herself? What do you think of her? Use some adjectives to describe her self-image and your description of her.
3. What kind of person is Editha? Hypocritical? Selfish? Idealistic? Please explain.

Kate Chopin (1850 –1904)

Kate Chopin is best remembered for her local color stories about the Louisiana life of her day. She was deeply concerned with women's lives and their continual struggles to create an identity of their own in patriarchal society; she was bold in exploring such taboo subjects as miscegenation, divorce, and female sexuality.

Chopin was born in St. Louis, Missouri. Her Irish immigrant father was a successful businessman who died in a tragic train wreck when his daughter was four years old. Her mother, grandmother, and great-grandmother were active, pious Catholics of French heritage. She grew up in the company of strong, loving women from whom she learned independence and the power of language.

She entered St. Louis Academy of the Sacred Heart at nine years old and graduated in 1868. She was well-read in English and French, and was most strongly influenced by such French writers as Flaubert, Zola, and de Maupassant in her sense of life and her craft as a writer.

At the age of nineteen, she married Oscar Chopin and went to live in New Orleans, Louisiana. During the more than ten years she spent there, she became fascinated by the variety of Louisiana life, the rich mixture of cultures, and the many languages and dialects. In 1884, a year after her husband's sudden death, she returned to St. Louis with her six children and began to write.

The characters who inhabit Chopin's fictional world are generally Louisiana Creoles, descendants of the original French and Spanish colonists, and Cajuns, descendants of Louisiana's French Canadian settlers. While Chopin is interested in capturing the flavor of Louisiana life as she knew it, she also moves beyond local color to explore the characters of her time and place.

Her short stories were collected in two books, *Bayou Folk* (1894) and *A Night in Acadie* (1897). Her most famous novel is *The Awakening* (1899), which traces the sensual and sexual coming to consciousness of a young woman. Though now considered a classic, *The Awakening was* denounced by her contemporary reviewers, just as Whitman's *Leaves of Grass* had been half a century earlier. This reaction so stunned Chopin that she wrote little else throughout the rest of her life.

The Story of an Hour

Knowing that Mrs. Mallard was afflicted with a heart trouble, great care was taken to break to her as gently as possible the news of her husband's death.

It was her sister Josephine who told her, in broken sentences; veiled hints that revealed in half concealing. Her husband's friend Richards was there, too, near her. It was he who had been in the newspaper office when intelligence of the railroad disaster was received, with Brently Mallard's name leading the list of "killed." He had only taken the time to assure himself of its truth by a second telegram, and had hastened to forestall any less careful, less tender friend in bearing the sad message.

She did not hear the story as many women have heard the same, with a paralyzed inability to accept its significance. She wept at once, with sudden, wild abandonment, in her sister's arms. When the storm of grief had spent itself she went away to her room alone. She would have no one follow her.

There stood, facing the open window, a comfortable, roomy armchair. Into this she sank, pressed down by a physical exhaustion that haunted her body and seemed to reach into her soul.

She could see in the open square before her house the tops of trees that were all aquiver with the new spring life. The delicious breath of rain was in the air. In the street below a peddler was crying his wares. The notes of a distant song which some one was singing reached her faintly, and countless sparrows were twittering in the eaves.

There were patches of blue sky showing here and there through the clouds that had met and piled one above the other in the west facing her window.

She sat with her head thrown back upon the cushion of the chair, quite motionless, except when a sob came up into her throat and shook her, as a child who has cried itself to sleep continues to sob in its dreams.

She was young, with a fair, calm face, whose lines bespoke repression and even a certain strength. But now there was a dull stare in her eyes, whose gaze was fixed away off yonder on one of those patches of blue sky. It was not a glance of reflection, but rather indicated a suspension of intelligent thought.

There was something coming to her and she was waiting for it, fearfully. What was it? She did not know; it was too subtle and elusive to name. But she felt it, creeping out of the sky, reaching toward her through the sounds, the scents, the color that filled the air.

Now her bosom rose and fell tumultuously. She was beginning to recognize this thing that was approaching to possess her, and she was striving to beat it back with her will — as powerless as her two white slender hands would have been.

When she abandoned herself a little whispered word escaped her slightly parted lips. She said it over and over under her breath: "free, free, free!" The vacant stare and the look of terror that had followed it went from her eyes. They stayed keen and bright. Her pulses beat fast, and the coursing blood warmed and relaxed every inch of her body.

She did not stop to ask if it were or were not a monstrous joy that held her. A clear and exalted perception enabled her to dismiss the suggestion as trivial.

She knew that she would weep again when she saw the kind, tender hands folded in death; the face that had never looked save with love upon her, fixed and gray and dead. But she saw beyond that bitter moment a long procession of years to come that would belong to her absolutely. And she opened and spread her arms out to them in welcome.

There would be no one to live for during those coming years; she would live for herself. There would be no powerful will bending hers in that blind persistence with which men and women believe they have a right to impose a private will upon a fellow-creature. A kind intention or a cruel intention made the act seem no less a crime as she looked upon it in that brief moment of illumination.

And yet she had loved him — sometimes. Often she had not. What did it matter! What could love, the unsolved mystery, count for in face of this possession of self-assertion which she suddenly recognized as the strongest impulse of her being!

"Free! Body and soul free!" she kept whispering.

Josephine was kneeling before the closed door with her lips to the keyhole, imploring for admission. "Louise, open the door! I beg, open the door — you will make yourself ill. What are you doing, Louise? For heaven's sake open the door."

"Go away. I am not making myself ill." No; she was drinking in a very elixir of life through that open window.

Her fancy was running riot along those days ahead of her. Spring days, and summer days, and all sorts of days that would be her own. She breathed a quick prayer that life might be long. It was only yesterday she had thought with a shudder that life might be long.

She arose at length and opened the door to her sister's importunities. There was a feverish triumph in her eyes, and she carried herself unwittingly like a goddess of Victory. She clasped her sister's waist, and together they descended the stairs. Richards stood waiting for them at the bottom.

Some one was opening the front door with a latchkey. It was Brently Mallard who entered, a little travel-stained, composedly carrying his grip-sack and umbrella. He had been far from the scene of accident, and did not even know there had been one. He stood amazed at Josephine's piercing cry; at Richards' quick motion to screen him from the view of his wife.

But Richards was too late.

When the doctors came they said she had died of heart disease — of joy that kills.

▶▶ Questions for Consideration and Discussion

1. What's Mrs. Mallard's reaction when learning her husband's death? What's your comment on the issues of marital love, conjugal domination and subordination (usually husband's dominance over wife), and personal freedom?
2. Among the three types of irony — verbal irony, situational irony, and dramatic irony — which type(s) of irony is/are used?

Edwin Arlington Robinson (1869 – 1935)

Edwin Arlington Robinson is best known for his brief "story and portrait" poems about his fictional New England "Tilbury Town" and its inhabitants. As a winner of three Pulitzer Prizes — the first came to him in 1922 — he has been regarded as a major American poet.

Robinson was born in a tiny village in Maine and grew up in Gardiner, Maine, on which he modeled Tilbury Town. When he was a high school student, he practiced writing in intricate verse form under the guidance of a local poet. He continued to write during the two years he attended Harvard University. In 1893, financial problems forced Robinson to leave college and return home. He did, however, manage to publish two books of poems, *The Torrent and the Night Before* (1896) and *The Children of the Night* (1897), at his own expense. Many of these poems and those published in later volumes deal with themes of personal failure and despair. The family's financial difficulties, along with the failure and early death of both of Robinson's older brothers, may also have been reflected in these themes.

At twenty-eight, Robinson moved to New York City, where he lived in semi-poverty and wrote without much of a readership. His life was made somewhat easier in 1902 when President Theodore Roosevelt, an admirer of his work, appointed him to a post in the New York Custom House where Herman Melville had once been employed. However, Robinson's first real success did not come until 1910, with the publication of *The Town down the River*. In time he was awarded three Pulitzer Prizes and became the best American poet between the generation of Whitman and Dickinson and that of Robert Frost, Ezra Pound, and William Carlos Williams.

In technique and style, Robinson is a traditionalist, but he is daringly realistic in his subject matter. Most of his poems attempt to tell the "truth" about Tilbury Town. To a Realist like Robinson, that truth mainly includes alienation, disillusionment, sadness, tragedy, frustration, and waste. The particular flavor of Robinson's best poems springs from his mixture of realism with irony and even humor.

Richard Cory
(1896)

Whenever Richard Cory went down town,
We people on the pavement looked at him:
He was a gentleman from sole to crown,
Clean favored, and imperially slim.

5   And he was always quietly arrayed,
And he was always human when he talked;
But still he fluttered pulses when he said,
"Good-morning," and he glittered when he walked.

And he was rich — yes, richer than a king —
10   And admirably schooled in every grace:
In fine, we thought that he was everything
To make us wish that we were in his place.

So on we worked, and waited for the light,
15   And went without the meat, and cursed the bread;
And Richard Cory, one calm summer night,
Went home and put a bullet through his head.

Miniver Cheevy
(1910)

Miniver Cheevy, child of scorn,
    Grew lean while he assailed the seasons;
He wept that he was ever born,
    And he had reasons.

5   Miniver loved the days of old
    When swords were bright and steeds were prancing;
The vision of a warrior bold
    Would set him dancing.

Miniver sighed for what was not,
10   And dreamed, and rested from his labors;

He dreamed of Thebes① and Camelot②,
    And Priam's③ neighbors.

Miniver mourned the ripe renown
    That made so many a name so fragrant;
15   He mourned Romance, now on the town,
    And Art, a vagrant.

Miniver loved the Medici④,
    Albeit he had never seen one;
He would have sinned incessantly
20   Could he have been one.

Miniver cursed the commonplace
    And eyed a khaki suit with loathing;
He missed the medieval grace
    Of iron clothing.

25   Miniver scorned the gold he sought,
    But sore annoyed was he without it;
Miniver thought, and thought, and thought,
    And thought about it.

Miniver Cheevy, born too late,
30   Scratched his head and kept on thinking;
    Miniver coughed, and called it fate,
    And kept on drinking.

Eros Turannos

(1914)

She fears him, and will always ask
    What fated her to choose him;
She meets in his engaging mask

---

① Thebes: leading city-state of ancient Greece.
② Camelot: legendary site in England of King Arthur's court and Round Table.
③ Priam: King of Troy during the Trojan War.
④ Medici: rich, powerful family of Florence, Italy, in the fourteenth, fifteenth, and sixteenth centuries.

All reasons to refuse him;
15   But what she meets and what she fears
Are less than are the downward years,
Drawn slowly to the foamless weirs
   Of age, were she to lose him.

Between a blurred sagacity
10   That once had power to sound him,
And Love, that will not let him be
   The Judas that she found him,
Her pride assuages her almost,
As if it were alone the cost. —
15   He sees that he will not be lost,
   And waits and looks around him.

A sense of ocean and old trees
   Envelops and allures him;
Tradition, touching all he sees
20   Beguiles and reassures him;
And all her doubts of what he says
Are dimmed with what she knows of days —
Till even prejudice delays
   And fades, and she secures him.

25   The falling leaf inaugurates
   The reign of her confusion;
The pounding wave reverberates
   The dirge of her illusion;
And home, where passion lived and died,
30   Becomes a place where she can hide,
While all the town and harbor side
   Vibrate with her seclusion.

We tell you, tapping on our brows,
   The story as it should be, —
35   As if the story of a house
   Were told, or ever could be;
We'll have no kindly veil between
Her visions and those we have seen, —
As if we guessed what hers have been,

40 Or what they are or would be.

Meanwhile we do no harm; for they
 That with a god have striven,
Not hearing much of what we say,
 Take what the god has given;
45 Though like waves breaking it may be,
 Or like a changed familiar tree,
 Or like a stairway to the sea
 Where down the blind are driven.

▷▷ Questions for Consideration and Discussion

1. What's the "surprise" ending of "Richard Cory"? What effect does Cory's final action seem to have on everyone in Tilbury Town? What does Tilbury Town's reaction to Cory's life and death suggest about human understanding?

2. Basically, how does Cheevy see himself? How do we see him? What do you think really causes his unhappiness?

3. From whose point of view is "Eros Turannos" narrated? Did the woman marry out of love? Why did she choose to marry the man? What is the townspeople's attitude toward this matter?

4. We have learned about three unhappy characters in Robinson's "Richard Cory," "Miniver Cheevy," and "Eros Turannos." Could these characters be found only in a small town at the turn of the 20th century? Please explain.

American Naturalism

As stated at the beginning of this chapter, Naturalism is an offshoot of Realism; it is commonly understood as an extension or intensification of realism. It emphasizes a biological and socioeconomic determinism. Before turning to the leading naturalists and their work, the scientific and philosophic backgrounds of Naturalism require some elaboration.

One of the most far-reaching intellectual events of the last half of the 19th century was the publication, in 1859, of Charles Darwin's *On the Origin of Species*. This book, together with his *Descent of Man* (1870), hypothesized, on the basis of massive physical evidence, that over the millennia humans had evolved from "lower" forms of life; that humans were special not because God had created them in God's image (as the Bible taught), but because they had successfully adapted to changing environmental conditions; and that in the struggle for living, only the fittest survived. In the 1870s, English philosopher Herbert Spencer applied Darwin's evolutionary theory to social relations. This was enthusiastically welcomed by many leading American businessmen. For instance, Andrew Carnegie, on behalf of the successful industrialists, argued that unrestrained competition was the equivalent of a law of nature designed to eliminate those unfit for the new economic order.

Another response to Darwin was to accept the deterministic implications of evolutionary theory and to use them to account for the behavior of characters in literary works. This meant that characters were conceived as more or less complex combinations of inherited attributes and habits resulting from socioeconomic forces. As Émile Zola (1840 – 1902), the influential French theorist and novelist, put the matter in his essay "The Experimental Novel" (1880):

> In short, we must operate with characters, passions, human and social data as the chemist and the physicist work on inert bodies, as the physiologist works on living bodies. Determinism governs everything. It is scientific investigation; it is experimental reasoning that combats one by one the hypotheses of the idealists and will replace novels of pure imagination by novels of observation and experiment.

Inspired by these ideas, some American writers adopted aspects of this so-called naturalistic view of human kind. Stephen Crane, Theodore Dreiser, Jack London, and Frank Norris are usually identified as the leading figures of American Naturalism. Generally speaking, the characters these Naturalist writers examine are from the fringes and lower depths of contemporary society, and the characters' fates are the products of degenerate heredity, a sordid environment, and a good deal of bad luck. In naturalist fiction, characters are often caught within forces of nature or of society that are beyond their understanding or control. For instance, in Jack London's short story "To Build a Fire," the main character is crushed by the overwhelming force of the Arctic cold. Tim Haskins, a farmer in Hamlin Garland's short story "Under the Lion's Paw," suffers beneath an economic force that he is not equipped to fight. The young soldier Henry Fleming in Stephen Crane's *The Red Badge of Courage* (1895) usually must act under the shadow of larger forces that he cannot know or understand. Theodore Dreiser's *Sister Carrie* (1900) is a prime example of naturalism in that the author, as intrusive narrator, makes his comments, from time to time, on the forces behind the characters' behaviors: He tries to be amoral in the view of human life, neither condemning nor praising the characters for actions beyond their control.

It is important to point out that American naturalist writers didn't simply cobble their understandings of Darwin, Spencer, or Zola into some rigid, absolutist, dogmatic mode. Rather, they responded to naturalistic notions in diverse and innovative ways. On the one hand, they explored how people were shaped by their biological, environmental, and other material forces. On the other hand, they allowed, in different degrees, for the value of human beings, for their potential to make some measurable sense out of their experience, and for their capacity to act compassionately under the most adverse circumstances. For instance, Stephen Crane was no absolutist in naturalistic determinism. He believed, as he said of the titular character of *Maggie: A Girl of the Streets* (1893), that environment counts for a great deal in determining human fate. But not every person born in a slum ends up as a hoodlum, drunk, or suicide. Moreover, "a great deal" is not the same as everything. He observes in his short story "The Open Boat" (1898) that nature is not hostile, only "indifferent, flatly indifferent." In *The Red Badge of Courage*, as the story draws to its end, Henry Fleming responds to the chaos and violence that surround him with alternating surges of panic and self-congratulation, not as a man who has fully understood himself and his place in the world. This may show that Crane, like most naturalists, is more ambiguous, more accepting of paradoxes than rigidly embracing the notion of naturalism.

It should also be pointed out that although the naturalist literature described the world with brutal realism, it sometimes aimed at bettering the world through social reform or individual inspiration. For example, Frank Norris and Hamlin Garland, in portraying the plight of the Western and Midwestern farmers, hoped to bring this desperate situation to the eyes of the American public so to improve it. For another example, on reading Stephen Crane's "The Open Boat," we are left with the thought that precisely because human beings are exposed to a savage world of chance where death is always imminent, people should not only learn the art of sympathetic identification with others but also practice solidarity. Without this deeply felt human connection, human experience is meaningless.

▶▶ Questions for Consideration and Discussion

1. Are you for or against literary naturalism? Why?
2. Can you identify some forces that have helped to shape your way of life or the kind of person you are now?

Stephen Crane (1871 – 1900)

Stephen Crane lived a short life — he died of tuberculosis at twenty-eight — but he accomplished an enormous achievement within his brief span of existence. Hemingway said in his *Green Hills of Africa* (1935): "The good writers are Henry James, Stephen Crane, and Mark Twain. That's not the order they're good in. There is no order for good writers."

Stephen Crane lived a life of rebellion — against his strict upbringing, his school and university, and the society which he considered poorly regulated and unjust. As the fourteenth and the youngest child of a Methodist minister in New Jersey, Crane first chafed against the constraints of his structured family life. The restrictions of university life didn't agree with him any better. He studied in two of higher education institutes, but he never graduated, for he was unable to accept the routine of academic life. During his one semester stay at Syracuse University, he spent more time playing baseball than studying. Yet, during that semester he had already begun work on his first novel, *Maggie: A Girl of the Streets*.

After leaving Syracuse, Crane moved to New York City, the inevitable destination for a young man with literary ambitions and a desire to experience the fullness of life. There he found work as a journalist. He was only twenty when he heard Hamlin Garland lecture on Realism in fiction. Inspired, Crane resumed work on *Maggie: A Girl of the Streets*, a novella about a young girl born in the slums of New York who, during her short life, is driven to prostitution and suicide. The book was rejected by several editors who felt that the American public was not ready for so un-Romantic a tale. Apparently they were right. When, in 1893, Crane borrowed money from his brother to have *Maggie* published, though a few writers praised the book, it did not sell.

Nevertheless, Crane began work on another novel. He called it *The Red Badge of Courage: An Episode of the American Civil War*. *The Red Badge of Courage* was serialized in 1894 and published in book form one year later. It was a resounding success and has become one of America's classic novels.

Crane, of course, was too young to have experienced the Civil War firsthand. He was strongly influenced, however, by the realistic novels of the Russian master Leo Tolstoy, and in order to get a sense of the "reality" of battle, he also met and talked with Civil War veterans. Fascinated with danger and war (though temperamentally a gentle person), he went to Greece to cover the Greco-Turkish War in 1897 and the Spanish-American War in 1898. These experiences proved to him that the feelings he had portrayed chiefly from his imagination in *The Red Badge of Courage* were indeed accurate descriptions of what it felt like to be in battle.

Most of Crane's other fiction and nonfiction are grounded in personal experience. "The Open Boat" (1897) is based on his experience of being shipwrecked while traveling to Cuba; "The Blue Hotel" (1898) is set in the American West, which he visited in the course of his career as journalist. Crane also wrote some poetry, collected in two volumes — *The Black Riders* (1895) and *War is Kind* (1899). Crane's later works declined in power, but *The Red Badge of Courage* will always hold a high place in the history of the American novel.

It is true that *The Red Badge of Courage* is set in the Civil War. But it would be a mistake to read it as a Civil War novel. It is an "episode" of the war; the war only provides a backdrop. We never find out much about the war itself; for instance, we do not learn what battle is being described, when it took place, or what role it played in the outcome of the war. Like the soldiers in the novel, we see only a fragment of the total picture. Our full view is that of a young man swinging wildly between confidence and fear, understanding and bewilderment. This shows that Crane wanted to give one soldier's impression of the war, not a journalistic account. This style of writing is called impressionism, a writing style that presents an author's or a character's impressions of an experience, rather than a more realistic description of it. Therefore, Crane is also regarded as an early example of American impressionism.

The Red Badge of Courage
(Excerpt)
Chapter 1

The cold passed reluctantly from the earth, and the retiring fogs revealed an army stretched out on the hills, resting. As the landscape changed from brown to green, the army awakened, and began to tremble with eagerness at the noise of rumors. It cast its eyes upon the roads, which were growing from long troughs of liquid mud to proper thoroughfares. A river, amber-tinted in the shadow of its banks, purled at the army's feet; and at night, when the stream had become of a sorrowful blackness, one could see across it the red, eyelike gleam of hostile camp-fires set in the low brows of distant hills.

Once a certain tall soldier developed virtues and went resolutely to wash a shirt. He came flying back from a brook waving his garment bannerlike. He was swelled with a tale he had heard from a reliable friend, who had heard it from a truthful cavalryman, who had heard it from his trustworthy brother, one of the orderlies at division headquarters. He adopted the important air of a herald in red and gold.

"We're goin' t' move t'morrah — sure," he said pompously to a group in the company street. "We're goin' 'way up the river, cut across, an' come around in behint 'em."

To his attentive audience he drew a loud and elaborate plan of a very brilliant campaign. When he had finished, the blue-clothed① men scattered into small arguing groups between the rows of squat brown huts. A negro teamster who had been dancing upon a cracker box with the hilarious encouragement of twoscore soldiers was deserted. He sat mournfully down. Smoke drifted lazily from a multitude of quaint chimneys.

"It's a lie! That's all it is — a thunderin' lie!" said another private loudly. His smooth face was flushed, and his hands were thrust sulkily into his trouser's pockets. He took the matter as an affront to him. "I don't believe the derned old army's ever going to move. We're set. I've got ready to move eight times in the last two weeks, and we ain't moved yet."

The tall soldier felt called upon to defend the truth of a rumor he himself had introduced. He and the loud one came near to fighting over it.

A corporal began to swear before the assemblage. He had just put a costly board floor in his house, he said. During the early spring he had refrained from adding extensively to the comfort of his environment because he had felt that the army might start on the march at any moment. Of late, however, he had been impressed that they were in a sort of eternal camp.

Many of the men engaged in a spirited debate. One outlined in a peculiarly lucid manner all the plans of the commanding general. He was opposed by men who advocated that there were other plans of campaign. They clamored at each other, numbers making futile bids for the popular attention. Meanwhile, the soldier who had fetched the rumor bustled about with much importance. He was continually assailed by questions.

"What's up, Jim?"

"Th' army's goin' t' move."

"Ah, what yeh talkin' about? How yeh know it is?"

"Well, yeh kin b'lieve me er not, jest as yeh like. I don't care a hang."

There was much food for thought in the manner in which he replied. He came near to convincing them by disdaining to produce proofs. They grew much excited over it.

There was a youthful private who listened with eager ears to the words of the tall soldier and to the varied comments of his comrades. After receiving a fill of discussions concerning marches and attacks, he went to his hut and crawled through an intricate hole that served it as a door. He wished to be alone with some new thoughts that had lately come to him.

He lay down on a wide bunk that stretched across the end of the room. In the other end, cracker boxes were made to serve as furniture. They were grouped about the fireplace. A picture from an illustrated weekly was upon the log walls, and three rifles were paralleled on pegs. Equipments hung on handy projections, and some tin dishes lay upon a small pile of firewood. A folded tent was serving as a roof. The sunlight, without, beating upon it, made it

---

① blue-clothed: During the American Civil War, Union soldiers of the North wore blue uniforms; Confederate soldiers of the South wore grey uniforms.

glow a light yellow shade. A small window shot an oblique square of whiter light upon the cluttered floor. The smoke from the fire at times neglected the clay chimney and wreathed into the room, and this flimsy chimney of clay and sticks made endless threats to set ablaze the whole establishment.

The youth was in a little trance of astonishment. So they were at last going to fight. On the morrow, perhaps, there would be a battle, and he would be in it. For a time he was obliged to labor to make himself believe. He could not accept with assurance an omen that he was about to mingle in one of those great affairs of the earth.

He had, of course, dreamed of battles all his life — of vague and bloody conflicts that had thrilled him with their sweep and fire. In visions he had seen himself in many struggles. He had imagined peoples secure in the shadow of his eagle-eyed prowess. But awake he had regarded battles as crimson blotches on the pages of the past. He had put them as things of the bygone with his thought-images of heavy crowns and high castles. There was a portion of the world's history which he had regarded as the time of wars, but it, he thought, had been long gone over the horizon and had disappeared forever.

From his home his youthful eyes had looked upon the war in his own country with distrust. It must be some sort of a play affair. He had long despaired of witnessing a Greeklike struggle. Such would be no more, he had said. Men were better, or more timid. Secular and religious education had effaced the throat-grappling instinct, or else firm finance held in check the passions.

He had burned several times to enlist. Tales of great movements shook the land. They might not be distinctly Homeric, but there seemed to be much glory in them. He had read of marches, sieges, conflicts, and he had longed to see it all. His busy mind had drawn for him large pictures extravagant in color, lurid with breathless deeds.

But his mother had discouraged him. She had affected to look with some contempt upon the quality of his war ardor and patriotism. She could calmly seat herself and with no apparent difficulty give him many hundreds of reasons why he was of vastly more importance on the farm than on the field of battle. She had had certain ways of expression that told him that her statements on the subject came from a deep conviction. Moreover, on her side, was his belief that her ethical motive in the argument was impregnable.

At last, however, he had made firm rebellion against this yellow light thrown upon the color of his ambitions. The newspapers, the gossip of the village, his own picturings, had aroused him to an uncheckable degree. They were in truth fighting finely down there. Almost every day the newspaper printed accounts of a decisive victory.

One night, as he lay in bed, the winds had carried to him the clangoring of the church bell as some enthusiast jerked the rope frantically to tell the twisted news of a great battle. This voice of the people rejoicing in the night had made him shiver in a prolonged ecstasy of excitement. Later, he had gone down to his mother's room and had spoken thus: "Ma, I'm going to enlist."

"Henry, don't you be a fool," his mother had replied. She had then covered her face with the quilt. There was an end to the matter for that night.

Nevertheless, the next morning he had gone to a town that was near his mother's farm and had enlisted in a company that was forming there. When he had returned home his mother was milking the brindle cow. Four others stood waiting. "Ma, I've enlisted," he had said to her diffidently. There was a short silence. "The Lord's will be done, Henry," she had finally replied, and had then continued to milk the brindle cow.

When he had stood in the doorway with his soldier's clothes on his back, and with the light of excitement and expectancy in his eyes almost defeating the glow of regret for the home bonds, he had seen two tears leaving their trails on his mother's scarred cheeks.

Still, she had disappointed him by saying nothing whatever about returning with his shield or on it. ① He had privately primed himself for a beautiful scene. He had prepared certain sentences which he thought could be used with touching effect. But her words destroyed his plans. She had doggedly peeled potatoes and addressed him as follows: "You watch out, Henry, an' take good care of yerself in this here fighting business — you watch, an' take good care of yerself. Don't go a-thinkin' you can lick the hull rebel army at the start, because yeh can't. Yer jest one little feller amongst a hull lot of others, and yeh've got to keep quiet an' do what they tell yeh. I know how you are, Henry.

"I've knet yeh eight pair of socks, Henry, and I've put in all yer best shirts, because I want my boy to be jest as warm and comf'able as anybody in the army. Whenever they get holes in 'em, I want yeh to send 'em right-away back to me, so's I kin dern② 'em.

"An' allus be careful an' choose yer comp'ny. There's lots of bad men in the army, Henry. The army makes 'em wild, and they like nothing better than the job of leading off a young feller like you, as ain't never been away from home much and has allus had a mother, an' a-learning 'em to drink and swear. Keep clear of them folks, Henry. I don't want yeh to ever do anything, Henry, that yeh would be 'shamed to let me know about. Jest think as if I was a-watchin' yeh. If yeh keep that in yer mind allus, I guess yeh'll come out about right.

"Yeh must allus remember yer father, too, child, an' remember he never drunk a drop of licker in his life, and seldom swore a cross oath.

"I don't know what else to tell yeh, Henry, excepting that yeh must never do no shirking, child, on my account. If so be a time comes when yeh have to be kilt or do a mean thing, why, Henry, don't think of anything 'cept what's right, because there's many a woman has to bear up 'ginst sech things these times, and the Lord'll take keer of us all.

"Don't forgit about the socks and the shirts, child; and I've put a cup of blackberry jam with yer bundle, because I know yeh like it above all things. Good-by, Henry. Watch out, and be a good boy."

He had, of course, been impatient under the ordeal of this speech. It had not been quite

---

① returning with his shield or on it: In Greek literature, soldiers going off to war were advised to return alive (with shield) or dead (carried on the shield).

② dern: dam; repair the holes in.

what he expected, and he had borne it with an air of irritation. He departed feeling vague relief.

Still, when he had looked back from the gate, he had seen his mother kneeling among the potato parings. Her brown face, upraised, was stained with tears, and her spare form was quivering. He bowed his head and went on, feeling suddenly ashamed of his purposes.

From his home he had gone to the seminary to bid adieu to many schoolmates. They had thronged about him with wonder and admiration. He had felt the gulf now between them and had swelled with calm pride. He and some of his fellows who had donned blue were quite overwhelmed with privileges for all of one afternoon, and it had been a very delicious thing. They had strutted.

A certain light-haired girl had made vivacious fun at his martial spirit, but there was another and darker girl whom he had gazed at steadfastly, and he thought she grew demure and sad at sight of his blue and brass. As he had walked down the path between the rows of oaks, he had turned his head and detected her at a window watching his departure. As he perceived her, she had immediately begun to stare up through the high tree branches at the sky. He had seen a good deal of flurry and haste in her movement as she changed her attitude. He often thought of it.

On the way to Washington his spirit had soared. The regiment was fed and caressed at station after station until the youth had believed that he must be a hero. There was a lavish expenditure of bread and cold meats, coffee, and pickles and cheese. As he basked in the smiles of the girls and was patted and complimented by the old men, he had felt growing within him the strength to do mighty deeds of arms.

After complicated journeyings with many pauses, there had come months of monotonous life in a camp. He had had the belief that real war was a series of death struggles with small time in between for sleep and meals; but since his regiment had come to the field the army had done little but sit still and try to keep warm.

He was brought then gradually back to his old ideas. Greeklike struggles would be no more. Men were better, or more timid. Secular and religious education had effaced the throat-grappling instinct, or else firm finance held in check the passions.

He had grown to regard himself merely as a part of a vast blue demonstration. His province was to look out, as far as he could, for his personal comfort. For recreation he could twiddle his thumbs and speculate on the thoughts which must agitate the minds of the generals. Also, he was drilled and drilled and reviewed, and drilled and drilled and reviewed.

The only foes he had seen were some pickets along the river bank. They were a sun-tanned, philosophical lot, who sometimes shot reflectively at the blue pickets. When reproached for this afterward, they usually expressed sorrow, and swore by their gods that the guns had exploded without their permission. The youth, on guard duty one night, conversed across the stream with one of them. He was a slightly ragged man, who spat skillfully between his shoes and possessed a great fund of bland and infantile assurance. The youth liked him personally.

"Yank," the other had informed him, "yer a right dum good feller." This sentiment, floating to him upon the still air, had made him temporarily regret war.

Various veterans had told him tales. Some talked of gray, bewhiskered hordes who were advancing with relentless curses and chewing tobacco with unspeakable valor; tremendous bodies of fierce soldiery who were sweeping along like the Huns. Others spoke of tattered and eternally hungry men who fired despondent powders. "They'll charge through hell's fire an' brimstone t' git a holt on a haversack, an' sech stomachs ain't a'lastin' long," he was told. From the stories, the youth imagined the red, live bones sticking out through slits in the faded uniforms.

Still, he could not put a whole faith in veteran's tales, for recruits were their prey. They talked much of smoke, fire, and blood, but he could not tell how much might be lies. They persistently yelled "Fresh fish!" at him, and were in no wise to be trusted.

However, he perceived now that it did not greatly matter what kind of soldiers he was going to fight, so long as they fought, which fact no one disputed. There was a more serious problem. He lay in his bunk pondering upon it. He tried to mathematically prove to himself that he would not run from a battle.

Previously he had never felt obliged to wrestle too seriously with this question. In his life he had taken certain things for granted, never challenging his belief in ultimate success, and bothering little about means and roads. But here he was confronted with a thing of moment. It had suddenly appeared to him that perhaps in a battle he might run. He was forced to admit that as far as war was concerned he knew nothing of himself.

A sufficient time before he would have allowed the problem to kick its heels at the outer portals of his mind, but now he felt compelled to give serious attention to it.

A little panic-fear grew in his mind. As his imagination went forward to a fight, he saw hideous possibilities. He contemplated the lurking menaces of the future, and failed in an effort to see himself standing stoutly in the midst of them. He recalled his visions of broken-bladed glory, but in the shadow of the impending tumult he suspected them to be impossible pictures.

He sprang from the bunk and began to pace nervously to and fro. "Good Lord, what's th' matter with me?" he said aloud.

He felt that in this crisis his laws of life were useless. Whatever he had learned of himself was here of no avail. He was an unknown quantity. He saw that he would again be obliged to experiment as he had in early youth. He must accumulate information of himself, and meanwhile he resolved to remain close upon his guard lest those qualities of which he knew nothing should everlastingly disgrace him. "Good Lord!" he repeated in dismay.

After a time the tall soldier slid dexterously through the hole. The loud private followed. They were wrangling.

"That's all right," said the tall soldier as he entered. He waved his hand expressively. "You can believe me or not, jest as you like. All you got to do is sit down and wait as quiet as you can. Then pretty soon you'll find out I was right."

His comrade grunted stubbornly. For a moment he seemed to be searching for a formidable reply. Finally he said: "Well, you don't know everything in the world, do you?"

"Didn't say I knew everything in the world," retorted the other sharply. He began to stow various articles snugly into his knapsack.

The youth, pausing in his nervous walk, looked down at the busy figure. "Going to be a battle, sure, is there, Jim?" he asked.

"Of course there is," replied the tall soldier. "Of course there is. You jest wait 'til to-morrow, and you'll see one of the biggest battles ever was. You jest wait."

"Thunder!" said the youth.

"Oh, you'll see fighting this time, my boy, what'll be regular out-and-out fighting," added the tall soldier, with the air of a man who is about to exhibit a battle for the benefit of his friends.

"Huh!" said the loud one from a corner.

"Well," remarked the youth, "like as not this story'll turn out jest like them others did."

"Not much it won't," replied the tall soldier, exasperated. "Not much it won't. Didn't the cavalry all start this morning?" He glared about him. No one denied his statement. "The cavalry started this morning," he continued. "They say there ain't hardly any cavalry left in camp. They're going to Richmond, or some place, while we fight all the Johnnies①. It's some dodge like that. The regiment's got orders, too. A feller what seen 'em go to headquarters told me a little while ago. And they're raising blazes all over camp — anybody can see that."

"Shucks!" said the loud one.

The youth remained silent for a time. At last he spoke to the tall soldier. "Jim!"

"What?"

"How do you think the reg'ment'll do?"

"Oh, they'll fight all right, I guess, after they once get into it," said the other with cold judgment. He made a fine use of the third person. "There's been heaps of fun poked at 'em because they're new, of course, and all that; but they'll fight all right, I guess."

"Think any of the boys'll run?" persisted the youth.

"Oh, there may be a few of 'em run, but there's them kind in every regiment, 'specially when they first goes under fire," said the other in a tolerant way. "Of course it might happen that the hull kit-and-boodle② might start and run, if some big fighting came first-off, and then again they might stay and fight like fun. But you can't bet on nothing. Of course they ain't never been under fire yet, and it ain't likely they'll lick the hull rebel army all-to-oncet③ the first time; but I think they'll fight better than some, if worse than others. That's the way I figger.

---

① Johnnies: Confederate soldiers of the South were called "Johnny Rebs"; Union soldiers of the North, "Billy Yanks."

② kit-and-boodle: everybody; a variation of "kit and caboodle", meaning a group of persons or things.

③ all-to-oncet: all at once.

They call the reg'ment 'Fresh fish' and everything; but the boys come of good stock, and most of 'em'll fight like sin after they oncet git shootin'," he added, with a mighty emphasis on the last four words.

"Oh, you think you know — " began the loud soldier with scorn.

The other turned savagely upon him. They had a rapid altercation, in which they fastened upon each other various strange epithets.

The youth at last interrupted them. "Did you ever think you might run yourself, Jim?" he asked. On concluding the sentence he laughed as if he had meant to aim a joke. The loud soldier also giggled.

The tall private waved his hand. "Well," said he profoundly, "I've thought it might get too hot for Jim Conklin in some of them scrimmages, and if a whole lot of boys started and run, why, I s'pose I'd start and run. And if I once started to run, I'd run like the devil, and no mistake. But if everybody was a-standing and a-fighting, why, I'd stand and fight. Be jiminey, I would. I'll bet on it. "

"Huh!" said the loud one.

The youth of this tale felt gratitude for these words of his comrade. He had feared that all of the untried men possessed great and correct confidence. He now was in a measure reassured.

Chapter 9

The youth fell back in the procession until the tattered soldier was not in sight. Then he started to walk on with the others.

But he was amid wounds. The mob of men was bleeding. Because of the tattered soldier's question he now felt that his shame could be viewed. He was continually casting sidelong glances to see if the men were contemplating the letters of guilt he felt burned into his brow.

At times he regarded the wounded soldiers in an envious way. He conceived persons with torn bodies to be peculiarly happy. He wished that he, too, had a wound, a red badge of courage.

The spectral soldier was at his side like a stalking reproach. The man's eyes were still fixed in a stare into the unknown. His gray, appalling face had attracted attention in the crowd, and men, slowing to his dreary pace, were walking with him. They were discussing his plight, questioning him and giving him advice. In a dogged way he repelled them, signing to them to go on and leave him alone. The shadows of his face were deepening and his tight lips seemed holding in check the moan of great despair. There could be seen a certain stiffness in the movements of his body, as if he were taking infinite care not to arouse the passion of his wounds. As he went on, he seemed always looking for a place, like one who goes to choose a grave.

Something in the gesture of the man as he waved the bloody and pitying soldiers away made the youth start as if bitten. He yelled in horror. Tottering forward he laid a quivering hand upon the man's arm. As the latter slowly turned his waxlike features toward him the youth screamed:

"Gawd! Jim Conklin!"

The tall soldier made a little commonplace smile. "Hello, Henry," he said.

The youth swayed on his legs and glared strangely. He stuttered and stammered. "Oh, Jim — oh, Jim — oh, Jim — "

The tall soldier held out his gory hand. There was a curious red and black combination of new blood and old blood upon it. "Where yeh been, Henry?" he asked. He continued in a monotonous voice, "I thought mebbe yeh got keeled over. There's been thunder t' pay t'-day. I was worryin' about it a good deal."

The youth still lamented. "Oh, Jim — oh, Jim — oh, Jim — "

"Yeh know," said the tall soldier, "I was out there." He made a careful gesture. "An', Lord, what a circus! An', b'jiminey, I got shot — I got shot. Yes, b'jiminey, I got shot." He reiterated this fact in a bewildered way, as if he did not know how it came about.

The youth put forth anxious arms to assist him, but the tall soldier went firmly as if propelled. Since the youth's arrival as a guardian for his friend, the other wounded men had ceased to display much interest. They occupied themselves again in dragging their own tragedies toward the rear.

Suddenly, as the two friends marched on, the tall soldier seemed to be overcome by a tremor. His face turned to a semblance of gray paste. He clutched the youth's arm and looked all about him, as if dreading to be overheard. Then he began to speak in a shaking whisper:

"I tell yeh what I'm 'fraid of, Henry — I'll tell yeh what I'm 'fraid of. I'm 'fraid I'll fall down — an' them yeh know — them damned artillery wagons — they like as not 'll run over me. That's what I'm 'fraid of — "

The youth cried out to him hysterically: "I'll take care of yeh, Jim! I'll take care of yeh! I swear t' Gawd I will!"

"Sure — will yeh, Henry?" the tall soldier beseeched.

"Yes — yes — I tell yeh — I'll take care of yeh, Jim!" protested the youth. He could not speak accurately because of the gulpings in his throat.

But the tall soldier continued to beg in a lowly way. He now hung babelike to the youth's arm. His eyes rolled in the wildness of his terror. "I was allus a good friend t' yeh, wa'n't I, Henry? I've allus been a pretty good feller, ain't I? An' it ain't much t' ask, is it? Jest t' pull me along outer th' road? I'd do it fer you, wouldn't I, Henry?"

He paused in piteous anxiety to await his friend's reply.

The youth had reached an anguish where the sobs scorched him. He strove to express his loyalty, but he could only make fantastic gestures.

However, the tall soldier seemed suddenly to forget all those fears. He became again the grim, stalking specter of a soldier. He went stonily forward. The youth wished his friend to lean upon him, but the other always shook his head and strangely protested. "No — no — no —

leave me be — leave me be — "

His look was fixed again upon the unknown. He moved with mysterious purpose, and all of the youth's offers he brushed aside. " No — no — leave me be — leave me be — "

The youth had to follow.

Presently the latter heard a voice talking softly near his shoulder. Turning he saw that it belonged to the tattered soldier. " Ye'd better take 'im outa th' road, pardner. There's a batt'ry comin' helitywhoop down th' road an' he'll git runned over. He's a goner anyhow in about five minutes — yeh kin see that. Ye'd better take 'im outa th' road. Where th' blazes does hi git his stren'th from?"

"Lord knows!" cried the youth. He was shaking his hands helplessly.

He ran forward presently and grasped the tall soldier by the arm. "Jim! Jim!" he coaxed, "come with me. "

The tall soldier weakly tried to wrench himself free. "Huh," he said vacantly. He stared at the youth for a moment. At last he spoke as if dimly comprehending. "Oh! Inteh th' fields? Oh!"

He started blindly through the grass.

The youth turned once to look at the lashing riders and jouncing guns of the battery. He was startled from this view by a shrill outcry from the tattered man.

"Gawd! He's runnin'!"

Turning his head swiftly, the youth saw his friend running in a staggering and stumbling way toward a little clump of bushes. His heart seemed to wrench itself almost free from his body at this sight. He made a noise of pain. He and the tattered man began a pursuit. There was a singular race.

When he overtook the tall soldier he began to plead with all the words he could find. "Jim — Jim — what are you doing — what makes you do this way — you'll hurt yerself. "

The same purpose was in the tall soldier's face. He protested in a dulled way, keeping his eyes fastened on the mystic place of his intentions. "No — no — don't tech me — leave me be — leave me be — "

The youth, aghast and filled with wonder at the tall soldier, began quaveringly to question him. "Where yeh goin', Jim? What you thinking about? Where you going? Tell me, won't you, Jim?"

The tall soldier faced about as upon relentless pursuers. In his eyes there was a great appeal. "Leave me be, can't yeh? Leave me be for a minnit. "

The youth recoiled. " Why, Jim," he said, in a dazed way, " what's the matter with you?"

The tall soldier turned and, lurching dangerously, went on. The youth and the tattered soldier followed, sneaking as if whipped, feeling unable to face the stricken man if he should again confront them. They began to have thoughts of a solemn ceremony. There was something rite-like in these movements of the doomed soldier. And there was a resemblance in him to a devotee of a mad religion, blood-sucking, muscle-wrenching, bone-crushing. They were awed and afraid. They hung back lest he have at command a dreadful weapon.

At last, they saw him stop and stand motionless. Hastening up, they perceived that his face wore an expression telling that he had at last found the place for which he had struggled. His spare figure was erect; his bloody hands were quietly at his side. He was waiting with patience for something that he had come to meet. He was at the rendezvous. They paused and stood, expectant.

There was a silence.

Finally, the chest of the doomed soldier began to heave with a strained motion. It increased in violence until it was as if an animal was within and was kicking and tumbling furiously to be free.

This spectacle of gradual strangulation made the youth writhe, and once as his friend rolled his eyes, he saw something in them that made him sink wailing to the ground. He raised his voice in a last supreme call.

"Jim — Jim — Jim — "

The tall soldier opened his lips and spoke. He made a gesture. "Leave me be — don't tech me — leave me be — "

There was another silence while he waited.

Suddenly his form stiffened and straightened. Then it was shaken by a prolonged ague. He stared into space. To the two watchers there was a curious and profound dignity in the firm lines of his awful face.

He was invaded by a creeping strangeness that slowly enveloped him. For a moment the tremor of his legs caused him to dance a sort of hideous hornpipe. His arms beat wildly about his head in expression of implike enthusiasm.

His tall figure stretched itself to its full height. There was a slight rending sound. Then it began to swing forward, slow and straight, in the manner of a falling tree. A swift muscular contortion made the left shoulder strike the ground first.

The body seemed to bounce a little way from the earth. "God!" said the tattered soldier.

The youth had watched, spellbound, this ceremony at the place of meeting. His face had been twisted into an expression of every agony he had imagined for his friend.

He now sprang to his feet and, going closer, gazed upon the pastelike face. The mouth was open and the teeth showed in a laugh.

As the flap of the blue jacket fell away from the body, he could see that the side looked as if it had been chewed by wolves.

The youth turned, with sudden, livid rage, toward the battlefield. He shook his fist. He seemed about to deliver a philippic.

"Hell — "

The red sun was pasted in the sky like a wafer.

▶ Questions for Consideration and Discussion

1. What's the tall soldier's name? The loud soldier's? The youth's? What is suggested by the fact that Crane withholds the names of his characters until well into the story?

2. What does Chapter One imply about the new recruits' understanding of the events in which they participated? How does this reflect the naturalistic view?

3. How is the description in this novel similar to and different from what you have read about elsewhere or seen in war films?

Theodore Dreiser (1871 –1945)

Theodore Dreiser is now best remembered as the author of *Sister Carrie* (1900), the most significant work of naturalism in English, and of *An American Tragedy* (1925), one of America's great novels.

Dreiser was born in Indiana. He was the eleventh of thirteen children. His father, a German immigrant who was severe and emotionally distant, was not successful in providing for his large family.

Dreiser's unhappy childhood haunted him throughout his life. The large family moved from house to house in Indiana dogged by poverty, insecurity, and internal division. One of his brothers, Paul, became a famous popular songwriter, but other brothers and sisters lived turbulent and unrespectable lives.

From the age of 15, Dreiser was on his own, earning meager support from a variety of menial jobs. A high-school teacher financed him to study a year at Indiana University in 1889, but Dreiser's real education came from experience and independent reading and thinking.

In 1892, by persistence and good luck, Dreiser got his first newspaper job with the *Chicago Globe*. Over the next decade, as an itinerant journalist, Dreiser slowly groped his way to authorship, testing what he knew from his own life against what he had learned from reading Charles Darwin, Thomas Huxley, Herbert Spencer, late-nineteenth-century scientists and social scientists who lent support to the view that nature and society had no divine sanction, that human beings, just as much as other species, were participants in an evolutionary process in which only those who adapted successfully to their environments survived.

Dreiser's first work is *Sister Carrie* (1900), a novel telling the story of Carrie Meeber, a young country girl from Wisconsin who comes to Chicago as a result of being attracted by the prospect of excitement in the rapidly growing Midwestern urban center.

There she is seduced first by a traveling salesman, Charles Drouett, then by George Hurstwood, a married middle-aged manager of a saloon. After closing one night, Hurstwood steals ten thousand dollars from the safe in the bar; then he and Carrie end up settling down in New York City, where he slowly deteriorates while she becomes a successful actress. They eventually part company and, unknown to Carrie, Hurstwood commits suicide.

Mainly because the novel depicts an amoral story of a "fallen" woman's success, it was virtually suppressed by its publisher, who printed but refused to promote the book. Since its reissue in 1907, it has steadily risen in popularity and scholarly acceptance as one of the key works in the Dreiser canon.

Dreiser's next great work is *Jennie Gerhardt* (1911). It is about the doomed love between a rich man and a poor woman. In the story a young woman, Jennie, is seduced by a senator. She bears a child out of wedlock but sacrifices her own interests to avoid harming her lover's career. It takes seriously the reality of gentleness, selflessness, and loyalty, though in the end materialism and pressures associated with wealth and social position prevail.

After *Jennie Gerhardt*, he wrote three novels which he described as a "Trilogy of Desire": *The Financier* (1912), *The Titan* (1914), and *The Stoic* (not published until 1947). In these three novels Dreiser shifted his attention from helpless protagonists to powerful individuals who assume dominant roles in business and society.

The year of 1925 witnessed the publication of Dreiser's greatest and most successful novel, *An American Tragedy*. This novel is based on a much publicized murder in Upstate New York in 1906. Clyde Griffiths is a poor boy who dreams of a life of luxury and status. When his prospect for marrying a wealthy girl is threatened by his pregnant girlfriend, a factory worker with whom he has had a relationship, Clyde plans to murder her by drowning while they go boating. When the moment arrives, he lacks the nerve to do so. However, he leaves her to drown after their boat accidentally tips over during an outing on a deserted lake so that it would seem like an accident. Much of the novel dwells on the capture of Clyde, the investigation and prosecution of the case, and the harrowing details of Clyde's imprisonment and execution. The novel was an immediate best-seller. It confirmed Dreiser's status as one of the leading writers of his time.

During the last two decades of his life, Dreiser turned to polemical writing, and also other genres — poetry, travel books, and autobiography. He visited the Soviet Union in 1927 and published *Dreiser Looks at Russia* the following year. In the 1930s, like many other American intellectuals and writers, Dreiser was increasingly attracted by the philosophical program of the Communist party. He published two nonfiction books presenting a critical perspective on capitalist America, *Tragic America* (1931) and *America Is Worth Saving* (1941). He joined the Communist Party about five months before his death on December 28, 1945.

Dreiser was fascinated by ideas and human destinies. He was interested in human motives and behavior and the particularities of the environments that helped to shape them.

Sister Carrie

(Excerpt)

Chapter 1 The Magent Attracting: A Waif amid Forces

When Caroline Meeber boarded the afternoon train for Chicago, her total outfit consisted of a small trunk, a cheap imitation alligator-skin satchel, a small lunch in a paper box, and a yellow leather snap purse, containing her ticket, a scrap of paper with her sister's address in Van Buren Street, and four dollars in money. It was in August, 1889. She was eighteen years of age, bright, timid, and full of the illusions of ignorance and youth. Whatever touch of regret at parting characterised her thoughts, it was certainly not for advantages now being given up. A gush of tears at her mother's farewell kiss, a touch in her throat when the cars clacked by the flour mill where her father worked by the day, a pathetic sigh as the familiar green environs of the village passed in review, and the threads which bound her so lightly to girlhood and home were irretrievably broken.

To be sure there was always the next station, where one might descend and return. There was the great city, bound more closely by these very trains which came up daily. Columbia City was not so very far away, even once she was in Chicago. What, pray, is a few hours — a few hundred miles? She looked at the little slip bearing her sister's address and wondered. She gazed at the green landscape, now passing in swift review, until her swifter thoughts replaced its impression with vague conjectures of what Chicago might be.

When a girl leaves her home at eighteen, she does one of two things. Either she falls into saving hands and becomes better, or she rapidly assumes the cosmopolitan standard of virtue and becomes worse. Of an intermediate balance, under the circumstances, there is no possibility. The city has its cunning wiles, no less than the infinitely smaller and more human tempter. There are large forces which allure with all the soulfulness of expression possible in the most cultured human. The gleam of a thousand lights is often as effective as the persuasive light in a wooing and fascinating eye. Half the undoing of the unsophisticated and natural mind is accomplished by forces wholly superhuman. A blare of sound, a roar of life, a vast array of human hives, appeal to the astonished senses in equivocal terms. Without a counsellor at hand to whisper cautious interpretations, what falsehoods may not these things breathe into the unguarded ear! Unrecognized for what they are, their beauty, like music, too often relaxes, then weakens, then perverts the simpler human perceptions.

Caroline, or Sister Carrie, as she had been half affectionately termed by the family, was possessed of a mind rudimentary in its power of observation and analysis. Self-interest with her was high, but not strong. It was, nevertheless, her guiding characteristic. Warm with the fancies of youth, pretty with the insipid prettiness of the formative period, possessed of a figure promising eventual shapeliness and an eye alight with certain native intelligence, she was a fair example of the middle American class — two generations removed from the emigrant. Books were beyond her interest — knowledge a sealed book. In the intuitive graces she was still crude. She could scarcely toss her head gracefully. Her hands were almost ineffectual. The feet, though small, were set flatly. And yet she was interested in her charms, quick to understand the keener pleasures of life, ambitious to gain in material things. A half-equipped little knight she was, venturing to reconnoiter the mysterious city and dreaming wild dreams of some vague, far-off supremacy, which should make it prey and subject — the proper penitent, groveling at a woman's slipper.

"That," said a voice in her ear, "is one of the prettiest little resorts in Wisconsin."

"Is it?" she answered nervously.

The train was just pulling out of Waukesha. For some time she had been conscious of a man behind. She felt him observing her mass of hair. He had been fidgeting, and with natural intuition she felt a certain interest growing in that quarter. Her maidenly reserve, and a certain sense of what was conventional under the circumstances, called her to forestall and deny this familiarity, but the daring and magnetism of the individual, born of past experiences and triumphs, prevailed. She answered.

He leaned forward to put his elbows upon the back of her seat and proceeded to make himself volubly agreeable.

"Yes, that is a great resort for Chicago people. The hotels are swell. You are not familiar with this part of the country, are you?"

"Oh, yes, I am," answered Carrie. "That is, I live at Columbia City. I have never been through here, though."

"And so this is your first visit to Chicago," he observed.

All the time she was conscious of certain features out of the side of her eye. Flush, colorful cheeks, a light moustache, a grey fedora hat. She now turned and looked upon him in full, the instincts of self-protection and coquetry mingling confusedly in her brain.

"I didn't say that," she said.

"Oh," he answered, in a very pleasing way and with an assumed air of mistake, "I thought you did."

Here was a type of the travelling canvasser for a manufacturing house — a class which at that time was first being dubbed by the slang of the day "drummers." He came within the meaning of a still newer term, which had sprung into general use among Americans in 1880, and which concisely expressed the thought of one whose dress or manners are calculated to elicit the admiration of susceptible young women — a "masher. " His suit was of a striped and crossed pattern of brown wool, new at that time, but since become familiar as a business suit. The low crotch of the vest revealed a stiff shirt bosom of white and pink stripes. From his coat sleeves protruded a pair of linen cuffs of the same pattern, fastened with large, gold plate buttons, set with the common yellow agates known as "cat's-eyes. " His fingers bore several rings — one, the ever-enduring heavy seal — and from his vest dangled a neat gold watch chain, from which was suspended the secret insignia of the Order of Elks. The whole suit was rather tight-fitting, and was finished off with heavy-soled tan shoes, highly polished, and the grey fedora hat. He was, for the order of intellect represented, attractive, and whatever he had to recommend him, you may be sure was not lost upon Carrie, in this, her first glance.

Lest this order of individual should permanently pass, let me put down some of the most striking characteristics of his most successful manner and method. Good clothes, of course, were the first essential, the things without which he was nothing. A strong physical nature, actuated by a keen desire for the feminine, was the next. A mind free of any consideration of the problems or forces of the world and actuated not by greed, but an insatiable love of variable pleasure. His method was always simple. Its principal element was daring, backed, of course, by an intense desire and admiration for the sex. Let him meet with a young woman once and he would approach her with an air of kindly familiarity, not unmixed with pleading, which would result in most cases in a tolerant acceptance. If she showed any tendency to coquetry he would be apt to straighten her tie, or if she "took up" with him at all, to call her by her first name. If he visited a department store it was to lounge familiarly over the counter and ask some leading questions. In more exclusive circles, on the train or in waiting stations, he went slower. If some seemingly vulnerable object appeared he was all attention — to pass the compliments of the day, to lead the way to the parlor car, carrying her grip, or, failing that, to take a seat next her with the hope of being able to court her to her destination. Pillows, books, a footstool, the shade lowered; all these figured in the things which he could do. If, when she reached her destination he did not alight and attend her baggage for her, it was because, in his own estimation, he had signally failed.

A woman should some day write the complete philosophy of clothes. No matter how young, it is one of the things she wholly comprehends. There is an indescribably faint line in the matter of man's apparel which somehow divides for her those who are worth glancing at and those who are not. Once an individual has passed this faint line on the way downward he will get no glance from her. There is another line at which the dress of a man will cause her to study her own. This line the individual at her elbow now marked for Carrie. She became conscious of an inequality. Her own plain blue dress, with its black cotton tape trimmings, now seemed to her shabby. She felt the worn state of her shoes.

"Let's see," he went on, "I know quite a number of people in your town. Morgenroth the clothier and Gibson the dry goods man. "

"Oh, do you?" she interrupted, aroused by memories of longings their show windows had cost her.

At last he had a clew to her interest, and followed it deftly. In a few minutes he had come about into her seat. He talked of sales of clothing, his travels, Chicago, and the amusements of that city.

"If you are going there, you will enjoy it immensely. Have you relatives?"

"I am going to visit my sister," she explained.

"You want to see Lincoln Park," he said, "and Michigan Boulevard. They are putting up great buildings there. It's a second New York — great. So much to see — theatres, crowds, fine houses — oh, you'll like that."

There was a little ache in her fancy of all he described. Her insignificance in the presence of so much magnificence faintly affected her. She realized that hers was not to be a round of pleasure, and yet there was something promising in all the material prospect he set forth. There was something satisfactory in the attention of this individual with his good clothes. She could not help smiling as he told her of some popular actress of whom she reminded him. She was not silly, and yet attention of this sort had its weight.

"You will be in Chicago some little time, won't you?" he observed at one turn of the now easy conversation.

"I don't know," said Carrie vaguely — a flash vision of the possibility of her not securing employment rising in her mind.

"Several weeks, anyhow," he said, looking steadily into her eyes.

There was much more passing now than the mere words indicated. He recognized the indescribable thing that made up for fascination and beauty in her. She realized that she was of interest to him from the one standpoint which a woman both delights in and fears. Her manner was simple, though for the very reason that she had not yet learned the many little affectations with which women conceal their true feelings. Some things she did appeared bold. A clever companion — had she ever had one — would have warned her never to look a man in the eyes so steadily.

"Why do you ask?" she said.

"Well, I'm going to be there several weeks. I'm going to study stock at our place and get new samples. I might show you 'round."

"I don't know whether you can or not. I mean I don't know whether I can. I shall be living with my sister, and — "

"Well, if she minds, we'll fix that." He took out his pencil and a little pocket note-book as if it were all settled. "What is your address there?"

She fumbled her purse which contained the address slip.

He reached down in his hip pocket and took out a fat purse. It was filled with slips of paper, some mileage books, a roll of greenbacks. It impressed her deeply. Such a purse had never been carried by any one attentive to her. Indeed, an experienced traveler, a brisk man of the world, had never come within such close range before. The purse, the shiny tan shoes, the smart new suit, and the air with which he did things, built up for her a dim world of fortune, of which he was the centre. It disposed her pleasantly toward all he might do.

He took out a neat business card, on which was engraved Bartlett, Caryoe & Company, and down in the left-hand corner, Chas. H. Drouet.

"That's me," he said, putting the card in her hand and touching his name. "It's pronounced Drew-eh. Our family was French, on my father's side."

She looked at it while he put up his purse. Then he got out a letter from a bunch in his coat pocket. "This is the house I travel for," he went on, pointing to a picture on it, "corner of State and Lake." There was pride in his voice. He felt that it was something to be connected with such a place, and he made her feel that way.

"What is your address?" he began again, fixing his pencil to write.

She looked at his hand.

"Carrie Meeber," she said slowly. "Three hundred and fifty-four West Van Buren Street, care S. C. Hanson."

He wrote it carefully down and got out the purse again. "You'll be at home if I come around Monday night?" he said.

"I think so," she answered.

How true it is that words are but the vague shadows of the volumes we mean. Little audible links, they are, chaining together great inaudible feelings and purposes. Here were these two, bandying little phrases, drawing purses, looking at cards, and both unconscious of how inarticulate all their real feelings were. Neither was wise enough to be sure of the working of the mind of the other. He could not tell how his luring succeeded.

She could not realize that she was drifting, until he secured her address. Now she felt that she had yielded something — he, that he had gained a victory. Already they felt that they were somehow associated. Already he took control in directing the conversation. His words were easy. Her manner was relaxed.

They were nearing Chicago. Signs were everywhere numerous. Trains flashed by them. Across wide stretches of flat, open prairie they could see lines of telegraph poles stalking across the fields toward the great city. Far away were indications of suburban towns, some big smokestacks towering high in the air.

Frequently there were two-story frame houses standing out in the open fields, without fence or trees, lone outposts of the approaching army of homes.

To the child, the genius with imagination, or the wholly untraveled, the approach to a great city for the first time is a wonderful thing. Particularly if it be evening — that mystic period between the glare and gloom of the world when life is changing from one sphere or condition to another. Ah, the promise of the night. What does it not hold for the weary! What old illusion of hope is not here forever repeated! Says the soul of the toiler to itself, "I shall soon be free. I shall be in the ways and the hosts of the merry. The streets, the lamps, the lighted chamber set for dining, are for me. The theatre, the halls, the parties, the ways of rest and the paths of song — these are mine in the night." Though all humanity be still enclosed in the shops, the thrill runs abroad. It is in the air. The dullest feel something which they may not always express or describe. It is the lifting of the burden of toil.

Sister Carrie gazed out of the window. Her companion, affected by her wonder, so contagious are all things, felt anew some interest in the city and pointed out its marvels.

"This is Northwest Chicago," said Drouet. "This is the Chicago River," and he pointed to a little muddy creek, crowded with the huge masted wanderers from far-off waters nosing the black-posted banks. With a puff, a clang, and a clatter of rails it was gone. "Chicago is getting to be a great town," he went on. "It's a wonder. You'll find lots to see here."

She did not hear this very well. Her heart was troubled by a kind of terror. The fact that she was alone, away from home, rushing into a great sea of life and endeavor, began to tell. She could not help but feel a little choked for breath — a little sick as her heart beat so fast. She half closed her eyes and tried to think it was nothing, that Columbia City was only a little way off.

"Chicago! Chicago!" called the brakeman, slamming open the door. They were rushing into a more crowded yard, alive with the clatter and clang of life. She began to gather up her poor little grip and closed her hand firmly upon her purse. Drouet arose, kicked his legs to straighten his trousers, and seized his clean yellow grip.

"I suppose your people will be here to meet you?" he said. "Let me carry your grip."

"Oh, no," she said. "I'd rather you wouldn't. I'd rather you wouldn't be with me when I meet my sister."

"All right," he said in all kindness. "I'll be near, though, in case she isn't here, and take you out there safely."

"You're so kind," said Carrie, feeling the goodness of such attention in her strange situation.

"Chicago!" called the brakeman, drawing the word out long. They were under a great shadowy train shed, where the lamps were already beginning to shine out, with passenger cars all about and the train moving at a snail's pace. The people in the car were all up and crowding about the door.

"Well, here we are," said Drouet, leading the way to the door. "Good-bye, till I see you Monday."

"Good-bye," she answered, taking his proffered hand.

"Remember, I'll be looking till you find your sister."

She smiled into his eyes.

They filed out, and he affected to take no notice of her. A lean-faced, rather commonplace woman recognized Carrie on the platform and hurried forward.

"Why, Sister Carrie!" she began, and there was embrace of welcome.

Carrie realized the change of affectional atmosphere at once. Amid all the maze, uproar, and novelty she felt cold reality taking her by the hand. No world of light and merriment. No round of amusement. Her sister carried with her most of the grimness of shift and toil.

"Why, how are all the folks at home?" she began; "how is father, and mother?"

Carrie answered, but was looking away. Down the aisle, toward the gate leading into the waiting-room and the street, stood Drouet. He was looking back. When he saw that she saw him and was safe with her sister he turned to go, sending back the shadow of a smile. Only Carrie saw it. She felt something lost to her when he moved away. When he disappeared she felt his absence thoroughly. With her sister she was much alone, a lone figure in a tossing, thoughtless sea.

Chapter 47   The Way of the Beaten: a Harp in the Wind

...

And now Carrie had attained that which in the beginning seemed life's object, or at least, such fraction of it as human beings ever attain of their original desires. She could look about on her gowns and carriage, her furniture and bank account. Friends there were, as the world takes it — those who would bow and smile in acknowledgment of her success. For these she had once craved. Applause there was, and publicity — once far off, essential things, but now grown trivial and indifferent. Beauty also — her type of loveliness — and yet she was lonely. In her rocking-chair she sat, when not otherwise engaged — singing and dreaming.

Thus in life there is ever the intellectual and the emotional nature — the mind that reasons, and the mind that feels. Of one come the men of action — generals and statesmen; of the other, the poets and dreamers — artists all.

As harps in the wind, the latter respond to every breath of fancy, voicing in their moods all the ebb and flow of the ideal.

Man has not yet comprehended the dreamer any more than he has the ideal. For him the laws and morals of the world are unduly severe. Ever hearkening to the sound of beauty, straining for the flash of its distant wings, he watches to follow, wearying his feet in travelling. So watched Carrie, so followed, rocking and singing.

And it must be remembered that reason had little part in this. Chicago dawning, she saw the city offering more of loveliness than she had ever known, and instinctively, by force of her moods alone, clung to it. In fine raiment and elegant surroundings, men seemed to be contented. Hence, she drew near these things. Chicago, New York; Drouet, Hurstwood; the world of fashion and the world of stage — these were but incidents. Not them, but that which they represented, she longed for. Time proved the representation false.

Oh, the tangle of human life! How dimly as yet we see. Here was Carrie, in the beginning poor, unsophisticated, emotional; responding with desire to everything most lovely in life, yet finding herself turned as by a wall. Laws to say: "Be allured, if you will, by everything lovely, but draw not nigh unless by righteousness." Convention to say: "You shall not better your situation save by honest labor." If honest labor be unremunerative and difficult to endure; if it be the long, long road which never reaches beauty, but wearies the feet and the heart; if the drag to follow beauty be such that one abandons the admired way, taking rather the despised path leading to her dreams quickly, who shall cast the first stone? Not evil, but longing for that which is better, more often directs the steps of the erring. Not evil, but goodness more often allures the feeling mind unused to reason.

Amid the tinsel and shine of her state walked Carrie, unhappy. As when Drouet took her, she had thought: "Now am I lifted into that which is best"; as when Hurstwood seemingly offered her the better way: "Now am I happy." But since the world goes its way past all who will not partake of its folly, she now found herself alone. Her purse was open to him whose need was greatest. In her walks on Broadway, she no longer thought of the elegance of the creatures who passed her. Had they more of that peace and beauty which glimmered afar off, then were they to be envied.

Drouet abandoned his claim and was seen no more. Of Hurstwood's death she was not even aware. A slow, black boat setting out from the pier at Twenty-seventh Street upon its weekly errand bore, with many others, his nameless body to the Potter's Field.

Thus passed all that was of interest concerning these twain in their relation to her. Their influence upon her life is explicable alone by the nature of her longings. Time was when both represented for her all that was most potent in earthly success. They were the personal representatives of a state most blessed to attain — the titled ambassadors of comfort and peace, aglow with their credentials. It is but natural that when the world which they represented no longer allured her, its ambassadors should be discredited. Even had Hurstwood returned in his original beauty and glory, he could not now have allured her. She had learned that in his world, as in her own present state, was not happiness.

Sitting alone, she was now an illustration of the devious ways by which one who feels, rather than reasons, may be led in the pursuit of beauty. Though often disillusioned, she was still waiting for that halcyon day when she should be led forth among dreams become real. Ames had pointed out a farther step, but on and on beyond that, if accomplished, would lie others for her. It was forever to be the pursuit of that radiance of delight which tints the distant hilltops of the world.

Oh, Carrie, Carrie! Oh, blind strivings of the human heart! Onward, onward, it saith, and where beauty leads, there it follows. Whether it be the tinkle of a lone sheep bell o'er some quiet landscape, or the glimmer of beauty in sylvan places, or the show of soul in some passing eye, the heart knows and makes answer, following. It is when the feet weary and hope seems vain that the heartaches and the longings arise. Know, then, that for you is neither surfeit nor content. In your rocking-chair, by your window dreaming, shall you long, alone. In your rocking-chair, by your window, shall you dream such happiness as you may never feel.

▶ Questions for Consideration and Discussion

1. What are identified as instances of "forces" in the opening chapter of *Sister Carrie*? Please analyze the naturalistic ideas suggested in this chapter.

2. *Sister Carrie* is narrated by intrusive narrator, which means an omniscient narrator who, in addition to reporting the events of a novel's story, offers comments on characters and events. What do you think is the advantage of this narrative

technique in relating this naturalistic story?

3. In the last section of Chapter 47 (the final chapter of the novel), the narrator claims that though Carrie gets what she originally craves for, she is unhappy. What do you think brings most extent of happiness?

4. Please expound through using textual evidence that the fiction is not a love story, rather, it could be called a Bildungsroman, to some extent.

Jack London (1876 – 1916)

Jack London is best remembered for his enduringly popular stories that involve the primitive struggle of individuals in the context of irresistible natural forces such as the wild sea or the Arctic wasteland. Among such stories are the classic novels *The Call of the Wild* (1903) and *The Sea Wolf* (1904).

London was born in San Francisco. He didn't receive much schooling. From about age thirteen he supported himself with a series of menial and dangerous jobs, struggling for survival.

Beginning in 1895, London, who had loved to read as a boy, determined that he must have an education. He entered Oakland High School and worked hard to finish. He then attended the University of California at Berkeley, but left after one semester because of a shortage of money. He was lured away by the great Klondike Gold Rush of 1897 – 1898. After he returned from his gold-seeking adventures, he attempted to earn a living by setting his adventures down on paper. His endeavor was very successful. By early 1899 he had published one of his most famous stories, *The White Silence*. Then, *An Odyssey of the North* appeared in the *Atlantic Monthly's* first issue of 1900; this led in turn to publication in April 1900 of the first collection of his stories, *The Son of the Wolf*. By his twenty-eighth birthday, he was well on his way to becoming the first American millionaire writer solely by virtue of his publications. By the time he died in 1916, London had become the best-selling American author around the world. In his writing career of less than twenty years, he produced twenty novels, two hundred stories, more than four hundred nonfiction works, and thousands of letters.

Jack London embraced both Marxist socialism and the dark views of Nietzsche and Darwinism. He believed in both the inevitable triumph of the working class and the evolutionary necessity of the survival of the fittest. His sincere intellectual and personal involvement in the socialist movement is recorded in such novels and polemical works as *The People of the Abyss* (1903), *War of the Classes* (1905), *The Iron Heel* (1908), and *Revolution* (1910). The tension between his "opposed" beliefs is most vividly projected in his autobiographical novel *Martin Eden* (1909).

His short story "The Law of Life" is set in Alaska. It was written when London was about 25 years old. The characters are members of a nomadic native tribe whose customs are shaped by the harsh conditions of the Arctic.

The Law of Life

Old Koskoosh listened greedily. Though his sight had long since faded, his hearing was still acute, and the slightest sound penetrated to the glimmering intelligence which yet abode behind the withered forehead, but which no longer gazed forth upon the things of the world. Ah! That was Sit-cum-to-ha, shrilly anathematizing the dogs as she cuffed and beat them into the harnesses. Sit-cum-to-ha was his daughter's daughter, but she was too busy to waste a thought upon her broken grandfather, sitting alone there in the snow, forlorn and helpless. Camp must be broken. The long trail waited while the short day refused to linger. Life called her, and the duties of life, not death. And he was very close to death now.

The thought made the old man panicky for the moment, and he stretched forth a palsied hand which wandered tremblingly over the small heap of dry wood beside him. Reassured that it was indeed there, his hand returned to the shelter of his mangy furs, and he again fell to listening. The sulky crackling of half-frozen hides told him that the chief's moose-skin lodge had been struck, and even then was being rammed and jammed into portable compass. The chief was his son, stalwart and strong, head man of the tribesmen, and a mighty hunter. As the women toiled with the camp luggage, his voice rose, chiding them for their slowness. Old Koskoosh strained his ears. It was the last time he would hear that voice. There went Geehow's lodge! And Tusken's! Seven, eight, nine; only the shaman's could be still standing. There! They were at work upon it now. He could hear the shaman grunt as he piled it on the sled. A child whimpered, and a woman soothed it with soft, crooning gutturals. Little Koo-tee, the old man thought, a fretful child, and not overstrong. It would die soon, perhaps, and they would burn a hole through the frozen tundra and pile rocks above to keep the wolverines away. Well, what did it matter? A few years at best, and as many an empty belly as a full one. And in the end, Death waited, ever-hungry and hungriest of them all.

What was that? Oh, the men lashing the sleds and drawing tight the thongs. He listened, who would listen no more. The whip-lashes snarled and bit among the dogs. Hear them whine! How they hated the work and the trail! They were off! Sled after sled churned slowly away into the silence. They were gone. They had passed out of his life, and he faced the last bitter hour alone. No. The snow crunched beneath a moccasin; a man stood beside him; upon his head a hand rested gently. His son was good to do this thing. He remembered other old men whose sons had not waited after the tribe. But his son had. He wandered away into the past, till the young man's voice brought him back.

"Is it well with you?" he asked.

And the old man answered, "It is well. "

"There be wood beside you," the younger man continued, "and the fire burns bright. The morning is gray, and the cold has broken. It will snow presently. Even now it is snowing. "

"Ay, even now it is snowing. "

"The tribesmen hurry. Their bales are heavy, and their bellies flat with lack of feasting. The trail is long and they travel fast. I go now. It is well?"

"It is well. I am as a last year's leaf, clinging lightly to the stem. The first breath that blows, and I fall. My voice is become like an old woman's. My eyes no longer show me the way of my feet, and my feet are heavy, and I am tired. It is well. "

He bowed his head in content till the last noise of the complaining snow had died away, and he knew his son was beyond recall. Then his hand crept out in haste to the wood. It alone stood between him and the eternity that yawned in upon him. At last the measure of his life was a handful of fagots. One by one they would go to feed the fire, and just so, step by step, death would creep upon him. When the last stick had surrendered up its heat, the frost would begin to gather strength. First his feet would yield, then his hands; and the numbness would travel, slowly, from the extremities to the body. His head would fall forward upon his knees, and he would rest. It was easy. All men must die.

He did not complain. It was the way of life, and it was just. He had been born close to the earth, close to the earth had he lived, and the law thereof was not new to him. It was the law of all flesh. Nature was not kindly to the flesh. She had no concern for that concrete thing called the individual. Her interest lay in the species, the race. This was the deepest abstraction old Koskoosh's barbaric mind was capable of, but he grasped it firmly. He saw it exemplified in all life. The rise of the sap, the bursting greenness of the willow bud, the fall of the yellow leaf — in this alone was told the whole history. But one task did Nature set the individual. Did he not perform it, he died. Did he perform it, it was all the same, he died. Nature did not care; there were plenty who were obedient, and it was only the obedience in this matter, not the obedient, which lived and lived always. The tribe of Koskoosh was very old. The old men he had known when a boy, had known old men before them. Therefore it was true that the tribe lived, that it stood for the obedience of all its members, way down into the forgotten past, whose very resting-places were unremembered. They did not count; they were episodes. They had passed away like clouds from a summer sky. He also was an episode, and would pass away. Nature did not care. To life she set one task, gave one law. To perpetuate was the task of life, its law was death. A maiden was a good creature to look upon, full-breasted and strong, with spring to her step and light in her eyes. But her task was yet before her. The light in her eyes brightened, her step quickened, she was now bold with the young men, now timid, and she gave them of her own unrest. And ever she grew fairer and yet fairer to look upon, till some hunter, able no longer to withhold himself, took her to his lodge to cook and toil for him and to become the mother of his children. And with the coming of her offspring her looks left her. Her limbs dragged and shuffled, her eyes dimmed and bleared, and only the little children found joy against the withered cheek of the old squaw by the fire.

Her task was done. But a little while, on the first pinch of famine or the first long trail, and she would be left, even as he had been left, in the snow, with a little pile of wood. Such was the law. He placed a stick carefully upon the fire and resumed his meditations. It was the same everywhere, with all things. The mosquitoes vanished with the first frost. The little tree-squirrel crawled away to die. When age settled upon the rabbit it became slow and heavy, and could no longer outfoot its enemies. Even the big bald-face grew clumsy and blind and quarrelsome, in the end to be dragged down by a handful of yelping huskies. He remembered how he had abandoned his own father on an upper reach of the Klondike one winter, the winter before the missionary came with his talk-books and his box of medicines. Many a time had Koskoosh smacked his lips over the recollection of that box, though now his mouth refused to moisten. The "painkiller" had been especially good. But the missionary was a bother after all, for he brought no meat into the camp, and he ate heartily, and the hunters grumbled. But he chilled his lungs on the divide by the Mayo①, and the dogs afterwards nosed the stones away and fought over his bones.

Koskoosh placed another stick on the fire and harked back deeper into the past. There was the time of the Great Famine, when the old men crouched empty-bellied to the fire, and let fall from their lips dim traditions of the ancient day when the Yukon ran wide open for three winters, and then lay frozen for three summers. He had lost his mother in that famine. In the summer the salmon run had failed, and the tribe looked forward to the winter and the coming of the caribou. Then the winter came, but with it there were no caribou. Never had the like been known, not even in the lives of the old men. But the caribou did not come, and it was the seventh year, and the rabbits had not replenished, and the dogs were naught but bundles of bones. And through the long darkness the children wailed and died, and the women, and the old men; and not one in ten of the tribe lived to meet the sun when it came back in the spring. That was a famine!

But he had seen times of plenty, too, when the meat spoiled on their hands, and the dogs were fat and worthless with overeating — times when they let the game go unkilled, and the women were fertile, and the lodges were cluttered with sprawling men-children and women-children. Then it was the men became high-stomached, and revived ancient quarrels, and crossed the divides to the south to kill the Pellys②, and to the west that they might sit by the dead fires of the Tananas. He remembered, when a boy, during a time of plenty, when he saw a moose pulled down by the wolves. Zing-ha lay with him in the snow and watched — Zing-ha, who later became the craftiest of hunters, and who, in the end, fell through an air-hole on the Yukon. They found him, a month afterward, just as he had crawled halfway out and frozen stiff to the ice.

But the moose. Zing-ha and he had gone out that day to play at hunting after the manner

---

① the Mayo: a small river in the Yukon Territory in northwestern Canada.
② the Pellys: the Pellys probably refer to native peoples who lived near the Pelly River.

of their fathers. On the bed of the creek they struck the fresh track of a moose, and with it the tracks of many wolves. "An old one," Zing-ha, who was quicker at reading the sign, said — "an old one who cannot keep up with the herd. The wolves have cut him out from his brothers, and they will never leave him." And it was so. It was their way. By day and by night, never resting, snarling on his heels, snapping at his nose, they would stay by him to the end. How Zing-ha and he felt the blood-lust quicken! The finish would be a sight to see!

Eager-footed, they took the trail, and even he, Koskoosh, slow of sight and an unversed tracker, could have followed it blind, it was so wide. Hot were they on the heels of the chase, reading the grim tragedy, fresh-written, at every step. Now they came to where the moose had made a stand. Thrice the length of a grown man's body, in every direction, had the snow been stamped about and uptossed. In the midst were the deep impressions of the splay-hoofed game, and all about, everywhere, were the lighter footmarks of the wolves. Some, while their brothers harried the kill, had lain to one side and rested. The full-stretched impress of their bodies in the snow was as perfect as though made the moment before. One wolf had been caught in a wild lunge of the maddened victim and trampled to death. A few bones, well picked, bore witness.

Again, they ceased the uplift of their snowshoes at a second stand. Here the great animal had fought desperately. Twice had he been dragged down, as the snow attested, and twice had he shaken his assailants clear and gained footing once more. He had done his task long since, but none the less was life dear to him. Zing-ha said it was a strange thing, a moose once down to get free again; but this one certainly had. The shaman would see signs and wonders in this when they told him.

And yet again, they come to where the moose had made to mount the bank and gain the timber. But his foes had laid on from behind, till he reared and fell back upon them, crushing two deep into the snow. It was plain the kill was at hand, for their brothers had left them untouched. Two more stands were hurried past, brief in time-length and very close together. The trail was red now, and the clean stride of the great beast had grown short and slovenly. Then they heard the first sounds of the battle — not the full-throated chorus of the chase, but the short, snappy bark which spoke of close quarters and teeth to flesh. Crawling up the wind, Zing-ha bellied it through the snow, and with him crept he, Koskoosh, who was to be chief of the tribesmen in the years to come. Together they shoved aside the under branches of a young spruce and peered forth. It was the end they saw.

The picture, like all of youth's impressions, was still strong with him, and his dim eyes watched the end played out as vividly as in that far-off time. Koskoosh marvelled at this, for in the days which followed, when he was a leader of men and a head of councillors, he had done great deeds and made his name a curse in the mouths of the Pellys, to say naught of the strange white man he had killed, knife to knife, in open fight.

For long he pondered on the days of his youth, till the fire died down and the frost bit deeper. He replenished it with two sticks this time, and gauged his grip on life by what remained. If Sit-cum-to-ha had only remembered her grandfather, and gathered a larger armful, his hours would have been longer. It would have been easy. But she was ever a careless child, and honored not her ancestors from the time the Beaver, son of the son of Zing-ha, first cast eyes upon her. Well, what mattered it? Had he not done likewise in his own quick youth? For a while he listened to the silence. Perhaps the heart of his son might soften, and he would come back with the dogs to take his old father on with the tribe to where the caribou ran thick and the fat hung heavy upon them.

He strained his ears, his restless brain for the moment stilled. Not a stir, nothing. He alone took breath in the midst of the great silence. It was very lonely. Hark! What was that? A chill passed over his body. The familiar, long-drawn howl broke the void, and it was close at hand. Then on his darkened eyes was projected the vision of the moose — the old bull moose — the torn flanks and bloody sides, the riddled mane, and the great branching horns, down low and tossing to the last. He saw the flashing forms of gray, the gleaming eyes, the lolling tongues, the slavered fangs. And he saw the inexorable circle close in till it became a dark point in the midst of the stamped snow.

A cold muzzle thrust against his cheek, and at its touch his soul leaped back to the present. His hand shot into the fire and dragged out a burning faggot. Overcome for the nonce by his hereditary fear of man, the brute retreated, raising a prolonged call to his brothers; and greedily they answered, till a ring of crouching, jaw-slobbered gray was stretched round about. The old man listened to the drawing in of this circle. He waved his brand wildly, and sniffs turned to snarls; but the panting brutes refused to scatter. Now one wormed his chest forward, dragging his haunches after, now a second, now a third; but never a one drew back. Why should he cling to life? he asked, and dropped the blazing stick into the snow. It sizzled and went out. The circle grunted uneasily, but held its own. Again he saw the last stand of the old bull moose, and Koskoosh dropped his head wearily upon his knees. What did it matter after all? Was it not the law of life?

▶▶ Questions for Consideration and Discussion

1. The narrator claims that "Nature was not kindly to the flesh. She had no concern for that concrete thing called the individual. Her interest lay in the species, the race," and that "Nature did not care; there were plenty who were obedient, and it was only the obedience in this matter, not the obedient, which lived and lived always." Do you agree or disagree? Please elaborate.

2. According to Koskoosh's last thoughts, do you think this attitude toward death is ultimately hopeful or hopeless? Please explain.

Part IV

From World War I to World War II

(1914–1945)

Part IV

From World War I to World War II

(1914–1945)

Chapter 5

American Modernism

Historical Background

American modernism was the phenomenon of international modernism transplanted and transformed in the American context.

The word *modernism* derives from *modern*, which principally means *new*, *different from what is traditional*. This suggests that both the context and the text of modernist literature are different from those of the previous eras.

The pivotal event of the Modernist era was World War Ⅰ, which began in 1914 and lasted four years. Before the war, people anticipated the new century with great optimism. But the brutality of the large-scale modern war — in which tanks, machine guns, planes, and poison gas caused death and destruction on a scale unmatched — shocked and appalled people so much that their view of the world and of humanity changed radically.

World War Ⅰ was a conflict among European powers, with Germany, Austria-Hungary, Turkey, and Bulgaria on one side, England, France, Belgium, Serbia, Russia, and Italy on the other side. The United States kept out of the war until 1917, when it entered as an ally of England and France.

American participation in the war marked a crucial stage in the nation's evolution to a world power. In the meantime, it took no time for American artists and thinkers to realize that this brutal modern world war was so different from imaginary heroism.

To tell the truth, American losses were not great in absolute terms: Fewer men were killed than in the Civil War, and among the American casualties more soldiers were killed by disease than in battle. Moreover, there was no fighting on American ground. But the sense of a great civilization being destroyed or destroying itself, the feeling of social breakdown, and the strong consciousness of individual powerlessness became part of the American experiences as a result of direct involvement in World

War Ⅰ. Consequently, people in general had a feeling of fear, disorientation, and on occasion, liberation. They were certain that an old order had ended, but they were uncertain as to what might arise. This kind of mentality has been called the "modern temper," which was partly shaped by World War Ⅰ.

The modern temper was also shaped by forces internal to the United States. These forces — urbanization, industrialization, and immigration — had long been at work, but between the wars the pace quickened. Technological advancement was another important force. New inventions and the use thereof at large changed the way people lived as well as the outlook people had. For instance, the telephone, the radio, motion pictures, and the widespread availability of books, newspapers, and magazines created a new kind of connectedness and a new kind of culture called mass culture. By far the most powerful technological influence between the wars came from the automobile, the "horseless carriage." Henry Ford's development of Assembly-line techniques for producing automobiles made cars become cheap enough for most Americans to own one. Cars not only allowed people to travel from place to place with a speed impossible before, but also remarkably reshaped the structure of American industry and occupations, and altered America dramatically.

Alongside the influence of modern science and technology was the impact of the ideas of some great thinkers. The two thinkers whose ideas had the greatest impact on the period were the Austrian Sigmund Freud (1856 – 1939) and the German Karl Marx (1818 – 1883).

Freud invented the practice of psychoanalysis. According to his theory, the "mind" is a complex energy-system that has three structural elements — *id*, *ego*, and *super-ego*. The *id* is that part of the mind in which is situated the instinctual desires which require satisfaction. The *super-ego* is that part which contains the "conscience," namely, socially-acquired control mechanisms which have been internalized, while the *ego* is the conscious self that is created by the dynamic tensions and interactions between the *id* and the *super-ego* and has the task of reconciling their conflicting demands with the requirements of external reality. To put it differently, the "self" is a dynamism shaped by tension-filled negotiations between the individual desires (*id*) and the pressures from civilization (*super-ego*). When a person's instinctual desire (*id*) is deemed by *super-ego* as reprehensible, it is not destroyed but repressed into the unconscious, from where it exerts a determining force upon the conscious mind, and can cause the dysfunctional behavior. Freud, with this basic theory, shattered the old certainty that the "self" is a conscious rational entity. Freud's influence is enormous and widely felt in literature, art, socio-cultural criticism, and modern medicine.

Karl Marx believed that capitalism contained the seeds of its own destruction; that communism was the inevitable end to the process of evolution begun with feudalism and passing through capitalism and socialism; that the root of all behavior was economic and that the leading feature of economic life was the division of society into antagonistic classes based on a relation to the means of production; and that the ideas of any particular society represented the interests of its dominant class.

To sum up, life in the early 20th century seemed suddenly different. The modern mind found all the aforementioned new knowledge exciting. But, it was also bewildered by the conflicting philosophies and ways of life. For example, both Freud and Marx seemed to espouse a kind of determinism that countered long-standing American beliefs in free will and free choice, and Marxist socialism and communism went counter to traditional American beliefs in free enterprise and competition in the marketplace.

The interwar period encompassed two decades. Each decade had its own specificities.

The 1920s has been popularly called "the Roaring Twenties." Repulsed by the senseless slaughter of the war and perplexed by the new changes, many Americans expressed a desperate yet creative hysteria in jazz rhythms, outrageous fashions, careless motorcar driving, etc. On October 29, 1929, however, the excitement ended with the crashing of the New York stock market. In fact, the crash was worldwide. Millions of Americans were unemployed; many more people lost their life savings.

The 1930s saw Americans struggle to restore and restructure the nation's economy. Unfortunately, the dismal situation was made worse by the Dust Bowl drought in the Midwest. In 1932, Franklin D. Roosevelt was elected American president. His series of liberal reforms — for instance, the creation of jobs in the public sector by the federal government and the implementation of social security, welfare, and unemployment insurance — cushioned the worst effects of the Depression and avoided the revolution that many had thought inevitable. Real prosperity did not return, however, until World War II prompted a great expansion in industry. In a way, the outbreak of World War II was relative to the worldwide Depression, because the social unrest it caused led to the rise of fascist dictators in Europe: Francisco Franco in Spain, Benito Mussolini in Italy, and Adolf Hitler in Germany. Hitler's program, which was to make Germany rich and strong by conquering the rest of Europe, led inexorably to World War II.

American Modernism

In the early 20th century, people's lives were drastically different compared with before. In both Europe and America, there seemed to have been a strong awareness of some sort of "break" with the past. In response to this type of temperament, the artists created arts that looked very different from the traditional in form and content. Movements in all the arts overlapped and succeeded one another with amazingly rapid speed — Imagism, Cubism, Dadaism, Vorticism, and many others. The new artists shared a desire to capture the complexity of modern life, to focus on the variety and confusion of the 20th century by reshaping and sometimes discarding the ideas and habits of the 19th century. For instance, painter Pablo Picasso, instead of reproducing what one sees from a single perspective, showed multiple perspectives in one painting, while composer Arnold Schoenberg abandoned the traditional eight-note scale and created music using twelve-tone scale. At the heart of the modernist aesthetic lay the conviction that the previously sustaining structures of human life, whether social, political, religious, or artistic, had been either destroyed or falsely shown up. Therefore, the way to create arts had to be renovated.

The literature produced under the influence of the modern temper is retrospectively called modernism by literary critics. Used in the broadest sense, the term *modernism* is a catchall phrase for any kind of literary production in the interwar period that deals with the modern world. More narrowly, it refers to work that represents the breakdown to traditional society under the pressures of modernity. In this sense, much modernist literature is actually anti-modern, because it interprets modernity as an experience of loss. In the English world, the primary landmarks of modernist literature are James Joyce's fiction *Ulysses* and T.S. Eliot's long poem *The Waste Land* (both published in 1922).

The Era of Modernism was indeed the era of the New. "Make it new," Ezra Pound once said in Europe, both as a definition of modernism and as a call to his fellow modernist writers. Many writers abandoned the traditional, and experimented with the new. Thus, modernism is pluralistic in style and inclusive of diverse responses to the human conditions in the modern world.

I. The Main Features of Modernist Writing

The following are some major characteristics of literary modernism.

1. **Avant-garde**   Modernist literature is characterized chiefly by a rejection of the

19th century traditions. For instance, the conventions of realism were abandoned by Franz Kafka and other novelists, while many modernist poets rejected traditional meters in favor of free verse. The visual appearance of poetry was another means of breaking with traditions, for example, E. E. Cummings' poems are noted for lowercase letters in strange places and words spaced oddly on a page.

2. **Adopting modern psychology** Most great modernist writers were interested in the workings of the human mind; thus, they were impacted by modern psychology and William James' notion of the "stream of consciousness." They created characters who, like real people, think by leaping from association to association in a continuous flow of ideas that seem to go in several directions at once. T. S. Eliot, William Faulkner, and Irish writer James Joyce made this stream-of-consciousness style famous.

3. **Construction of fragments** Modernist literature is often fragmentary, reflecting not only the "stream of consciousness" but also the modernist perception of the 20th century as a jumble of conflicting ideas. Most modernists believed that high-flown writing might conceal the real, rather than convey the real; that the form of a story, with its beginning, complications, and resolutions, might be mere artifice imposed on the flux and fragmentation of experience.

4. **Shorter in length** Compared with earlier writings, modernist literature is notable for what it omits — the explanations, interpretations, connections, summaries, etc. A typical modernist work seems to begin arbitrarily, to advance without explanation, and to end without resolution, consisting of vivid segments juxtaposed without cushioning or integrating transitions. The average novel became quite a bit shorter than it had been in the 19th century, when a novel was expected to fill two or even three volumes.

5. **Unconventional narrative points of view** Fictions in previous stages often feature an authoritative narrator who knows every character's mind, but modernist fiction tends to be written in the first person point of view, or to limit the reader to one character's point of view, or to use multiple points of view. The selected point of view is sometimes the point of view of a naive or marginal person — a child or an outsider. For instance, *The Great Gatsby* (1925) by F. Scott Fitzgerald is narrated by Gatsby's neighbor Nick Carraway, a marginal character. Another example is William Faulkner's masterpiece *The Sound and the Fury* (1929). It has four sections, each with a different narrator, each supplying a different piece of the plot. Three of the narrators are brothers: Benjy, the idiot; Quentin, the suicide; and Jason, the business failure. Each of them, for different reasons, mourns the loss of their sister Caddie. In these

three sections, the narration jumps freely in time and place. Only the last section is told from a traditionally omniscient point of view and provides a sequential narration. The use of these narrative techniques accords with the modernist sense that "truth" does not exist objectively but is the product of a personal interaction with reality. By doing so, the author can convey better the reality of confusion rather than the myth of certainty.

6. **Requirement of reader's participation** Modernist literature often insists the readers participate and draw their own conclusions. The Modernist shows rather than tells, suggests rather than asserts, making use of symbols and images instead of statements. Therefore, readers have to decide what meaning is conveyed by the symbols or images. Additionally, because modernist fiction tends to upset chronological development and looks fragmentary, a typical modernist work may appear to lack coherence. But, actually it does retain a degree of coherence, which the reader has to dig out. Thus, reading modernist literature is a challenging thing.

7. **A renewed interest in the "old" and non-Western cultures** It is noteworthy that some modernists seemed contradictory: When they were innovatively creating new styles of modernist literature, they attached themselves to the old, searching history for the "best" and most useful things they could find among the World's literature, mythologies, religions, philosophies, and social systems; many modernist works are unified by reference to myth. For example, James Joyce's reference to the Greek mythological king character Ulysses in *Ulysses*, Ezra Pound's Asian element in his poetry, and T. S. Eliot's anthropological allusions.

8. **Irony and ambiguity** Irony and ambiguity are not unique modernist traits; however, they are pretty preeminent rhetorical modes in modernism. They reflect a general disillusionment in the social, economic, and spiritual values of the Western world.

II. The Interaction of Modernism and American Regional Traditionalism

Because modernism was an international movement, it seemed, in some people's eyes, to conflict with the American tradition in literature. Hence, it was not automatically accepted by American writers. The degree to which American writers adopted modernist techniques varied greatly. Many writers integrated modernist ideas and methods with American subject matter: They chose to identify themselves with the American scene and to root their work in a specific region. In their works they treated their regions sometimes in a celebratory way, sometimes in a critical way. Carl Sandburg, Edgar Lee Masters, Sherwood Anderson, and Willa Cather worked with the

Midwest; Cather grounded her later work in the Southwest; Robinson Jeffers and John Steinbeck wrote about California; Edwin Arlington Robinson and Robert Frost identified their work with New England; William Faulkner, Catherine Anne Porter, Thomas Wolfe, Ellen Glasgow, and Margaret Mitchell wrote about the South (Mitchell's 1936 novel *Gone with the Wind*, the recipient of the 1937 Pulitzer Prize, is one of the best-known Southern novels.). Some writers attempted to speak for the nation as a whole, as the title of John Dos Passos's *U. S. A.* clearly shows.

Ⅲ. The American Expatriates and the Lost Generation

Many American writers of this period lived in Europe for part, if not all, of their lives. Gertrude Stein moved to Paris in 1903, and made France her home for the remainder of her life; Ezra Pound went to London in 1908 and made his home in Italy after 1925; T. S. Eliot moved to England in 1914 and settled there permanently. These expatriates left the United States because they thought their country lacked in a tradition of high culture, and they could not thrive artistically in their native land. As leading modernists, they helped, encouraged, and influenced many other American expatriate writers of the time, including Robert Frost who spent years in Europe from 1912 to 1915, Ernest Hemingway who was wounded in World War Ⅰ and stayed in Paris after the war, and F. Scott Fitzgerald who moved to Europe in 1924 and stayed there until 1931. Gertrude Stein once told the young Hemingway, "You are all a lost generation," and the term has been used again and again to describe the people of the postwar years living in confusion and despair because of the war, especially the Americans who remained in Paris as a colony of expatriates. These so-called "Lost Generation" writers, for instance Hemingway, went to Gertrude Stein's salon often. With no doubt, Hemingway was a typical representative of the Lost Generation writers. His *The Sun Also Rises* (1926) and *A Farewell to Arms* (1929) depict the sense of "loss."

Ⅳ. The Jazz Age and the Harlem Renaissance

The 1920s has been called the Jazz Age, when New Orleans musicians moved "up the river" to Chicago, and the theatres of New York's Harlem pulsed with Jazz music. Hence the 1920s has also been called the Roaring Twenties. Jazz Age was characterized by extravagance and hedonism. It was a reaction to the austerity and hardship of the wartime years. The roaring of the decade served to mask a quiet pain. The spokesman of the Jazz Age is F. Scott Fitzgerald, whose *The Great Gatsby* masterfully depicts the roaring and the pain.

The 1920s was also a decade in which African Americans made themselves a permanent part of the nation's cultural life. In 1915, as a direct result of the industrial needs of World War I , opportunities opened for African Americans in the factories of the North, therefore the so-called Great Migration out of the South began. In the 1920s, African Americans who thronged to New York City's Harlem District turned Harlem into a vigorous, fertile center for black cultural activities. As W. E. B. Du Bois and others urged the expression of racial pride, black writers focused on their own lives, culture, and identity. The fresh and new subjects as well as skillful writing attracted publishers and readers to the works of many black writers, including Langston Hughes, Jean Toomer, Countee Cullen, and later, Zora Neale Hurston. However, with the economic depression of the 1930s, the Harlem Renaissance faded.

V. The Rise of American Drama

Drama in America developed slowly as a self-conscious literary form. The comprehensible reasons may be that theaters such as the elitist European ones of the 18th century would not flourish at the same time in America that was only an infant democracy, and the melodrama of the 19th century would not attract serious American writers, who did not turn to drama until Realism and Expressionism began to appear on the stage. As late as 1920, the year that witnessed Eugene O'Neill's *Beyond the Horizon*, America produced a world-recognized playwright.

European influence on American theatre was strong. By 1915, Henrik Ibsen in Norway and George Bernard Shaw in England had shown that the theatre could be an arena for serious ideas, while the psychological dramas of August Strindberg, the symbolic work of Maurice Maeterlinck, and the sophisticated cynicism of Arthur Schnitzer provided other models.

In the beginning of the 20th century, so-called " little theaters " sprang up throughout the United States. Willing to produce original works by unknown talents, these little theaters encouraged serious playwrights. Eugene O'Neill (1888 – 1953) began his career as a writer for a little theatre company named the Provincetown Players, which was founded by Pulitzer Prize winning playwright Susan Glaspell (1876 – 1948) and her husband.

The plays of Eugene O'Neill reflect his New England background and Irish American heritage. They not only display the realism and the interest in modern psychology characteristic of Ibsen and Strindberg, but also reflect the modernist experimentation of the early 20th century: In *The Great God Brown* (1926), characters don and remove masks while they are speaking; in *Strange Interlude* (1928), the characters' thoughts are heard by the audience.

Led by O'Neill, American drama flourished between the two world wars. Elmer Rice wrote a portrait of tenement life called *Street Scene* (1929); Clifford Odets explored serious social problems in *Awake and Sing*! (1935) and *Waiting for Lefty* (1935). Maxwell Anderson wrote plays in verse, and George S. Kaufman and Moss Hart entertained audiences with their witty satires. In this interwar period, many of the poets and fictionists also wrote plays, for example, Ernest Hemingway, E. E. Cummings, William Faulkner, T. S. Eliot, and John Steinbeck. It was in this period that drama moved decisively into the American literary mainstream.

The 1920s and 1930s also saw the development of a strictly American form, the musical comedy, which reached its peak after World War II.

VI. The Depression Era's Proletarian Literature

Depression era literature was blunt and direct in its social criticism. John Dos Passos (1896 – 1970), James T. Farrell (1904 – 1979), and John Steinbeck (1902 – 1968) are the major writers of this subgroup, with John Steinbeck being the most eminent representative. He focused his attention on poor, working-class people who struggled against social and economic odds for a decent life. His masterpiece, *The Grapes of Wrath* (1939), won the Pulitzer Prize in 1940, and the story was made into a memorable movie starring Henry Fonda in the same year.

▷▷ Questions for Consideration and Discussion

1. "Modern" means *new*, *different from what is traditional*. Are things that are "modern" always good? Name a number of modern things that you think are good, and some other modern things that you think are not good. Explain to your deskmate why you think so.
2. What's your interpretation of some modernists' seemingly contradictory practice of attaching themselves to the world's ancient literature?
3. In what way do the theories of William James and Sigmund Freud remarkably influence literary modernism? Are you convinced by their ideas?

Ezra Pound (1885 – 1972)

Ezra Pound was the driving force behind modernist literature. He is especially remembered for his campaign for "imagism," a name he coined for a new kind of poetry.

Born in a small town in Idaho, Pound grew up in a suburb of Philadelphia and attended the University of Pennsylvania. He wanted to become a poet when he was an undergraduate. This motivated his graduate studies in languages — French, Italian, Old English, and Latin — at the University of Pennsylvania, where he received his MA in 1906.

Convinced that his country had no place for him and that a country with no place for him had no place for art, at age twenty-three, he left for Europe in 1908. Thinking that the United States was a culturally backward nation, he longed to produce a sophisticated, worldly poetry on behalf of his country. In Europe he wrote poetry and criticism, and translated verse from different languages. He also served as an overseas editor for Chicago's *Poetry* magazine. He used this position to nurture the careers of many writers, such as Robert Frost and T. S. Eliot.

Primarily influenced by classical Chinese poetry and Japanese Haiku, in 1912 Pound founded the literary movement of Imagism, which called for "direct treatment of the ' thing. '" Instead of having the poet tell us what we should be feeling, Pound wanted an image to produce the emotion, to "speak for itself. "

Although his view of poetry would seem to exclude the long poem as a workable form, Pound could not overcome the traditional belief that a really great poem had to be long. He hoped to write such a poem himself, a poem for his time, which would unite biography and history by representing the total content of his mind and memory. To this end, in 1915 he began working on his *Cantos*, in which he combined his own ideas with materials from different cultures and languages, historical texts, and newspaper articles.

After 1925, Pound made his home in Italy. There he devoted his life to socio-economic thought. His survey of history persuaded him that the ideal society was a hierarchy with a strong leader and an agricultural economy. Accordingly, he became an admirer of Benito Mussolini and he greeted the Italian fascist dictator as deliverer. When World War II broke out, he voluntarily served the Italian government by making numerous English-language radio broadcasts beamed at England and the United States in which he vilified the Jews, President Roosevelt, and American society in general. After the war he was arrested and imprisoned by American troops in Pisa. This experience was reflected in what is perhaps his greatest poetic achievement, *The Pisan Cantos*. He was held in an open-air cage at the prison camp for weeks before he finally was brought back to the United States to be tried for treason. The trial did not take place, however, because the court accepted a psychiatric report to the effect that Pound was "insane and mentally unfit to be tried. " From 1946 to 1958 he was a patient and a prisoner in St. Elizabeth's Hospital for the criminally insane in Washington, D. C.

In 1958, the efforts of a committee of writers succeeded in winning Pound's release, and he returned to Italy, where he died at the age of eighty-seven. He remains one of the most controversial poets of the era.

His "In a Station of the Metro" is a classic of imagist poem; "the metro" refers to Paris Subway. "A Pact" depicts the change of his attitude toward Walt Whitman. And "The River-Merchant's Wife: A Letter" is his adaptation from Chinese Tang Dynasty poet Li Bai's poem "Song of Changgan."[①] Pound adapted Li Bai's poem from the papers of Ernest Fenollosa.

In a Station of the Metro

The apparition of these faces in the crowd;
Petals on a wet, black bough.

A Pact

I make a pact with you, Walt Whitman —
I have detested you long enough.
I come to you as a grown child
Who has had a pig-headed father;
5   I am old enough now to make friends.
It was you that broke the new wood,
Now is a time for carving.
We have one sap and one root —
Let there be commerce[②] between us.

The River-Merchant's Wife: A Letter

While my hair was still cut straight across my forehead
I played about the front gate, pulling flowers.
You came by on bamboo stilts, playing horse,
You walked about my seat, playing with blue plums.

---

① "Song of Changgan":《长干行》。

② commerce: an exchange of views and attitudes.

5   And we went on living in the village of Chōkan:
Two small people, without dislike or suspicion.

At fourteen I married My Lord you.
I never laughed, being bashful.
Lowering my head, I looked at the wall.
10   Called to, a thousand times, I never looked back.

At fifteen I stopped scowling,
I desired my dust to be mingled with yours
Forever and forever, and forever.
Why should I climb the look out?

15   At sixteen you departed,
You went into far Ku-tō-en, by the river of swirling eddies,
And you have been gone five months.
The monkeys make sorrowful noise overhead.

You dragged your feet when you went out.
20   By the gate now, the moss is grown, the different mosses,
Too deep to clear them away!
The leaves fall early this autumn, in wind.
The paired butterflies are already yellow with August
Over the grass in the West garden;
25   They hurt me.
I grow older.
If you are coming down through the narrows of the river Kiang,
Please let me know beforehand,
And I will come out to meet you
30   As far as Chō-fū-Sa.

▶▶ Questions for Consideration and Discussion

1. In "In a Station of the Metro," what two images are juxtaposed? Pound once wrote, "Painters realize that what matters is form and color. The image is the poet's pigment." In what way is this poem like a painting?

2. In "A Pact," what extended metaphor does the poet use in lines 6 to 9? Please discuss with your partner in what way Pound and Whitman are alike?

3. Compare Li Bai's original poem "Song of Changgan" (《长干行》) with Pound's

translation of it, namely "The River-Merchant's Wife: A Letter." Do you think Pound uses Imagist ideas well in his translation? If you translate the poem, how will you do the job differently?

T. S. Eliot(1888 – 1965)

Along with Ezra Pound, T. S. Eliot did more to revolutionize poetry in the 20th century than any other poets. He was awarded the Nobel Prize for literature in 1948.

Eliot was born in St. Louis, Missouri, into a distinguished family that provided him with the best education available. He attended Harvard University for both undergraduate and graduate work (1906 – 1910, 1911 – 1914). He studied at the Sorbonne in Paris from 1910 to 1911 and at Oxford from 1915 to 1916. It was in England, when he was twenty-six, that Eliot met Pound who would champion his art and serve as an editor of his poems.

In 1915, through Pound's effort, *Poetry* magazine published T. S. Eliot's "The Love Song of J. Alfred Prufrock." Often called the first modernist poem, this poem captures the emptiness and alienation many people felt living in modern, impersonal cities. However, when it first came out, the poem baffled, even angered, many readers. They found its subject matter "un-poetic," its fragmented structure off-putting, and its allusions difficult to understand.

The same month "Prufrock" was published, Eliot married Vivien Haigh-Wood. For six years he worked as a teacher and a bank clerk. In his spare time he wrote numerous literary essays; he began his best-known work, *The Waste Land*, in 1921 and finished it in a Swiss sanatorium while recovering from a mental collapse brought on by overwork, marital problems, and general depression. He accepted some alterations suggested by his wife. But Pound's editing had altered *The Waste Land* so significantly that it has been claimed that Pound should be given due credit as the co-author of this masterpiece.

The Waste Land consists of five discontinuous segments, each composed of fragments incorporating multiple voices and characters, literary and historical allusions, vignettes of contemporary life, surrealistic images, as well as myths and legends. Many readers interpreted *The Waste Land* as a monumental critique of Western culture; they regarded Eliot as spokesman for the "disillusioned" generation. However, Eliot saw it as a purely personal piece of "rhythmical grumbling."

The Waste Land brought Eliot international acclaim but not happiness. Eliot was facing great strain in his marriage and in his bank clerk job. Eventually, he began a new, more satisfying career as a book editor and found a purpose in life by converting to the Church of England. In poems such as "The Hollow Men" (1925), "Ash Wednesday" (1930), and his another masterpiece *Four Quartets* (1943), he described the importance and difficulty of belief in a spiritually impoverished world.

In the latter years of his life, Eliot wrote several plays: *Murder in the Cathedral* (1935), *The Family Reunion* (1939), *The Cocktail Party* (1949), *The Confidential Clerk* (1953), and *The Elder Statesman* (1959), all religious in theme.

In recognition of his achievement, in 1948 Eliot was awarded the Nobel Prize for Literature.

The Love Song of J. Alfred Prufrock

S'io credesse che mia risposta fosse
A persona che mai tornasse al mondo,
Questa fiamma staria senza piu scosse.
Ma percioche giammai di questo fondo
Non torno vivo alcun, s'i'odo il vero,
Senza tema d'infamia ti rispondo. [1]

Let us go then, you and I,
When the evening is spread out against the sky
Like a patient etherized upon a table;
Let us go, through certain half-deserted streets,
5   The muttering retreats
Of restless nights in one-night cheap hotels
And sawdust restaurants with oyster-shells:
Streets that follow like a tedious argument
Of insidious intent
10   To lead you to an overwhelming question…
Oh, do not ask, "What is it?"

---

[1] The inscription is in Italian language, taken from Dante's *Inferno*, Chapter 27, lines 61 to 66. The speaker, Guido da Montefeltro, consumed in flame as punishment for giving false counsel, confesses his shame without fear of its being reported since he believes — wrongly — that Dante cannot return to earth. The words mean: "If I believed that my reply were being made to one who would ever return to the world, this flame would shake no more; but since, if what I hear is true, none ever did return alive from this depth, I answer you without fear of dishonor."

Let us go and make our visit.

In the room the women come and go
Talking of Michelangelo.

15   The yellow fog that rubs its back upon the window-panes,
        The yellow smoke that rubs its muzzle on the window-panes,
        Licked its tongue into the corners of the evening,
        Lingered upon the pools that stand in drains,
        Let fall upon its back the soot that falls from chimneys,
20   Slipped by the terrace, made a sudden leap,
        And seeing that it was a soft October night,
        Curled once about the house, and fell asleep.

        And indeed there will be time①
        For the yellow smoke that slides along the street,
25   Rubbing its back upon the window-panes;
        There will be time, there will be time
        To prepare a face to meet the faces that you meet;
        There will be time to murder and create,
        And time for all the works and days② of hands
30   That lift and drop a question on your plate;
        Time for you and time for me,
        And time yet for a hundred indecisions,
        And for a hundred visions and revisions,
        Before the taking of a toast and tea.

35   In the room the women come and go
        Talking of Michelangelo.

        And indeed there will be time
        To wonder, "Do I dare?" and, "Do I dare?"
        Time to turn back and descend the stair,
40   With a bald spot in the middle of my hair —
        (They will say: "How his hair is growing thin!")

---

① And indeed there will be time: an echo of Andrew Marvell's poem "To His Coy Mistress"
    (1681): "Had we but world enough and time."
② works and days: *Works and Days* is a didactic poem about farming by the Greek Poet Hesiod (8th
    century B. C.).

My morning coat, my collar mounting firmly to the chin,
My necktie rich and modest, but asserted by a simple pin —
(They will say: "But how his arms and legs are thin!")
45   Do I dare
Disturb the universe?
In a minute there is time
For decisions and revisions which a minute will reverse.

For I have known them all already, known them all:
50   Have known the evenings, mornings, afternoons,
I have measured out my life with coffee spoons;
I know the voices dying with a dying fall[①]
Beneath the music from a farther room.
    So how should I presume?

55   And I have known the eyes already, known them all —
The eyes that fix you in a formulated phrase,
And when I am formulated, sprawling on a pin,
When I am pinned and wriggling on the wall,
Then how should I begin
60   To spit out all the butt-ends of my days and ways?
    And how should I presume?

And I have known the arms already, known them all —
Arms that are braceleted and white and bare
(But in the lamplight, downed with light brown hair!)
65   Is it perfume from a dress
That makes me so digress?
Arms that lie along a table, or wrap about a shawl.
    And should I then presume?
    And how should I begin?

· · · · ·

70   Shall I say, I have gone at dusk through narrow streets
And watched the smoke that rises from the pipes
Of lonely men in shirt-sleeves, leaning out of windows? ...

I should have been a pair of ragged claws

---

①   a dying fall: an echo of Duke Orsino's invocation of music in Shakespeare's *Twelfth Night* (1.1.4):
"If music be the food of love, play on...That strain again! It had a dying fall."

Scuttling across the floors of silent seas.

. . . . .

75   And the afternoon, the evening, sleeps so peacefully!
     Smoothed by long fingers,
     Asleep ... tired ... or it malingers,
     Stretched on the floor, here beside you and me.
     Should I, after tea and cakes and ices,
80   Have the strength to force the moment to its crisis?
     But though I have wept and fasted, wept and prayed,
     Though I have seen my head (grown slightly bald) brought in upon a
          platter①,
     I am no prophet — and here's no great matter;
     I have seen the moment of my greatness flicker,
85   And I have seen the eternal Footman hold my coat, and snicker,
     And in short, I was afraid.

     And would it have been worth it, after all,
     After the cups, the marmalade, the tea,
     Among the porcelain, among some talk of you and me,
90   Would it have been worth while,
     To have bitten off the matter with a smile,
     To have squeezed the universe into a ball
     To roll it towards some overwhelming question,
     To say: "I am Lazarus②, come from the dead,
95   Come back to tell you all, I shall tell you all" —
     If one, settling a pillow by her head
          Should say: "That is not what I meant at all;
          That is not it, at all."

     And would it have been worth it, after all,
100 Would it have been worth while,
     After the sunsets and the door yards and the sprinkled streets,
     After the novels, after the teacups, after the skirts that trail along the
          floor —

---

①   my head(grown slightly bald) brought in upon a platter: The head of the prophet John the Baptist,
    who was killed at the behest of Princess Salome, was brought to her on a platter (Matthew 14:1 –
    11.
②   Lazarus: The resurrection of Lazarus is recounted in John 11:1 – 44, in which Jesus resurrected
    Lazarus from the dead.

And this, and so much more? —

It is impossible to say just what I mean!

105　But as if a magic lantern threw the nerves in patterns on a screen:

Would it have been worthwhile

If one, settling a pillow or throwing off a shawl,

And turning toward the window, should say:

　　"That is not it at all,

110　　That is not what I meant, at all."

　　　　　　　　· · · · ·

No! I am not Prince Hamlet, nor was meant to be;

Am an attendant lord, one that will do

To swell a progress①, start a scene or two,

Advise the prince; no doubt, an easy tool,

115　Deferential, glad to be of use,

Politic, cautious, and meticulous;

Full of high sentence, but a bit obtuse;

At times, indeed, almost ridiculous —

Almost, at times, the Fool.

120　I grow old ... I grow old...

I shall wear the bottoms of my trousers rolled.

Shall I part my hair behind? Do I dare to eat a peach?

I shall wear white flannel trousers, and walk upon the beach.

I have heard the mermaids singing, each to each.

125　I do not think that they will sing to me.

I have seen them riding seaward on the waves

Combing the white hair of the waves blown back

When the wind blows the water white and black.

We have lingered in the chambers of the sea

130　By sea-girls wreathed with seaweed red and brown

Till human voices wake us, and we drown.

▶ Questions for Consideration and Discussion

1. Does "The Love Song of J. Alfred Prufrock" fit your expectation of a love song?
   Why or why not? What do you think happens to Prufrock in this poem? Please cite

---

① progress: a journey or procession made by royal courts and often portrayed on Elizabethan stages.

from the poem to support your assumption.

2. Why would Prufrock think of himself as "you and I," or "we"? According to his monologue, what's his mood or feelings?

3. Compare the "I" in this poem and the "I" in "Song of Myself." How are the two speakers different? Which persona do you identify with?

Robert Frost (1874 – 1963)

Robert Frost, one of the most popular American poets of the 20th century, was a four-time winner of the Pulitzer Prize.

Although he identified himself with New England, Frost was born in San Francisco, California, and lived there until eleven years old, when his father died. Following his father's passing, his mother moved the family to New England, where she supported the family by working as a school teacher. Frost's mother wrote poetry, and it was his mother who introduced him to the works of the English Romantic writers, the New England Transcendentalists, and the poets of her native Scotland.

Frost attended Dartmouth College and Harvard during the 1890s, but he left each college after a short period of time on account of his frustration with academic life. Preferring real-life experiences to academic learning, he thereafter worked as a mill hand, journalist, farmer, and schoolteacher.

At age twenty-six, Frost moved to a farm in New Hampshire, where he got to know the rugged landscape and inhabitants of rural New England. Between farm chores, he began his career as a poet. Unable to get his poems published, in 1912 Frost sold his farm and moved to England along with his wife and four children.

In London, Frost became acquainted with Ezra Pound and his associates. Frost worked on his poetry and found a publisher for his first book, *A Boy's Will* (1913), which was reviewed favorably by Pound. Pound recommended Frost's poems to American editors and helped get his second book, *North of Boston*, published in 1914. *North of Boston* was widely praised by critics in both America and England, and the favorable reception persuaded Frost to return to America in 1915. He bought another farm in New Hampshire and prospered financially through sales of his books and papers, along with teaching and lecturing at various colleges. The success he enjoyed for the rest of his life, however, came too late to cancel the bitterness left by his earlier struggles. Moreover, he endured personal tragedy: A son committed suicide, and a daughter had a complete mental collapse.

Despite the debt of gratitude he owed Pound and other modernists, Frost never subscribed to the tenets of Modernism. Surely he was familiar with the ideas of William James and other modern psychologists, but he was equally familiar with the works of Emerson, Thoreau, and other 19th century masters. In his work we find traces of the Romantic love of nature, we also find a modern sense of irony; we find signs of Thoreau's love of isolation, we also find tint of Hawthorne's dark vision; we find Longfellow's traditional craftsmanship and Dickinson's dry humor, we also find some realistic characterization.

Throughout the 1920s Frost's poetic practices changed very little. His later books include *Mountain Interval* (1916), *New Hampshire* (1923), and *West-Running Brook* (1928). And these books confirmed the impression he had created in *North of Boston*.

Stopping by Woods on a Snowy Evening

Whose woods these are I think I know.
His house is in the village though;
He will not see me stopping here
To watch his woods fill up with snow.

5   My little horse must think it queer
To stop without a farmhouse near
Between the woods and frozen lake
The darkest evening of the year.

He gives his harness bells a shake
10   To ask if there is some mistake.
The only other sound's the sweep
Of easy wind and downy flake.

The woods are lovely, dark and deep,
But I have promises to keep,
15   And miles to go before I sleep,
And miles to go before I sleep.

Mending Wall

Something there is that doesn't love a wall,
That sends the frozen-ground-swell under it,

And spills the upper boulders in the sun;
And makes gaps even two can pass abreast.

5   The work of hunters is another thing:
I have come after them and made repair
Where they have left not one stone on a stone,
But they would have the rabbit out of hiding,
To please the yelping dogs. The gaps I mean,
10   No one has seen them made or heard them made,
But at spring mending-time we find them there.

I let my neighbor know beyond the hill;
And on a day we meet to walk the line
And set the wall between us once again.
15   We keep the wall between us as we go.

To each the boulders that have fallen to each.
And some are loaves and some so nearly balls
20   We have to use a spell to make them balance:
"Stay where you are until our backs are turned!"
We wear our fingers rough with handling them.
Oh, just another kind of out-door game,
One on a side. It comes to little more:
There where it is we do not need the wall:
He is all pine and I am apple orchard.
25   My apple trees will never get across
And eat the cones under his pines, I tell him.
He only says, "Good fences make good neighbors. "

Spring is the mischief in me, and I wonder
If I could put a notion in his head:
30   "Why do they make good neighbors? Isn't it
Where there are cows? But here there are no cows.
Before I built a wall I'd ask to know
What I was walling in or walling out,
And to whom I was like to give offence.
35   Something there is that doesn't love a wall,
That wants it down. " I could say "Elves" to him,
But it's not elves exactly, and I'd rather
He said it for himself. I see him there

Bringing a stone grasped firmly by the top
40   In each hand, like an old-stone savage armed.
He moves in darkness as it seems to me,
Not of woods only and the shade of trees.
He will not go behind his father's saying,
And he likes having thought of it so well
45   He says again, "Good fences make good neighbors."

The Road Not Taken

Two roads diverged in a yellow wood,
And sorry I could not travel both
And be one traveler, long I stood
And looked down one as far as I could
5   To where it bent in the undergrowth;

Then took the other, as just as fair,
And having perhaps the better claim,
Because it was grassy and wanted wear;
Though as for that the passing there
10   Had worn them really about the same,

And both that morning equally lay
In leaves no step had trodden black.
Oh, I kept the first for another day!
Yet knowing how way leads on to way,
15   I doubted if I should ever come back.

I shall be telling this with a sigh
Somewhere ages and ages hence:
Two roads diverged in a wood, and I —
I took the one less traveled by,
20   And that has made all the difference.

Nothing Gold Can Stay

Nature's first green is gold,
Her hardest hue to hold.

Her early leaf's a flower;

But only so an hour.

5 Then leaf subsides to leaf,

So Eden sank to grief,

So dawn goes down to day.

Nothing gold can stay.

Fire and Ice

Some say the world will end in fire,

Some say in ice.

From what I've tasted of desire

I hold with those who favor fire.

5 But if it had to perish twice,

I think I know enough of hate

To say that for destruction ice

Is also great

And would suffice.

Questions for Consideration and Discussion

1. In "Stopping by Woods on a Snowy Evening," why does the speaker stop? Is he the owner of the woods? According to the suggestion of the poem, what would the speaker like to do if he hasn't had promises to keep?

2. In "Mending Wall," what are the causes of the wall's damage? What kind of damage does the speaker focus on? Does his attitude toward the wall sound controversial? Please cite from the poem for explanation. What might walls and fences symbolize in the poem?

3. In "The Road Not Taken," why does the speaker's mind stay focused on the road not taken? What are the clues that suggest that the road is more than a tangible road but "a road of life"? Have you ever encountered any dilemma in your life? How did you make your final decision?

4. Do you agree with Robert Frost's point that nothing gold can stay? Why or why not?

5. In "Fire and Ice," what do the two emotions have in common? Explain the irony in the poem.

Sherwood Anderson（1876－1941）

Sherwood Anderson is now best remembered for his short-story sequence *Winesburg, Ohio* (1919), which is his third book.

Anderson was born in southern Ohio. He was the third of seven children in the family, headed by a father whose training and skill as a harness maker were becoming useless in the new world of the automobile. Anderson's father moved the family from place to place in search of work. In this unsettled, transitory life, it was the stamina and tenderness of Anderson's mother that supplied coherence and security for the children. In 1894, the family finally settled down in the town of Clyde, Ohio, which became the model for his fictional town Winesburg.

Anderson did not start his writing career until he was approaching middle age. In 1912, he abandoned his successful business career and his marriage in Ohio and moved to Chicago. There he took a job in advertising and joined the so-called Chicago Group — including novelist Theodore Dreiser and poet Carl Sandburg — whose activities were creating the Chicago Renaissance.

Anderson's first major publication was *Windy McPherson's Son* (1916), about a man who runs away from a small Iowa town in futile search for life's meaning. His second novel was *Marching Men* (1917), about a charismatic lawyer who tries but fails to reorganize the factory system in a small town. These books reveal three of Anderson's preoccupations: the individual quest for self and social betterment; the small-town environment; and the distrust of modern industrial society. However, in these two novels, the interest in human psychology and the sense of conflict between inner and outer worlds that appear in his later works was missing.

In 1916, Anderson began writing and publishing the tales that were brought together in his third book *Winesburg, Ohio*. Consisting of twenty-three thematically related sketches and stories, *Winesburg, Ohio* was "half individual tales, half long novel form," as the author himself described it. In simple, realistic language, Anderson dramatized crucial episodes in the lives of his characters. The narrative is united by the appearance of George Willard, a young reporter for the local newspaper, who is in revolt against the narrowness of the small-town life and acts as a counterpoint to the other people of the town. The book ends with the death of George's mother and his departure from the town. With the help of the narrator, whose vision is larger than that of George Willard, the reader can see how the lives of the characters have been profoundly distorted by loneliness, isolation, dissatisfaction with their world, and frustration in their attempts to find something good.

After *Winesburg, Ohio*, Anderson continued writing for two decades. But he was never again as successful as he had been with the Winesburg stories. His best later work was in short stories, published in three volumes: *The Triumph of the Egg* (1921), *Horses and Men* (1923), and *Death in the Woods and Other Stories* (1933). He also wrote a number of novels, including *Poor White* (1920), *Many Marriages* (1923), *Beyond Desire* (1932), and *Kit Brandon* (1936), as well as free verse, prose poems, plays, essays, and autobiography.

Anderson died at sea on the way to South America while on a goodwill mission for the State Department on March 8, 1941. After his death, Anderson's reputation soon declined, but in the 1970s, scholars and critics have found a new interest in his work. Undeniably, his simple and direct style, his use of the point of view of outsider characters, among other techniques, were important influences on other writers, for example he helped nurture the early careers of Hemingway and William Faulkner, whom he had met in Paris and New Orleans respectively, though neither Hemingway nor Faulkner was willing to admit that they had been influenced by him.

"Adventure" is typical of the Winesburg stories in its realism and its theme of loneliness and isolation.

Winesburg, Ohio

(Excerpt)

Adventure

Alice Hindman, a woman of twenty-seven when George Willard was a mere boy, had lived in Winesburg all her life. She clerked in Winney's Dry Goods Store and lived with her mother, who had married a second husband.

Alice's step-father was a carriage painter, and given to drink. His story is an odd one. It will be worth telling some day.

At twenty-seven Alice was tall and somewhat slight. Her head was large and overshadowed her body. Her shoulders were a little stooped and her hair and eyes brown. She was very quiet but beneath a placid exterior a continual ferment went on.

When she was a girl of sixteen and before she began to work in the store, Alice had an affair with a young man. The young man, named Ned Currie, was older than Alice. He, like George Willard, was employed on the *Winesburg Eagle* and for a long time he went to see Alice almost every evening. Together the two walked under the trees through the streets of the town and talked of what they would do with their lives. Alice was then a very pretty girl and Ned Currie took her into his arms and kissed her. He became excited and said things he did not intend to say and Alice, betrayed by her desire to have something beautiful come into her rather narrow life, also grew excited. She also talked. The outer crust of her life, all of her natural diffidence and reserve, was torn away and she gave herself over to the emotions of love. When, late in the fall of her sixteenth year, Ned Currie went away to Cleveland where he hoped to get a place on a city newspaper and rise in the world, she wanted to go with him. With a trembling voice she told him what was in her mind. "I will work and you can work," she said. "I do not want to harness you to a needless expense that will prevent your making progress. Don't marry me now. We will get along without that and we can be together. Even though we live in the same house no one will say anything. In the city we will be unknown and people will pay no attention to us."

Ned Currie was puzzled by the determination and abandon of his sweetheart and was also deeply touched. He had wanted the girl to become his mistress but changed his mind. He wanted to protect and care for her. "You don't know what you're talking about," he said sharply; "you may be sure I'll let you do no such thing. As soon as I get a good job I'll come back. For the present you'll have to stay here. It's the only thing we can do."

On the evening before he left Winesburg to take up his new life in the city, Ned Currie went to call on Alice. They walked about through the streets for an hour and then got a rig from Wesley Moyer's livery and went for a drive in the country. The moon came up and they found themselves unable to talk. In his sadness the young man forgot the resolutions he had made regarding his conduct with the girl.

They got out of the buggy at a place where a long meadow ran down to the bank of Wine Creek and there in the dim light became lovers. When at midnight they returned to town they were both glad. It did not seem to them that anything that could happen in the future could blot out the wonder and beauty of the thing that had happened. "Now we will have to stick to each other, whatever happens we will have to do that," Ned Currie said as he left the girl at her father's door.

The young newspaper man did not succeed in getting a place on a Cleveland paper and went west to Chicago. For a time he was lonely and wrote to Alice almost every day. Then he was caught up by the life of the city; he began to make friends and found new interests in life. In Chicago he boarded at a house where there were several women. One of them attracted his attention and he forgot Alice in Winesburg. At the end of a year he had stopped writing letters, and only once in a long time, when he was lonely or when he went into one of the city parks and saw the moon shining on the grass as it had shone that night on the meadow by Wine Creek, did he think of her at all.

In Winesburg the girl who had been loved grew to be a woman. When she was twenty-two years old her father, who owned a harness repair shop, died suddenly. The harness maker was an old soldier, and after a few months his wife received a widow's pension. She used the first money she got to buy a loom and became a weaver of carpets, and Alice got a place in Winney's store. For a number of years nothing could have induced her to believe that Ned Currie would not in the end return to her.

She was glad to be employed because the daily round of toil in the store made the time of waiting seem less long and uninteresting. She began to save money, thinking that when she had saved two or three hundred dollars she would follow her lover to the city and try if her presence would not win back his affections.

Alice did not blame Ned Currie for what had happened in the moonlight in the field, but felt that she could never marry another man. To her the thought of giving to another what she still felt could belong only to Ned seemed monstrous. When other young men tried to attract her attention she would have nothing to do with them. "I am his wife and shall remain his wife whether he comes back or not," she whispered to herself, and for all of her willingness to support herself could not have understood the growing modern idea of a woman's owning herself and giving and taking for her own ends in life.

Alice worked in the dry goods store from eight in the morning until six at night and on three evenings a week went back to the store to stay from seven until nine. As time passed and she became more and more lonely she began to practice the devices common to lonely people. When at night she went upstairs into her own room she knelt on the floor to pray and in her prayers whispered things she wanted to say to her lover. She became attached to inanimate objects, and because it was her own, could not bear to have anyone touch the furniture of her room. The trick of saving money, begun for a purpose, was carried on after the scheme of going to the city to find Ned Currie had been given up. It became a fixed habit, and when she needed new clothes she did not get them. Sometimes on rainy afternoons in the store she got out her bank book and, letting it lie open before her, spent hours dreaming impossible dreams of saving money enough so that the interest would support both herself and her future husband.

"Ned always liked to travel about," she thought. "I'll give him the chance. Some day when we are married and I can save both his money and my own, we will be rich. Then we can travel together all over the world. "

In the dry goods store weeks ran into months and months into years as Alice waited and dreamed of her lover's return. Her employer, a grey old man with false teeth and a thin grey mustache that drooped down over his mouth, was not given to conversation, and sometimes, on rainy days and in the winter when a storm raged in Main Street, long hours passed when no customers came in. Alice arranged and rearranged the stock. She stood near the front window where she could look down the deserted street and thought of the evenings when she had walked with Ned Currie and of what he had said. "We will have to stick to each other now. " The words echoed and re-echoed through the mind of the maturing woman. Tears came into her eyes. Sometimes when her employer had gone out and she was alone in the store she put her head on the counter and wept. "Oh, Ned, I am waiting," she whispered over and over, and all the time the creeping fear that he would never come back grew stronger within her.

In the spring when the rains have passed and before the long hot days of summer have come, the country about Winesburg is delightful. The town lies in the midst of open fields, but beyond the fields are pleasant patches of woodlands. In the wooded places are many little cloistered nooks, quiet places where lovers go to sit on Sunday afternoons. Through the trees they look out across the fields and see farmers at work about the barns or people driving up and down on the roads. In the town bells ring and occasionally a train passes, looking like a toy thing in the distance.

For several years after Ned Currie went away Alice did not go into the wood with the other young people on Sunday, but one day after he had been gone for two or three years and when her loneliness seemed unbearable, she put on her best dress and set out. Finding a little sheltered place from which she could see the town and a long stretch of the fields, she sat down. Fear of age and ineffectuality took possession of her. She could not sit still, and arose. As she stood looking out over the land something, perhaps the thought of never ceasing life as it expresses itself in the flow of the seasons, fixed her mind on the passing years. With a shiver of dread, she realized that for her the beauty and freshness of youth had passed. For the first time she felt that she had been cheated. She did not blame Ned Currie and did not know what to blame. Sadness swept over her. Dropping to her knees, she tried to pray, but instead of prayers words of protest came to her lips. "It is not going to come to me. I will never find happiness. Why do I tell myself lies?" she cried, and an odd sense of relief came with this, her first bold attempt to face the fear that had become a part of her everyday life.

In the year when Alice Hindman became twenty-five two things happened to disturb the dull uneventfulness of her days. Her mother married Bush Milton, the carriage painter of Winesburg, and she herself became a member of the Winesburg Methodist Church. Alice joined the church because she had become frightened by the loneliness of her position in life. Her mother's second marriage had emphasized her isolation. "I am becoming old and queer. If Ned comes he will not want me. In the city where he is living men are perpetually young. There is so much going on that they do not have time to grow old," she told herself with a grim little smile, and went resolutely about the business of becoming acquainted with people. Every Thursday evening when the store had closed she went to a prayer meeting in the basement of the church and on Sunday evening attended a meeting of an organization called The Epworth League.

When Will Hurley, a middle-aged man who clerked in a drug store and who also belonged to the church, offered to walk home with her she did not protest. "Of course I will not let him make a practice of being with me, but if he comes to see me once in a long time there can be no harm in that," she told herself, still determined in her loyalty to Ned Currie.

Without realizing what was happening, Alice was trying feebly at first, but with growing determination, to get a new hold upon life. Beside the drug clerk she walked in silence, but sometimes in the darkness as they went stolidly along she put out her hand and touched softly the folds of his coat. When he left her at the gate before her mother's house she did not go indoors, but stood for a moment by the door. She wanted to call to the drug clerk, to ask him to sit with her in the darkness on the porch before the house, but was afraid he would not understand. "It is not him that I want," she told herself; "I want to avoid being so much alone. If I am not careful I will grow unaccustomed to being with people."

During the early fall of her twenty-seventh year a passionate restlessness took possession of Alice. She could not bear to be in the company of the drug clerk, and when, in the evening, he came to walk with her she sent him away. Her mind became intensely active and when, weary from the long hours of standing behind the counter in the store, she went home and crawled into bed, she could not sleep. With staring eyes she looked into the darkness. Her imagination, like a child awakened from long sleep, played about the room. Deep within her there was something that would not be cheated by phantasies and that demanded some definite answer from life.

Alice took a pillow into her arms and held it tightly against her breasts. Getting out of bed, she arranged a blanket so that in the darkness it looked like a form lying between the sheets and, kneeling beside the bed, she caressed it, whispering words over and over, like a refrain. "Why doesn't something happen? Why am I left here alone?" she muttered. Although she sometimes thought of Ned Currie, she no longer depended on him. Her desire had grown vague. She did not want Ned Currie or any other man. She wanted to be loved, to have something answer the call that was growing louder and louder within her.

And then one night when it rained Alice had an adventure. It frightened and confused her. She had come home from the store at nine and found the house empty. Bush Milton had gone off to town and her mother to the house of a neighbor. Alice went upstairs to her room and undressed in the darkness. For a moment she stood by the window hearing the rain beat against the glass and then a strange desire took possession of her. Without stopping to think of what she intended to do, she ran downstairs through the dark house and out into the rain. As she stood on the little grass plot before the house and felt the cold rain on her body a mad desire to run naked through the streets took possession of her.

She thought that the rain would have some creative and wonderful effect on her body. Not for years had she felt so full of youth and courage. She wanted to leap and run, to cry out, to find some other lonely human and embrace him. On the brick sidewalk before the house a man stumbled homeward. Alice started to run. A wild, desperate mood took possession of her. "What do I care who it is. He is alone, and I will go to him," she thought; and then without stopping to consider the possible result of her madness, called softly. "Wait!" she cried. "Don't go away. Whoever you are, you must wait."

The man on the sidewalk stopped and stood listening. He was an old man and somewhat deaf. Putting his hand to his mouth, he shouted. "What? What say?" he called.

Alice dropped to the ground and lay trembling. She was so frightened at the thought of what she had done that when the man had gone on his way she did not dare get to her feet, but crawled on hands and knees through the grass to the house. When she got to her own room she bolted the door and drew her dressing table across the doorway. Her body shook as with a chill and her hands trembled so that she had difficulty getting into her nightdress. When she got into bed she buried her face in the pillow and wept brokenheartedly. "What is the matter with me? I will do something dreadful if I am not careful," she thought, and turning her face to the wall, began trying to force herself to face bravely the fact that many people must live and die alone, even in Winesburg.

>> **Questions for Consideration and Discussion**

1. What is the adventure in the story? What reasons combine to drive Alice to take such an adventure?
2. Is Alice's outcry heard by anybody in the town? What does this symbolize? What counsel would you give to Alice?
3. Have you experienced extreme loneliness? Share your experience with your deskmate and discuss the ways to get rid of loneliness.

Ernest Hemingway (1899 – 1961)

As a journalist, novelist, short-story writer, the winner of Nobel Prize for literature in 1954, Hemingway has been regarded as one of the finest literary stylists of the 20th century. His distinctively economical, crisp, unadorned style left American literature permanently changed. He brought a hard-bitten realism into American fiction.

Hemingway's writings and his life experiences were closely related; he wrote about those aspects of life that he had personally experienced.

Hemingway, the second of six children, was born and raised in Oak Park, Illinois. His mother was a music teacher and a lover of high culture. His father was a successful physician who enjoyed hunting and fishing. As a result, Hemingway spent many of his boyhood summers hunting and fishing near his family's summer house, and it was then that he developed the masculine ideal that is reflected in much of his work. Outdoor adventures would remain a part of his life and his writing.

After high school, Hemingway took a job with the *Kansas City Star*. In the short time that Hemingway worked for the newspaper, he learned some stylistic lessons that would later influence his fiction. When writing newspaper articles, journalists were encouraged to use short sentences, short paragraphs and active verbs to better convey compression, clarity, and immediacy. Hemingway later said: "Those were the best rules I ever learned for the business of writing. I've never forgotten them."

When the United States entered World War I in 1917, Hemingway was eager to go. An eye problem barred him from the army, so he joined the ambulance corps of the Italian army and was wounded in battle. The experiences of war and of being wounded were traumatic; Hemingway returned to them in one way or another in all his later writing.

After the war, Hemingway went to Paris, then considered as the literary capital of the world. There he came to know Gertrude Stein, Sherwood Anderson, Ezra Pound, F. Scott Fitzgerald, and others in the large community of expatriate artistic and literary

Americans. He was influenced or helped by them in one way or another. His posthumous memoir *A Moveable Feast* (1964) contains vivid portraits of Pound, Stein, Fitzgerald and some other American artists in this group.

In 1926, his novel *The Sun Also Rises* appeared. Narrated by Jake Barnes whose World War I wounds have left him sexually impotent, the novel depicts Jake's efforts to live according to a self-conscious code of dignity, of "grace under pressure." Barnes finds an ideal in the rich tradition of Spanish peasant life, especially as epitomized in bullfighting and the bullfighter. This book brilliantly captures Hemingway's years in Paris as one of the "lost generation." It also presents the stripped-down "Hemingway style" at its finest. "I always try to write on the principle of the iceberg," he told an interviewer. "There is seven-eighths of it under water for every part that shows."

Hemingway's other well-known novels include *A Farewell to Arms* (1929), *For Whom the Bell Tolls* (1940), and *The Old Man and the Sea* (1952). *A Farewell to Arms* describes a romance between an American army officer, Frederick Henry, and a British nurse, Catherine Barkley. The two run away from war, trying to make "a separate peace," but this idyll is shattered when Catherine dies in childbirth. This fiction well epitomizes the negative feelings of post-World War I : the meaninglessness of modern life, a sense of loss (particularly the loss of love), disillusionment, grief, frustration, and despair. *For Whom the Bell Tolls* draws on Hemingway's experiences in Spain as a war correspondent. It is an epic story set in the Spanish Civil War.

A fan of bullfighting, Hemingway wrote two nonfiction books on the subject: *Death in the Afternoon* and *The Dangerous Summer*.

After World War II, with his fourth wife — also his last wife — journalist Mary Welsh, Hemingway made his home in Cuba, where he wrote *The Old Man and the Sea* (1952), a short novel written as one text without breaks. It recounts an old fisherman Santiago's fishing journey, his long and lonely struggle with a fish and the sea, and his victory in defeat. In *The Old Man and the Sea*, Hemingway shifted his focus from human affairs to the vital contacts between species as well as between creatures and the rest of nature. The old man, like most Hemingway's heroes, lives dangerously, by personal codes of honor, courage, and endurance. This short novel won a Pulitzer Prize in 1953 and was central to his Nobel Prize in 1954.

Hemingway traveled a lot and was badly hurt in Africa in October 1953 in the crash of a small plane. The crash damaged his mental and physical health, and he never fully recovered. Subject increasingly to despair and an incapacitating paranoia, he was hospitalized several times before he killed himself in 1961.

A Farewell to Arms

(Excerpt)

Chapter 41

One morning I awoke about three o'clock hearing Catherine stirring in the bed.

"Are you all right, Cat?"

"I've been having some pains, darling."

"Regularly?"

"No, not very."

"If you have them at all regularly we'll go to the hospital."

I was very sleepy and went back to sleep. A little while later I woke again.

"Maybe you'd better call up the doctor," Catherine said. "I think maybe this is it."

I went to the phone and called the doctor. "How often are the pains coming?" he asked.

"How often are they coming, Cat?"

"I should think every quarter of an hour."

"You should go to the hospital, then," the doctor said. "I will dress and go there right away myself."

I hung up and called the garage near the station to send up a taxi. No one answered the phone for a long time. Then I finally got a man who promised to send up a taxi at once. Catherine was dressing. Her bag was all packed with the things she would need at the hospital and the baby things. Outside in the hall I rang for the elevator. There was no answer. I went downstairs. There was no one downstairs except the night-watchman. I brought the elevator up myself, put Catherine's bag in it, she stepped in and we went down. The night-watchman opened the door for us and we sat outside on the stone slabs beside the stairs down to the driveway and waited for the taxi. The night was clear and the stars were out. Catherine was very excited.

"I'm so glad it's started," she said. "Now in a little while it will be all over."

"You're a good brave girl."

"I'm not afraid. I wish the taxi would come, though."

We heard it coming up the street and saw its headlights. It turned into the driveway and I helped Catherine in and the driver put the bag up in front.

"Drive to the hospital," I said.

We went out of the driveway and started up the hill.

At the hospital we went in and I carried the bag. There was a woman at the desk who wrote down Catherine's name, age, address, relatives and religion, in a book. She said she had no religion and the woman drew a line in the space after that word. She gave her name as Catherine Henry.

"I will take you up to your room," she said. We went up in an elevator. The woman stopped it and we stepped out and followed her down a hall. Catherine held tight to my arm.

"This is the room," the woman said. "Will you please undress and get into bed? Here is a night-gown for you to wear."

"I have a night-gown," Catherine said.

"It is better for you to wear this night-gown," the woman said.

I went outside and sat on a chair in the hallway.

"You can come in now," the woman said from the doorway. Catherine was lying in the narrow bed wearing a plain, square-cut night-gown that looked as though it were made of rough sheeting. She smiled at me.

"I'm having fine pains now," she said. The woman was holding her wrist and timing the pains with a watch.

"That was a big one," Catherine said. I saw it on her face.

"Where's the doctor?" I asked the woman.

"He's lying down sleeping. He will be here when he is needed."

"I must do something for Madame, now," the nurse said. "Would you please step out again?"

I went out into the hall. It was a bare hall with two windows and closed doors all down the corridor. It smelled of hospital. I sat on the chair and looked at the floor and prayed for Catherine.

"You can come in," the nurse said. I went in.

"Hello, darling," Catherine said.

"How is it?"

"They are coming quite often now." Her face drew up. Then she smiled.

"That was a real one. Do you want to put your hand on my back again, nurse?"

"If it helps you," the nurse said.

"You go away, darling," Catherine said. "Go out and get something to eat. I may do this for a long time the nurse says."

"The first labor is usually protracted," the nurse said.

"Please go out and get something to eat," Catherine said. "I'm fine, really."

"I'll stay awhile," I said.

The pains came quite regularly, then slackened off. Catherine was very excited. When the pains were bad she called them good ones. When they started to fall off she was disappointed and ashamed.

"You go out, darling," she said. "I think you are just making me self-conscious." Her face tied up. "There. That was better. I so want to be a good wife and have this child without any foolishness. Please go and get some breakfast, darling, and then come back. I won't miss you. Nurse is splendid to me."

"You have plenty of time for breakfast," the nurse said.

"I'll go then. Good-by, sweet."

"Good-by," Catherine said, "and have a fine breakfast for me too."

"Where can I get breakfast?" I asked the nurse.

"There's a café down the street at the square," she said. "It should be open now."

Outside it was getting light. I walked down the empty street to the café. There was a light in the window. I went in and stood at the zinc bar and an old man served me a glass of white wine and a brioche. The brioche was yesterday's. I dipped it in the wine and then drank a glass of coffee.

"What do you do at this hour?" the old man asked.

"My wife is in labor at the hospital."

"So. I wish you good luck."

"Give me another glass of wine."

He poured it from the bottle slopping it over a little so some ran down on the zinc. I drank this glass, paid and went out. Outside along the street were the refuse cans from the houses waiting for the collector. A dog was nosing at one of the cans.

"What do you want?" I asked and looked in the can to see if there was anything I could pull out for him; there was nothing on top but coffee-grounds, dust and some dead flowers.

"There isn't anything, dog," I said. The dog crossed the street. I went up the stairs in the hospital to the floor Catherine was on and down the hall to her room. I knocked on the door. There was no answer. I opened the door; the room was empty, except for Catherine's bag on a chair and her dressing-gown hanging on a hook on the wall. I went out and down the hall, looking for somebody. I found a nurse.

"Where is Madame Henry?"

"A lady has just gone to the delivery room."

"Where is it?"

"I will show you."

She took me down to the end of the hall. The door of the room was partly open. I could see Catherine lying on a table, covered by a sheet. The nurse was on one side and the doctor stood on the other side of the table beside some cylinders. The doctor held a rubber mask attached to a tube in one hand.

"I will give you a gown and you can go in," the nurse said. "Come in here, please."

She put a white gown on me and pinned it at the neck in back with a safety pin.

"Now you can go in," she said. I went into the room.

"Hello, darling," Catherine said in a strained voice. "I'm not doing much."

"You are Mr. Henry?" the doctor asked.

"Yes. How is everything going, doctor?"

"Things are going very well," the doctor said. "We came in here where it is easy to give gas for the pains."

"I want it now," Catherine said. The doctor placed the rubber mask over her face and turned a dial and I watched Catherine breathing deeply and rapidly. Then she pushed the mask away. The doctor shut off the petcock.

"That wasn't a very big one. I had a very big one a while ago. The doctor made me go clear out, didn't you, doctor?" Her voice was strange. It rose on the word doctor.

The doctor smiled.

"I want it again," Catherine said. She held the rubber tight to her face and breathed fast. I heard her moaning a little. Then she pulled the mask away and smiled.

"That was a big one," she said. "That was a very big one. Don't you worry, darling. You go away. Go have another breakfast."

"I'll stay," I said.

We had gone to the hospital about three o'clock in the morning. At noon Catherine was still in the delivery room. The pains had slackened again. She looked very tired and worn now but she was still cheerful.

"I'm not any good, darling," she said. "I'm so sorry. I thought I would do it very easily. Now — there's one — " she reached out her hand for the mask and held it over her face. The doctor moved the dial and watched her. In a little while it was over.

"It wasn't much," Catherine said. She smiled. "I'm a fool about the gas. It's wonderful."

"We'll get some for the home," I said.

"There one comes," Catherine said quickly. The doctor turned the dial and looked at his watch.

"What is the interval now?" I asked.

"About a minute."

"Don't you want lunch?"

"I will have something pretty soon," he said.

"You must have something to eat, doctor," Catherine said. "I'm so sorry I go on so long. Couldn't my husband give me the gas?"

"If you wish," the doctor said. "You turn it to the numeral two."

"I see," I said. There was a marker on a dial that turned with a handle.

"I want it now," Catherine said. She held the mask tight to her face. I turned the dial to number two and when Catherine put down the mask I turned it off. It was very good of the doctor to let me do something.

"Did you do it, darling?" Catherine asked. She stroked my wrist.

"Sure."

"You're so lovely." She was a little drunk from the gas.

"I will eat from a tray in the next room," the doctor said. "You can call me any moment." While the time passed I watched him eat, then, after a while, I saw that he was lying down and smoking a cigarette. Catherine was getting very tired.

"Do you think I'll ever have this baby?" she asked.

"Yes, of course you will."

"I try as hard as I can. I push down but it goes away. There it comes. Give it to me."

At two o'clock I went out and had lunch. There were a few men in the café sitting with coffee and glasses of kirsch or marc on the tables. I sat down at a table. "Can I eat?" I asked the waiter.

"It is past time for lunch."

"Isn't there anything for all hours?"

"You can have choucroute."

"Give me choucroute and beer."

"A demi or a bock?"

"A light demi."

The waiter brought a dish of sauerkraut with a slice of ham over the top and a sausage buried in the hot wine-soaked cabbage. I ate it and drank the beer. I was very hungry. I watched the people at the tables in the café. At one table they were playing cards. Two men at the table next me were talking and smoking. The café was full of smoke. The zinc bar, where I had breakfasted, had three people behind it now; the old man, a plump woman in a black dress who sat behind a counter and kept track of everything served to the tables, and a boy in an apron. I wondered how many children the woman had and what it had been like.

When I was through with the choucroute I went back to the hospital. The street was all clean now. There were no refuse cans out. The day was cloudy but the sun was trying to come through.

I rode upstairs in the elevator, stepped out and went down the hall to Catherine's room, where I had left my white gown. I put it on and pinned it in back at the neck. I looked in the glass and saw myself looking like a fake doctor with a beard. I went down the hall to the delivery room. The door was closed and I knocked. No one answered so I turned the handle and went in. The doctor sat by Catherine. The nurse was doing something at the other end of the room.

"Here is your husband," the doctor said.

"Oh, darling, I have the most wonderful doctor," Catherine said in a very strange voice. "He's been telling me the most wonderful story and when the pain came too badly he put me all the way out. He's wonderful. You're wonderful, doctor."

"You're drunk," I said.

"I know it," Catherine said. "But you shouldn't say it." Then, "Give it to me. Give it to me." She clutched hold of the mask and breathed short and deep, pantingly, making the respirator click. Then she gave a long sigh and the doctor reached with his left hand and lifted away the mask.

"That was a very big one," Catherine said. Her voice was very strange. "I'm not going to die now, darling. I'm past where I was going to die. Aren't you glad?"

"Don't you get in that place again."

"I won't. I'm not afraid of it though. I won't die, darling."

"You will not do any such foolishness," the doctor said. "You would not die and leave your husband."

"Oh, no. I won't die. I wouldn't die. It's silly to die. There it comes. Give it to me."

After a while the doctor said, "You will go out, Mr. Henry, for a few moments and I will make an examination."

"He wants to see how I am doing," Catherine said. "You can come back afterward, darling, can't he, doctor?"

"Yes," said the doctor. "I will send word when he can come back."

I went out the door and down the hall to the room where Catherine was to be after the baby came. I sat in a chair there and looked at the room. I had the paper in my coat that I had bought when I went out for lunch and I read it. It was beginning to be dark outside and I turned the light on to read. After a while I stopped reading and turned off the light and watched it get dark outside. I wondered why the doctor did not send for me. Maybe it was better I was away. He probably wanted me away for a while. I looked at my watch. If he did not send for me in ten minutes I would go down anyway.

Poor, poor dear Cat. And this was the price you paid for sleeping together. This was the end of the trap. This was what people got for loving each other. Thank God for gas, anyway. What must it have been like before there were anesthetics. Once it started, they were in the mill-race. Catherine had a good time in the time of pregnancy. It wasn't bad. She was hardly ever sick. She was not awfully uncomfortable until toward the last. So now they got her in the end. You never got away with anything. Get away hell! It would have been the same if we had been married fifty times. And what if she should die? She won't die. People don't die in childbirth nowadays. That was what all husbands thought. Yes, but what if she should die? She won't die. She's just having a bad time. The initial labor is usually protracted. She's only having a bad time. Afterward we'd say what a bad time and Catherine would say it wasn't really so bad. But what if she should die? She can't die. Yes, but what if she should die? She can't, I tell you. Don't be a fool. It's just a bad time. It's just nature giving her hell. It's only the first labor, which is almost always protracted. Yes, but what if she should die? She can't die. Why would she die? What reason is there for her to die? There's just a child that has to be born, the by-product of good nights in Milan. It makes trouble and is born and then you look after it and get fond of it maybe. But what if she should die? She won't die. But what if she should die? She won't. She's all right. But what if she should die? She can't die. But what if she should die? Hey, what about that? What if she should die?

The doctor came into the room.

"How does it go, doctor?"

"It doesn't go," he said.

"What do you mean?"

"Just that. I made an examination — " He detailed the result of the examination. "Since then I've waited to see. But it doesn't go."

"What do you advise?"

"There are two things. Either a high forceps delivery which can tear and be quite dangerous besides being possibly bad for the child, and a Caesarean."①

---

① Caesarean: Caesarean section, or C-section, is an operation to deliver a baby through a cut made in the mother's tummy and womb in order to safely lift the baby out.

"What is the danger of a Caesarean?" What if she should die!

"It should be no greater than the danger of an ordinary delivery. "

"Would you do it yourself?"

"Yes. I would need possibly an hour to get things ready and to get the people I would need. Perhaps a little less. "

"What do you think?"

"I would advise a Caesarean operation. If it were my wife I would do a Caesarean. "

"What are the after effects?"

"There are none. There is only the scar. "

"What about infection?"

"The danger is not so great as in a high forceps delivery. "

"What if you just went on and did nothing?"

"You would have to do something eventually. Mrs. Henry is already losing much of her strength. The sooner we operate now the safer. "

"Operate as soon as you can," I said.

"I will go and give the instructions. "

I went into the delivery room. The nurse was with Catherine who lay on the table, big under the sheet, looking very pale and tired.

"Did you tell him he could do it?" she asked.

"Yes. "

"Isn't that grand. Now it will be all over in an hour. I'm almost done, darling. I'm going all to pieces. Please give me that. It doesn't work. Oh, it doesn't work!"

"Breathe deeply. "

"I am. Oh, it doesn't work any more. It doesn't work!"

"Get another cylinder," I said to the nurse.

"That is a new cylinder. "

"I'm just a fool, darling," Catherine said. "But it doesn't work any more. " She began to cry. "Oh, I wanted so to have this baby and not make trouble, and now I'm all done and all gone to pieces and it doesn't work. Oh, darling, it doesn't work at all. I don't care if I die if it will only stop. Oh, please, darling, please make it stop. There it comes. Oh Oh Oh!" She breathed sobbingly in the mask.

"It doesn't work. It doesn't work. It doesn't work. Don't mind me, darling. Please don't cry. Don't mind me. I'm just gone all to pieces. You poor sweet. I love you so and I'll be good again. I'll be good this time. Can't they give me something? If they could only give me something. "

"I'll make it work. I'll turn it all the way. "

"Give it to me now. "

I turned the dial all the way and as she breathed hard and deep her hand relaxed on the mask. I shut off the gas and lifted the mask. She came back from a long way away.

"That was lovely, darling. Oh, you're so good to me. "

"You be brave, because I can't do that all the time. It might kill you. "

"I'm not brave any more, darling. I'm all broken. They've broken me. I know it now. "

"Everybody is that way. "

"But it's awful. They just keep it up till they break you. "

"In an hour it will be over. "

"Isn't that lovely? Darling, I won't die, will I?"

"No. I promise you won't. "

"Because I don't want to die and leave you, but I get so tired of it and I feel I'm going to die. "

"Nonsense. Everybody feels that. "

"Sometimes I know I'm going to die. "

"You won't. You can't. "

"But what if I should?"

"I won't let you. "

"Give it to me quick. Give it to me!"

Then afterward, "I won't die. I won't let myself die. "

"Of course you won't. "

"You'll stay with me?"

"Not to watch it. "

"No, just to be there. "

"Sure. I'll be there all the time. "

"You're so good to me. There, give it to me. Give me some more. It's not working!"

I turned the dial to three and then four. I wished the doctor would come back. I was afraid of the numbers above two.

Finally a new doctor came in with two nurses and they lifted Catherine onto a wheeled stretcher and we started down the hall. The stretcher went rapidly down the hall and into the elevator where everyone had to crowd against the wall to make room; then up, then an open door and out of the elevator and down the hall on rubber wheels to the operating room. I did not recognize the doctor with his cap and mask on. There was another doctor and more nurses.

"They've got to give me something," Catherine said. " They've got to give me something. Oh please, doctor, give me enough to do some good!"

One of the doctors put a mask over her face and I looked through the door and saw the bright small amphitheatre of the operating room.

"You can go in the other door and sit up there," a nurse said to me. There were benches behind a rail that looked down on the white table and the lights. I looked at Catherine. The mask was over her face and she was quiet now. They wheeled the stretcher forward. I turned away and walked down the hall. Two nurses were hurrying toward the entrance to the gallery.

"It's a Caesarean," one said. "They're going to do a Caesarean. "

The other one laughed, "We're just in time. Aren't we lucky?" They went in the door that led to the gallery.

Another nurse came along. She was hurrying too.

"You go right in there. Go right in," she said.

"I'm staying outside."

She hurried in. I walked up and down the hall. I was afraid to go in. I looked out the window. It was dark but in the light from the window I could see it was raining. I went into a room at the far end of the hall and looked at the labels on bottles in a glass case. Then I came out and stood in the empty hall and watched the door of the operating room.

A doctor came out followed by a nurse. He held something in his two hands that looked like a freshly skinned rabbit and hurried across the corridor with it and in through another door. I went down to the door he had gone into and found them in the room doing things to a new-born child. The doctor held him up for me to see. He held him by the heels and slapped him.

"Is he all right?"

"He's magnificent. He'll weigh five kilos."

I had no feeling for him. He did not seem to have anything to do with me. I felt no feeling of fatherhood.

"Aren't you proud of your son?" the nurse asked. They were washing him and wrapping him in something. I saw the little dark face and dark hand, but I did not see him move or hear him cry. The doctor was doing something to him again. He looked upset.

"No," I said. "He nearly killed his mother."

"It isn't the little darling's fault. Didn't you want a boy?"

"No," I said. The doctor was busy with him. He held him up by the feet and slapped him. I did not wait to see it. I went out in the hall. I could go in now and see. I went in the door and a little way down the gallery. The nurses who were sitting at the rail motioned for me to come down where they were. I shook my head. I could see enough where I was.

I thought Catherine was dead. She looked dead. Her face was gray, the part of it that I could see. Down below, under the light, the doctor was sewing up the great long, forcep-spread, thick-edged, wound. Another doctor in a mask gave the anesthetic. Two nurses in masks handed things. It looked like a drawing of the Inquisition. I knew as I watched I could have watched it all, but I was glad I hadn't. I do not think I could have watched them cut, but I watched the wound closed into a high welted ridge with quick skilful-looking stitches like a cobbler's, and was glad. When the wound was closed I went out into the hall and walked up and down again. After a while the doctor came out.

"How is she?"

"She is all right. Did you watch?"

He looked tired.

"I saw you sew up. The incision looked very long."

"You thought so?"

"Yes. Will that scar flatten out?"

"Oh, yes. "

After a while they brought out the wheeled stretcher and took it very rapidly down the hallway to the elevator. I went along beside it. Catherine was moaning. Downstairs they put her in the bed in her room. I sat in a chair at the foot of the bed. There was a nurse in the room. I got up and stood by the bed. It was dark in the room. Catherine put out her hand. "Hello, darling," she said. Her voice was very weak and tired.

"Hello, you sweet. "

"What sort of baby was it?"

"Sh — don't talk," the nurse said.

"A boy. He's long and wide and dark. "

"Is he all right?"

"Yes," I said. "He's fine. "

I saw the nurse look at me strangely.

"I'm awfully tired," Catherine said. "And I hurt like hell. Are you all right, darling?"

"I'm fine. Don't talk. "

"You were lovely to me. Oh, darling, I hurt dreadfully. What does he look like?"

"He looks like a skinned rabbit with a puckered-up old-man's face. "

"You must go out," the nurse said. "Madame Henry must not talk. "

"I'll be outside. "

"Go and get something to eat. "

"No. I'll be outside. " I kissed Catherine. She was very gray and weak and tired.

"May I speak to you?" I said to the nurse. She came out in the hall with me. I walked a little way down the hall.

"What's the matter with the baby?" I asked.

"Didn't you know?"

"No. "

"He wasn't alive. "

"He was dead?"

"They couldn't start him breathing. The cord was caught around his neck or something. "

"So he's dead. "

"Yes. It's such a shame. He was such a fine big boy. I thought you knew. "

"No," I said. "You better go back in with Madame. "

I sat down on the chair in front of a table where there were nurses' reports hung on clips at the side and looked out of the window. I could see nothing but the dark and the rain falling across the light from the window. So that was it. The baby was dead. That was why the doctor looked so tired. But why had they acted the way they did in the room with him? They supposed he would come around and start breathing probably. I had no religion but I knew he ought to have been baptized. But what if he never breathed at all. He hadn't. He had never been alive. Except in Catherine. I'd felt him kick there often enough. But I hadn't for a week.

Maybe he was choked all the time. Poor little kid. I wished the hell I'd been choked like that. No I didn't. Still there would not be all this dying to go through. Now Catherine would die. That was what you did. You died. You did not know what it was about. You never had time to learn. They threw you in and told you the rules and the first time they caught you off base they killed you. Or they killed you gratuitously like Aymo①. Or gave you the syphilis like Rinaldi②. But they killed you in the end. You could count on that. Stay around and they would kill you.

Once in camp I put a log on top of the fire and it was full of ants. As it commenced to burn, the ants swarmed out and went first toward the centre where the fire was; then turned back and ran toward the end. When there were enough on the end they fell off into the fire. Some got out, their bodies burnt and flattened, and went off not knowing where they were going. But most of them went toward the fire and then back toward the end and swarmed on the cool end and finally fell off into the fire. I remember thinking at the time that it was the end of the world and a splendid chance to be a messiah and lift the log off the fire and throw it out where the ants could get off onto the ground. But I did not do anything but throw a tin cup of water on the log, so that I would have the cup empty to put whiskey in before I added water to it. I think the cup of water on the burning log only steamed the ants.

So now I sat out in the hall and waited to hear how Catherine was. The nurse did not come out, so after a while I went to the door and opened it very softly and looked in. I could not see at first because there was a bright light in the hall and it was dark in the room. Then I saw the nurse sitting by the bed and Catherine's head on a pillow, and she was all flat under the sheet. The nurse put her finger to her lips, then stood up and came to the door.

"How is she?" I asked.

"She's all right," the nurse said. "You should go and have your supper and then come back if you wish."

I went down the hall and then down the stairs and out the door of the hospital and down the dark street in the rain to the café. It was brightly lighted inside and there were many people at the tables. I did not see a place to sit, and a waiter came up to me and took my wet coat and hat and showed me a place at a table across from an elderly man who was drinking beer and reading the evening paper. I sat down and asked the waiter what the plat du jour③ was.

"Veal stew — but it is finished."

"What can I have to eat?"

"Ham and eggs, eggs with cheese, or choucroute."

"I had choucroute this noon," I said.

"That's true," he said. "That's true. You ate choucroute this noon." He was a middle-aged man with a bald top to his head and his hair slicked over it. He had a kind face.

---

① Aymo:one of ambulance drivers.

② Rinald:an Italian lieutenant and surgeon, Henry's roomate and friend.

③ plat du jour: the special or featured dish of the day on a restaurant menu.

"What do you want? Ham and eggs or eggs with cheese?"

"Ham and eggs," I said, "and beer."

"A demi-blonde?"

"Yes," I said.

"I remembered," he said. "You took a demi-blonde this noon."

I ate the ham and eggs and drank the beer. The ham and eggs were in a round dish — the ham underneath and the eggs on top. It was very hot and at the first mouthful I had to take a drink of beer to cool my mouth. I was hungry and I asked the waiter for another order. I drank several glasses of beer. I was not thinking at all but read the paper of the man opposite me. It was about the break through on the British front. When he realized I was reading the back of his paper he folded it over. I thought of asking the waiter for a paper, but I could not concentrate. It was hot in the café and the air was bad. Many of the people at the tables knew one another. There were several card games going on. The waiters were busy bringing drinks from the bar to the tables. Two men came in and could find no place to sit. They stood opposite the table where I was. I ordered another beer. I was not ready to leave yet. It was too soon to go back to the hospital. I tried not to think and to be perfectly calm. The men stood around but no one was leaving, so they went out. I drank another beer. There was quite a pile of saucers now on the table in front of me. The man opposite me had taken off his spectacles, put them away in a case, folded his paper and put it in his pocket and now sat holding his liqueur glass and looking out at the room. Suddenly I knew I had to get back. I called the waiter, paid the reckoning, got into my coat, put on my hat and started out the door. I walked through the rain up to the hospital.

Upstairs I met the nurse coming down the hall.

"I just called you at the hotel," she said. Something dropped inside me.

"What is wrong?"

"Mrs. Henry has had a hemorrhage."

"Can I go in?"

"No, not yet. The doctor is with her."

"Is it dangerous?"

"It is very dangerous." The nurse went into the room and shut the door. I sat outside in the hall. Everything was gone inside of me. I did not think. I could not think. I knew she was going to die and I prayed that she would not. Don't let her die. Oh, God, please don't let her die. I'll do anything for you if you won't let her die. Please, please, please, dear God, don't let her die. Dear God, don't let her die. Please, please, please don't let her die. God please make her not die. I'll do anything you say if you don't let her die. You took the baby but don't let her die. That was all right but don't let her die. Please, please, dear God, don't let her die.

The nurse opened the door and motioned with her finger for me to come. I followed her into the room. Catherine did not look up when I came in. I went over to the side of the bed. The doctor was standing by the bed on the opposite side. Catherine looked at me and smiled.

I bent down over the bed and started to cry.

"Poor darling," Catherine said very softly. She looked gray.

"You're all right, Cat," I said. "You're going to be all right."

"I'm going to die," she said; then waited and said, "I hate it."

I took her hand.

"Don't touch me," she said. I let go of her hand. She smiled. "Poor darling. You touch me all you want."

"You'll be all right, Cat. I know you'll be all right."

"I meant to write you a letter to have if anything happened, but I didn't do it."

"Do you want me to get a priest or any one to come and see you?"

"Just you," she said. Then a little later, "I'm not afraid. I just hate it."

"You must not talk so much," the doctor said.

"All right," Catherine said.

"Do you want me to do anything, Cat? Can I get you anything?"

Catherine smiled, "No." Then a little later, "You won't do our things with another girl, or say the same things, will you?"

"Never."

"I want you to have girls, though."

"I don't want them."

"You are talking too much," the doctor said. "Mr. Henry must go out. He can come back again later. You are not going to die. You must not be silly."

"All right," Catherine said. "I'll come and stay with you nights," she said. It was very hard for her to talk.

"Please go out of the room," the doctor said. "You cannot talk." Catherine winked at me, her face gray. "I'll be right outside," I said.

"Don't worry, darling," Catherine said. "I'm not a bit afraid. It's just a dirty trick."

"You dear, brave sweet."

I waited outside in the hall. I waited a long time. The nurse came to the door and came over to me. "I'm afraid Mrs. Henry is very ill," she said. "I'm afraid for her."

"Is she dead?"

"No, but she is unconscious."

It seems she had one hemorrhage after another. They couldn't stop it. I went into the room and stayed with Catherine until she died. She was unconscious all the time, and it did not take her very long to die.

Outside the room, in the hall; I spoke to the doctor, "Is there anything I can do to-night?"

"No. There is nothing to do. Can I take you to your hotel?"

"No, thank you. I am going to stay here a while."

"I know there is nothing to say. I cannot tell you — "

"No," I said. "There's nothing to say."

"Good-night," he said. "I cannot take you to your hotel?"

"No, thank you."

"It was the only thing to do," he said. "The operation proved — "

"I do not want to talk about it," I said.

"I would like to take you to your hotel."

"No, thank you."

He went down the hall. I went to the door of the room.

"You can't come in now," one of the nurses said.

"Yes I can," I said.

"You can't come in yet."

"You get out," I said. "The other one too."

But after I had got them out and shut the door and turned off the light it wasn't any good. It was like saying good-bye to a statue. After a while I went out and left the hospital and walked back to the hotel in the rain.

▶ Questions for Consideration and Discussion

1. In this chapter, two living creatures are mentioned alongside human beings: dog and ants. In what light are they mentioned? What meaning is conveyed through the mention?

2. What modernistic traits are identifiable in this chapter?

3. What does the ending episode of this chapter (also of this fiction) suggest about Henry's future? How can the fiction be justifiably called fiction from the lost generation?

F. Scott Fitzgerald (1896 – 1940)

Though Fitzgerald's life ran roughly parallel to the first four decades of the 20th century, it is with the 1920s that his reputation as a novelist is associated; he has been called Spokesman of the Roaring Twenties; he is best known for his fiction that depicts America's "Jazz Age."

Fitzgerald was born into a fairly well-to-do family in St. Paul, Minnesota. He attended, but never graduated from Princeton University. There he mingled with the moneyed classes from the East coast, and he was greatly obsessed with them the remainder of his life.

In 1917 he was drafted into the army, but the war ended before he saw active service. While he was stationed in Alabama, he met and courted Zelda Zayre, a local belle. But Zelda rejected him. In 1919 he went to New York City, determined to make a fortune and win Zelda. Amazingly, he succeeded. In 1920 he published his first novel *This Side of Paradise* (a novel about college life), and it became an instant success. A week after the novel came out, Scott and Zelda were married and together they commenced a rich life of endless parties. They spent more than Fitzgerald made from the publications of his writings: *Flappers and Philosophers* (1921), *Tales of the Jazz Age* (1922), and *The Beautiful and Damned* (1922).

In 1924, the Fitzgeralds moved to Europe to live less expensively. They made friends with such American expatriates as Gertrude Stein, Ezra Pound, and Ernest Hemingway. During this time Fitzgerald published his best-known and most successful novel, *The Great Gatsby* (1925), and another book of short stories, *All the Sad Young Men* (1926). He wrote and wrote. However, despite the pace at which he worked, the Fitzgeralds could not get out of debt. He became an alcoholic. Zelda broke down in 1930 and spent most of her remaining years in mental institutions.

In 1931 Fitzgerald reestablished himself permanently in the United States, and in 1934 he published *Tender is the Night*, a novel following the decline of a young American psychiatrist whose personal energies are sapped, and his career corroded by his marriage and his own weakness of character. As in *The Great Gatsby*, the protagonist begins as a disciple of the work ethic and turns into a pursuer of wealth, thus the American Dream turns into a nightmare. But this novel did not sell well. In 1937 Fitzgerald turned to Hollywood screenwriting. He died of a heart attack in Hollywood at the age of forty-four.

In the 1920s and 1930s, Fitzgerald was equally famous as a writer and as a celebrity author whose lifestyle seemed to symbolize the two decades: In the 1920s he stood for all-night partying, drinking, and the pursuit of pleasure, while in the 1930s he stood for the gloomy aftermath of excess. His private life, in many ways, seemed to symbolize the eras before and after the stock market crash of 1929. Fitzgerald once said "Sometimes I don't know whether Zelda and I are real or whether we are characters in one of my novels."

The Great Gatsby is set in New York City and Long Island during the 1920s. Nick Carraway, the narrator, is a young Princeton man, who works as a bond broker in Manhattan. He becomes involved in the life of his rich and shady neighbor at Long Island, Jay Gatsby, who is entertaining hundreds of guests at lavish parties. Gatsby reveals to Nick that he and Nick's cousin Daisy Buchanan had a brief affair before the war; however, during the war Daisy married Tom Buchanan, who literally bought her love. Gatsby says he lost Daisy because he had no money, but he is still in love with her. He persuades Nick to bring him and Daisy together again. "You can't repeat the past ," Nick says to Gatsby. Gatsby tries to convince Daisy to leave Tom, who, in turn, reveals that Gatsby has made his money from bootlegging. "They're a rotten crowd," Nick shouts to Gatsby. "You're worth the whole damn bunch put together. " Daisy, driving Gatsby's car, hits and kills Tom's mistress Myrtle Wilson without knowing her identity. Gatsby remains silent to protect Daisy, but Tom tells Myrtle's husband that it is Gatsby who killed his wife (which is a lie). Wilson murders Gatsby and then commits suicide. Nick is left to arrange Gatsby's funeral, attended only by Gatsby's father and one former guest.

The above is the story the fiction tells. However, the way the story is narrated is far more meaningful, for Nick's own judgment is often in question. Nick is both moved and repelled by the tale he tells, and his attitude toward Gatsby is both sympathetic and critical. The fiction can be called a *complex* study of the American dream embodied by Gatsby. But the road he takes — through greedy and quick amassing of wealth and through equating wealth with American Dream — is wrong.

The structure of *The Great Gatsby* is compact, the style is dazzling, and its images of automobiles, parties and garbage heaps seem to capture the contradictions of a consumer society.

The Great Gatsby

(Excerpt)

Chapter 3

There was music from my neighbor's house through the summer nights. In his blue gardens men and girls came and went like moths among the whisperings and the champagne and the stars. At high tide in the afternoon I watched his guests diving from the tower of his raft or taking the sun on the hot sand of his beach while his two motor-boats slit the waters of the Sound, drawing aquaplanes over cataracts of foam. On week-ends his Rolls-Royce became an omnibus, bearing parties to and from the city, between nine in the morning and long past midnight, while his station wagon scampered like a brisk yellow bug to meet all trains. And on Mondays eight servants including an extra gardener toiled all day with mops and scrubbing-brushes and hammers and garden-shears, repairing the ravages of the night before.

Every Friday five crates of oranges and lemons arrived from a fruiterer in New York — every Monday these same oranges and lemons left his back door in a pyramid of pulpless halves. There was a machine in the kitchen which could extract the juice of two hundred oranges in half an hour, if a little button was pressed two hundred times by a butler's thumb.

At least once a fortnight a corps of caterers came down with several hundred feet of canvas and enough colored lights to make a Christmas tree of Gatsby's enormous garden. On buffet tables, garnished with glistening hors-d'oeuvre, spiced baked hams crowded against salads of harlequin designs and pastry pigs and turkeys bewitched to a dark gold.

In the main hall a bar with a real brass rail was set up, and stocked with gins and liquors and with cordials so long forgotten that most of his female guests were too young to know one from another.

By seven o'clock the orchestra has arrived — no thin five-piece affair but a whole pitful of oboes and trombones and saxophones and viols and cornets and piccolos and low and high drums. The last swimmers have come in from the beach now and are dressing upstairs; the cars from New York are parked five deep in the drive, and already the halls and salons and verandas are gaudy with primary colors and hair shorn in strange new ways and shawls beyond the dreams of Castile. The bar is in full swing and floating rounds of cocktails permeate the garden outside until the air is alive with chatter and laughter and casual innuendo and introductions forgotten on the spot and enthusiastic meetings between women who never knew each other's names.

The lights grow brighter as the earth lurches away from the sun and now the orchestra is playing yellow cocktail music and the opera of voices pitches a key higher. Laughter is easier, minute by minute, spilled with prodigality, tipped out at a cheerful word. The groups change more swiftly, swell with new arrivals, dissolve and form in the same breath — already there are wanderers, confident girls who weave here and there among the stouter and more stable, become for a sharp, joyous moment the center of a group and then excited with triumph glide on through the sea-change of faces and voices and color under the constantly changing light.

Suddenly one of these gypsies in trembling opal, seizes a cocktail out of the air, dumps it down for courage and moving her hands like Frisco dances out alone on the canvas platform. A momentary hush; the orchestra leader varies his rhythm obligingly for her and there is a burst of chatter as the erroneous news goes around that she is Gilda Gray's understudy from the "Follies." The party has begun.

I believe that on the first night I went to Gatsby's house I was one of the few guests who had actually been invited. People were not invited — they went there. They got into automobiles which bore them out to Long Island and somehow they ended up at Gatsby's door. Once there they were introduced by somebody who knew Gatsby and after that they conducted themselves according to the rules of behavior associated with amusement parks. Sometimes they came and went without having met Gatsby at all, came for the party with a simplicity of heart that was its own ticket of admission.

I had been actually invited. A chauffeur in a uniform of robin's egg blue crossed my lawn early that Saturday morning with a surprisingly formal note from his employer — the honor would be entirely Gatsby's, it said, if I would attend his "little party" that night. He had seen me several times and had intended to call on me long before but a peculiar combination of circumstances had prevented it — signed Jay Gatsby in a majestic hand.

Dressed up in white flannels I went over to his lawn a little after seven and wandered around rather ill-at-ease among swirls and eddies of people I didn't know — though here and there was a face I had noticed on the commuting train. I was immediately struck by the number of young Englishmen dotted about; all well dressed, all looking a little hungry and all talking in low earnest voices to solid and prosperous Americans. I was sure that they were selling something: bonds or insurance or automobiles. They were, at least, agonizingly aware of the easy money in the vicinity and convinced that it was theirs for a few words in the right key.

As soon as I arrived I made an attempt to find my host but the two or three people of whom I asked his whereabouts stared at me in such an amazed way and denied so vehemently any knowledge of his movements that I slunk off in the direction of the cocktail table — the only place in the garden where a single man could linger without looking purposeless and alone.

I was on my way to get roaring drunk from sheer embarrassment when Jordan Baker came out of the house and stood at the head of the marble steps, leaning a little backward and looking with contemptuous interest down into the garden.

Welcome or not, I found it necessary to attach myself to someone before I should begin to address cordial remarks to the passers-by.

"Hello!" I roared, advancing toward her. My voice seemed unnaturally loud across the garden.

"I thought you might be here," she responded absently as I came up. "I remembered you lived next door to — "

She held my hand impersonally, as a promise that she'd take care of me in a minute, and gave ear to two girls in twin yellow dresses who stopped at the foot of the steps.

"Hello!" they cried together. "Sorry you didn't win."

That was for the golf tournament. She had lost in the finals the week before.

"You don't know who we are," said one of the girls in yellow, "but we met you here about a month ago."

"You've dyed your hair since then," remarked Jordan, and I started, but the girls had moved casually on and her remark was addressed to the premature moon, produced like the supper, no doubt, out of a caterer's basket. With Jordan's slender golden arm resting in mine we descended the steps and sauntered about the garden. A tray of cocktails floated at us through the twilight and we sat down at a table with the two girls in yellow and three men, each one introduced to us as Mr. Mumble.

"Do you come to these parties often?" inquired Jordan of the girl beside her.

"The last one was the one I met you at," answered the girl, in an alert, confident voice. She turned to her companion: "Wasn't it for you, Lucille?"

It was for Lucille, too.

"I like to come," Lucille said. "I never care what I do, so I always have a good time. When I was here last I tore my gown on a chair, and he asked me my name and address — inside of a week I got a package from Croirier's with a new evening gown in it."

"Did you keep it?" asked Jordan.

"Sure I did. I was going to wear it tonight, but it was too big in the bust and had to be altered. It was gas blue with lavender beads. Two hundred and sixty-five dollars."

"There's something funny about a fellow that'll do a thing like that," said the other girl eagerly. "He doesn't want any trouble with ANYbody."

"Who doesn't?" I inquired.

"Gatsby. Somebody told me — "

The two girls and Jordan leaned together confidentially.

"Somebody told me they thought he killed a man once."

A thrill passed over all of us. The three Mr. Mumbles bent forward and listened eagerly.

"I don't think it's so much THAT," argued Lucille skeptically; "it's more that he was a German spy during the war."

One of the men nodded in confirmation.

"I heard that from a man who knew all about him, grew up with him in Germany," he assured us positively.

"Oh, no," said the first girl, "it couldn't be that, because he was in the American army during the war." As our credulity switched back to her she leaned forward with enthusiasm. "You look at him sometimes when he thinks nobody's looking at him. I'll bet he killed a man."

She narrowed her eyes and shivered. Lucille shivered. We all turned and looked around for Gatsby. It was testimony to the romantic speculation he inspired that there were whispers about him from those who found little that it was necessary to whisper about in this world.

The first supper — there would be another one after midnight — was now being served, and Jordan invited me to join her own party who were spread around a table on the other side of the garden. There were three married couples and Jordan's escort, a persistent undergraduate given to violent innuendo, and obviously under the impression that sooner or later Jordan was going to yield him up her person to a greater or lesser degree. Instead of rambling, this party had preserved a dignified homogeneity, and assumed to itself the function of representing the staid nobility of the countryside — East Egg condescending to West Egg, and carefully on guard against its spectroscopic gayety.

"Let's get out," whispered Jordan, after a somehow wasteful and inappropriate half hour. "This is much too polite for me."

We got up, and she explained that we were going to find the host — I had never met him, she said, and it was making me uneasy. The undergraduate nodded in a cynical, melancholy way.

The bar, where we glanced first, was crowded but Gatsby was not there.

She couldn't find him from the top of the steps, and he wasn't on the veranda. On a chance we tried an important-looking door, and walked into a high Gothic library, panelled with carved English oak, and probably transported complete from some ruin overseas.

A stout, middle-aged man with enormous owl-eyed spectacles was sitting somewhat drunk on the edge of a great table, staring with unsteady concentration at the shelves of books. As we entered he wheeled excitedly around and examined Jordan from head to foot.

"What do you think?" he demanded impetuously.

"About what?"

He waved his hand toward the book-shelves.

"About that. As a matter of fact you needn't bother to ascertain. I ascertained. They're real. "

"The books?"

He nodded.

"Absolutely real — have pages and everything. I thought they'd be a nice durable cardboard. Matter of fact, they're absolutely real. Pages and — Here! Lemme show you. "

Taking our skepticism for granted, he rushed to the bookcases and returned with Volume One of the "Stoddard Lectures. "

"See!" he cried triumphantly. "It's a bona-fide piece of printed matter. It fooled me. This fella's a regular Belasco. It's a triumph. What thoroughness! What realism! Knew when to stop, too — didn't cut the pages. But what do you want? What do you expect?"

He snatched the book from me and replaced it hastily on its shelf muttering that if one brick was removed the whole library was liable to collapse.

"Who brought you?" he demanded. "Or did you just come? I was brought. Most people were brought. "

Jordan looked at him alertly, cheerfully, without answering.

"I was brought by a woman named Roosevelt," he continued. "Mrs. Claud Roosevelt. Do you know her? I met her somewhere last night. I've been drunk for about a week now, and I thought it might sober me up to sit in a library. "

"Has it?"

"A little bit, I think. I can't tell yet. I've only been here an hour. Did I tell you about the books? They're real. They're — "

"You told us. "

We shook hands with him gravely and went back outdoors.

There was dancing now on the canvas in the garden, old men pushing young girls backward in eternal graceless circles, superior couples holding each other tortuously, fashionably, and keeping in the corners — and a great number of single girls dancing individualistically or relieving the orchestra for a moment of the burden of the banjo or the traps. By midnight the hilarity had increased. A celebrated tenor had sung in Italian, and a notorious contralto had sung in jazz, and between the numbers people were doing "stunts" all over the garden, while happy, vacuous bursts of laughter rose toward the summer sky. A pair of stage twins, who turned out to be the girls in yellow, did a baby act in costume, and champagne was served in glasses bigger than finger bowls. The moon had risen higher, and floating in the Sound was a triangle of silver scales, trembling a little to the stiff, tinny drip of the banjoes on the lawn.

I was still with Jordan Baker. We were sitting at a table with a man of about my age and a rowdy little girl, who gave way upon the slightest provocation to uncontrollable laughter. I was enjoying myself now. I had taken two finger-bowls of champagne, and the scene had changed before my eyes into something significant, elemental, and profound.

At a lull in the entertainment the man looked at me and smiled.

"Your face is familiar," he said, politely. "Weren't you in the Third Division during the war?"

"Why, yes. I was in the Ninth Machine-Gun Battalion."

"I was in the Seventh Infantry until June nineteen-eighteen. I knew I'd seen you somewhere before."

We talked for a moment about some wet, gray little villages in France. Evidently he lived in this vicinity, for he told me that he had just bought a hydroplane, and was going to try it out in the morning.

"Want to go with me, old sport? Just near the shore along the Sound."

"What time?"

"Any time that suits you best."

It was on the tip of my tongue to ask his name when Jordan looked around and smiled.

"Having a gay time now?" she inquired.

"Much better." I turned again to my new acquaintance. "This is an unusual party for me. I haven't even seen the host. I live over there — " I waved my hand at the invisible hedge in the distance, "and this man Gatsby sent over his chauffeur with an invitation." For a moment he looked at me as if he failed to understand.

"I'm Gatsby," he said suddenly.

"What!" I exclaimed. "Oh, I beg your pardon."

"I thought you knew, old sport. I'm afraid I'm not a very good host."

He smiled understandingly — much more than understandingly. It was one of those rare smiles with a quality of eternal reassurance in it, that you may come across four or five times in life. It faced — or seemed to face — the whole external world for an instant, and then concentrated on you with an irresistible prejudice in your favor. It understood you just so far as you wanted to be understood, believed in you as you would like to believe in yourself and assured you that it had precisely the impression of you that, at your best, you hoped to convey. Precisely at that point it vanished — and I was looking at an elegant young rough-neck, a year or two over thirty, whose elaborate formality of speech just missed being absurd. Some time before he introduced himself I'd got a strong impression that he was picking his words with care.

Almost at the moment when Mr. Gatsby identified himself, a butler hurried toward him with the information that Chicago was calling him on the wire. He excused himself with a small bow that included each of us in turn.

"If you want anything just ask for it, old sport," he urged me. "Excuse me. I will rejoin you later."

When he was gone I turned immediately to Jordan — constrained to assure her of my surprise. I had expected that Mr. Gatsby would be a florid and corpulent person in his middle years.

"Who is he?" I demanded. "Do you know?"

"He's just a man named Gatsby."

"Where is he from, I mean? And what does he do?"

"Now YOU're started on the subject," she answered with a wan smile. "Well, he told me once he was an Oxford man."

A dim background started to take shape behind him but at her next remark it faded away.

"However, I don't believe it."

"Why not?"

"I don't know," she insisted, "I just don't think he went there."

Something in her tone reminded me of the other girl's "I think he killed a man," and had the effect of stimulating my curiosity. I would have accepted without question the information that Gatsby sprang from the swamps of Louisiana or from the lower East Side of New York. That was comprehensible. But young men didn't — at least in my provincial inexperience I believed they didn't — drift coolly out of nowhere and buy a palace on Long Island Sound.

"Anyhow he gives large parties," said Jordan, changing the subject with an urbane distaste for the concrete. "And I like large parties. They're so intimate. At small parties there isn't any privacy."

There was the boom of a bass drum, and the voice of the orchestra leader rang out suddenly above the echolalia of the garden.

"Ladies and gentlemen," he cried. "At the request of Mr. Gatsby we are going to play for you Mr. Vladimir Tostoff's latest work which attracted so much attention at Carnegie Hall last May. If you read the papers you know there was a big sensation." He smiled with jovial condescension, and added "Some sensation!" whereupon everybody laughed.

"The piece is known," he concluded lustily, "as Vladimir Tostoff's JAZZ HISTORY OF THE WORLD."

The nature of Mr. Tostoff's composition eluded me, because just as it began my eyes fell on Gatsby, standing alone on the marble steps and looking from one group to another with approving eyes. His tanned skin was drawn attractively tight on his face and his short hair looked as though it were trimmed every day. I could see nothing sinister about him. I wondered if the fact that he was not drinking helped to set him off from his guests, for it seemed to me that he grew more correct as the fraternal hilarity increased.

When the JAZZ HISTORY OF THE WORLD was over, girls were putting their heads on men's shoulders in a puppyish, convivial way, girls were swooning backward playfully into men's arms, even into groups, knowing that some one would arrest their falls — but no one swooned backward on Gatsby, and no French bob touched Gatsby's shoulder, and no singing quartets were formed with Gatsby's head for one link.

"I beg your pardon."

Gatsby's butler was suddenly standing beside us.

"Miss Baker?" he inquired. "I beg your pardon but Mr. Gatsby would like to speak to you alone."

"With me?" she exclaimed in surprise.

"Yes, madame."

She got up slowly, raising her eyebrows at me in astonishment, and followed the butler toward the house. I noticed that she wore her evening dress, all her dresses, like sports clothes — there was a jauntiness about her movements as if she had first learned to walk upon golf courses on clean, crisp mornings.

I was alone and it was almost two. For some time confused and intriguing sounds had issued from a long, many-windowed room which overhung the terrace. Eluding Jordan's undergraduate, who was now engaged in an obstetrical conversation with two chorus girls, and who implored me to join him, I went inside.

The large room was full of people. One of the girls in yellow was playing the piano, and beside her stood a tall, red haired young lady from a famous chorus, engaged in song. She had drunk a quantity of champagne, and during the course of her song she had decided, ineptly, that everything was very, very sad — she was not only singing, she was weeping too. Whenever there was a pause in the song she filled it with gasping, broken sobs, and then took up the lyric again in a quavering soprano. The tears coursed down her cheeks — not freely, however, for when they came into contact with her heavily beaded eyelashes they assumed an inky color, and pursued the rest of their way in slow black rivulets. A humorous suggestion was made that she sing the notes on her face, whereupon she threw up her hands, sank into a chair, and went off into a deep vinous sleep.

"She had a fight with a man who says he's her husband," explained a girl at my elbow.

I looked around. Most of the remaining women were now having fights with men said to be their husbands. Even Jordan's party, the quartet from East Egg, were rent asunder by dissension. One of the men was talking with curious intensity to a young actress, and his wife, after attempting to laugh at the situation in a dignified and indifferent way, broke down entirely and resorted to flank attacks — at intervals she appeared suddenly at his side like an angry diamond, and hissed: "You promised!" into his ear.

The reluctance to go home was not confined to wayward men. The hall was at present occupied by two deplorably sober men and their highly indignant wives. The wives were sympathizing with each other in slightly raised voices.

"Whenever he sees I'm having a good time he wants to go home."

"Never heard anything so selfish in my life."

"We're always the first ones to leave."

"So are we."

"Well, we're almost the last tonight," said one of the men sheepishly. "The orchestra left half an hour ago."

In spite of the wives' agreement that such malevolence was beyond credibility, the dispute ended in a short struggle, and both wives were lifted, kicking, into the night.

As I waited for my hat in the hall the door of the library opened and Jordan Baker and Gatsby came out together. He was saying some last word to her, but the eagerness in his manner tightened abruptly into formality as several people approached him to say goodbye.

Jordan's party were calling impatiently to her from the porch, but she lingered for a moment to shake hands.

"I've just heard the most amazing thing," she whispered. "How long were we in there?"

"Why, about an hour."

"It was — simply amazing," she repeated abstractedly. "But I swore I wouldn't tell it and here I am tantalizing you." She yawned gracefully in my face. "Please come and see me… Phone book…Under the name of Mrs. Sigourney Howard… My aunt…" She was hurrying off as she talked — her brown hand waved a jaunty salute as she melted into her party at the door.

Rather ashamed that on my first appearance I had stayed so late, I joined the last of Gatsby's guests, who were clustered around him. I wanted to explain that I'd hunted for him early in the evening and to apologize for not having known him in the garden.

"Don't mention it," he enjoined me eagerly. "Don't give it another thought, old sport." The familiar expression held no more familiarity than the hand which reassuringly brushed my shoulder. "And don't forget we're going up in the hydroplane tomorrow morning, at nine o'clock."

Then the butler, behind his shoulder: "Philadelphia wants you on the phone, sir."

"All right, in a minute. Tell them I'll be right there…Good night."

"Good night."

"Good night." He smiled — and suddenly there seemed to be a pleasant significance in having been among the last to go, as if he had desired it all the time. "Good night, old sport … Good night."

But as I walked down the steps I saw that the evening was not quite over. Fifty feet from the door a dozen headlights illuminated a bizarre and tumultuous scene. In the ditch beside the road, right side up, but violently shorn of one wheel, rested a new coupé which had left Gatsby's drive not two minutes before. The sharp jut of a wall accounted for the detachment of the wheel, which was now getting considerable attention from half a dozen curious chauffeurs. However, as they had left their cars blocking the road, a harsh, discordant din from those in the rear had been audible for some time, and added to the already violent confusion of the scene.

A man in a long duster had dismounted from the wreck and now stood in the middle of the road, looking from the car to the tire and from the tire to the observers in a pleasant, puzzled way.

"See!" he explained. "It went in the ditch."

The fact was infinitely astonishing to him, and I recognized first the unusual quality of wonder, and then the man — it was the late patron of Gatsby's library.

"How'd it happen?"

He shrugged his shoulders.

"I know nothing whatever about mechanics," he said decisively.

"But how did it happen? Did you run into the wall?"

"Don't ask me," said Owl Eyes, washing his hands of the whole matter. "I know very little about driving — next to nothing. It happened, and that's all I know."

"Well, if you're a poor driver you oughtn't to try driving at night."

"But I wasn't even trying," he explained indignantly, "I wasn't even trying."

An awed hush fell upon the bystanders.

"Do you want to commit suicide?"

"You're lucky it was just a wheel! A bad driver and not even TRYing!"

"You don't understand," explained the criminal. "I wasn't driving. There's another man in the car."

The shock that followed this declaration found voice in a sustained "Ah-h-h!" as the door of the coupé swung slowly open. The crowd — it was now a crowd — stepped back involuntarily, and when the door had opened wide there was a ghostly pause. Then, very gradually, part by part, a pale, dangling individual stepped out of the wreck, pawing tentatively at the ground with a large uncertain dancing shoe.

Blinded by the glare of the headlights and confused by the incessant groaning of the horns, the apparition stood swaying for a moment before he perceived the man in the duster.

"Wha's matter?" he inquired calmly. "Did we run outa gas?"

"Look!"

Half a dozen fingers pointed at the amputated wheel — he stared at it for a moment, and then looked upward as though he suspected that it had dropped from the sky.

"It came off," some one explained.

He nodded.

"At first I din' notice we'd stopped."

A pause. Then, taking a long breath and straightening his shoulders, he remarked in a determined voice:

"Wonder'ff tell me where there's a gas'line station?"

At least a dozen men, some of them little better off than he was, explained to him that wheel and car were no longer joined by any physical bond.

"Back out," he suggested after a moment. "Put her in reverse."

"But the WHEEL'S off!"

He hesitated.

"No harm in trying," he said.

The caterwauling horns had reached a crescendo and I turned away and cut across the lawn toward home. I glanced back once. A wafer of a moon was shining over Gatsby's house, making the night fine as before, and surviving the laughter and the sound of his still glowing garden. A sudden emptiness seemed to flow now from the windows and the great doors, endowing with complete isolation the figure of the host, who stood on the porch, his hand up in a formal gesture of farewell.

Reading over what I have written so far, I see I have given the impression that the events of three nights several weeks apart were all that absorbed me. On the contrary, they were merely casual events in a crowded summer, and, until much later, they absorbed me infinitely less than my personal affairs.

Most of the time I worked. In the early morning the sun threw my shadow westward as I hurried down the white chasms of lower New York to the Probity Trust. I knew the other clerks and young bond-salesmen by their first names, and lunched with them in dark, crowded restaurants on little pig sausages and mashed potatoes and coffee. I even had a short affair with a girl who lived in Jersey City and worked in the accounting department, but her brother began throwing mean looks in my direction, so when she went on her vacation in July I let it blow quietly away.

I took dinner usually at the Yale Club — for some reason it was the gloomiest event of my day — and then I went upstairs to the library and studied investments and securities for a conscientious hour. There were generally a few rioters around, but they never came into the library, so it was a good place to work. After that, if the night was mellow, I strolled down Madison Avenue past the old Murray Hill Hotel, and over Thirty-third Street to the Pennsylvania Station.

I began to like New York, the racy, adventurous feel of it at night, and the satisfaction that the constant flicker of men and women and machines gives to the restless eye. I liked to walk up Fifth Avenue and pick out romantic women from the crowd and imagine that in a few minutes I was going to enter into their lives, and no one would ever know or disapprove. Sometimes, in my mind, I followed them to their apartments on the corners of hidden streets, and they turned and smiled back at me before they faded through a door into warm darkness. At the enchanted metropolitan twilight I felt a haunting loneliness sometimes, and felt it in others — poor young clerks who loitered in front of windows waiting until it was time for a solitary restaurant dinner — young clerks in the dusk, wasting the most poignant moments of night and life.

Again at eight o'clock, when the dark lanes of the Forties were five deep with throbbing taxi cabs, bound for the theatre district, I felt a sinking in my heart. Forms leaned together in the taxis as they waited, and voices sang, and there was laughter from unheard jokes, and lighted cigarettes outlined unintelligible gestures inside. Imagining that I, too, was hurrying toward gayety and sharing their intimate excitement, I wished them well.

For a while I lost sight of Jordan Baker, and then in midsummer I found her again. At first I was flattered to go places with her, because she was a golf champion, and every one knew her name. Then it was something more. I wasn't actually in love, but I felt a sort of tender curiosity. The bored haughty face that she turned to the world concealed something — most affectations conceal something eventually, even though they don't in the beginning — and one day I found what it was. When we were on a house-party together up in Warwick, she left a borrowed car out in the rain with the top down, and then lied about it — and suddenly I remembered the story about her that had eluded me that night at Daisy's. At her first big golf tournament there was a row that nearly reached the newspapers — a suggestion that she had moved her ball from a bad lie in the semi-final round. The thing approached the proportions of a scandal — then died away. A caddy retracted his statement, and the only other witness admitted that he might have been mistaken. The incident and the name had remained together in my mind.

Jordan Baker instinctively avoided clever, shrewd men, and now I saw that this was because she felt safer on a plane where any divergence from a code would be thought impossible. She was incurably dishonest. She wasn't able to endure being at a disadvantage, and given this unwillingness, I suppose she had begun dealing in subterfuges when she was very young in order to keep that cool, insolent smile turned to the world and yet satisfy the demands of her hard, jaunty body.

It made no difference to me. Dishonesty in a woman is a thing you never blame deeply — I was casually sorry, and then I forgot. It was on that same house party that we had a curious conversation about driving a car. It started because she passed so close to some workmen that our fender flicked a button on one man's coat.

"You're a rotten driver," I protested. "Either you ought to be more careful, or you oughtn't to drive at all."

"I am careful."

"No, you're not."

"Well, other people are," she said lightly.

"What's that got to do with it?"

"They'll keep out of my way," she insisted. "It takes two to make an accident."

"Suppose you met somebody just as careless as yourself."

"I hope I never will," she answered. "I hate careless people. That's why I like you."

Her gray, sun-strained eyes stared straight ahead, but she had deliberately shifted our relations, and for a moment I thought I loved her. But I am slow-thinking and full of interior rules that act as brakes on my desires, and I knew that first I had to get myself definitely out of that tangle back home. I'd been writing letters once a week and signing them: "Love, Nick," and all I could think of was how, when that certain girl played tennis, a faint mustache of perspiration appeared on her upper lip. Nevertheless there was a vague understanding that had to be tactfully broken off before I was free.

Every one suspects himself of at least one of the cardinal virtues, and this is mine: I am one of the few honest people that I have ever known.

Chapter 9

After two years I remember the rest of that day, and that night and the next day, only as an endless drill of police and photographers and newspaper men in and out of Gatsby's front door. A rope stretched across the main gate and a policeman by it kept out the curious, but little boys soon discovered that they could enter through my yard, and there were always a few of them clustered open-mouthed about the pool. Someone with a positive manner, perhaps a detective, used the expression "madman" as he bent over Wilson's body that afternoon, and the adventitious authority of his voice set the key for the newspaper reports next morning.

Most of those reports were a nightmare — grotesque, circumstantial, eager, and untrue. When Michaelis's testimony at the inquest brought to light Wilson's suspicions of his wife I thought the whole tale would shortly be served up in racy pasquinade — but Catherine①, who might have said anything, didn't say a word. She showed a surprising amount of character about it too — looked at the coroner with determined eyes under that corrected brow of hers, and swore that her sister had never seen Gatsby, that her sister was completely happy with her husband, that her sister had been into no mischief whatever. She convinced herself of it and cried into her handkerchief, as if the very suggestion was more than she could endure. So Wilson was reduced to a man "deranged by grief" in order that the case might remain in its simplest form. And it rested there.

But all this part of it seemed remote and unessential. I found myself on Gatsby's side, and alone. From the moment I telephoned news of the catastrophe to West Egg village, every surmise about him, and every practical question, was referred to me. At first I was surprised and confused; then, as he lay in his house and didn't move or breathe or speak, hour upon hour, it grew upon me that I was responsible, because no one else was interested — interested, I mean, with that intense personal interest to which every one has some vague right at the end.

I called up Daisy half an hour after we found him, called her instinctively and without hesitation. But she and Tom had gone away early that afternoon, and taken baggage with them.

"Left no address?"

"No."

"Say when they'd be back?"

"No."

"Any idea where they are? How I could reach them?"

"I don't know. Can't say."

I wanted to get somebody for him. I wanted to go into the room where he lay and reassure him: "I'll get somebody for you, Gatsby. Don't worry. Just trust me and I'll get somebody for you — "

Meyer Wolfshiem's② name wasn't in the phone book. The butler gave me his office address on Broadway, and I called Information, but by the time I had the number it was long after five, and no one answered the phone.

"Will you ring again?"

"I've rung them three times."

"It's very important."

---

① Catherine is the younger sister of Myttle Wilson, sister-in-law to George Wilson. Catherine is aware of her sister's secret affair with Tom.

② Meyer Wolfshiem: Meyer Wolfshiem was a business associate and a friend of Gatsby's.

"Sorry. I'm afraid no one's there."

I went back to the drawing room and thought for an instant that they were chance visitors, all these official people who suddenly filled it. But, as they drew back the sheet and looked at Gatsby with unmoved eyes, his protest continued in my brain:

"Look here, old sport, you've got to get somebody for me. You've got to try hard. I can't go through this alone."

Some one started to ask me questions, but I broke away and going upstairs looked hastily through the unlocked parts of his desk — he'd never told me definitely that his parents were dead. But there was nothing — only the picture of Dan Cody, a token of forgotten violence, staring down from the wall.

Next morning I sent the butler to New York with a letter to Wolfshiem, which asked for information and urged him to come out on the next train. That request seemed superfluous when I wrote it. I was sure he'd start when he saw the newspapers, just as I was sure there'd be a wire from Daisy before noon — but neither a wire nor Mr. Wolfshiem arrived, no one arrived except more police and photographers and newspaper men.

When the butler brought back Wolfshiem's answer I began to have a feeling of defiance, of scornful solidarity between Gatsby and me against them all.

> *Dear Mr. Carraway. This has been one of the most terrible shocks of my life to me I hardly can believe it that it is true at all. Such a mad act as that man did should make us all think. I cannot come down now as I am tied up in some very important business and cannot get mixed up in this thing now. If there is anything I can do a little later let me know in a letter by Edgar. I hardly know where I am when I hear about a thing like this and am completely knocked down and out.*
> *Yours truly,*
> *MEYER WOLFSHIEM*

And then hasty addenda beneath:
Let me know about the funeral etc. do not know his family at all.

When the phone rang that afternoon and Long Distance said Chicago was calling I thought this would be Daisy at last. But the connection came through as a man's voice, very thin and far away.

"This is Slagle speaking…"

"Yes?" The name was unfamiliar.

"Hell of a note, isn't it? Get my wire?"

"There haven't been any wires."

"Young Parke's in trouble," he said rapidly. "They picked him up when he handed the bonds over the counter. They got a circular from New York giving 'em the numbers just five minutes before. What d'you know about that, hey? You never can tell in these hick towns — "

"Hello!" I interrupted breathlessly. "Look here — this isn't Mr. Gatsby. Mr. Gatsby's dead. "

There was a long silence on the other end of the wire, followed by an exclamation... then a quick squawk as the connection was broken.

I think it was on the third day that a telegram signed Henry C. Gatz arrived from a town in Minnesota. It said only that the sender was leaving immediately and to postpone the funeral until he came.

It was Gatsby's father, a solemn old man, very helpless and dismayed, bundled up in a long cheap ulster against the warm September day. His eyes leaked continuously with excitement, and when I took the bag and umbrella from his hands he began to pull so incessantly at his sparse gray beard that I had difficulty in getting off his coat. He was on the point of collapse, so I took him into the music room and made him sit down while I sent for something to eat. But he wouldn't eat, and the glass of milk spilled from his trembling hand.

"I saw it in the Chicago newspaper," he said. "It was all in the Chicago newspaper. I started right away. "

"I didn't know how to reach you. "

His eyes, seeing nothing, moved ceaselessly about the room.

"It was a madman," he said. "He must have been mad. "

"Wouldn't you like some coffee?" I urged him.

"I don't want anything. I'm all right now, Mr. — "

"Carraway. "

"Well, I'm all right now. Where have they got Jimmy?"

I took him into the drawing-room, where his son lay, and left him there. Some little boys had come up on the steps and were looking into the hall; when I told them who had arrived, they went reluctantly away.

After a little while Mr. Gatz opened the door and came out, his mouth ajar, his face flushed slightly, his eyes leaking isolated and unpunctual tears. He had reached an age where death no longer has the quality of ghastly surprise, and when he looked around him now for the first time and saw the height and splendor of the hall and the great rooms opening out from it into other rooms, his grief began to be mixed with an awed pride. I helped him to a bedroom upstairs; while he took off his coat and vest I told him that all arrangements had been deferred until he came.

"I didn't know what you'd want, Mr. Gatsby — "

"Gatz is my name. "

" — Mr. Gatz. I thought you might want to take the body west. "

He shook his head.

"Jimmy always liked it better down East. He rose up to his position in the East. Were you a friend of my boy's, Mr. — ?"

"We were close friends. "

"He had a big future before him, you know. He was only a young man but he had a lot of brain power here. "

He touched his head impressively and I nodded.

"If he'd of lived he'd of been a great man. A man like James J. Hill. ① He'd of helped build up the country. "

"That's true," I said, uncomfortably.

He fumbled at the embroidered coverlet, trying to take it from the bed, and lay down stiffly — was instantly asleep.

That night an obviously frightened person called up and demanded to know who I was before he would give his name.

"This is Mr. Carraway," I said.

"Oh — " He sounded relieved. "This is Klipspringer. "

I was relieved too for that seemed to promise another friend at Gatsby's grave. I didn't want it to be in the papers and draw a sightseeing crowd so I'd been calling up a few people myself. They were hard to find.

"The funeral's tomorrow," I said. "Three o'clock, here at the house. I wish you'd tell anybody who'd be interested. "

"Oh, I will," he broke out hastily. "Of course I'm not likely to see anybody, but if I do. "

His tone made me suspicious.

"Of course you'll be there yourself. "

"Well, I'll certainly try. What I called up about is — "

"Wait a minute," I interrupted. "How about saying you'll come?"

"Well, the fact is — the truth of the matter is that I'm staying with some people up here in Greenwich and they rather expect me to be with them tomorrow. In fact there's a sort of picnic or something. Of course I'll do my very best to get away. "

I ejaculated an unrestrained " Huh!" and he must have heard me for he went on nervously:

"What I called up about was a pair of shoes I left there. I wonder if it'd be too much trouble to have the butler send them on. You see they're tennis shoes and I'm sort of helpless without them. My address is care of B. F. — "

I didn't hear the rest of the name because I hung up the receiver.

After that I felt a certain shame for Gatsby — one gentleman to whom I telephoned implied that he had got what he deserved. However, that was my fault, for he was one of those who used to sneer most bitterly at Gatsby on the courage of Gatsby's liquor and I should have known better than to call him.

The morning of the funeral I went up to New York to see Meyer Wolfshiem; I couldn't seem to reach him any other way. The door that I pushed open on the advice of an elevator

---

① James J. Hill: James J. Hill was a railroad magnate responsible for greatly expanding railways into the U. S. Northwest during the late 19th century.

boy was marked "The Swastika Holding Company" and at first there didn't seem to be any one inside. But when I'd shouted "Hello" several times in vain an argument broke out behind a partition and presently a lovely Jewess appeared at an interior door and scrutinized me with black hostile eyes.

"Nobody's in," she said. "Mr. Wolfshiem's gone to Chicago."

The first part of this was obviously untrue for someone had begun to whistle "The Rosary," tunelessly, inside.

"Please say that Mr. Carraway wants to see him."

"I can't get him back from Chicago, can I?"

At this moment a voice, unmistakably Wolfshiem's, called "Stella!" from the other side of the door.

"Leave your name on the desk," she said quickly. "I'll give it to him when he gets back."

"But I know he's there."

She took a step toward me and began to slide her hands indignantly up and down her hips.

"You young men think you can force your way in here any time," she scolded. "We're getting sickantired of it. When I say he's in Chicago, he's in ChiCAgo."

I mentioned Gatsby.

"Oh-oh!" She looked at me over again. "Will you just — what was your name?"

She vanished. In a moment Meyer Wolfshiem stood solemnly in the doorway, holding out both hands. He drew me into his office, remarking in a reverent voice that it was a sad time for all of us, and offered me a cigar.

"My memory goes back to when I first met him," he said. "A young major just out of the army and covered over with medals he got in the war. He was so hard up he had to keep on wearing his uniform because he couldn't buy some regular clothes. First time I saw him was when he come into Winebrenner's poolroom at Forty-third Street and asked for a job. He hadn't eat anything for a couple of days. 'Come on have some lunch with me,' I sid. He ate more than four dollars' worth of food in half an hour."

"Did you start him in business?" I inquired.

"Start him! I made him."

"Oh."

"I raised him up out of nothing, right out of the gutter. I saw right away he was a fine appearing, gentlemanly young man, and when he told me he was an Oggsford① I knew I could use him good. I got him to join up in the American Legion and he used to stand high there. Right off he did some work for a client of mine up to Albany. We were so thick like that in everything — " He held up two bulbous fingers " — always together."

I wondered if this partnership had included the World's Series transaction in 1919.

"Now he's dead," I said after a moment. "You were his closest friend, so I know you'll

---

① Oggsford: "Oggsford" is mispronunciation of "Oxford".

want to come to his funeral this afternoon."

"I'd like to come."

"Well, come then."

The hair in his nostrils quivered slightly and as he shook his head his eyes filled with tears.

"I can't do it — I can't get mixed up in it," he said.

"There's nothing to get mixed up in. It's all over now."

"When a man gets killed I never like to get mixed up in it in any way. I keep out. When I was a young man it was different — if a friend of mine died, no matter how, I stuck with them to the end. You may think that's sentimental but I mean it — to the bitter end."

I saw that for some reason of his own he was determined not to come, so I stood up.

"Are you a college man?" he inquired suddenly.

For a moment I thought he was going to suggest a "gonnegtion"① but he only nodded and shook my hand.

"Let us learn to show our friendship for a man when he is alive and not after he is dead," he suggested. "After that my own rule is to let everything alone."

When I left his office the sky had turned dark and I got back to West Egg in a drizzle. After changing my clothes I went next door and found Mr. Gatz walking up and down excitedly in the hall. His pride in his son and in his son's possessions was continually increasing and now he had something to show me.

"Jimmy sent me this picture." He took out his wallet with trembling fingers. "Look there."

It was a photograph of the house, cracked in the corners and dirty with many hands. He pointed out every detail to me eagerly. "Look there!" and then sought admiration from my eyes. He had shown it so often that I think it was more real to him now than the house itself.

"Jimmy sent it to me. I think it's a very pretty picture. It shows up well."

"Very well. Had you seen him lately?"

"He come out to see me two years ago and bought me the house I live in now. Of course we was broke up when he run off from home but I see now there was a reason for it. He knew he had a big future in front of him. And ever since he made a success he was very generous with me."

He seemed reluctant to put away the picture, held it for another minute, lingeringly, before my eyes. Then he returned the wallet and pulled from his pocket a ragged old copy of a book called "Hopalong Cassidy."

"Look here, this is a book he had when he was a boy. It just shows you."

He opened it at the back cover and turned it around for me to see.

On the last fly-leaf was printed the word SCHEDULE, and the date September 12th, 1906. And underneath:

---

① gonnegtion: "gonnegtion" is mispronounciation of "connection".

Rise from bed	6:00 A.M.
Dumbbell exercise and wall-scaling	6:15 — 6:30
Study electricity, etc.	7:15 — 8:15
Work	8:30 — 4:30 P.M.
Baseball and sports	4:30 — 5:00
Practice elocution, poise and how to attain it	5:00 — 6:00
Study needed inventions	7:00 — 9:00

GENERAL RESOLVES

No wasting time at Shafters or a [name, indecipherable]

No more smokeing or chewing

Bath every other day

Read one improving book or magazine per week

Save $5.00 [crossed out] $3.00 per week

Be better to parents

"I come across this book by accident," said the old man. "It just shows you, don't it?"

"It just shows you."

"Jimmy was bound to get ahead. He always had some resolves like this or something. Do you notice what he's got about improving his mind? He was always great for that. He told me I et like a hog once and I beat him for it."

He was reluctant to close the book, reading each item aloud and then looking eagerly at me. I think he rather expected me to copy down the list for my own use.

A little before three the Lutheran minister arrived from Flushing and I began to look involuntarily out the windows for other cars. So did Gatsby's father. And as the time passed and the servants came in and stood waiting in the hall, his eyes began to blink anxiously and he spoke of the rain in a worried uncertain way. The minister glanced several times at his watch so I took him aside and asked him to wait for half an hour. But it wasn't any use. Nobody came.

About five o'clock our procession of three cars reached the cemetery and stopped in a thick drizzle beside the gate — first a motor hearse, horribly black and wet, then Mr. Gatz and the minister and I in the limousine, and, a little later, four or five servants and the postman from West Egg in Gatsby's station wagon, all wet to the skin. As we started through the gate into the cemetery I heard a car stop and then the sound of someone splashing after us over the soggy ground. I looked around. It was the man with owl-eyed glasses whom I had found marvelling over Gatsby's books in the library one night three months before.

I'd never seen him since then. I don't know how he knew about the funeral or even his name. The rain poured down his thick glasses and he took them off and wiped them to see the protecting canvas unrolled from Gatsby's grave.

I tried to think about Gatsby then for a moment but he was already too far away and I could only remember, without resentment, that Daisy hadn't sent a message or a flower. Dimly I heard someone murmur: "Blessed are the dead that the rain falls on," and then the owl-eyed man said "Amen to that," in a brave voice.

We straggled down quickly through the rain to the cars. Owl-Eyes spoke to me by the gate.

"I couldn't get to the house," he remarked.

"Neither could anybody else."

"Go on!" He started. "Why, my God! they used to go there by the hundreds."

He took off his glasses and wiped them again outside and in.

"The poor son-of-a-bitch," he said.

...

Gatsby's house was still empty when I left — the grass on his lawn had grown as long as mine. One of the taxi drivers in the village never took a fare past the entrance gate without stopping for a minute and pointing inside; perhaps it was he who drove Daisy and Gatsby over to East Egg the night of the accident and perhaps he had made a story about it all his own. I didn't want to hear it and I avoided him when I got off the train.

I spent my Saturday nights in New York because those gleaming, dazzling parties of his were with me so vividly that I could still hear the music and the laughter faint and incessant from his garden and the cars going up and down his drive. One night I did hear a material car there and saw its lights stop at his front steps. But I didn't investigate. Probably it was some final guest who had been away at the ends of the earth and didn't know that the party was over.

On the last night, with my trunk packed and my car sold to the grocer, I went over and looked at that huge incoherent failure of a house once more. On the white steps an obscene word, scrawled by some boy with a piece of brick, stood out clearly in the moonlight and I erased it, drawing my shoe raspingly along the stone. Then I wandered down to the beach and sprawled out on the sand.

Most of the big shore places were closed now and there were hardly any lights except the shadowy, moving glow of a ferryboat across the Sound. And as the moon rose higher the inessential houses began to melt away until gradually I became aware of the old island here that flowered once for Dutch sailors' eyes — a fresh, green breast of the new world. Its vanished trees, the trees that had made way for Gatsby's house, had once pandered in whispers to the last and greatest of all human dreams; for a transitory enchanted moment man must have held his breath in the presence of this continent, compelled into an aesthetic contemplation he neither understood nor desired, face to face for the last time in history with something commensurate to his capacity for wonder.

And as I sat there brooding on the old, unknown world, I thought of Gatsby's wonder when he first picked out the green light at the end of Daisy's dock. He had come a long way to this blue lawn and his dream must have seemed so close that he could hardly fail to grasp it.

He did not know that it was already behind him, somewhere back in that vast obscurity beyond the city, where the dark fields of the republic rolled on under the night.

Gatsby believed in the green light, the orgastic future that year by year recedes before us. It eluded us then, but that's no matter — tomorrow we will run faster, stretch out our arms farther... And one fine morning —

So we beat on, boats against the current, borne back ceaselessly into the past.

Questions for Consideration and Discussion

1. In Chapter 3 of *The Great Gatsby*, did the partygoers treat Gatsby's place as a public amusement park or a private property? Before the narrator chanced to meet Gatsby, what rumors did some of the people say concerning Gatsby's identity? What did Jordan say about Gatsby's history?

2. In Chapter 3 (actually throughout this whole fiction), careless driving is depicted by Nick Carraway. When Nick reproached Jordan for not being a careful driver, Jordan responded, saying that other people would keep out of her way and that it took two careless people to make an accident. What's your comment on Jordan's psychology? If two careless people encounter one another, what will be the result?

3. The man with owl-eyed spectacles makes his appearance in both Chapter 3 and Chapter 9. What does he do in these chapters?

4. In both these two chapters, telephone repeatedly becomes part of the story plot. Please discuss how telephone discourse pushes the story forward.

5. Compare Gatsby's Schedule (as shown by his father) in Chapter 9 with Benjamin Franklin's schedule. In what ways are the two schedules similar and in what ways are they different?

John Steinbeck (1902 – 1968)

John Steinbeck, the Nobel Prize winner for literature in 1962, is best known for his fiction set in his native California during the Depression of the 1930s.

Steinbeck was born in Salinas, California. He supported himself from boyhood, working at a variety of manual jobs. This experience provided firsthand observation of the attitudes, manners, and language of the working people (in particular the migrant farm workers), laid the foundation of his sympathy with them, and established the characteristic tone of his novels.

When he was unable to complete his college studies at Stanford University, Steinbeck made his way to New York City on a cattle boat, hoping to get his early writing published. Failing this, he worked briefly as a newspaper reporter and then returned to California, where he continued to write while taking an assortment of jobs. During World War II he returned to Journalism, serving as a war correspondent in Italy.

Today, Steinbeck is primarily remembered for three of his many novels: *In Dubious Battle* (1936), *Of Mice and Men* (1937), and *The Grapes of Wrath* (1939). Among the three, *The Grapes of Wrath*, his Pulitzer Prize-winning novel, is the most important.

The subject of *In Dubious Battle* was a fruit pickers' strike. *Of Mice and Men* tells of the tragic friendship of two migrant workers. *The Grapes of Wrath* is an epic depiction of the Joad family, who, after losing their land in Oklahoma, migrated westward to California on U. S. Highway 66 looking for, but not finding, a better life. Through the struggles of their journey and the disillusionment that awaits them, they learn how poor, exploited people can unite as a community to survive. Combining naturalist and symbolist techniques to depict the characters' plights, the novel expresses compassion, outrage, and admiration for the working people. It remains one of the most powerfully moving books written about the Great Depression. Its impact has been compared to that of Harriet Beecher Stowe's *Uncle Tom's Cabin*. It provoked a wide debate about the hard lot of migrant laborers, and helped to put an agricultural reform into effect. Ma Joad's outcry sums up the sense of the times: "We ain' gonna die out. People is goin' on — changin' a little, maybe, but goin' right on."

Steinbeck's novels and stories usually offer a strong sense of social justice, a heightened sensitivity to the colors and textures of the American landscape, and a compelling plot. He is a regionalist as well as a naturalist.

Steinbeck won the Nobel Prize in 1962 for his overall achievements.

The Grapes of Wrath
(Excerpt)

Chapter 5

The owners of the land came onto the land, or more often a spokesman for the owners came. They came in closed cars, and they felt the dry earth with their fingers, and sometimes they drove big earth augers into the ground for soil tests. The tenants, from their sun-beaten dooryards, watched uneasily when the closed cars drove along the fields. And at last the owner men drove into the dooryards and sat in their cars to talk out of the windows. The tenant men stood beside the cars for a while, and then squatted on their hams and found sticks with which to mark the dust.

In the open doors the women stood looking out, and behind them the children — corn-headed children, with wide eyes, one bare foot on top of the other bare foot, and the toes working. The women and the children watched their men talking to the owner men. They were silent.

Some of the owner men were kind because they hated what they had to do, and some of them were angry because they hated to be cruel, and some of them were cold because they had long ago found that one could not be an owner unless one were cold. And all of them were caught in something larger than themselves. Some of them hated the mathematics that drove them, and some were afraid, and some worshiped the mathematics because it provided a refuge from thought and from feeling. If a bank or a finance company owned the land, the owner man said, The Bank — or the Company — needs — wants — insists — must have — as though the Bank or the Company were a monster, with thought and feeling, which had ensnared them. These last would take no responsibility for the banks or the companies because they were men and slaves, while the banks were machines and masters all at the same time. Some of the owner men were a little proud to be slaves to such cold and powerful masters. The owner men sat in the cars and explained. You know the land is poor. You've scrabbled at it long enough, God knows.

The squatting tenant men nodded and wondered and drew figures in the dust, and yes, they knew, God knows. If the dust only wouldn't fly. If the top would only stay on the soil, it might not be so bad.

The owner men went on leading to their point: You know the land's getting poorer. You know what cotton does to the land; robs it, sucks all the blood out of it.

The squatters nodded — they knew, God knew. If they could only rotate the crops they might pump blood back into the land.

Well, it's too late. And the owner men explained the workings and the thinkings of the monster that was stronger than they were. A man can hold land if he can just eat and pay taxes; he can do that.

Yes, he can do that until his crops fail one day and he has to borrow money from the bank.

But — you see, a bank or a company can't do that, because those creatures don't breathe air, don't eat side-meat. They breathe profits; they eat the interest on money. If they don't get it, they die the way you die without air, without side-meat. It is a sad thing, but it is so. It is just so.

The squatting men raised their eyes to understand. Can't we just hang on? Maybe the next year will be a good year. God knows how much cotton next year. And with all the wars — God knows what price cotton will bring. Don't they make explosives out of cotton? And uniforms? Get enough wars and cotton'll hit the ceiling. Next year, maybe. They looked up questioningly.

We can't depend on it. The bank — the monster has to have profits all the time. It can't wait. It'll die. No, taxes go on. When the monster stops growing, it dies. It can't stay one size.

Soft fingers began to tap the sill of the car window, and hard fingers tightened on the restless drawing sticks. In the doorways of the sun-beaten tenant houses, women sighed and then shifted feet so that the one that had been down was now on top, and the toes working. Dogs came sniffing near the owner cars and wetted on all four tires one after another. And chickens lay in the sunny dust and fluffed their feathers to get the cleansing dust down to the skin. In the little sties the pigs grunted inquiringly over the muddy remnants of the slops.

The squatting men looked down again. What do you want us to do? We can't take less share of the crop — we're half starved now. The kids are hungry all the time. We got no clothes, torn an' ragged. If all the neighbors weren't the same, we'd be ashamed to go to meeting.

And at last the owner men came to the point. The tenant system won't work any more. One man on a tractor can take the place of twelve or fourteen families. Pay him a wage and take all the crop. We have to do it. We don't like to do it. But the monster's sick. Something's happened to the monster.

But you'll kill the land with cotton. We know. We've got to take cotton quick before the land dies. Then we'll sell the land. Lots of families in the East would like to own a piece of land.

The tenant men looked up alarmed. But what'll happen to us? How'll we eat?

You'll have to get off the land. The plows'll go through the dooryard.

And now the squatting men stood up angrily. Grampa took up the land, and he had to kill the Indians and drive them away. And Pa was born here, and he killed weeds and snakes. Then a bad year came and he had to borrow a little money. An' we was born here. There in the door — our children born here. And Pa had to borrow money. The bank owned the land then, but we stayed and we got a little bit of what we raised.

We know that — all that. It's not us, it's the bank. A bank isn't like a man. Or an owner with fifty thousand acres, he isn't like a man either. That's the monster.

Sure, cried the tenant men, but it's our land. We measured it and broke it up. We were born on it, and we got killed on it, died on it. Even if it's no good, it's still ours. That's what makes it ours — being born on it, working it, dying on it. That makes ownership, not a paper with numbers on it.

We're sorry. It's not us. It's the monster. The bank isn't like a man.

Yes, but the bank is only made of men.

No, you're wrong there — quite wrong there. The bank is something else than men. It happens that every man in a bank hates what the bank does, and yet the bank does it. The bank is something more than men, I tell you. It's the monster. Men made it, but they can't control it.

The tenants cried, Grampa killed Indians, Pa killed snakes for the land. Maybe we can kill banks — they're worse than Indians and snakes. Maybe we got to fight to keep our land, like Pa and Grampa did.

And now the owner men grew angry. You'll have to go.

But it's ours, the tenant men cried. We —

No. The bank, the monster owns it. You'll have to go.

We'll get our guns, like Grampa when the Indians came. What then?

Well — first the sheriff, and then the troops. You'll be stealing if you try to stay, you'll be murderers if you kill to stay. The monster isn't men, but it can make men do what it wants.

But if we go, where'll we go? How'll we go? We got no money.

We're sorry, said the owner men. The bank, the fifty-thousand-acre owner can't be responsible. You're on land that isn't yours. Once over the line maybe you can pick cotton in the fall. Maybe you can go on relief. Why don't you go on west to California? There's work there, and it never gets cold. Why, you can reach out anywhere and pick an orange. Why, there's always some kind of crop to work in. Why don't you go there? And the owner men started their cars and rolled away.

The tenant men squatted down on their hams again to mark the dust with a stick, to figure, to wonder. Their sunburned faces were dark, and their sun-whipped eyes were light. The women moved cautiously out of the doorways toward their men, and the children crept behind the women, cautiously, ready to run. The bigger boys squatted beside their fathers, because that made them men. After a time the women asked, What did he want?

And the men looked up for a second, and the smolder of pain was in their eyes. We got to get off.

Where'll we go? the women asked.

We don't know. We don't know.

And the women went quickly, quietly back into the houses and herded the children ahead of them. They knew that a man so hurt and so perplexed may turn in anger, even on people he loves. They left the men alone to figure and to wonder in the dust.

After a time perhaps the tenant man looked about — at the pump put in ten years ago, with a goose-neck handle and iron flowers on the spout, at the chopping block where a thousand chickens had been killed, at the hand plow lying in the shed, and the patent crib hanging in the rafters over it.

The children crowded about the women in the houses. What we going to do, Ma? Where we going to go?

The women said, We don't know, yet. Go out and play. But don't go near your father. He might whale you if you go near him. And the women went on with the work, but all the time they watched the men squatting in the dust — perplexed and figuring.

The tractors came over the roads and into the fields, great crawlers moving like insects, having the incredible strength of insects. They crawled over the ground, laying the track and rolling on it and picking it up. Diesel tractors, puttering while they stood idle; they thundered when they moved, and then settled down to a droning roar. Snubnosed monsters, raising the dust and sticking their snouts into it, straight down the country, across the country, through fences, through dooryards, in and out of gullies in straight lines. They did not run on the ground, but on their own roadbeds. They ignored hills and gulches, water courses, fences, houses.

The man sitting in the iron seat did not look like a man; gloved, goggled, rubber dust mask over nose and mouth, he was a part of the monster, a robot in the seat. The thunder of the cylinders sounded through the country, became one with the air and the earth, so that earth and air muttered in sympathetic vibration. The driver could not control it — straight across country it went, cutting through a dozen farms and straight back. A twitch at the controls could swerve the cat', but the driver's hands could not twitch because the monster that built the tractors, the monster that sent the tractor out, had somehow got into the driver's hands, into his brain and muscle, had goggled him and muzzled him — goggled his mind, muzzled his speech, goggled his perception, muzzled his protest. He could not see the land as it was, he could not smell the land as it smelled; his feet did not stamp the clods or feel the warmth and power of the earth. He sat in an iron seat and stepped on iron pedals. He could not cheer or beat or curse or encourage the extension of his power, and because of this he could not cheer or whip or curse or encourage himself. He did not know or own or trust or beseech the land. If a seed dropped did not germinate, it was nothing. If the young thrusting plant withered in drought or drowned in a flood of rain, it was no more to the driver than to the tractor.

He loved the land no more than the bank loved the land. He could admire the tractor — its machined surfaces, its surge of power, the roar of its detonating cylinders; but it was not his tractor. Behind the tractor rolled the shining disks, cutting the earth with blades — not plowing but surgery, pushing the cut earth to the right where the second row of disks cut it and pushed it to the left; slicing blades shining, polished by the cut earth. And pulled behind the disks, the harrows combing with iron teeth so that the little clods broke up and the earth lay smooth. Behind the harrows, the long seeders — twelve curved iron penes erected in the foundry, orgasms set by gears, raping methodically, raping without passion. The driver sat in his iron seat and he was proud of the straight lines he did not will, proud of the tractor he did not own or love, proud of the power he could not control. And when that crop grew, and was harvested, no man had crumbled a hot clod in his fingers and let the earth sift past his fingertips. No man had touched the seed, or lusted for the growth. Men ate what they had not raised, had no connection with the bread. The land bore under iron, and under iron gradually died; for it was not loved or hated, it had no prayers or curses.

At noon the tractor driver stopped sometimes near a tenant house and opened his lunch: sandwiches wrapped in waxed paper, white bread, pickle, cheese, Spam, a piece of pie branded like an engine part. He ate without relish. And tenants not yet moved away came out to see him, looked curiously while the goggles were taken off, and the rubber dust mask, leaving white circles around the eyes and a large white circle around nose and mouth. The exhaust of the tractor puttered on, for fuel is so cheap it is more efficient to leave the engine running than to heat the Diesel nose for a new start. Curious children crowded close, ragged children who ate their fried dough as they watched. They watched hungrily the unwrapping of the sandwiches, and their hunger-sharpened noses smelled the pickle, cheese, and Spam. They didn't speak to the driver. They watched his hand as it carried food to his mouth. They did not watch him chewing; their eyes followed the hand that held the sandwich. After a while the tenant who could not leave the place came out and squatted in the shade beside the tractor.

"Why, you're Joe Davis's boy!"

"Sure," the driver said.

"Well, what you doing this kind of work for — against your own people?"

"Three dollars a day. I got damn sick of creeping for my dinner — and not getting it. I got a wife and kids. We got to eat. Three dollars a day, and it comes every day."

"That's right," the tenant said. "But for your three dollars a day fifteen or twenty families can't eat at all. Nearly a hundred people have to go out and wander on the roads for your three dollars a day. Is that right?"

And the driver said, "Can't think of that. Got to think of my own kids. Three dollars a day, and it comes every day. Times are changing, mister, don't you know? Can't make a living on the land unless you've got two, five, ten thousand acres and a tractor. Crop land isn't for little guys like us any more. You don't kick up a howl because you can't make Fords, or because you're not the telephone company. Well, crops are like that now. Nothing to do about it. You try to get three dollars a day someplace. That's the only way."

The tenant pondered. "Funny thing how it is. If a man owns a little property, that property is him, it's part of him, and it's like him. If he owns property only so he can walk on it and handle it and be sad when it isn't doing well, and feel fine when the rain falls on it, that property is him, and some way he's bigger because he owns it. Even if he isn't successful he's big with his property. That is so."

And the tenant pondered more. "But let a man get property he doesn't see, or can't take time to get his fingers in, or can't be there to walk on it — why, then the property is the man. He can't do what he wants, he can't think what he wants. The property is the man, stronger than he is. And he is small, not big. Only his possessions are big — and he's the servant of his property. That is so, too."

The driver munched the branded pie and threw the crust away. "Times are changed, don't you know? Thinking about stuff like that don't feed the kids. Get your three dollars a day, feed your kids. You got no call to worry about anybody's kids but your own. You get a reputation for talking like that, and you'll never get three dollars a day. Big shots won't give you three dollars a day if you worry about anything but your three dollars a day."

"Nearly a hundred people on the road for your three dollars. Where will we go?"

"And that reminds me," the driver said, "you better get out soon. I'm going through the dooryard after dinner."

"You filled in the well this morning."

"I know. Had to keep the line straight. But I'm going through the dooryard after dinner. Got to keep the lines straight. And — well, you know Joe Davis, my old man, so I'll tell you this. I got orders wherever there's a family not moved out — if I have an accident — you know, get too close and cave the house in a little — well, I might get a couple of dollars. And my youngest kid never had no shoes yet."

"I built it with my hands. Straightened old nails to put the sheathing on. Rafters are wired to the stringers with baling wire. It's mine. I built it. You bump it down — I'll be in the window with a rifle. You even come too close and I'll pot you like a rabbit. "

"It's not me. There's nothing I can do. I'll lose my job if I don't do it. And look — suppose you kill me? They'll just hang you, but long before you're hung there'll be another guy on the tractor, and he'll bump the house down. You're not killing the right guy. "

"That's so," the tenant said. "Who gave you orders? I'll go after him. He's the one to kill. "

"You're wrong. He got his orders from the bank. The bank told him, ' Clear those people out or it's your job. ' "

"Well, there's a president of the bank. There's a board of directors. I'll fill up the magazine of the rifle and go into the bank. "

The driver said, "Fellow was telling me the bank gets orders from the East. The orders were, ' Make the land show profit or we'll close you up. ' "

"But where does it stop? Who can we shoot? I don't aim to starve to death before I kill the man that's starving me. "

"I don't know. Maybe there's nobody to shoot. Maybe the thing isn't men at all. Maybe like you said, the property's doing it. Anyway I told you my orders. "

"I got to figure," the tenant said. "We all got to figure. There's some way to stop this. It's not like lightning or earthquakes. We've got a bad thing made by men, and by God that's something we can change. " The tenant sat in his doorway, and the driver thundered his engine and started off, tracks falling and curving, harrows combing, and the phalli of the seeder slipping into the ground. Across the dooryard the tractor cut, and the hard, foot-beaten ground was seeded field, and the tractor cut through again; the uncut space was ten feet wide. And back he came. The iron guard bit into the house-corner, crumbled the wall, and wrenched the little house from its foundation so that it fell sideways, crushed like a bug. And the driver was goggled and a rubber mask covered his nose and mouth. The tractor cut a straight line on, and the air and the ground vibrated with its thunder. The tenant man stared after it, his rifle in his hand. His wife was beside him, and the quiet children behind. And all of them stared after the tractor.

▶ Questions for Consideration and Discussion

1. How are the land owners portrayed and presented?
2. What is/are compared to a monster? How do you like the comparison?
3. What naturalistic view is represented in the chapter?
4. What point made by the author/narrator impresses you most? Why?

William Faulkner(1897 – 1962)

William Faulkner, the recipient of the Nobel Prize for Literature in 1950, is a literary giant from the American South who is best remembered as the creator of fictional cosmos "Yoknapatawpha County. " He is both an avant-garde modernist and a writer of the agrarian American South.

Faulkner came from an old southern family named Falkner, which Faulkner changed by adding "u" in his own name. He grew up in Oxford, Mississippi. His family was proud of its southern heritage, especially of his paternal great-grandfather, who had served as a Colonel in the Confederate Army, lawyer, railroad builder, financier, politician, and author of a popular Romantic novel, *The White Rose of Memphis*. When Faulkner, in third grade, was asked what he wanted to do when he grew up, his prompt reply was: "I want to be a writer like my great-granddaddy. "

Like many writers of his generation, Faulkner was eager to go off to war. He joined the Royal Flying Corps in Canada and was still under training when the war was over. He returned to the United States, attended the University of Mississippi for a year, drifted from one job to another and wrote poetry. In 1925, he went to New Orleans, where, for the first time, he met and mingled with literary people, including Sherwood Anderson, who encouraged Faulkner to develop his own style, to concentrate on prose, and to use his region for material. Faulkner wrote his first novel, *Soldier's Pay*, in New Orleans, and with the recommendation of Anderson it was published in 1926. He learned about the experimental writing of James Joyce and of the ideas of Sigmund Freud.

Faulkner spent most of his remaining years in his native town Oxford, working on his novels and short stories at a farm. He set the majority of his later fiction in his native region, which he renamed Yoknapatawpha County. In this locale of his imaginative world, Faulkner populated with a broad spectrum of remarkable characters — farmers, hunters, aristocrats, businessmen, former black slaves, dispossessed Indians, and several generations of whole families moving on different levels of southern society. Each story and each novel contributes to the construction of a whole. Their theme is the decay of the old South (as represented by the Sartoris and Compson families) and the emergence of ruthless and brash newcomers (represented by the Snopeses).

Now, William Faulkner is best remembered for his sequence of modernist novels, *The Sound and the Fury* (1929) (Faulkner's favorite novel), *As I Lay Dying* (1930), *Light in August* (1931), and *Absalom, Absalom!* (1936). After *Absalom, Absalom!* Faulkner continued to write novels and short stories, but none of them was as highly regarded as his early sequence of books. During World War II Faulkner's popularity declined further. His books went out of print, and he supported himself by screenwriting. However, the publication of *The Portable Faulkner* (an anthology of his writings) in 1946 made his national reputation soar again. He already had a major reputation abroad, especially in France, where his work in translation was influential. In 1948, he published his antiracist novel *Intruder in the Dust*. This novel occasioned the award of the Noble Prize in 1950.

He died of a heart attack at the age of 65 in 1962.

The short story "Dry September," herein anthologized, was published in 1931.

Dry September

I

Through the bloody September twilight, aftermath of sixty-two rainless days, it had gone like a fire in dry grass — the rumor, the story, whatever it was. Something about Miss Minnie Cooper and a Negro. Attacked, insulted, frightened: none of them, gathered in the barber shop on that Saturday evening where the ceiling fan stirred, without freshening it, the vitiated air sending back upon them, in recurrent surges of stale pomade and lotion, their own stale breath and odors, knew exactly what had happened.

"Except it wasn't Will Mayes," a barber said. He was a man of middle age; a thin, sand-colored man with a mild face, who was shaving a client. "I know Will Mayes. He's a good nigger. And I know Miss Minnie Cooper, too."

"What do you know about her?" a second barber said.

"Who is she?" the client said. "A young girl?"

"No," the barber said. "She's about forty, I reckon. She ain't married. That's why I don't believe — "

"Believe, hell!" a hulking youth in a sweat-stained silk shirt said. "Won't you take a white woman's word before a nigger's?"

"I don't believe Will Mayes did it," the barber said. "I know Will Mayes."

"Maybe you know who did it, then. Maybe you already got him out of town, you damn niggerlover."

"I don't believe anybody did anything. I don't believe anything happened. I leave it to you fellows if them ladies that get old without getting married don't have notions that a man cant — "

"Then you are a hell of a white man," the client said. He moved under the cloth. The youth had sprung to his feet.

"You don't?" he said. "Do you accuse a white woman of lying?"

The barber held the razor poised above the half-risen client. He did not look around.

"It's this durn weather," another said. "It's enough to make a man do anything. Even to her."

Nobody laughed. The barber said in his mild, stubborn tone: "I ain't accusing nobody of nothing. I just know and you fellows know how a woman that never — "

"You damn niggerlover!" the youth said.

"Shut up, Butch," another said. "We'll get the facts in plenty of time to act."

"Who is? Who's getting them?" the youth said. "Facts, hell! I — "

"You're a fine white man," the client said. "Ain't you?" In his frothy beard he looked like a desert rat in the moving pictures. "You tell them, Jack," he said to the youth. "If there ain't any white men in this town, you can count on me, even if I ain't only a drummer and a stranger."

"That's right, boys," the barber said. "Find out the truth first. I know Will Mayes."

"Well, by God!" the youth shouted. "To think that a white man in this town — "

"Shut up, Butch," the second speaker said. "We got plenty of time."

The client sat up. He looked at the speaker. "Do you claim that anything excuses a nigger attacking a white woman? Do you mean to tell me you are a white man and you'll stand for it? You better go back North where you came from. The South don't want your kind here."

"North what?" the second said. "I was born and raised in this town."

"Well, by God!" the youth said. He looked about with a strained, baffled gaze, as if he was trying to remember what it was he wanted to say or to do. He drew his sleeve across his sweating face. "Damn if I'm going to let a white woman — "

"You tell them, Jack," the drummer said. "By God, if they — "

The screen door crashed open. A man stood in the floor, his feet apart and his heavy-set body poised easily. His white shirt was open at the throat; he wore a felt hat. His hot, bold glance swept the group. His name was McLendon. He had commanded troops at the front in France and had been decorated for valor.

"Well," he said, "are you going to sit there and let a black son rape a white woman on the streets of Jefferson?"

Butch sprang up again. The silk of his shirt clung flat to his heavy shoulders. At each armpit was a dark halfmoon. "That's what I been telling them! That's what I — "

"Did it really happen?" a third said. "This ain't the first man scare she ever had, like Hawkshaw says. Wasn't there something about a man on the kitchen roof, watching her undress, about a year ago?"

"What?" the client said. "What's that?" The barber had been slowly forcing him back into the chair; he arrested himself reclining, his head lifted, the barber still pressing him down.

McLendon whirled on the third speaker. "Happen? What the hell difference does it make? Are you going to let the black sons get away with it until one really does it?"

"That's what I'm telling them!" Butch shouted. He cursed, long and steady, pointless.

"Here, here," a fourth said. "Not so loud. Don't talk so loud."

"Sure," McLendon said; "no talking necessary at all. I've done my talking. Who's with me?" He poised on the balls of his feet, roving his gaze.

The barber held the drummer's face down, the razor poised. "Find out the facts first, boys. I know Willy Mayes. It wasn't him. Let's get the sheriff and do this thing right."

McLendon whirled upon him his furious, rigid face. The barber did not look away. They looked like men of different races. The other barbers had ceased also above their prone clients. "You mean to tell me," McLendon said, "that you'd take a nigger's word before a white woman's? Why, you damn niggerloving — "

The third speaker rose and grasped McLendon's arm; he too had been a soldier. "Now, now. Let's figure this thing out. Who knows anything about what really happened?"

"Figure out hell!" McLendon jerked his arm free. "All that're with me get up from there. The ones that ain't — " He roved his gaze, dragging his sleeve across his face.

Three men rose. The drummer in the chair sat up. "Here," he said, jerking at the cloth about his neck. "Get this rag off me. I'm with him. I don't live here, but by God, if our mothers and wives and sisters — " He smeared the cloth over his face and flung it to the floor. McLendon stood in the floor and cursed the others. Another rose and moved toward him. The remainder sat uncomfortable, not looking at one another, then one by one they rose and joined him.

The barber picked the cloth from the floor. He began to fold it neatly. "Boys, don't do that. Will Mayes never done it. I know."

"Come on," McLendon said. He whirled. From his hip pocket protruded the butt of a heavy automatic pistol. They went out. The screen door crashed behind them reverberant in the dead air.

The barber wiped the razor carefully and swiftly, and put it away, and ran to the rear, and took his hat from the wall. "I'll be back as soon as I can," he said to the other barbers. "I can't let — " He went out, running. The two other barbers followed him to the door and caught it on the re-bound, leaning out and looking up the street after him. The air was flat and dead. It had a metallic taste at the base of the tongue.

"What can he do?" the first said. The second one was saying "Jees Christ, Jees Christ" under his breath. "I'd just as lief be Will Mayes as Hawk, if he gets McLendon riled."

"Jees Christ, Jees Christ," the second whispered.

"You reckon he really done it to her?" the first said.

II

She was thirty-eight or thirty-nine. She lived in a small frame house with her invalid mother and a thin, sallow, un-flagging aunt, where each morning between ten and eleven she would appear on the porch in a lace-trimmed boudoir cap, to sit swinging in the porch swing until noon. After dinner she lay down for a while, until the afternoon began to cool. Then, in one of the three or four new voile dresses which she had each summer, she would go downtown to spend the afternoon in the stores with the other ladies, where they would handle the goods and haggle over the prices in cold, immediate voices, without any intention of buying.

She was of comfortable people — not the best in Jefferson, but good people enough — and she was still on the slender side of ordinary looking, with a bright, faintly haggard manner and dress. When she was young she had a slender, nervous body and a sort of hard vivacity which had enabled her for a time to ride upon the crest of the town's social life as exemplified by the high school party and church social period of her contemporaries while still children enough to be unclassconscious.

She was the last to realize that she was losing ground; that those among whom she had been a little brighter and louder flame than any other were beginning to learn the pleasure of snobbery — male — and retaliation — female. That was when her face began to wear that bright, haggard look. She still carried it to parties on shadowy porticoes and summer lawns, like a mask or a flag, with that bafflement of furious repudiation of truth in her eyes. One evening at a party she heard a boy and two girls, all schoolmates, talking. She never accepted another invitation.

She watched the girls with whom she had grown up as they married and got homes and children, but no man ever called on her steadily until the children of the other girls had been calling her "aunty" for several years, the while their mothers told them in bright voices about how popular Aunt Minnie had been as a girl. Then the town began to see her driving on Sunday afternoons with the cashier in the bank. He was a widower of about forty — a high-colored man, smelling always faintly of the barber shop or of whisky. He owned the first automobile in town, a red runabout; Minnie had the first motoring bonnet and veil the town ever saw. Then the town began to say: "Poor Minnie." "But she is old enough to take care of herself," others said. That was when she began to ask her old schoolmates that their children call her "cousin" instead of "aunty."

It was twelve years now since she had been relegated into adultery by public opinion, and eight years since the cashier had gone to a Memphis bank, returning for one day each Christmas, which he spent at an annual bachelors' party at a hunting club on the river. From behind their curtains the neighbors would see the party pass, and during the over-the-way Christmas day visiting they would tell her about him, about how well he looked, and how they heard that he was prospering in the city, watching with bright, secret eyes her haggard, bright face. Usually by that hour there would be the scent of whisky on her breath. It was supplied her by a youth, a clerk at the soda fountain: "Sure; I buy it for the old gal. I reckon she's entitled to a little fun."

Her mother kept to her room altogether now; the gaunt aunt ran the house. Against that background Minnie's bright dresses, her idle and empty days, had a quality of furious unreality. She went out in the evenings only with women now, neighbors, to the moving pictures. Each afternoon she dressed in one of the new dresses and went downtown alone, where her young "cousins" were already strolling in the late afternoons with their delicate, silken heads and thin, awkward arms and conscious hips, clinging to one another or shrieking and giggling with paired boys in the soda fountain when she passed and went on along the serried store fronts, in the doors of which the sitting and lounging men did not even follow her with their eyes any more.

III

The barber went swiftly up the street where the sparse lights, insect-swirled, glared in rigid and violent suspension in the lifeless air. The day had died in a pall of dust; above the darkened square, shrouded by the spent dust, the sky was as clear as the inside of a brass bell. Below the cast was a rumor of the twice-waxed moon.

When he overtook them McLendon and three others were getting into a car parked in an alley. McLendon stooped his thick head, peering out beneath the top. "Changed your mind, did you?" he said. "Damn good thing; by God, tomorrow when this town hears about how you talked tonight — "

"Now, now," the other ex-soldier said. "Hawkshaw's all right. Come on, Hawk, jump in. "

"Will Mayes never done it, boys," the barber said. "If anybody done it. Why, you all know well as I do there ain't any town where they got better niggers than us. And you know how a lady will kind of think things about men when there ain't any reason to, and Miss Minnie anyway — "

"Sure, sure," the soldier said. "We're just going to talk to him a little; that's all. "

"Talk hell!" Butch said. "When we're through with the — "

"Shut up, for God's sake!" the soldier said. "Do you want everybody in town — "

"Tell them, by God!" McLendon said. "Tell every one of the sons that'll let a white woman — "

"Let's go; let's go: here's the other car." The second car slid squealing out of a cloud of dust at the alley mouth. McLendon started his car and took the lead. Dust lay like fog in the street. The street lights hung nimbused as in water. They drove on out of town.

A rutted lane turned at right angles. Dust hung above it too, and above all the land. The dark bulk of the ice plant, where the Negro Mayes was night watchman, rose against the sky. "Better stop here, hadn't we?" the soldier said. McLendon did not reply. He hurled the car up and slammed to a stop, the headlights glaring on the blank wall.

"Listen here, boys," the barber said; "if he's here, don't that prove he never done it? Don't it? If it was him, he would run. Don't you see he would?" The second car came up and stopped. McLendon got down; Butch sprang down beside him. "Listen, boys," the barber said.

"Cut the lights off!" McLendon said. The breathless dark rushed down. There was no sound in it save their lungs as they sought air in the parched dust in which for two months they had lived; then the diminishing crunch of McLendon's and Butch's feet, and a moment later McLendon's voice:

"Will! ... Will!"

Below the cast the wan hemorrhage of the moon increased. It heaved above the ridge, silvering the air, the dust, so that they seemed to breathe, live, in a bowl of molten lead. There was no sound of nightbird nor insect, no sound save their breathing and a faint ticking of contracting metal about the cars. Where their bodies touched one another they seemed to sweat dryly, for no more moisture came. "Christ! " a voice said; "let's get out of here. "

But they didn't move until vague noises began to grow out of the darkness ahead; then they got out and waited tensely in the breathless dark. There was another sound: a blow, a hissing expulsion of breath and McLendon cursing in undertone. They stood a moment longer, then they ran forward. They ran in a stumbling clump, as though they were fleeing something. "Kill him, kill the son," a voice whispered. McLendon flung them back.

"Not here," he said. "Get him into the car." "Kill him, kill the black son!" the voice murmured. They dragged the Negro to the car. The barber had waited beside the car. He could feel himself sweating and he knew he was going to be sick at the stomach.

"What is it, captains?" the Negro said. "I ain't done nothing. 'Fore God, Mr. John." Someone produced handcuffs. They worked busily about the Negro as though he were a post, quiet, intent, getting in one another's way. He submitted to the handcuffs, looking swiftly and constantly from dim face to dim face. "Who's here, captains?" he said, leaning to peer into the faces until they could feel his breath and smell his sweaty reek. He spoke a name or two. "What you all say I done, Mr. John?"

Mclendon jerked the car door open. "Get in!" he said.

The Negro did not move. "What you all going to do with me, Mr. John? I ain't done nothing. White folks, captains, I ain't done nothing: I swear 'fore God." He called another name.

"Get in!" McLendon said. He struck the Negro. The others expelled their breath in a dry hissing and struck him with random blows and he whirled and cursed them, and swept his manacled hands across their faces and slashed the barber upon the mouth, and the barber struck him also. "Get him in there," McLendon said. They pushed at him. He ceased struggling and got in and sat quietly as the others took their places. He sat between the barber and the soldier, drawing his limbs in so as not to touch them, his eyes going swiftly and constantly from face to face. Butch clung to the running board. The car moved on. The barber nursed his mouth with his handkerchief.

"What's the matter, Hawk?" the soldier said.

"Nothing," the barber said. They regained the highroad and turned away from town. The second car dropped back out of the dust. They went on, gaining speed; the final fringe of houses dropped behind.

"Goddamn, he stinks!" the soldier said.

"We'll fix that," the drummer in front beside McLendon said. On the running board Butch cursed into the hot rush of air. The barber leaned suddenly forward and touched McLendon's arm.

"Let me out, John," he said.

"Jump out, niggerlover," McLendon said without turning his head. He drove swiftly. Behind them the sourceless lights of the second car glared in the dust. Presently McLendon turned into a narrow road. It was rutted with disuse. It led back to an abandoned brick kiln — a series of reddish mounds and weed- and vine-choked vats without bottom. It had been used for pasture once, until one day the owner missed one of his mules. Although he prodded carefully in the vats with a long pole, he could not even find the bottom of them.

"John," the barber said.

"Jump out, then," McLendon said, hurling the car along the ruts. Beside the barber the Negro spoke: "Mr. Henry."

The barber sat forward. The narrow tunnel of the road rushed up and past. Their motion was like an extinct furnace blast: cooler, but utterly dead. The car bounded from rut to rut.

"Mr. Henry," the Negro said.

The barber began to tug furiously at the door. "Look out, there!" the soldier said, but the barber had already kicked the door open and swung onto the running board. The soldier leaned across the Negro and grasped at him, but he had already jumped. The car went on without checking speed.

The impetus hurled him crashing through dust-sheathed weeds, into the ditch. Dust puffed about him, and in a thin, vicious crackling of sapless stems he lay choking and retching until the second car passed and died away. Then he rose and limped on until he reached the highroad and turned toward town, brushing at his clothes with his hands. The moon was higher, riding high and clear of the dust at last, and after a while the town began to glare beneath the dust. He went on, limping. Presently he heard cars and the glow of them grew in the dust behind him and he left the road and crouched again in the weeds until they passed. McLendon's car came last now. There were four people in it and Butch was not on the running board.

They went on; the dust swallowed them; the glare and the sound died away. The dust of them hung for a while, but soon the eternal dust absorbed it again. The barber climbed back onto the road and limped on toward town.

IV

As she dressed for supper on that Saturday evening, her own flesh felt like fever. Her hands trembled among the hooks and eyes, and her eyes had a feverish look, and her hair swirled crisp and crackling under the comb. While she was still dressing the friends called for her and sat while she donned her sheerest underthings and stockings and a new voile dress. "Do you feel strong enough to go out?" they said, their eyes bright too, with a dark glitter. "When you have had time to get over the shock, you must tell us what happened. What he said and did; everything."

In the leafed darkness, as they walked toward the square, she began to breathe deeply, something like a swimmer preparing to dive, until she ceased trembling, the four of them walking slowly because of the terrible heat and out of solicitude for her. But as they neared the square she began to tremble again, walking with her head up, her hands clenched at her sides, their voices about her murmurous, also with that feverish, glittering quality of their eyes.

They entered the square, she in the center of the group, fragile in her fresh dress. She was trembling worse. She walked slower and slower, as children eat ice cream, her head up and her eyes bright in the haggard banner of her face, passing the hotel and the coatless drummers in chairs along the curb looking around at her: "that's the one: see? The one in pink in the middle." "Is that her? What did they do with the nigger? Did they — ?" "Sure. He's all right." "All right, is he?" "Sure. He went on a little trip." Then the drug store, where even the young men lounging in the door-way tipped their hats and followed with their eyes the motion of her hips and legs when she passed.

They went on, passing the lifted hats of the gentlemen, the suddenly ceased voices, deferent, protective. "Do you see?" the friends said. Their voices sounded like long, hovering sighs of hissing exultation. "There's not a Negro on the square. Not one."

They reached the picture show. It was like a miniature fairyland with its lighted lobby and colored lithographs of life caught in its terrible and beautiful mutations. Her lips began to tingle. In the dark, when the picture began, it would be all right; she could hold back the laughing so it would not waste away so fast and so soon. So she hurried on before the turning faces, the undertones of low astonishment, and they took their accustomed places where she could see the aisle against the silver glare and the young men and girls coming in two and two against it.

The lights flicked away; the screen glowed silver, and soon life began to unfold, beautiful and passionate and sad, while still the young men and girls entered, scented and sibilant in the half dark, their paired backs in silhouette delicate and sleek, their slim, quick bodies awkward, divinely young, while beyond them the silver dream accumulated, inevitably on and on. She began to laugh. In trying to suppress it, it made more noise than ever; heads began to turn. Still laughing, her friends raised her and led her out, and she stood at the curb, laughing on a high, sustained note, until the taxi came up and they helped her in.

They removed the pink voile and the sheer underthings and the stockings, and put her to bed, and cracked ice for her temples, and sent for the doctor. He was hard to locate, so they ministered to her with hushed ejaculations, renewing the ice and fanning her. While the ice was fresh and cold she stopped laughing and lay still for a time, moaning only a little. But soon the laughing welled again and her voice rose screaming.

"Shhhhhhhhhhh! Shhhhhhhhhhhhhh!" They said, freshening the icepack, smoothing her hair, examining it for gray; "poor girl!" Then to one another: "Do you suppose anything really happened?" their eyes darkly aglitter, secret and passionate. "Shhhhhhhhhh! Poor girl! Poor Minnie!"

V

It was midnight when McLendon drove up to his neat new house. It was trim and fresh as a birdcage and almost as small, with its clean, green-and-white paint. He locked the car and mounted the porch and entered. His wife rose from a chair beside the reading lamp. McLendon stopped in the floor and stared at her until she looked down.

"Look at that clock," he said, lifting his arm, pointing. She stood before him, her face lowered, a magazine in her hands. Her face was pale, strained, and weary-looking. "Haven't I told you about sitting up like this, waiting to see when I come in?"

"John," she said. She laid the magazine down. Poised on the balls of his feet, he glared at her with his hot eyes, his sweating face.

"Didn't I tell you?" He went toward her. She looked up then. He caught her shoulder. She stood passive, looking at him.

He went on through the house, ripping off his shirt, and on the dark, screened porch at the rear he stood and mopped his head and shoulders with the shirt and flung it away. He took the pistol from his hip and laid it on the table beside the bed, and sat on the bed and removed his shoes, and rose and slipped his trousers off. He was sweating again already, and he stooped and hunted furiously for the shirt. At last he found it and wiped his body again, and, with his body pressed against the dusty screen, he stood panting. There was no movement, no sound, not even an insect. The dark world seemed to lie stricken beneath the cold moon and the lidless stars.

▶▶ Questions for Consideration and Discussion

1. What effect is achieved by the abrupt shifts of point of view among the five sections of the story?

2. Besides time and place, setting can also include the weather — which, in some stories, may be crucial. In what way does climate seem as substantial as any character in "Dry September"? Do you think that climate can play an important role in determining people's behaviors? Please explain.

3. What purpose does Hawkshaw serve in the story?

4. The four seasons of the year are often analogized to human's stages of life-time. In what way do you think "Dry September" is a perfect title to the story?

Eugene O'Neill (1888 – 1953)

Eugene O'Neill, the winner of four Pulitzer Prizes for Drama and the 1936 Nobel Prize for Literature, is America's first major — as well as premier — playwright, the first to explore serious themes in the theater and to experiment with theatrical conventions. He enjoys the distinguishing credit of raising American dramatic theater from its narrow origins to an art form respected around the world.

O'Neill was born into an actor's family. His father James O'Neill made a fortune playing the lead role in the popular melodrama *The Count of Monte Cristo*, which he played on tour more than five thousand times. His mother Ella Quinlan hated backstage life and escaped her misery by taking morphine. His older brother James Jr. , born in 1878 and during most of Eugene's childhood away at various boarding schools, ended up becoming an actor and an alcoholic.

During O'Neill's childhood, his parents toured for part of every year, lived in New York City hotels for another part, and spent summers at their home in New London, Connecticut. Young Eugene spent much of his early years on national tours with his parents.

O'Neill went to good preparatory schools and started college at Princeton in 1906. But he quit after a year. For the next five years, he drank and drifted. He eloped, but the marriage was quickly terminated. He shipped out to sea for a year, and he searched for gold in South Africa. But most of the time, he spent in Greenwich Village — an area of lower Manhattan that was becoming home to artists and political radicals. In 1912, O'Neill became ill with tuberculosis, and was inspired to become a playwright while reading during his recovery.

Many of O'Neill's first plays were grim one-acters based on his experiences at sea. In the 1920s, he rejected realism in an effort to capture on the stage the forces behind human life. His plays became longer, and he began to experiment with techniques to convey inner emotions — the world of the mind, of memories and fears.

O'Neill's father had died in 1920, his mother in 1921, and his brother in 1923. During the mid-1920s, O'Neill became interested in dramatizing the complicated pattern of his family's life. He was influenced by the ideas of Sigmund Freud: the power of irrational drives; the existence of a subconscious; the roles of repression, suppression and inhibition in the formation of personality in adult suffering; the importance of sex; and above all, the lifelong influence of parents.

The 1920s witnessed O'Neill to win Pulitzer Prizes for three of his plays: *Beyond the Horizon* (1920), *Anna Christie* (1922), *Strange Interlude* (1928). He was awarded the Nobel Prize for Literature in 1936. However, today, he is best known for the work he wrote after his Nobel Prize, particularly his two later plays, *The Iceman Cometh* (1946) and *Long Day's Journey into Night*, which was published in 1956 and awarded Pulitzer Prize the following year.

Long Day's Journey into Night, O'Neill's semi-autobiography, is probably his most famous work. It concerns the Tyrone family — consisting of father James, mother Mary, and their sons Jamie and Edmund. James is a miserly actor; Mary is addicted to morphine; Jamie is alcoholic; and Edmund is ill with tuberculosis. "Long Day" refers to the time-dimensional setting of the play, which takes place during one day.

The play is set on a single day, but for the Tyrones, the implication is that every day is exactly the same. The Tyrones are at the mercy of the past, and they are haunted by their old memories, old dreams and ambitions, and old disappointments. This results in the fact that every day is full of the same arguments, dismays, and regrets. It is a literal day in the lives of the Tyrones, but it is also the Tyrones' journey through life toward death. Each Tyrone was both a victim and an oppressor. The audience's sympathy shifts throughout the play, alternately condemning and forgiving each character.

O'Neill called the drama "a play of old sorrow, written in tears and blood. " As he lay dying, he sent the drama in a sealed envelope to his publisher, stipulating that it should only be opened and read "twenty-five years after my death. " Even then, it should never be performed. Fortunately, O'Neill's widow disobeyed O'Neill's instructions and allowed it to be staged.

O'Neill began to suffer from Parkinson's disease in the 1930s and lived in relative seclusion for the last twenty years of his life.

Long Day's Journey into Night
(Excerpt)

CHARACTERS:
JAMES TYRONE
MARY CAVAN TYRONE, *James Tyrone's wife*
JAMES TYRONE, JR., *their elder son*
EDMUND TYRONE, *their younger son*
CATHLEEN, *second girl* ①

SCENES:
> ACT 1 *Living room of the Tyrones' summer home* 8:30 a. m. *of a day in August*, 1912
> ACT 2 SCENE 1 *The same, around* 12:45
> SCENE 2 *The same, about a half hour later*
> ACT 3 *The same, around* 6:30 *that evening*
> ACT 4 *The same, around midnight*

---

① second girl: a female house-servant.

Act 3

SCENE — *The same. It is around half past six in the evening. Dusk is gathering in the living room, an early dusk due to the fog which has rolled in from the Sound and is like a white curtain drawn down outside the windows. From a lighthouse beyond the harbor's mouth, a foghorn is heard at regular intervals, moaning like a mournful whale in labor, and from the harbor itself, intermittently, comes the warning ringing of bells on yachts at anchor.*

The tray with the bottle of whiskey, glasses, and pitcher of ice water is on the table, as it was in the pre-luncheon scene of the previous act.

MARY *and the second girl,* CATHLEEN, *are discovered. The latter is standing at left of table. She holds an empty whiskey glass in her hand as if she'd forgotten she had it. She shows the effects of drink. Her stupid, good-humored face wears a pleased and flattered simper.*

MARY *is paler than before and her eyes shine with unnatural brilliance. The strange detachment in her manner has intensified. She has hidden deeper within herself and found refuge and release in a dream where present reality is but an appearance to be accepted and dismissed unfeelingly — even with a hard cynicism — or entirely ignored. There is at times an uncanny gay, free youthfulness in her manner, as if in spirit she were released to become again, simply and without self-consciousness, the naive, happy, chattering schoolgirl of her convent days. She wears the dress into which she had changed for her drive to town, a simple, fairly expensive affair, which would be extremely becoming if it were not for the careless, almost slovenly way she wears it. Her hair is no longer fastidiously in place. It has a slightly disheveled, lopsided look. She talks to CATHLEEN with a confiding familiarity, as if the second girl were an old, intimate friend. As the curtain rises, she is standing by the screen door looking out. A moan of the foghorn is heard.*

MARY: [*amused — girlishly*] That foghorn! Isn't it awful, Cathleen?

CATHLEEN: [*talks more familiarly than usual but never with intentional impertinence because she sincerely likes her mistress*] It is indeed, Ma'am. It's like a banshee.

MARY: [*Goes on as if she hadn't heard. In nearly all the following dialogue there is the feeling that she has* CATHLEEN *with her merely as an excuse to keep talking.*] I don't mind it tonight. Last night it drove me crazy. I lay awake worrying until I couldn't stand it any more.

CATHLEEN: Bad cess to it①. I was scared out of my wits riding back from town. I thought that ugly monkey, Smythe, would drive us in a ditch or against a tree. You couldn't see your hand in front of you. I'm glad you had me sit in back with you, Ma'am. If I'd been in

---

① Bad cess to it: Bad luck to it (Irish).

front with that monkey — He can't keep his dirty hands to himself. Give him half a chance and he's pinching me on the leg or you-know-where — asking your pardon, Ma'am, but it's true.

MARY: [*dreamily*] It wasn't the fog I minded, Cathleen, I really love fog.

CATHLEEN: They say it's good for the complexion.

MARY: It hides you from the world and the world from you. You feel that everything has changed, and nothing is what it seemed to be. No one can find or touch you any more.

CATHLEEN: I wouldn't care so much if Smythe was a fine, handsome man like some chauffeurs I've seen — I mean, if it was all in fun, for I'm a decent girl. But for a shriveled runt like Smythe — ! I've told him, you must think I'm hard up that I'd notice a monkey like you. I've warned him, one day I'll give a clout that'll knock him into next week. And so I will!

MARY: It's the foghorn I hate. It won't let you alone. It keeps reminding you, and warning you, and calling you back. [*She smiles strangely.*] But it can't tonight. It's just an ugly sound. It doesn't remind me of anything. [*She gives a teasing, girlish laugh.*] Except, perhaps, Mr. Tyrone's snores. I've always had such fun teasing him about it. He has snored ever since I can remember, especially when he's had too much to drink, and yet he's like a child, he hates to admit it. [*She laughs, coming to the table.*] Well, I suppose I snore at times, too, and I don't like to admit it. So I have no right to make fun of him, have I? [*She sits on the rocker at right of table.*]

CATHLEEN: Ah, sure, everybody healthy snores. It's a sign of sanity, they say. [*then, worriedly*] What time is it, Ma'am? I ought to go back in the kitchen. The damp is in Bridget's rheumatism and she's like a raging devil. She'll bite my head off.

[*She puts her glass on the table and makes a movement toward the back parlor.*]

MARY: [*with a flash of apprehension*] No, don't go, Cathleen. I don't want to be alone, yet.

CATHLEEN: You won't be for long. The Master and the boys will be home soon.

MARY: I doubt if they'll come back for dinner. They have too good an excuse to remain in the barrooms where they feel at home.

[CATHLEEN stares at her, stupidly puzzled, MARY goes on smilingly]
Don't worry about Bridget. I'll tell her I kept you with me, and you can take a big drink of whiskey to her when you go. She won't mind then.

CATHLEEN: [*grins — at her ease again*] No, Ma'am. That's the one thing can make her cheerful. She loves her drop.

MARY: Have another drink yourself, if you wish, Cathleen.

CATHLEEN: I don't know if I'd better, Ma'am. I can feel what I've had already, [*reaching for the bottle*] Well, maybe one more won't harm. [*She pours a drink.*] Here's your good health, Ma'am. [*She drinks without bothering about a chaser.*]

MARY: [*dreamily*] I really did have good health once, Cathleen. But that was long ago.

CATHLEEN: [*worried again*] The Master's sure to notice what's gone from the bottle. He has the eye of a hawk for that.

MARY: [*amusedly*] Oh, we'll play Jamie's trick on him. Just measure a few drinks of water and pour them in.

CATHLEEN: [*does this — with a silly giggle*] God save me, it'll be half water. He'll know by the taste.

MARY: [*indifferently*] No, by the time he comes home he'll be too drunk to tell the difference. He has such a good excuse, he believes, to drown his sorrows.

CATHLEEN: [*philosophically*] Well, it's a good man's failing. I wouldn't give a trauneen① for a teetotaler. They've no high spirits, [*then, stupidly puzzled*] Good excuse? You mean Master Edmund, Ma'am? I can tell the Master is worried about him.

MARY: [*stiffens defensively — but in a strange way the reaction has a mechanical quality, as if it did not penetrate to real emotion*] Don't be silly, Cathleen. Why should he be? A touch of grippe is nothing. And Mr. Tyrone never is worried about anything, except money and property and the fear he'll end his days in poverty. I mean, deeply worried. Because he cannot really understand anything else. [*She gives a little laugh of detached, affectionate amusement.*] My husband is a very peculiar man, Cathleen.

CATHLEEN: [*vaguely resentful*] Well, he's a fine, handsome, kind gentleman just the same, Ma'am. Never mind his weakness.

MARY: Oh, I don't mind. I've loved him dearly for thirty-six years. That proves I know he's lovable at heart and can't help being what he is, doesn't it?

CATHLEEN: [*hazily reassured*] That's right, Ma'am. Love him dearly, for any fool can see he worships the ground you walk on. [*fighting the effect of her last drink and trying to be soberly conversational*] Speaking of acting, Ma'am, how is it you never went on the stage?

MARY: [*resentfully*] I? What put that absurd notion in your head? I was brought up in a respectable home and educated in the best convent in the Middle West. Before I met Mr. Tyrone I hardly knew there was such a thing as a theater. I was a very pious girl. I even dreamed of becoming a nun. I've never had the slightest desire to be an actress.

CATHLEEN: [*bluntly*] Well, I can't imagine you a holy nun, Ma'am. Sure, you never darken the door of a church, God forgive you.

_____

① trauneen: coin of very low value (Irish).

MARY: [*ignores this*] I've never felt at home in the theater. Even though Mr. Tyrone has made me go with him on all his tours, I've had little to do with the people in his company, or with anyone on the stage. Not that I have anything against them. They have always been kind to me, and I to them. But I've never felt at home with them. Their life is not my life. It has always stood between me and — [*She gets up — abruptly*] But let's not talk of old things that couldn't be helped. [*She goes to the porch door and stares out.*] How thick the fog is. I can't see the road. All the people in the world could pass by and I would never know. I wish it was always that way. It's getting dark already. It will soon be night, thank goodness. [*She turns back — vaguely*] It was kind of you to keep me company this afternoon, Cathleen. I would have been lonely driving uptown alone.

CATHLEEN: Sure, wouldn't I rather ride in a fine automobile than stay here and listen to Bridget's lies about her relations? It was like a vacation, Ma'am. [*She pauses — then stupidly*] There was only one thing I didn't like.

MARY: [*vaguely*] What was that, Cathleen?

CATHLEEN: The way the man in the drugstore acted when I took in the prescription for you. [*indignantly*] The impidence① of him!

MARY: [*with stubborn blankness*] What are you talking about? What drugstore? What prescription? [*then hastily, as* CATHLEEN *stares in stupid amazement*] Oh, of course, I'd forgotten. The medicine for the rheumatism in my hands. What did the man say? [*then with indifference*] Not that it matters, as long as he filled the prescription.

CATHLEEN: It mattered to me, then! I'm not used to being treated like a thief. He gave me a long look and says insultingly, "Where did you get hold of this?" and I says, "It's none of your damned business, but if you must know, it's for the lady I work for, Mrs. Tyrone, who's sitting out in the automobile." That shut him up quick. He gave a look out at you and said, "Oh," and went to get the medicine.

MARY: [*vaguely*] Yes, he knows me. [*She sits in the armchair at right rear of table. She adds in a calm, detached voice*] It's a special kind of medicine. I have to take it because there is no other that can stop the pain — all the pain — I mean, in my hands. [*She raises her hands and regards them with melancholy sympathy. There is no tremor in them now.*] Poor hands! You'd never believe it, but they were once one of my good points, along with my hair and eyes, and I had a fine figure, too. [*Her tone has become more and more far-off and dreamy.*] They were a musician's hands. I used to love the piano. I worked so hard at my music in the Convent — if you can call it work when you do something you love. Mother Elizabeth and my music teacher both said I had more talent than any student they remembered. My father paid for special lessons. He spoiled me. He would do anything I

---

① impidence: impudence.

asked. He would have sent me to Europe to study after I graduated from the Convent. I might have gone — if I hadn't fallen in love with Mr. Tyrone. Or I might have become a nun. I had two dreams. To be a nun, that was the more beautiful one. To become a concert pianist, that was the other. [*She pauses, regarding her hands fixedly.* CATHLEEN *blinks her eyes to fight off drowsiness and a tipsy feeling.*] I haven't touched a piano in so many years. I couldn't play with such crippled fingers, even if I wanted to. For a time after my marriage I tried to keep up my music. But it was hopeless. One-night stands, cheap hotels, dirty trains, leaving children, never having a home — [*She stares at her hands with fascinated disgust.*] See, Cathleen, how ugly they are! So maimed and crippled! You would think they'd been through some horrible accident! [*She gives a strange little laugh.*] So they have, come to think of it. [*She suddenly thrusts her hands behind her back.*] I won't look at them. They're worse than the foghorn for reminding me — [*then with defiant self-assurance*] But even they can't touch me now. [*She brings her hands from behind her back and deliberately stares at them — calmly*] They're far away. I see them, but the pain has gone.

CATHLEEN: [*stupidly puzzled*] You've taken some of the medicine? It made you act funny, Ma'am. If I didn't know better, I'd think you'd a drop taken.

MARY: [*dreamily*] It kills the pain. You go back until at last you are beyond its reach. Only the past when you were happy is real. [*She pauses — then as if her words had been an evocation which called back happiness she changes in her whole manner and facial expression. She looks younger. There is a quality of an innocent convent girl about her, and she smiles shyly.*] If you think Mr. Tyrone is handsome now, Cathleen, you should have seen him when I first met him. He had the reputation of being one of the best looking men in the country. The girls in the Convent who had seen him act, or seen his photographs, used to rave about him. He was a great matinee idol then, you know. Women used to wait at the stage door just to see him come out. You can imagine how excited I was when my father wrote me he and James Tyrone had become friends, and that I was to meet him when I came home for Easter vacation. I showed the letter to all the girls, and how envious they were! My father took me to see him act first. It was a play about the French Revolution and the leading part was a nobleman. I couldn't take my eyes off him. I wept when he was thrown in prison — and then was so mad at myself because I was afraid my eyes and nose would be red. My father had said we'd go backstage to his dressing room right after the play, and so we did. [*She gives a little excited, shy laugh.*] I was so bashful all I could do was stammer and blush like a little fool. But he didn't seem to think I was a fool. I know he liked me the first moment we were introduced. [*coquettishly*] I guess my eyes and nose couldn't have been red, after all. I was really very pretty then, Cathleen. And he was handsomer than my wildest dream, in his make-up and his nobleman's costume that was so becoming to him. He was different from all ordinary men, like someone from another world. At the same time he was simple, and kind, and unassuming, not a bit stuck-up or vain. I fell in love right then. So did he, he told me afterwards. I forgot all about becoming a nun or a concert pianist. All I wanted was to be his wife. [*She pauses, staring before her with unnaturally bright, dreamy eyes, and a rapt, tender, girlish smile.*] Thirty-six years ago, but I can see it as clearly as if it were tonight! We've loved each other ever since. And in all those thirty-six years, there has never been a breath of scandal about him. I mean, with any other woman. Never since he met me. That has made me very happy, Cathleen. It has made me forgive so many other things.

CATHLEEN: [*fighting tipsy drowsiness — sentimentally*] He's a fine gentleman and you're a lucky woman, [*then, fidgeting*] Can I take the drink to Bridget, Ma'am? It must be near dinnertime and I ought to be in the kitchen helping her. If she don't get something to quiet her temper, she'll be after me with the cleaver.

MARY: [*with a vague exasperation at being brought back from her dream*] Yes, yes, go. I don't need you now.

CATHLEEN: [*with relief*] Thank you, Ma'am. [*She pours out a big drink and starts for the back parlor with it.*] You won't be alone long. The Master and the boys —

MARY: [*impatiently*] No, no, they won't come. Tell Bridget I won't wait. You can serve dinner promptly at half past six. I'm not hungry but I'll sit at the table and we'll get it over with.

CATHLEEN: You ought to eat something, Ma'am. It's a queer medicine if it takes away your appetite.

MARY: [*has begun to drift into dreams again — reacts mechanically*] What medicine? I don't know what you mean, [*in dismissal*] You better take the drink to Bridget.

CATHLEEN: Yes, Ma'am.

[*She disappears through the back parlor, MARY waits until she hears the pantry door close behind her. Then she settles back in relaxed dreaminess, staring fixedly at nothing. Her arms rest limply along the arms of the chair, her hands with long, warped, swollen-knuckled, sensitive fingers drooping in complete calm. It is growing dark in the room. There is a pause of dead quiet. Then from the world outside comes the melancholy moan of the foghorn, followed by a chorus of bells, muffled by the fog, from the anchored craft in the harbor. MARY's face gives no sign she has heard, but her hands jerk and the fingers automatically play for a moment on the air. She frowns and shakes her head mechanically as if a fly had walked across her mind. She suddenly loses all the girlish quality and is an aging, cynically sad, embittered woman.*]

MARY: [*bitterly*] You're a sentimental fool. What is so wonderful about that first meeting between a silly romantic schoolgirl and a matinee idol? You were much happier before you knew he existed, in the Convent when you used to pray to the Blessed Virgin. [*longingly*] If I could only find the faith I lost, so I could pray again! [*She pauses — then begins to recite the Hail Mary in a flat, empty tone.*] "Hail, Mary, full of grace! The Lord is with Thee; blessed art Thou among women. " [*sneeringly*] You expect the Blessed Virgin to be fooled by a lying dope fiend reciting words! You can't hide from her! [*She springs to her feet. Her hands fly up to pat her hair distractedly.*] I must go upstairs. I haven't taken enough. When you start again you never know exactly how much you need. [*She goes toward the front parlor — then stops in the doorway as she hears the sound of voices from the front path. She starts guiltily.*] That must be them — [*She hurries back to sit down. Her face sets in stubborn defensiveness — resentfully*] Why are they coming back? They don't want to. And I'd much rather be alone. [*Suddenly her whole manner changes. She becomes pathetically relieved and eager.*] Oh, I'm so glad they've come! I've been so horribly lonely! [*The front door is heard closing and* TYRONE *calls uneasily from the hall.*]

TYRONE: Are you there, Mary?

[*The light in the hall is turned on and shines through the front parlor to fall on* MARY.]

MARY: [*rises from her chair, her face lighting up lovingly — with excited eagerness*] I'm here, dear. In the living room. I've been waiting for you.

[TYRONE *comes in through the front parlor,* EDMUND *is behind him.* TYRONE *has had a lot to drink but beyond a slightly glazed look in his eyes and a trace of blur in his speech, he does not show it.* EDMUND *has also had more than a few drinks without much apparent effect, except that his sunken cheeks are flushed and his eyes look bright and feverish. They stop in the doorway to stare appraisingly at her. What they see fulfills their worst expectations. But for the moment* MARY *is unconscious of their condemning eyes. She kisses her husband and then* EDMUND. *Her manner is unnaturally effusive. They submit shrinkingly. She talks excitedly.*]

I'm so happy you've come. I had given up hope. I was afraid you wouldn't come home. It's such a dismal, foggy evening. It must be much more cheerful in the barrooms uptown, where there are people you can talk and joke with. No, don't deny it. I know how you feel. I don't blame you a bit. I'm all the more grateful to you for coming home. I was sitting here so lonely and blue. Come and sit down.

[*She sits at left rear of table,* EDMUND *at left of table, and* TYRONE *in the rocker at right of it.*]

Dinner won't be ready for a minute. You're actually a little early. Will wonders never cease. Here's the whiskey, dear. Shall I pour a drink for you? [*Without waiting for a reply she does so.*] And you, Edmund? I don't want to encourage you, but one before dinner, as an appetizer, can't do any harm.

[*She pours a drink for him. They make no move to take the drinks. She talks on as if unaware of their silence.*]

Where's Jamie? But, of course, he'll never come home so long as he has the price of a drink left. [She *reaches out and clasps her husband's hand — sadly*] I'm afraid Jamie has been lost to us for a long time, dear. [*Her face hardens.*] But we mustn't allow him to drag Edmund down with him, as he'd like to do. He's jealous because Edmund has always been the baby — just as he used to be of Eugene. He'll never be content until he makes Edmund as hopeless a failure as he is.

EDMUND: [*miserably*] Stop talking, Mama.

TYRONE: [*dully*] Yes, Mary, the less you say now — [*then to* EDMUND, *a bit tipsily*] All the same there's truth in your mother's warning. Beware of that brother of yours, or he'll poison life for you with his damned sneering serpent's tongue!

EDMUND: [*as before*] Oh, cut it out, Papa.

MARY: [*goes on as if nothing had been said*] It's hard to believe, seeing Jamie as he is now, that he was ever my baby. Do you remember what a healthy, happy baby he was, James? The one-night stands and filthy trains and cheap hotels and bad food never made him cross or sick. He was always smiling or laughing. He hardly ever cried. Eugene was the same, too, happy and healthy, during the two years he lived before I let him die through my neglect.

TYRONE: Oh, for the love of God! I'm a fool for coming home!

EDMUND: Papa! Shut up!

MARY: [*smiles with detached tenderness at* EDMUND] It was Edmund who was the crosspatch when he was little, always getting upset and frightened about nothing at all. [*She pats his hand — teasingly*] Everyone used to say, dear, you'd cry at the drop of a hat.

EDMUND: [*cannot control his bitterness*] Maybe I guessed there was a good reason not to laugh.

TYRONE: [*reproving and pitying*] Now, now, lad. You know better than to pay attention —

MARY: [*as if she hadn't heard — sadly again*] Who would have thought Jamie would grow up to disgrace us. You remember, James, for years after he went to boarding school, we received such glowing reports. Everyone liked him. All his teachers told us what a fine brain he had, and how easily he learned his lessons. Even after he began to drink and they had to expel him, they wrote us how sorry they were, because he was so likable and such a brilliant student. They predicted a wonderful future for him if he would only learn to take life seriously. [*She pauses — then adds with a strange, sad detachment*] It's such a pity. Poor Jamie! It's hard to understand — [*Abruptly a change comes over her. Her face hardens and she stares at her husband with accusing hostility.*] No, it isn't at all. You brought him up to be a boozer. Since he first opened his eyes, he's seen you drinking. Always a bottle on the bureau in the cheap hotel rooms! And if he had a nightmare when he was little, or a stomach-ache, your remedy was to give him a teaspoonful of whiskey to quiet him.

TYRONE:[*stung*] So I'm to blame because that lazy hulk has made a drunken loafer of himself? Is that what I came home to listen to? I might have known! When you have the poison in you, you want to blame everyone but yourself!

EDMUND: Papa! You told me not to pay attention. [*then, resentfully*] Anyway it's true. You did the same thing with me. I can remember that teaspoonful of booze every time I woke up with a nightmare.

MARY:[*in a detached reminiscent tone*] Yes, you were continually having nightmares as a child. You were born afraid. Because I was so afraid to bring you into the world. [*She pauses — then goes on with the same detachment*] Please don't think I blame your father, Edmund. He didn't know any better. He never went to school after he was ten. His people were the most ignorant kind of poverty-stricken Irish. I'm sure they honestly believed whiskey is the healthiest medicine for a child who is sick or frightened.

[TYRONE *is about to burst out in angry defense of his family but* EDMUND *intervenes.*]

EDMUND:[*sharply*] Papa! [*changing the subject*] Are we going to have this drink, or aren't we?

TYRONE:[*controlling himself — dully*] You're right. I'm a fool to take notice. [He picks up his glass listlessly.] Drink hearty, lad.

[EDMUND *drinks but* TYRONE *remains staring at the glass in his hand.* EDMUND *at once realizes how much the whiskey has been watered. He frowns, glancing from the bottle to his mother — starts to say something but stops.*]

MARY:[*in a changed tone — repentantly*] I'm sorry if I sounded bitter, James. I'm not. It's all so far away. But I did feel a little hurt when you wished you hadn't come home. I was so relieved and happy when you came, and grateful to you. It's very dreary and sad to be here alone in the fog with night falling.

TYRONE:[*moved*] I'm glad I came, Mary, when you act like your real self.

MARY: I was so lonesome I kept Cathleen with me just to have someone to talk to. [*Her manner and quality drift back to the shy convent girl again.*] Do you know what I was telling her, dear? About the night my father took me to your dressing room and I first fell in love with you. Do you remember?

TYRONE:[*deeply moved — his voice husky*] Can you think I'd ever forget, Mary?

[EDMUND *looks away from them, sad and embarrassed.*]

MARY:[*tenderly*] No. I know you still love me, James, in spite of everything.

TYRONE:[*His face works and he blinks back tears — with quiet intensity*] Yes! As God is my judge! Always and forever, Mary!

MARY: And I love you, dear, in spite of everything.

[*There is a pause in which* EDMUND *moves embarrassedly. The strange detachment comes over her manner again as if she were speaking impersonally of people seen from a distance.*]

But I must confess, James, although I couldn't help loving you, I would never have married you if I'd known you drank so much. I remember the first night your barroom friends had to help you up to the door of our hotel room, and knocked and then ran away before I came to the door. We were still on our honeymoon, do you remember?

TYRONE: [*with guilty vehemence*] I don't remember! It wasn't on our honeymoon! And I never in my life had to be helped to bed, or missed a performance!

MARY: [*as though he hadn't spoken*] I had waited in that ugly hotel room hour after hour. I kept making excuses for you. I told myself it must be some business connected with the theater. I knew so little about the theater. Then I became terrified. I imagined all sorts of horrible accidents. I got on my knees and prayed that nothing had happened to you — and then they brought you up and left you outside the door. [*She gives a little, sad sigh.*] I didn't know how often that was to happen in the years to come, how many times I was to wait in ugly hotel rooms. I became quite used to it.

EDMUND: [*bursts out with a look of accusing hate at his father*] Christ! No wonder — ! [*He controls himself — gruffly*] When is dinner, Mama? It must be time.

TYRONE: [*overwhelmed by shame which he tries to hide, fumbles with his watch*] Yes. It must be. Let's see. [*He stares at his watch without seeing it — pleadingly*] Mary! Can't you forget — ?

MARY: [*with detached pity*] No, dear. But I forgive. I always forgive you. So don't look so guilty. I'm sorry I remembered out loud. I don't want to be sad, or to make you sad. I want to remember only the happy part of the past. [*Her manner drifts back to the shy, gay convent girl.*] Do you remember our wedding, dear? I'm sure you've completely forgotten what my wedding gown looked like. Men don't notice such things. They don't think they're important. But it was important to me, I can tell you! How I fussed and worried! I was so excited and happy! My father told me to buy anything I wanted and never mind what it cost. The best is none too good, he said. I'm afraid he spoiled me dreadfully. My mother didn't. She was very pious and strict. I think she was a little jealous. She didn't approve of my marrying — especially an actor. I think she hoped I would become a nun. She used to scold my father. She'd grumble, "You never tell me, never mind what it costs, when I buy anything! You've spoiled that girl so. I pity her husband if she ever marries. She'll expect him to give her the moon. She'll never make a good wife." [*She laughs affectionately.*] Poor mother! [*She smiles at* TYRONE *with a strange, incongruous coquetry.*] But she was mistaken, wasn't she, James? I haven't been such a bad wife, have I?

TYRONE: [*huskily, trying to force a smile*] I'm not complaining, Mary.

MARY: [*a shadow of vague guilt crosses her face*] At least, I've loved you dearly, and done the best I could — under the circumstances. [*The shadow vanishes and her shy, girlish expression returns.*] That wedding gown was nearly the death of me and the dressmaker, too! [*She laughs.*] I was so particular. It was never quite good enough. At last she said she refused to touch it any more or she might spoil it, and I made her leave so I could be alone to examine myself in the mirror. I was so pleased and vain. I thought to myself, "Even if your nose and mouth and ears are a trifle too large, your eyes and hair and figure, and your hands, make up for it. You're just as pretty as any actress he's ever met, and you don't have to use paint." [*She pauses, wrinkling her brow in an effort of memory.*] Where is my wedding gown now, I wonder? I kept it wrapped up in tissue paper in my trunk. I used to hope I would have a daughter and when it came time for her to marry — She couldn't have bought a lovelier gown, and I knew, James, you'd never tell her, never mind the cost. You'd want her to pick up something at a bargain. It was made of soft, shimmering satin, trimmed with wonderful old duchesse lace, in tiny ruffles around the neck and sleeves, and worked in with the folds that were draped round in a bustle effect at the back. The basque① was boned and very tight. I remember I held my breath when it was fitted, so my waist would be as small as possible. My father even let me have duchesse lace on my white satin slippers, and lace with orange blossoms in my veil. Oh, how I loved that gown! It was so beautiful! Where is it now, I wonder? I used to take it out from time to time when I was lonely, but it always made me cry, so finally a long while ago — [*She wrinkles her forehead again.*] I wonder where I hid it? Probably in one of the old trunks in the attic. Some day I'll have to look. [*She stops, staring before her.* TYRONE *sighs, shaking his head hopelessly, and attempts to catch his son's eye, looking for sympathy, but* EDMUND *is staring at the floor.*]

TYRONE: [*forces a casual tone*] Isn't it dinner time, dear? [*with a feeble attempt at teasing*] You're forever scolding me for being late, but now I'm on time for once, it's dinner that's late.

[*She doesn't appear to hear him. He adds, still pleasantly*]

Well, if I can't eat yet, I can drink. I'd forgotten I had this.

[*He drinks his drink,* EDMUND *watches him.* TYRONE *scowls and looks at his wife with sharp suspicion — roughly*]

Who's been tampering with my whiskey? The damned stuff is half water! Jamie's been away and he wouldn't overdo his trick like this, anyway. Any fool could tell — Mary, answer

---

① basque: tight – fitting bodice.

me! [*with angry disgust*] I hope to God you haven't taken to drink on top of —

EDMUND: Shut up, Papa! [*to his mother, without looking at her*] You treated Cathleen and Bridget, isn't that it, Mama?

MARY: [*with indifferent casualness*] Yes, of course. They work hard for poor wages. And I'm the housekeeper, I have to keep them from leaving. Besides, I wanted to treat Cathleen because I had her drive uptown with me, and sent her to get my prescription filled.

EDMUND: For God's sake, Mama! You can't trust her! Do you want everyone on earth to know?

MARY: [*her face hardening stubbornly*] Know what? That I suffer from rheumatism in my hands and have to take medicine to kill the pain? Why should I be ashamed of that? [*turns on EDMUND with a hard, accusing antagonism — almost a revengeful enmity*] I never knew what rheumatism was before you were born! Ask your father!

[*EDMUND looks away, shrinking into himself*]

TYRONE: Don't mind her, lad. It doesn't mean anything. When she gets to the stage where she gives the old crazy excuse about her hands she's gone far away from us.

MARY: [*turns on him — with a strangely triumphant, taunting smile*] I'm glad you realize that, James! Now perhaps you'll give up trying to remind me, you and Edmund! [*abruptly, in a detached, matter-of-fact tone*] Why don't you light the light, James? It's getting dark. I know you hate to, but Edmund has proved to you that one bulb burning doesn't cost much. There's no sense letting your fear of the poorhouse make you too stingy.

TYRONE: [*reacts mechanically*] I never claimed one bulb cost much! It's having them on, one here and one there, that makes the Electric Light Company rich. [*He gets up and turns on the reading lamp — roughly*] But I'm a fool to talk reason to you. [*to EDMUND*] I'll get a fresh bottle of whiskey, lad, and we'll have a real drink. [*He goes through the back parlor.*]

MARY: [*with detached amusement*] He'll sneak around to the outside cellar door so the servants won't see him. He's really ashamed of keeping his whiskey padlocked in the cellar. Your father is a strange man, Edmund. It took many years before I understood him. You must try to understand and forgive him, too, and not feel contempt because he's close-fisted. His father deserted his mother and their six children a year or so after they came to America. He told them he had a premonition he would die soon, and he was homesick for Ireland, and wanted to go back there to die. So he went and he did die. He must have been a peculiar man, too. Your father had to go to work in a machine shop when he was only ten years old.

EDMUND: [*protests dully*] Oh, for Pete's sake, Mama. I've heard Papa tell that machine shop story ten thousand times.

MARY: Yes, dear, you've had to listen, but I don't think you've ever tried to understand.

EDMUND: [ignoring this — miserably] Listen, Mama! You're not so far gone yet you've forgotten everything. You haven't asked me what I found out this afternoon. Don't you care a damn?

MARY: [shakenly] Don't say that! You hurt me, dear!

EDMUND: What I've got is serious, Mama. Doc Hardy knows for sure now.

MARY: [stiffens into scornful, defensive stubbornness] That lying old quack! I warned you he'd invent — !

EDMUND: [miserably dogged] He called in a specialist to examine me, so he'd be absolutely sure.

MARY: [ignoring this] Don't tell me about Hardy! If you heard what the doctor at the sanatorium, who really knows something, said about how he'd treated me! He said he ought to be locked up! He said it was a wonder I hadn't gone mad! I told him I had once, that time I ran down in my nightdress to throw myself off the dock. You remember that, don't you? And yet you want me to pay attention to what Doctor Hardy says. Oh, no!

EDMUND: [bitterly] I remember, all right. It was right after that Papa and Jamie decided they couldn't hide it from me any more. Jamie told me. I called him a liar! I tried to punch him in the nose. But I knew he wasn't lying. [His voice trembles, his eyes begin to fill with tears] God, it made everything in life seem rotten!

MARY: [pitiably] Oh, don't. My baby! You hurt me so dreadfully!

EDMUND: [dully] I'm sorry, Mama. It was you who brought it up. [then with a bitter, stubborn persistence] Listen, Mama. I'm going to tell you whether you want to hear or not. I've got to go to a sanatorium.

MARY: [dazedly, as if this was something that had never occurred to her] Go away? [violently] No! I won't have it! How dare Doctor Hardy advise such a thing without consulting me! How dare your father allow him! What right has he? You are my baby! Let him attend to Jamie! [more and more excited and bitter] I know why he wants you sent to a sanatorium. To take you from me! He's always tried to do that. He's been jealous of every one of my babies! He kept finding ways to make me leave them. That's what caused Eugene's death. He's been jealous of you most of all. He knew I loved you most because —

EDMUND: [miserably] Oh, stop talking crazy, can't you, Mama! Stop trying to blame him. And why are you so against my going away now? I've been away a lot, and I've never noticed it broke your heart!

MARY: [bitterly] I'm afraid you're not very sensitive, after all. [sadly] You might have guessed, dear, that after I knew you knew — about me — I had to be glad whenever you were where you couldn't see me.

EDMUND: [*brokenly*] Mama! Don't! [*He reaches out blindly and takes her hand — but he drops it immediately, overcome by bitterness again.*] All this talk about loving me — and you won't even listen when I try to tell you how sick —

MARY: [*with an abrupt transformation into a detached bullying motherliness*] Now, now. That's enough! I don't care to hear because I know it's nothing but Hardy's ignorant lies.

[*He shrinks back into himself. She keeps on in a forced, teasing tone but with an increasing undercurrent of resentment.*]

You're so like your father, dear. You love to make a scene out of nothing so you can be dramatic and tragic. [*with a belittling laugh*] If I gave you the slightest encouragement, you'd tell me next you were going to die —

EDMUND: People do die of it. Your own father —

MARY: [*sharply*] Why do you mention him? There's no comparison at all with you. He had consumption. [*angrily*] I hate you when you become gloomy and morbid! I forbid you to remind me of my father's death, do you hear me?

EDMUND: [*his face hard — grimly*] Yes, I hear you, Mama. I wish to God I didn't! [*He gets upfront his chair and stands staring condemningly at her — bitterly*] It's pretty hard to take at times, having a dope fiend for a mother! [*She winces — all life seeming to drain from her face, leaving it with the appearance of a plaster cast. Instantly EDMUND wishes he could take back what he has said. He stammers miserably.*] Forgive me, Mama. I was angry. You hurt me.

[*There is a pause in which the foghorn and the ships' hells are heard.*]

MARY: [*goes slowly to the windows at right like an automaton — looking out, a blank, far-off quality in her voice*] Just listen to that awful foghorn. And the bells. Why is it fog makes everything sound so sad and lost, I wonder?

EDMUND: [*brokenly*] I — I can't stay here. I don't want any dinner. [*He hurries away through the front parlor. She keeps staring out the window until she hears the front door close behind him. Then she comes back and sits in her chair, the same blank look on her face.*]

MARY: [*vaguely*] I must go upstairs. I haven't taken enough. [*She pauses — then longingly*] I hope, sometime, without meaning it, I will take an overdose. I never could do it deliberately. The Blessed Virgin would never forgive me, then. [*She hears TYRONE returning and turns as he comes in, through the back parlor, with a bottle of whiskey he has just uncorked. He is fuming.*]

TYRONE: [*wrathfully*] The padlock is all scratched. That drunken loafer has tried to pick the lock with a piece of wire, the way he's done before, [*with satisfaction, as if this was a perpetual battle of wits with his elder son*] But I've fooled him this time. It's a special padlock a professional burglar couldn't pick. [*He puts the bottle on the tray and suddenly is aware of* EDMUND's *absence.*] Where's Edmund?

MARY: [*with a vague far-away air*] He went out. Perhaps he's going uptown again to find Jamie. He still has some money left, I suppose, and it's burning a hole in his pocket. He said he didn't want any dinner. He doesn't seem to have any appetite these days, [*then stubbornly*] But it's just a summer cold. [TYRONE *stares at her and shakes his head helplessly and pours himself a big drink and drinks it. Suddenly it is too much for her and she breaks out and sobs.*] Oh, James, I'm so frightened! [*She gets up and throws her arms around him and hides her face on his shoulder — sobbingly*] I know he's going to die!

TYRONE: Don't say that! It's not true! They promised me in six months he'd be cured.

MARY: You don't believe that! I can tell when you're acting! And it will be my fault. I should never have borne him. It would have been better for his sake. I could never hurt him then. He wouldn't have had to know his mother was a dope fiend — and hate her!

TYRONE: [*his voice quivering*] Hush, Mary, for the love of God! He loves you. He knows it was a curse put on you without your knowing or willing it. He's proud you're his mother! [*abruptly as he hears the pantry door opening*] Hush, now! Here comes Cathleen. You don't want her to see you crying.

[*She turns quickly away from him to the windows at right, hastily wiping her eyes. A moment later* CATHLEEN *appears in the back-parlor doorway. She is uncertain in her walk and grinning woozily.*]

CATHLEEN: [*starts guiltily when she sees* TYRONE — *with dignity*] Dinner is served, Sir. [*raising her voice unnecessarily*] Dinner is served, Ma'am. [*She forgets her dignity and addresses* TYRONE *with good-natured familiarity*] So you're here, are you? Well, well. Won't Bridget be in a rage! I told her the Madame said you wouldn't be home, [*then reading accusation in his eye*] Don't be looking at me that way. If I've a drop taken, I didn't steal it. I was invited. [*She turns with huffy dignity and disappears through the back parlor.*]

TYRONE: [*sighs — then summoning his actor's heartiness*] Come along, dear. Let's have our dinner. I'm hungry as a hunter.

MARY: [*comes to him — her face is composed in plaster again and her tone is remote*] I'm afraid you'll have to excuse me, James. I couldn't possibly eat anything. My hands pain me dreadfully. I think the best thing for me is to go to bed and rest. Good night dear. [*She kisses him mechanically and turns toward the front parlor.*]

TYRONE: [*harshly*] Up to take more of that God-damned poison, is that it? You'll be like a mad ghost before the night's over!

MARY: [*starts to walk away — blankly*] I don't know what you're talking about, James.

You say such mean, bitter things when you've drunk too much. You're as bad as Jamie or Edmund. [*She moves off through the front parlor. He stands a second as if not knowing what to do. He is a sad, bewildered, broken old man. He walks wearily off through the back parlor toward the dining room.*]

Questions for Consideration and Discussion

1. What is the symbolic meaning of the fog and Mary's glasses?
2. O'Neill saw each child's experiences as uniquely determined by particular parents; he saw the family, rather than the person, as the fundamental human unit. Do you agree or disagree? Please explain.
3. What advice would you give to Tyrone, to Mary, to Jamie, and to Edmund?

Part V

American Literature since World War II

(1945–)

Part IV

American Literature since
World War II

(1945-)

Chapter 6

American Contemporary Literature

Historical Background

As the Depression of the 1930s worsened, some countries turned to menacing dictators for leadership: Benito Mussolini in Italy, Adolf Hitler in Germany, and a military government in Japan. Soon Japanese troops invaded China, and Hitler's army stormed through Europe. World War II broke out.

The United States didn't join the Allies to oppose the Axis powers of Germany, Italy and Japan until December 7, 1941, when Japanese bombers attacked America's Pearl Harbor naval base, located in Honolulu, Hawaii. After years of the most devastating conflict the world had ever seen, America dropped two — the first and only two — atomic bombs on Japan in August 1945, bringing World War II to an abrupt end.

World War II brought great changes to the United States.

Above all, the war effort had required the U.S. to produce a great deal of goods badly needed in the war and thus boosted American industry dramatically. Plants that had manufactured different brands of automobiles, such as Chevrolets, Plymouths, and Fords now made B-24 Liberators and Grumman Avengers. Moreover, the devastation in Europe immediately after the war allowed American industries to dominate world markets, helping the wartime economic boom continue throughout the 1950s.

Generally speaking, postwar Americans did not seem as disillusioned as they had been after World War I. However, there were grave crises, too. After the war, the United States and the Soviet Union, former World War II Allied countries and victors, became tense rivals in a worldwide struggle for power, which resulted in the Cold War, the type of contest in which military strength was built up for deterrence rather than combat. Ideologically, the opposition was between Western capitalism and Soviet state socialism; militarily, the contest was expressed by the West's rebuilding Germany and forming the NATO, and by the Soviet Union's influencing Eastern European nations and forming the Warsaw Pact. American involvement in the Korean War (1950 – 1953) and the Vietnam War (1954 – 1975) was nothing but a demonstration of the Cold War mentality. It was also proof of America's assuming the role of world police.

Another new phenomenon World War II brought to America was the rising Civil Rights movement, a "freedom struggle" by African Americans in the 1950s and 1960s to gain equality. In theory, the Civil War in the 1860s had officially abolished slavery, but it didn't end discrimination against blacks, especially in the South. After Reconstruction (1865 – 1877), the Southern states created a legal system of discrimination against blacks known as Jim Crow Laws. Jim Crow Laws largely nullified the rights of citizenship previously granted them by federal law, by promoting "separate but equal" educational, social, and political policies. The fact of the matter, however, was that the policies were not fair or equal. This situation persisted well into the 20th century. During World War II, African Americans made enormous contributions to the final victory. One million black men and women served in the military — in segregated units. Many more worked in defense industries. As the war ended, blacks in the military and in civilian wartime jobs saw themselves as waging a "double victory" campaign to secure democracy abroad and equality for themselves in their own country. They naturally were unwilling to return to second-class status. In the meantime, the mainstream society, aware of the black people's contribution, could not continue to enforce segregation and other forms of prejudice as easily as before the war.

Numerous other factors also energized the civil rights movement. To begin with, on July 26, 1948, President Harry Truman signed two Executive Orders, barring racial discrimination in the civil service and mandating "equality of treatment and opportunity for all persons in the armed forces." Secondly, the postwar economic boom improved job opportunities for blacks. Higher income resulted in rising college enrollments for African Americans and increasing donations to civil rights organizations such as the National Association for the Advancement of Colored People (NAACP). Thirdly, the mass media, including fledgling television, publicized civil rights activism. Furthermore, television broadcasts that displayed the material prosperity enjoyed by middle-class whites fed African Americans' desires for a better standard of living.

International events also influenced the civil rights movement. Observers at home and abroad pointed out that the nation that claimed to represent the ideals of democracy and freedom in the Cold War denied civil rights to a substantial proportion of its own population. This provoked Americans of all colors to scrutinize racial discrimination.

An important catalyzing event occurred on December 1, 1955, when a black woman named Rosa Parks refused to give up her bus seat to a white man, and as a consequence was arrested for violating the city's segregation law in Montgomery, Alabama. The law required African Americans to sit in the back of city buses and to give up their seats to whites should the white section of the bus become full. The city's black residents, long tired of the indignities of segregation, began a boycott of city buses. They recruited Martin Luther King, Jr., a 27-year-old preacher, to head the Montgomery Improvement Association, the group which organized the boycott. Despite violence directed at Martin Luther King and his family — his home was bombed and his family's safety threatened — he continued to lead the boycott until, one year and a few weeks later, segregated seating was declared unconstitutional by the Supreme Court, and the city's buses were desegregated.

Although African Americans had sporadically demonstrated against segregation laws in previous decades, the Montgomery bus boycott became a turning point for their protests. It gained significant media attention for the civil rights cause, and it brought Martin Luther King to the fore as a leader.

A high point of the Civil Rights movement occurred on August 28, 1963: the March on Washington. More than 200,000 people, black and white, congregated in Washington, D. C., for the peaceful march. The main purpose of the march was to force civil rights legislation and establish job equality for everyone. Here, Martin Luther King, Jr. gave his famous speech "I Have a Dream," which quickly became a slogan for equality and freedom. President Kennedy, who had earlier tried to discourage the march, decided to use it to promote the passage of what became the Civil Rights Act of 1964. Unfortunately, before he could sign the legislation he initiated, Kennedy was assassinated in the fall of 1963. His successor, President Lyndon B. Johnson, signed the Civil Rights Act into law on July 2, 1964.

The Civil Rights movement has been noted by some activists, such as W. E. B. Du Bois, to have a kinship with the decolonization movements in European-controlled countries. To put it in another way, international anti-imperialist movements became, for African Americans, a metaphor for the civil rights movement in the United States. The Civil Rights movement went far beyond fighting to win equality for blacks. It also prompted gains for other ethnic populations, for people with disabilities, and for women as well. The surge of a new wave to feminism was easy to understand. During World War II, with three million men in uniform, the vastly expanded workforce had comprised an increasing number of women. After the war ended, many women were reluctant to return to homemaking, so that gradually women emerged as a political force on behalf of rights and opportunities in the workplace.

To sum up, the 1960s was arguably the most turbulent decade in American history. It saw many large-scale protests. Mainly, these protests were organized by Civil Rights activists, feminist activists, and anti-Vietnam War activists. These social activities produced new conditions and new ideas. But the decade also saw the assassinations of some famous leaders, including Martin Luther King, who was assassinated in 1968, four years after receiving the Nobel Peace Prize.

Since the late 1960s and early 1970s, the world has undergone some dramatic changes. With former colonies of European powers declaring independence one after another, colonialism came to an end, thus the world entered the postcolonial period. The Berlin Wall fell in 1989, and the Soviet Union dissolved in 1991. These two events supposedly indicate that the Cold War has ended and the world has entered post-Cold War period. However, despite the arrival of the postcolonial and post-Cold War eras, the colonial mentality and Cold War mentality persist. After the world stepped into the 21st century, the realities of today's world are too complex to be described only in post-colonial terms. The events of 9-11 in 2001 pushed the United States and the rest of the world into new chaos. The war against terrorism has become so complex that sometimes it is hard to determine where the frontlines are and what acts can be justifiably called antiterrorism operations — it has been suspected that under the name of antiterrorism, America has launched wars in which it performed deeds that reached beyond the norms of International Law.

Since the turn of the century, the wide use of computers and the on-going information revolution represented by internet-related technology have profoundly transformed the ways people perceive the world. Many Americans, like people elsewhere, feel that they live at the center of a globalized world. This feeling of being in a globalized space enhances both a sense of close-knit togetherness and a sharpened sense of difference. As a result, people become increasingly aware of globalism and multiculturalism.

All in all, when we stand at the end of the second decade of the 21st century and look retrospectively at the post-World War II years, we find that America has gone through the past 70 years with glamorous achievements but also with regrettable shames.

In each stage of human civilization, nationally or internationally, the ideas of great philosophers and thinkers influence people's outlook and worldview. After World War II, the two influential philosophical ideas in the United States are Existentialism and Deconstruction.

Existentialism informed and inspired a whole generation of American writers and artists in the 1950s and 1960s. Existentialism is, strictly speaking, a philosophy formulated in the first half of the 20th century, with Heidegger, Sartre, and Camus being the three main representatives. Of the three, Sartre is generally regarded as the formulator of its main version. The first and most important principle of existentialism is that existence precedes essence. With this principle, the existentialists reverse the main tradition in Western philosophy and the tradition of Christianity. According to Platonism-Christianity, what man ultimately becomes is the unfolding of his innate nature or essence; this essence of man reflects a pre-existent, eternal, and absolute Spirit or Idea. But the existentialist philosophers suggest that there is no such Spirit or Idea, and that there is no pre-established essence of humanity, and that each individual person is what he makes of himself by a succession of actions taken with the freedom of choice in a specific physical and historical context, and that the world, by itself, is purposeless and thus absurd. The idea of absurdity is central to existentialism.

The father of deconstruction is the French thinker Jacques Derrida. His ideas were brought to America by means of a series of university conferences and academic publications. His deconstructive criticism started with his "Structure, Sign and Play in the Discourse of the Human Sciences" in 1966. In 1967, he presented his basic views in three books: *Of Grammatology*, *Writing and Difference*, and *Speech and Phenomena*. He asserted that Western philosophy from Plato had been logocentric and the Western philosophical systems had been based on binary structure. This "logocentric" tradition of thought had attempted to establish grounds of certainty and truth by repressing the limitless instability of language, and had sought some absolute source or guarantee of meaning which could center or stabilize the uncertainties of signification. Derrida argues that the stable self-identity which we attribute to speech as the authentic source of meaning is illusory. Influenced by Derrida and his associates, such as Michel Foucault, Gilles Deleuze, Judith Butler, Jean Baudrillard, and Julia Kristeva, who have been called post-structrualist philosophers (Deconstruction and post-structuralism are often coterminous), American academics realized that what was accepted as absolute truth usually depended on rhetoric rather than fact, and the so-called "fact" itself was constructed by intellectual operations. For example, the Vietnam War had been presented to the American people through slogans rather than realities.

American Post-modernism

The American literature since 1945 is so varied that it is difficult to make generalizations about it.

In any previous period, a single term was able to be found to capture the general trends of American literature. However, no single phrase suffices to describe the variety of features of post-Word War II American literature. Though "postmodernism" has been used by literary academics, the term is notoriously ambiguous, implying either that modernism has been superseded or that it has continued into a new phase. Moreover, as a concept, the term is not without semantic problems. Like all "post-" designations, postmodernism refers to phenomena or ideas that come after modernism, however, it does not make clear when "modernism" ends and "postmodernism" begins. The term is further complicated on account of its interdisciplinary trait, because postmodernism is a concept that appears in a wide variety of fields, including art, architecture, music, film, literature, sociology, communications, fashion, and technology, each of which has a different history and thus a different way of marking the transition between the modern and the postmodern.

While modernism saw and represented the world as fragmented and incoherent, as an irrational collection of random events, and lamented the loss of meaning and structure in the modern world, postmodernism sees the same incoherence but celebrates the ridiculousness of trying to make meaning and order out of the irrational and random. In this sense, postmodernism is relatively coterminous with post-structuralism and deconstruction.

Postmodernism may be seen as a continuation of modernism's alienated mood and disorienting techniques, and at the same time as an abandonment of its determined quest for artistic coherence in a fragmented world.

Additionally, the term "postmodernism" cannot usefully serve as an inclusive description of all literature since the 1950s or 1960s, but is applied selectively to those works that display most evidently the moods and formal disconnections the novels and stories of such writers as Thomas Pynchon, Kurt Vonnegut, Italo Calvino, Vladimir Nabokov, and William S. Burroughs.

It is very hard, even dangerous, to define the main features of contemporany American literature, since there is no consensus. However, to facilitate our students' understanding, let's riskily attempt to do this job.

I. War Fictions as the Aftermath of World War II and the Beginning of the Cold War.

World War II offered prime material for a number of writers' writings, for instance: Norman Mailer's *The Naked and the Dead* (1948), James Jones' *From Here to Eternity* (1951), Irwin Shaw's *The Young Lions* (1948), Herman Wouk's *The Caine Mutiny* (1951). None of these authors glorify combat. Later, Joseph Heller, in his *Catch*-22 (1961), cast World War II in satirical and absurdist terms, arguing that war is laced with insanity. Thomas Pynchon, in his *Gravity's Rainbow* (1973), presented a complex, brilliant case parodying and displacing different versions of reality, and Kurt Vonnegut became one of the shining lights of the counterculture during the early 1970s following publication of *Slaughterhouse-Five* (1969).

II. A Continuation of Modernism

Postmodernism is a continuation of modernism. Modernism has given forms and techniques that post-World War II writers find inexhaustible. To put it in another way, postmodernism is dependent upon the modernist tradition.

III. High Variety and Diversity

After World War II, all Americans, men and women, both majority population and minority population, aspired to pursue personal freedom and individual self-expression. Literature sought to give a voice to those who had not previously been heard.

IV. A New View of Language

Despite the wide variety of styles, if there is any commonality in the period, it is an appreciation of and sometimes outright delight in language as a tool of literary expression. First of all, more emphasis is attached to language. It looks that as long as a character can talk, he survives. For instance, playwright Arthur Miller poses his character William "Willy" Loman in *Death of a Salesman* (1949) struggling to articulate his identity as an antihero, fighting to survive in a world so powerful as to overwhelm him. Four decades later, David Mamet's sales staff's slick talking manages to submerge all traces of reality beneath illusive meanings. One more example is that in Chinese American female writer Maxine Hong Kingston's *The Woman Warrior*, little Kingston says to a silent Chinese girl: "If you don't talk, you can't have a personality." Secondly, post-modernist writers view language as nothing more and nothing less than a system of "signs" or signifiers, which do not point to the signified in the external world, but only to themselves. To put it in another way, language, instead of representing truth or reality, only represents itself; and the so-called truths themselves are formulated and constructed with language only; and the so-called reality is simply the product of language, rather than genuine reality.

V. The Appearance of Nonfiction Novel and New Journalism

Deconstructionist criticism claims that there is no absolute objectivity; that all authors, journalist or not, write from their own points of view, which unavoidably bear a number of colorings and biases; and that what we think to be true is constructed by the author with language. Given all these factors, the lines between journalism and literature began to blur. People began to believe that characterization, imagery, symbol, and other literary techniques used by fiction writers were no longer the exclusive province of fiction but appropriate tools for an improved journalism. Thus newsworthy events began to be crafted in the manner of novels, while feature journalism reads more like a short story.

VI. The Emergence of Metafiction

Metafiction is fiction about fiction, or fiction that exposes how fiction writing is done. This means that metafiction openly comments on its own fictional status. Rather than claiming to convey some reality related to the external world, metafiction shows that a literary work represents nothing other than itself. The value of such work lies in the author, not the tale; the author frankly reveals how interesting the writer can make the process, how much evidence of imagination, intelligence, and creative personality shows through.

VII. The Influence of Existentialism

The central idea of existentialism is absurdity, which means a sense of being devoid of purpose. A contemporary person often feels the absurdity of the world, mainly as the effects of alienation due to capitalist modernization. The Beat Generation writings most prominently manifest the influence of Existentialism in the U.S., just as the Theatre of Absurd does in the UK. Other representative American titles that reflect on existentialist ideas include Saul Bellow's *Seize the Day*, Ralph Ellison's *Invisible Man*, and J. D. Salinger's *Catcher in the Rye*.

VIII. The Bloom of Southern Literature

Following the Southern Renaissance of the 1920s and 1930s, after World War II, as a result of the Civil Rights Movement, Southern literature grew thematically. More female and African American writers were accepted as integral parts of Southern literature, including such African American writers as Zora Neale Hurston and Alice Walker, along with white women writers such as Eudora Welty, Flannery O'Conner,

Ellen Glasgow, Carson McCullers, and Katherine Anne Porter, among many others. One of the most highly praised Southern novels of the 20th century, *To Kill a Mockingbird* by Harper Lee, won the Pulitzer Prize when it was published in 1960. Truman Capote, a New Orleans native, also found great success in the middle 20th century with *Breakfast at Tiffany's* (1958) and later his nonfiction *In Cold Blood* (1966). Another famous novel of the 1960s is *A Confederacy of Dunces* written by John Kennedy Toole but not published until 1980. It won the Pulitzer Prize in 1981 and has since become a cult classic. Southern poetry bloomed in the decades following World War II in large part thanks to the writing and efforts of Robert Penn Warren and James Dickey. Tennessee Williams was the most important dramatist that emerged in the South after World War II.

IX. The Massive Emergence of Ethnic Writers

The post-World War II era witnessed the increasing number of ethnic writers. The literature by African American writers experienced a new surge. The most impressive black writers include Ralph Ellison (best known for his novel *Invisible Man*), Alice Walker (best known for her fiction *The Color Purple*), and Toni Morrison, the first — and the only — American black who has been awarded the Nobel Prize for Literature in 1993. Jewish American writers also receive national and international recognition, such as Saul Bellow, Bernard Malamud, Isaac B. Singer, and Philip Roth. Other groups of ethnic writers are immensely impressive, too. For instance, Chinese American writers (such as Maxine Hong Kingston, Amy Tan, and Gish Jen), Japanese American writers, Mexican American writers, etc. Inspired by the new historical conditions, the ethnic writers portray in their works how the characters strive to seek their identity in a difficult world.

X. The Flourishing of Female Writers

As a result of the Feminist Movement, the post-World War II years saw the appearance of increasing number of female writers, either feminist or non-feminist, white or ethnic. No other period in American history has seen so many female writers creatively working in the literary arena.

XI. New Directions in Poetry

American poetry was transformed remarkably after World War II by Allen Ginsburg's *Howl* (1956) and Robert Lowell's *Life Studies* (1959). They are arguably the two most prominent poets of the post-World War II period. Allen Ginsberg is one of the leading figures of the Beat Generation, also one of the leading figures of the San

Francisco Renaissance. His *Howl*, with its open, experimental form, and strong oral emphasis, is a departure from the well-shaped lyric. Robert Lowell, a Bostonian, is credited as the precursor of the so-called "Confessional poetry," which explores and exposes the extreme moments of a person's individual experience, such as personal trauma, mental illness, sexuality, alcoholism, insanity, etc. It has been claimed that Lowell was, in part, inspired by the work of Ginsberg. Other significant poets of the school include Sylvia Plath, Elizabeth Bishop, Anne Sexton, and John Berryman. Apart from the Beat Generation and the Confessional school, two other parallel schools are Black Mountain school and New York school. Generally speaking, the poetry after World War II is wild, disquieting, oral stylish, dramatizing individual predicaments, and stressing angers. American poetry gradually moved farther from European traditions.

XII. The Bloom of American Drama

Following the great success of Eugene O'Neill, American drama continued to flourish after World War II. Two post-World War II playwrights who established reputation comparable to Eugene O'Neill are Tennessee Williams (1911 – 1983), and Arthur Miller (1915 – 2005). Tennessee Williams came from the Southern State of Mississippi. His best known plays are *The Glass Menagerie* (1945) and *A Streetcar Named Desire* (1947). Arthur Miller was born in New York. Among his most popular plays are *All My Sons* (1947), *Death of a Salesman* (1949), *The Crucible* (1953), and *A View from the Bridge* (1955, revised 1956). He is especially remembered for his *Death of a Salesman*, the Pulitzer Prize for Drama winner in 1949 and his *The Crucible*, a dramatized and partially fictionalized story of the Salem witch trials that took place in the Puritan Massachusetts Bay Colony in 1692. Miller wrote *The Crucible* as an allegory for McCarthyism in the early 1950s, when an anti-Communist crusade led by U. S. Senator Joseph McCarthy and others ruined innocent people's lives.

XIII. New Attention Paid to Native American Writers

Native American writers received new attention from mainstream culture. In 1969, N. Scott Momaday (1934 –) became the first and only Native American to win the Pulitzer Prize in Fiction for his novel *House Made of Dawn*. Published during a time of heightened cultural awareness in the late 1960s and early 1970s, *House Made of Dawn* not only produced a tremendous impact on the development of Native American literature, but also brought attention to other gifted Native American writers, such as Vine Deloria Jr. (1933 – 2005), whose *Custer Died for Your Sins: An Indian Manifesto* (1969) helped generate unprecedented national attention to Native American issues, Leslie Marmon Silko (1948 –), whose most well-known novel *Ceremony*

(1977) tells the story of a World War ∏ American Indian veteran returning home from the war to his poverty-stricken reservation, and James Welch (1940 – 2003), whose *Fools Crow* (1986) received several national literary awards. The most distinguished Native American writers in contemporary period include Louise Endrich (1954 –), whose novel *The Plague of Doves* was a finalist for the Pulitzer Prize for Fiction in 2009, and Sherman Alexie (1966 –), who has been considered as the most widely read Native American writer in the United States.

➤➤ Questions for Consideration and Discussion

1. What's your comment on the thought of existentialist philosophers? Do you think humans have stable essence or not? Existentialists believe "truth is subjectivity," do you believe this is true?

2. What's your comment on postmodernists' view of language? How would the view change your way of using language and interpreting other people's language? Existentialists believe "truth is subjectivity", do you believe this is true?

3. How would you explain the fact that on one hand the United States boasted of democracy and equality but on the other hand it remained prejudiced against African Americans?

4. Among the dramas Tennessee Williams and Arthur Miller created, which two titles sound most attractive? What do you think they most likely recount? Do research and see how your guess matches the subject matters.

▌ Joseph Heller(1923 – 1999)

Joseph Heller is best remembered for his fiction *Catch-22*, a representative work of black humor. To talk about Joseph Heller is to talk about *Catch-22* and black humor.

Heller was born into a Jewish family in New York City, where he received his high school education. In 1942, at age 19, he joined the U. S. Army Air Corps. Two years later he was sent to the Italian Front and served as a bombardier in the Mediterranean. His experience as a bombardier provided the inspiration for *Catch-22*, a satire on war and bureaucracy.

The novel is set in World War ∏. The protagonist Yossarian and his comrades are in an Air Force squadron stationed on an island in the Mediterranean Sea. Yossarian's main antagonist is Colonel Cathcart, whose goal in life is to become a general. Yossarian wants to stop flying missions so that he does not get killed, yet Cathcart's aim is to continue raising the number of required missions in order to impress his superiors. He uses Catch-22's unfair, illogical rules to keep the men flying. This creates a constant conflict between Yossarian and Colonel Cathcart. Yossarian's tent-mate, whose name is Orr, practices crashing every mission until he successfully escapes to Sweden in his last practice. Yossarian witnesses the death of Snowden, his pilot, and the death of Nately, his friend. Mentally troubled by these deaths, Yossarian refuses to fly any more missions. He visits Doctor Daneeka, pleading him to ground him on the basis of insanity, but the doctor tells him that he can't do that on account of army regulation Catch-22. In desperation, Yossarian wanders the streets of Rome and encounters every kind of human horror — rape, disease, murder. He is eventually arrested for being in Rome without a pass, and his superior officers, Colonel Cathcart and Colonel Korn, offer him a choice: He can either face a court-martial or be released and sent home on condition that he must state his support for their policy. Although he is tempted by their offer to send him back home, Yossarian chooses another way out — he decides to desert the army and flee to neutral Sweden, getting rid of the dehumanizing machinery of the military for good.

Catch-22 is a perfect example of dark humor, which is a kind of work in which disturbing or sinister subjects like death, disease, or warfare are treated with bitter amusement.

Within the book, "Catch-22" is a military rule, the self-contradictory circular logic. It is confusing. It is, in essence, a circular argument. Now, the phrase "Catch-22" has become a synonym for an absurd and self-contradictory dilemma.

Heller agrees that he attacks not only the absurdity of war but, in general, "the humbug, hypocrisy, cruelty and sheer stupidity of our mass society."

Catch-22
Chapter 5 Chief White Halfoat[①]
(Excerpt)

...

It was a horrible joke, but Doc Daneeka didn't laugh until Yossarian came to him one mission later and pleaded again, without any real expectation of success, to be grounded. Doc Daneeka snickered once and was soon immersed in problems of his own, which included Chief White Halfoat, who had been challenging him all that morning to Indian wrestle, and Yossarian, who decided right then and there to go crazy.

---

① Chief White Halfoat: A Native American soldier who shares a tent with Doctor Daneeka.

"You're wasting your time," Doc Daneeka was forced to tell him.

"Can you ground someone who's crazy?"

"Oh, sure. I have to. There's a rule saying I have to ground anyone who's crazy. "

"Then why don't you ground me? I'm crazy. Ask Clevinger. "

"Clevinger? Where is Clevinger? You find Clevinger and I'll ask him. "

"Then ask any of the others. They'll tell you how crazy I am. "

"They're crazy. "

"Then why don't you ground them?"

"Why don't they ask me to ground them?"

"Because they're crazy, that's why. "

"Of course they're crazy," Doc Daneeka replied. "I just told you they're crazy, didn't I? And you can't let crazy people decide whether you're crazy or not, can you?"

Yossarian looked at him soberly and tried another approach. "Is Orr crazy?"

"He sure is," Doc Daneeka said.

"Can you ground him?"

"I sure can. But first he has to ask me to. That's part of the rule. "

"Then why doesn't he ask you to?"

"Because he's crazy," Doc Daneeka said. "He has to be crazy to keep flying combat missions after all the close calls he's had. Sure, I can ground Orr. But first he has to ask me to. "

"That's all he has to do to be grounded?"

"That's all. Let him ask me. "

"And then you can ground him?" Yossarian asked.

"No. Then I can't ground him. "

"You mean there's a catch?"

"Sure there's a catch," Doc Daneeka replied. "Catch-22. Anyone who wants to get out of combat duty isn't really crazy. "

There was only one catch and that was Catch-22, which specified that a concern for one's own safety in the face of dangers that were real and immediate was the process of a rational mind. Orr was crazy and could be grounded. All he had to do was ask; and as soon as he did, he would no longer be crazy and would have to fly more missions. Orr would be crazy to fly more missions and sane if he didn't, but if he was sane then he had to fly them. If he flew them he was crazy and didn't have to; but if he didn't want to he was sane and had to. Yossarian was moved very deeply by the absolute simplicity of this clause of Catch-22 and let out a respectful whistle.

"That's some catch, that Catch-22," he observed.

"It's the best there is," Doc Daneeka agreed.

Yossarian saw it clearly in all its spinning reasonableness. There was an elliptical precision about its perfect pairs of parts that was graceful and shocking, like good modern art, and at times Yossarian wasn't quite sure that he saw it all, just the way he was never quite sure about good modern art or the flies Orr saw in Appleby's eyes. He had Orr's word to take for the flies in Appleby's eyes.

"Oh, they're there all right," Orr had assured him about the flies in Appleby's eyes after Yossarian's fist fight in the officers' club, "although he probably doesn't even know it. That's why he can't see things as they really are."

"How come he doesn't know it?" inquired Yossarian.

"Because he's got flies in his eyes," Orr explained with exaggerated patience. "How can he see he's got flies in his eyes if he's got flies in his eyes?" ...

Chapter 40 Catch-22

There was, of course, a catch.

"Catch-22?" inquired Yossarian.

"Of course," Colonel Korn answered pleasantly, after he had chased the mighty guard of massive M. P. s① out with an insouciant flick of his hand and a slightly contemptuous nod — most relaxed, as always, when he could be most cynical. His rimless square eyeglasses glinted with sly amusement as he gazed at Yossarian. "After all, we can't simply send you home for refusing to fly more missions and keep the rest of the men here, can we? That would hardly be fair to them."

"You're goddam right!" Colonel Cathcart blurted out, lumbering back and forth gracelessly like a winded bull, puffing and pouting angrily. "I'd like to tie him up hand and foot and throw him aboard a plane on every mission. That's what I'd like to do."

Colonel Korn motioned Colonel Cathcart to be silent and smiled at Yossarian. "You know, you really have been making things terribly difficult for Colonel Cathcart," he observed with flip good humor, as though the fact did not displease him at all. "The men are unhappy and morale is beginning to deteriorate. And it's all your fault."

"It's your fault," Yossarian argued, "for raising the number of missions."

"No, it's your fault for refusing to fly them," Colonel Korn retorted. "The men were perfectly content to fly as many missions as we asked as long as they thought they had no alternative. Now you've given them hope, and they're unhappy. So the blame is all yours."

"Doesn't he know there's a war going on?" Colonel Cathcart, still stamping back and forth, demanded morosely without looking at Yossarian.

"I'm quite sure he does," Colonel Korn answered. "That's probably why he refuses to fly them."

"Doesn't it make any difference to him?"

---

① M. P.: Military Police.

"Will the knowledge that there's a war going on weaken your decision to refuse to participate in it?" Colonel Korn inquired with sarcastic seriousness, mocking Colonel Cathcart.

"No, sir," Yossarian replied, almost returning Colonel Korn's smile.

"I was afraid of that," Colonel Korn remarked with an elaborate sigh, locking his fingers together comfortably on top of his smooth, bald, broad, shiny brown head. "You know, in all fairness, we really haven't treated you too badly, have we? We've fed you and paid you on time. We gave you a medal and even made you a captain."

"I never should have made him a captain," Colonel Cathcart exclaimed bitterly. "I should have given him a court-martial after he loused up that Ferrara mission and went around twice."

"I told you not to promote him," said Colonel Korn, "but you wouldn't listen to me."

"No you didn't. You told me to promote him, didn't you?"

"I told you not to promote him. But you just wouldn't listen."

"I should have listened."

"You never listen to me," Colonel Korn persisted with relish. "That's the reason we're in this spot."

"All right, gee whiz. Stop rubbing it in, will you?"

Colonel Cathcart burrowed his fists down deep inside his pockets and turned away in a slouch. "Instead of picking on me, why don't you figure out what we're going to do about him?"

"We're going to send him home, I'm afraid." Colonel Korn was chuckling triumphantly when he turned away from Colonel Cathcart to face Yossarian. "Yossarian, the war is over for you. We're going to send you home. You really don't deserve it, you know, which is one of the reasons I don't mind doing it. Since there's nothing else we can risk doing to you at this time, we've decided to return you to the States. We've worked out this little deal to — "

"What kind of deal?" Yossarian demanded with defiant mistrust.

Colonel Korn tossed his head back and laughed. "Oh, a thoroughly despicable deal, make no mistake about that. It's absolutely revolting. But you'll accept it quickly enough."

"Don't be too sure."

"I haven't the slightest doubt you will, even though it stinks to high heaven. Oh, by the way. You haven't told any of the men you've refused to fly more missions, have you?"

"No, sir," Yossarian answered promptly.

Colonel Korn nodded approvingly. "That's good. I like the way you lie. You'll go far in this world if you ever acquire some decent ambition."

"Doesn't he know there's a war going on?" Colonel Cathcart yelled out suddenly, and blew with vigorous disbelief into the open end of his cigarette holder.

"I'm quite sure he does," Colonel Korn replied acidly, "since you brought that identical point to his attention just a moment ago." Colonel Korn frowned wearily for Yossarian's benefit, his eyes twinkling swarthily with sly and daring scorn. Gripping the edge of Colonel Cathcart's desk with both hands, he lifted his flaccid haunches far back on the corner to sit with both short legs dangling freely. His shoes kicked lightly against the yellow oakwood, his sludge-brown socks, garterless, collapsed in sagging circles below ankles that were surprisingly small and white. "You know, Yossarian," he mused affably in a manner of casual reflection that seemed both derisive and sincere, "I really do admire you a bit. You're an intelligent person of great moral character who has taken a very courageous stand. I'm an intelligent person with no moral character at all, so I'm in an ideal position to appreciate it."

"These are very critical times," Colonel Cathcart asserted petulantly from a far corner of the office, paying no attention to Colonel Korn.

"Very critical times indeed," Colonel Korn agreed with a placid nod. "We've just had a change of command above, and we can't afford a situation that might put us in a bad light with either General Scheisskopf or General Peckem. Isn't that what you mean, Colonel?"

"Hasn't he got any patriotism?"

"Won't you fight for your country?" Colonel Korn demanded, emulating Colonel Cathcart's harsh, self-righteous tone. "Won't you give up your life for Colonel Cathcart and me?"

Yossarian tensed with alert astonishment when he heard Colonel Korn's concluding words. "What's that?" he exclaimed. "What have you and Colonel Cathcart got to do with my country? You're not the same."

"How can you separate us?" Colonel Korn inquired with ironical tranquility.

"That's right," Colonel Cathcart cried emphatically. "You're either for us or against us. There's no two ways about it."

"I'm afraid he's got you," added Colonel Korn. "You're either for us or against your country. It's as simple as that."

"Oh, no, Colonel. I don't buy that."

Colonel Korn was unruffled. "Neither do I, frankly, but everyone else will. So there you are."

"You're a disgrace to your uniform!" Colonel Cathcart declared with blustering wrath, whirling to confront Yossarian for the first time. "I'd like to know how you ever got to be a captain, anyway."

"You promoted him," Colonel Korn reminded sweetly, stifling a snicker. "Don't you remember?"

"Well, I never should have done it."

"I told you not to do it," Colonel Korn said. "But you just wouldn't listen to me."

"Gee whiz, will you stop rubbing it in?" Colonel Cathcart cried. He furrowed his brow and glowered at Colonel Korn through eyes narrow with suspicion, his fists clenched on his hips. "Say, whose side are you on, anyway?"

"Your side, Colonel. What other side could I be on?"

"Then stop picking on me, will you? Get off my back, will you?"

"I'm on your side, Colonel. I'm just loaded with patriotism."

"Well, just make sure you don't forget that." Colonel Cathcart turned away grudgingly after another moment, incompletely reassured, and began striding the floor, his hands kneading his long cigarette holder. He jerked a thumb toward Yossarian. "Let's settle with him. I know what I'd like to do with him. I'd like to take him outside and shoot him. That's what I'd like to do with him. That's what General Dreedle would do with him. "

"But General Dreedle isn't with us anymore," said Colonel Korn, "so we can't take him outside and shoot him. "

Now that his moment of tension with Colonel Cathcart had passed, Colonel Korn relaxed again and resumed kicking softly against Colonel Cathcart's desk. He returned to Yossarian. "So we're going to send you home instead. It took a bit of thinking, but we finally worked out this horrible little plan for sending you home without causing too much dissatisfaction among the friends you'll leave behind. Doesn't that make you happy?"

"What kind of plan? I'm not sure I'm going to like it. "

"I know you're not going to like it. " Colonel Korn laughed, locking his hands contentedly on top of his head again. "You're going to loathe it. It really is odious and certainly will offend your conscience. But you'll agree to it quickly enough. You'll agree to it because it will send you home safe and sound in two weeks, and because you have no choice. It's that or a court-martial. Take it or leave it. "

Yossarian snorted. "Stop bluffing, Colonel. You can't court-martial me for desertion in the face of the enemy. It would make you look bad and you probably couldn't get a conviction. "

"But we can court-martial you now for desertion from duty, since you went to Rome without a pass. And we could make it stick. If you think about it a minute, you'll see that you'd leave us no alternative. We can't simply let you keep walking around in open insubordination without punishing you. All the other men would stop flying missions, too. No, you have my word for it. We will court-martial you if you turn our deal down, even though it would raise a lot of questions and be a terrible black eye for Colonel Cathcart. "

Colonel Cathcart winced at the words "black eye" and, without any apparent premeditation, hurled his slender onyx-and-ivory cigarette holder down viciously on the wooden surface on his desk. "Jesus Christ!" he shouted unexpectedly. "I hate this goddam cigarette holder!" The cigarette holder bounced off the desk to the wall, ricocheted across the window sill to the floor and came to a stop almost where he was standing. Colonel Cathcart stared down at it with an irascible scowl. "I wonder if it's really doing me any good. "

"It's a feather in your cap with General Peckem, but a black eye for you with General Scheisskopf," Colonel Korn informed him with a mischievous look of innocence.

"Well, which one am I supposed to please?"

"Both. "

"How can I please them both? They hate each other. How am I ever going to get a feather in my cap from General Scheisskopf without getting a black eye from General Peckem?"

"March. "

"Yeah, march. That's the only way to please him. March. March. " Colonel Cathcart grimaced sullenly. "Some generals! They're a disgrace to their uniforms. If people like those two can make general, I don't see how I can miss."

"You're going to go far," Colonel Korn assured him with a flat lack of conviction, and turned back chuckling to Yossarian, his disdainful merriment increasing at the sight of Yossarian's unyielding expression of antagonism and distrust. "And there you have the crux of the situation. Colonel Cathcart wants to be a general and I want to be a colonel, and that's why we have to send you home."

"Why does he want to be a general?"

"Why? For the same reason that I want to be a colonel. What else have we got to do? Everyone teaches us to aspire to higher things. A general is higher than a colonel, and a colonel is higher than a lieutenant colonel. So we're both aspiring. And you know, Yossarian, it's a lucky thing for you that we are. Your timing on this is absolutely perfect, but I suppose you took that factor into account in your calculations."

"I haven't been doing any calculating," Yossarian retorted.

"Yes, I really do enjoy the way you lie," Colonel Korn answered. "Won't it make you proud to have your commanding officer promoted to general — to know you served in an outfit that averaged more combat missions per person than any other? Don't you want to earn more unit citations and more oak leaf clusters for your Air Medal? Where's your 'sprit de corps①? Don't you want to contribute further to this great record by flying more combat missions? It's your last chance to answer yes."

"No."

"In that case, you have us over a barrel — " said Colonel Korn without rancor.

"He ought to be ashamed of himself!"

" — And we have to send you home. Just do a few little things for us, and — "

"What sort of things?" Yossarian interrupted with belligerent misgiving.

"Oh, tiny, insignificant things. Really, this is a very generous deal we're making with you. We will issue orders returning you to the States — really, we will — and all you have to do in return is..."

"What? What must I do?"

Colonel Korn laughed curtly. "Like us."

Yossarian blinked. "Like you?"

"Like us."

"Like you?"

"That's right," said Colonel Korn, nodding, gratified immeasurably by Yossarian's guileless surprise and bewilderment. "Like us. Join us. Be our pal. Say nice things about us here and back in the States. Become one of the boys. Now, that isn't asking too much, is it?"

---

① 'sprit de corps: *spirit de corps* (French), group spirit.

"You just want me to like you? Is that all?"

"That's all."

"That's all?"

"Just find it in your heart to like us."

Yossarian wanted to laugh confidently when he saw with amazement that Colonel Korn was telling the truth.

"That isn't going to be too easy," he sneered.

"Oh, it will be a lot easier than you think," Colonel Korn taunted in return, undismayed by Yossarian's barb.

"You'll be surprised at how easy you'll find it to like us once you begin." Colonel Korn hitched up the waist of his loose, voluminous trousers. The deep black grooves isolating his square chin from his jowls were bent again in a kind of jeering and reprehensible mirth. "You see, Yossarian, we're going to put you on easy street. We're going to promote you to major and even give you another medal. Captain Flume is already working on glowing press releases describing your valor over Ferrara, your deep and abiding loyalty to your outfit and your consummate dedication to duty. Those phrases are all actual quotations, by the way. We're going to glorify you and send you home a hero, recalled by the Pentagon for morale and public-relations purposes. You'll live like a millionaire. Everyone will lionize you. You'll have parades in your honor and make speeches to raise money for war bonds. A whole new world of luxury awaits you once you become our pal. Isn't it lovely?"

Yossarian found himself listening intently to the fascinating elucidation of details. "I'm not sure I want to make speeches."

"Then we'll forget the speeches. The important thing is what you say to people here." Colonel Korn leaned forward earnestly, no longer smiling. "We don't want any of the men in the group to know that we're sending you home as a result of your refusal to fly more missions. And we don't want General Peckem or General Scheisskopf to get wind of any friction between us, either. That's why we're going to become such good pals."

"What will I say to the men who asked me why I refused to fly more missions?"

"Tell them you had been informed in confidence that you were being returned to the States and that you were unwilling to risk your life for another mission or two. Just a minor disagreement between pals, that's all."

"Will they believe it?"

"Of course they'll believe it, once they see what great friends we've become and when they see the press releases and read the flattering things you have to say about me and Colonel Cathcart. Don't worry about the men.

They'll be easy enough to discipline and control when you've gone. It's only while you're still here that they may prove troublesome. You know, one good apple can spoil the rest," Colonel Korn concluded with conscious irony. "You know — this would really be wonderful — you might even serve as an inspiration to them to fly more missions."

"Suppose I denounce you when I get back to the States?"

"After you've accepted our medal and promotion and all the fanfare? No one would believe you, the Army wouldn't let you, and why in the world should you want to? You're going to be one of the boys, remember?

You'll enjoy a rich, rewarding, luxurious, privileged existence. You'd have to be a fool to throw it all away just for a moral principle, and you're not a fool. Is it a deal?"

"I don't know."

"It's that or a court-martial."

"That's a pretty scummy trick I'd be playing on the men in the squadron, isn't it?"

"Odious," Colonel Korn agreed amiably, and waited, watching Yossarian patiently with a glimmer of private delight.

"But what the hell!" Yossarian exclaimed. "If they don't want to fly more missions, let them stand up and do something about it the way I did. Right?"

"Of course," said Colonel Korn.

"There's no reason I have to risk my life for them, is there?"

"Of course not."

Yossarian arrived at his decision with a swift grin. "It's a deal!" he announced jubilantly.

"Great," said Colonel Korn with somewhat less cordiality than Yossarian had expected, and he slid himself off Colonel Cathcart's desk to stand on the floor. He tugged the folds of cloth of his pants and undershorts free from his crotch and gave Yossarian a limp hand to shake. "Welcome aboard."

"Thanks, Colonel. I —"

"Call me Blackie, John. We're pals now."

"Sure, Blackie. My friends call me Yo-Yo. Blackie, I —"

"His friends call him Yo-Yo," Colonel Korn sang out to Colonel Cathcart. "Why don't you congratulate Yo-Yo on what a sensible move he's making?"

"That's a real sensible move you're making, Yo-Yo," Colonel Cathcart said, pumping Yossarian's hand with clumsy zeal.

"Thank you, Colonel, I —"

"Call him Chuck," said Colonel Korn.

"Sure, call me Chuck," said Colonel Cathcart with a laugh that was hearty and awkward. "We're all pals now."

"Sure, Chuck."

"Exit smiling," said Colonel Korn, his hands on both their shoulders as the three of them moved to the door.

"Come on over for dinner with us some night, Yo-Yo," Colonel Cathcart invited hospitably. "How about tonight? In the group dining room."

"I'd love to, sir."

"Chuck," Colonel Korn corrected reprovingly.

"I'm sorry, Blackie. Chuck. I can't get used to it."

"That's all right, pal."

"Sure, pal."

"Thanks, pal."

"Don't mention it, pal."

"So long, pal."

Yossarian waved goodbye fondly to his new pals and sauntered out onto the balcony corridor, almost bursting into song the instant he was alone. He was home free: he had pulled it off; his act of rebellion had succeeded; he was safe, and he had nothing to be ashamed of to anyone. He started toward the staircase with a jaunty and exhilarated air. A private in green fatigues saluted him. Yossarian returned the salute happily, staring at the private with curiosity. He looked strangely familiar. When Yossarian returned the salute, the private in green fatigues turned suddenly into Nately's whore and lunged at him murderously with a bone-handled kitchen knife that caught him in the side below his upraised arm. Yossarian sank to the floor with a shriek, shutting his eyes in overwhelming terror as he saw the girl lift the knife to strike at him again. He was already unconscious when Colonel Korn and Colonel Cathcart dashed out of the office and saved his life by frightening her away.

▶▶ Questions for Consideration and Discussion

1. What manifestations of black humor do you find in the excerpts?
2. What Catch-22 instances have you found around you in real life? What is your suggestion for the solution of such paradoxical situations?
3. Considering the thing that Colonel Cathcart and Colonel Korn proposed to have a "glowing press releases" composed for Yossarian who had actually behaved cowardly in the campaigns, what's your comment on the detachedness of "signifiers" and "the signified"?

‖ Saul Bellow(1915 – 2005)

Saul Bellow is one of the most outstanding novelists of the 20th century, enjoying parallel popularity with Hemingway and Faulkner. He was the recipient of the Noble Prize for Literature in 1976.

Saul Bellow, the youngest of four children of a Russian Jewish couple, was born in 1915 in Quebec, Canada and moved to Chicago when he was nine years old. He was educated first in the University of Chicago, then transferred to Northwestern University, where he took a degree in anthropology and sociology. The effects of his university education are everywhere evident in the novels he later wrote. His best-known works include *The Adventures of Augie March* (1953), *Seize the Day* (1956), *Henderson the Rain King* (1959), *Herzog* (1964), *Mr. Sammler's Planet* (1970), *Humboldt's Gift* (1975), and *Ravelstein* (2000).

During World War Ⅱ, Bellow joined the merchant marine, and during his service he completed his first novel, *Dangling Man* (1944). It is about a young Chicago man waiting to be drafted for the war. After the war, he taught, successively, at the University of Minnesota, New York University, Princeton University, and the University of Chicago.

In 1948, Bellow was awarded a Guggenheim Fellowship that allowed him to move to Paris, where he began writing *The Adventures of Augie March* (1953), a picaresque novel. *Seize the Day* is a short masterpiece centering on a calamitous day in the life of a failed forty-four-year-old New Yorker named Wilhelm Adler (also called Tommy Wilhelm in his first twenty years of life). Estranged from his vindictive wife and selfish father, Wilhelm loses his last seven hundred dollars as a result of being deceived by a quack psychologist Dr. Tamkin. He turns to his father for help, but the rich old man gives him nothing but advice and criticism. When he frantically searches for Dr. Tamkin, he is accidentally pushed by a crowd of people into a funeral parlor. As he stands next to the coffin of the unknown dead man, Wilhelm cries softly. He cries for the loss of another human being, for himself and his wasted life, and for the cold and uncaring humanity at large. Bellow's another 1950s' great work *Henderson the Rain King* concerns an American millionaire who pursues a mythic search for spiritual power in Africa and becomes a rain-maker and heir to a throne.

Bellow's best work in the 1960s is *Herzog*. The protagonist Moses Herzog is a forty-seven-year-old Jewish American whose career as a writer and an academic has encountered difficulty. Alone in an old house which he shares with rats, he is engaged in a whirlwind of mental activity and scrawls frantic letters which he never mails. Through these letters his life story is made known to the readers.

Mr. Sammler's Planet is set on a day, a night and the following day in April of 1969 in New York City, before the first Apollo lunar landings; everyone was talking about life on some other planet. The protagonist Mr. Sammler, a Holocaust survivor with Polish Jewish decent, is a displaced person in his seventies. In spite of other people's craziness with the promises of the future moon landings and endless possibilities, the Earth is still his planet which he defends with his human decency.

Humboldt's Gift won the 1976 Pulitzer Prize for Fiction and contributed to Bellow's winning the Nobel Prize in Literature the same year. It depicts the contrasting careers of two writers, Von Humboldt Fleisher and his protégé Charlie Citrine. Fleisher yearns to lift American society through art, but dies a failure. In contrast, Charlie Citrine makes a lot of money through his writing, especially from a Broadway play and a movie about a character named Von Trenck modeled after Fleisher.

Ravelstein is Saul Bellow's final novel. It is written in the form of a memoir. The narrator is in Paris with Abe Ravelstein, a renowned professor, and Nikki, his lover. Ravelstein, who is dying, asks the narrator to write a memoir about him after he dies. After Ravelstein's death, the narrator and his wife go on holiday to the Caribbean. The narrator catches a tropical disease and flies back to the United States to convalesce. Eventually, on regaining health, he decides to write the memoir.

Bellow sticks to realism and reflects the social evils and human sufferings prevalent in modern human society.

Most of his novels are philosophical representations of the isolation and predicament of the individual self in the modern American world. His approach to his characters and their obsessions is affirmative rather than ironic. His Nobel Prize award citation bespeaks well the spirit of his work: "For the human understanding and subtle analysis of contemporary culture that are combined in his work. "

Saul Bellow's Nobel Lecture

(December 12, 1976)

(Excerpt)

...

Every year we see scores of books and articles which tell the Americans what a state they are in — which make intelligent or simpleminded or extravagant or lurid or demented statements. All reflect the crises we are in while telling us what we must do about them; these analysts are produced by the very disorder and confusion they prescribe for. It is as a writer that I am considering their extreme moral sensitivity, their desire for perfection, their intolerance of the defects of society, the touching, the comical boundlessness of their demands, their anxiety, their irritability, their sensitivity, their tender-mindedness, their goodness, their convulsiveness, the recklessness with which they experiment with drugs and touch-therapies and bombs. The ex-Jesuit Malachi Martin in his book on the Church compares the modern American to Michelangelo's sculpture, *The Captive*. He sees " an unfinished struggle to emerge whole" from a block of matter. The American " captive" is beset in his struggle by "interpretations, admonitions, forewarnings and descriptions of himself by the self-appointed prophets, priests, judges and prefabricators of his travail," says Martin.

Let me take a little time to look more closely at this travail. In private life, disorder or near-panic. In families — for husbands, wives, parents, children — confusion; in civic behavior, in personal loyalties, in sexual practices (I will not recite the whole list; we are tired of hearing it) — further confusion. And with this private disorder goes public bewilderment. In the papers we read what used to amuse us in science fiction — *The New York Times* speaks of death rays and of Russian and American satellites at war in space. In the November *Encounter* so sober and responsible an economist as my colleague, Milton Friedman, declares that Great Britain by its public spending will soon go the way of poor countries like Chile. He is appalled by his own forecast. ...

You would think that one such article would be enough for a single number of a magazine but on another page of *Encounter* Professor Hugh Seton-Watson discusses George Kennan's recent survey of American degeneracy and its dire meaning for the world. Describing America's failure, Kennan speaks of crime, urban decay, drug-addiction, pornography, frivolity, deteriorated educational standards and concludes that our immense power counts for nothing. We cannot lead the world and, undermined by sinfulness, we may not be able to defend ourselves. Professor Seton-Watson writes, "Nothing can defend a society if its upper 100,000 men and women, both the decision-makers and those who help to mould the thinking of the decision-makers, are resolved to capitulate."

So much for the capitalist superpower. Now what about its ideological adversaries? I turn the pages of *Encounter* to a short study by Mr. George Watson, Lecturer in English at Cambridge, on the racialism of the Left. He tells us that Hyndman, the founder of the Social Democratic Federation, called the South African war the Jews' war; that the Webbs at times expressed racialist views (as did Ruskin, Carlyle and T. H. Huxley before them); he relates that Engels denounced the smaller Slav peoples of Eastern Europe as counter-revolutionary ethnic trash; and Mr. Watson in conclusion cites a public statement by Ulrike Meinhof of the West German "Red Army Faction" made at a judicial hearing in 1972 approving of "revolutionary extermination." For her, German anti-semitism of the Hitler period was essentially anticapitalist. "Auschwitz," she is quoted as saying, "meant that six million Jews were killed and thrown on the waste heap of Europe for what they were: money Jews (Geldjuden)."

I mention these racialists of the Left to show that for us there is no simple choice between the children of light and the children of darkness. Good and evil are not symmetrically distributed along political lines. But I have made my point; we stand open to all anxieties. The decline and fall of everything is our daily dread, we are agitated in private life and tormented by public questions.

And art and literature — what of them? Well, there is a violent uproar but we are not absolutely dominated by it. We are still able to think, to discriminate, and to feel. The purer, subtler, higher activities have not succumbed to fury or to nonsense. Not yet. Books continue to be written and read. It may be more difficult to reach the whirling mind of a modern reader but it is possible to cut through the noise and reach the quiet zone. In the quiet zone we may find that he is devoutly waiting for us. When complications increase, the desire for essentials increases too. The unending cycle of crises that began with the First World War has formed a kind of person, one who has lived through terrible, strange things, and in whom there is an observable shrinkage of prejudices, a casting off of disappointing ideologies, an ability to live with many kinds of madness, an immense desire for certain durable human goods — truth, for instance, or freedom, or wisdom. I don't think I am exaggerating; there is plenty of evidence for this. Disintegration? Well, yes. Much is disintegrating but we are experiencing also an odd kind of refining process. And this has been going on for a long time. Looking into Proust's *Time Regained* I find that he was clearly aware of it. His novel, describing French society during the Great War, tests the strength of his art. Without art, he insists, shirking no personal or collective horrors, we do not know ourselves or anyone else. Only art penetrates what pride, passion, intelligence and habit erect on all sides — the seeming realities of this world. There is another reality, the genuine one, which we lose sight of. This other reality is always sending us hints, which, without art, we can't receive. Proust calls these hints our "true impressions." The true impressions, our persistent intuitions, will, without art, be hidden from us and we will be left with nothing but a "terminology for practical ends which we falsely call life." Tolstoy put the matter in much the same way. A book like his *Ivan Ilyitch* also describes these same "practical ends" which conceal both life and death from us. In his final sufferings Ivan Ilyitch becomes an individual, a "character," by tearing down the concealments, by seeing through the "practical ends."

Proust was still able to keep a balance between art and destruction, insisting that art was a necessity of life, a great independent reality, a magical power. But for a long time art has not been connected, as it was in the past, with the main enterprise. The historian Edgar Wind tells us in *Art and Anarchy* that Hegel long ago observed that art no longer engaged the central energies of man. These energies were now engaged by science — a "relentless spirit of rational inquiry." Art had moved to the margins. There it formed "a wide and splendidly varied horizon." In an age of science people still painted and wrote poetry but, said Hegel, however splendid the gods looked in modern works of art and whatever dignity and perfection we might find "in the images of God the Father and the Virgin Mary" it was of no use: we no longer bent our knees. It is a long time since the knees were bent in piety. Ingenuity, daring exploration, freshness of invention replaced the art of "direct relevance." The most significant achievement of this pure art, in Hegel's view, was that, freed from its former responsibilities, it was no longer "serious." Instead it raised the soul through the "serenity of form above any painful involvement in the limitations of reality." I don't know who would make such a claim today for an art that raises the soul above painful involvements with reality. Nor am I sure that at this moment, it is the spirit of rational inquiry in pure science that engages the central energies of man. The center seems (temporarily perhaps) to be filled up with the crises I have been describing.

There were European writers in the 19th Century who would not give up the connection of literature with the main human enterprise. The very suggestion would have shocked Tolstoy and Dostoevski. But in the West a separation between great artists and the general public took place. They developed a marked contempt for the average reader and the bourgeois mass. The best of them saw clearly enough what sort of civilization Europe had produced, brilliant but unstable, vulnerable, fated to be overtaken by catastrophe, the historian Erich Auerbach tells us. Some of these writers, he says, produced "strange and vaguely terrifying works, or shocked the public by paradoxical and extreme opinions. Many of them took no trouble to facilitate the understanding of what they wrote — whether out of contempt for the public, the cult of their own inspiration, or a certain tragic weakness which prevented them from being at once simple and true. "

In the 20th century, theirs is still the main influence, for despite a show of radicalism and innovation our contemporaries are really very conservative. They follow their l9th-century leaders and hold to the old standard, interpreting history and society much as they were interpreted in the last century. What would writers do today if it would occur to them that literature might once again engage those "central energies," if they were to recognize that an immense desire had arisen for a return from the periphery, for what was simple and true?

Of course we can't come back to the center simply because we want to; but the fact that we are wanted might matter to us and the force of the crisis is so great that it may summon us back to such a center. But prescriptions are futile. One can't tell writers what to do. The imagination must find its own path. But one can fervently wish that they — that we — would come back from the periphery. We do not, we writers, represent mankind adequately. What account do Americans give of themselves, what accounts of them are given by psychologists, sociologists, historians, journalists, and writers? In a kind of contractual daylight they see themselves in the ways with which we are so desperately familiar. These images of contractual daylight, so boring to Robbe-Grillet and to me, originate in the contemporary world view: We put into our books the consumer, civil servant, football fan, lover, television viewer. And in the contractual daylight version their life is a kind of death. There is another life coming from an insistent sense of what we are which denies these daylight formulations and the false life — the death in life — they make for us. For it is false, and we know it, and our secret and incoherent resistance to it cannot stop, for that resistance arises from persistent intuitions. Perhaps humankind cannot bear too much reality, but neither can it bear too much unreality, too much abuse of the truth.

We do not think well of ourselves; we do not think amply about what we are. Our collective achievements have so greatly "exceeded" us that we "justify" ourselves by pointing to them. It is the jet plane in which we commonplace human beings have crossed the Atlantic in four hours that embodies such value as we can claim. Then we hear that this is closing time in the gardens of the West, that the end of our capitalist civilization is at hand. Some years ago Cyril Connolly wrote that we were about to undergo "a complete mutation, not merely to be defined as the collapse of the capitalist system, but such a sea-change in the nature of reality as could not have been envisaged by Karl Marx or Sigmund Freud. " This means that we are not yet sufficiently shrunken; we must prepare to be smaller still. I am not sure whether this should be called intellectual analysis or analysis by an intellectual. The disasters are disasters. It would be worse than stupid to call them victories as some statesmen have tried to do. But I am drawing attention to the fact that there is in the intellectual community a sizeable inventory of attitudes that have become respectable — notions about society, human nature, class, politics, sex, about mind, about the physical universe, the evolution of life. Few writers, even among the best, have taken the trouble to re-examine these attitudes or orthodoxies. Such attitudes only glow more powerfully in Joyce or D. H. Lawrence than in the books of lesser men; they are everywhere and no one challenges them seriously. Since the Twenties, how many novelists have taken a second look at D. H. Lawrence, or argued a different view of sexual potency or the effects of industrial civilization on the instincts? Literature has for nearly a century used the same stock of ideas, myths, strategies. "The most serious essayists of the last fifty years," says Robbe-Grillet. Yes, indeed. Essay after essay, book after book, confirm the most serious thoughts — Baudelairian, Nietzschean, Marxian, Psychoanalytic, etcetera — of these most serious essayists. What Robbe-Grillet says about character can be said also about these ideas, maintaining all the usual things about mass society, dehumanization and the rest. How weary we are of them. How poorly they represent us. The pictures they offer no more resemble us than we resemble the reconstructed reptiles and other monsters in a museum of paleontology. We are much more limber, versatile, better articulated, there is much more to us, we all feel it.

What is at the center now? At the moment, neither art nor science but mankind determining, in confusion and obscurity, whether it will endure or go under. The whole species — everybody — has gotten into the act. At such a time it is essential to lighten ourselves, to dump encumbrances, including the encumbrances of education and all organized platitudes, to make judgments of our own, to perform acts of our own. Conrad was right to appeal to that part of our being which is a gift. We must hunt for that under the wreckage of many systems. The failure of those systems may bring a blessed and necessary release from formulations, from an over-defined and misleading consciousness. With increasing frequency I dismiss as merely respectable opinions I have long held — or thought I held — and try to discern what I have really lived by, and what others live by. ...Our very vices, our mutilations, show how rich we are in thought and culture. How much we know. How much we even feel. The struggle that convulses us makes us want to simplify, to reconsider, to eliminate the tragic weakness which prevented writers — and readers — from being at once simple and true.

Writers are greatly respected. The intelligent public is wonderfully patient with them, continues to read them and endures disappointment after disappointment, waiting to hear from art what it does not hear from theology, philosophy, social theory, and what it cannot hear from pure science. Out of the struggle at the center has come an immense, painful longing for a broader, more flexible, fuller, more coherent, more comprehensive account of what we human beings are, who we are, and what this life is for. At the center humankind struggles with collective powers for its freedom, the individual struggles with dehumanization for the possession of his soul. If writers do not come again into the center it will not be because the center is pre-empted. It is not. They are free to enter. If they so wish.

The essence of our real condition, the complexity, the confusion, the pain of it is shown to us in glimpses, in what Proust and Tolstoy thought of as "true impressions." This essence reveals, and then conceals itself. When it goes away it leaves us again in doubt. But we never seem to lose our connection with the depths from which these glimpses come. The sense of our real powers, powers we seem to derive from the universe itself, also comes and goes. We are reluctant to talk about this because there is nothing we can prove, because our language is inadequate and because few people are willing to risk talking about it. They would have to say, "There is a spirit" and that is taboo. So almost everyone keeps quiet about it, although almost everyone is aware of it.

The value of literature lies in these intermittent "true impressions." A novel moves back and forth between the world of objects, of actions, of appearances, and that other world from which these "true impressions" come and which moves us to believe that the good we hang onto so tenaciously — in the face of evil, so obstinately — is no illusion.

No one who has spent years in the writing of novels can be unaware of this. The novel can't be compared to the epic, or to the monuments of poetic drama. But it is the best we can do just now. It is a sort of latter-day lean-to, a hovel in which the spirit takes shelter. A novel is balanced between a few true impressions and the multitude of false ones that make up most of what we call life. It tells us that for every human being there is a diversity of existences, that the single existence is itself an illusion in part, that these many existences signify something, tend to something, fulfill something; it promises us meaning, harmony and even justice. What Conrad said was true, art attempts to find in the universe, in matter as well as in the facts of life, what is fundamental, enduring, essential.

▶▶ Questions for Consideration and Discussion

1. Bellow claims that Proust holds the view that without art...we do not know ourselves or anyone else, that only art penetrates what pride, passion, intelligence and habit erect on all sides — the seeming realities of this world. Do you agree with Proust? Why or why not?

2. According to Bellow, the historian Edgar Wind tells us in *Art and Anarchy* that Hegel long ago observed that art no longer engaged the central energies of man, that these energies were now engaged by science — a "relentless spirit of rational inquiry," that art had moved to the margins, but Bellow thought that the center seemed "(temporarily perhaps) to be filled up with crises" he had been describing. What do you think is at the center now?

3. Bellow claims that the value of literature lies in the intermittent "true impressions," which are hints sent by the genuine reality which we lose sight of. What "true impressions" have you got from works of art you have studied?

▍ Flannery O'Connor (1925 –1964)

Flannery O'Connor, a female Southern writer with a Roman Catholic faith, was one of the twentieth century's finest writers of short stories. She is particularly acclaimed for her stories which combine comic with tragic and brutal.

O'Connor was born and brought up in Georgia. Her father Edward O'Connor died in 1941 from disseminated lupus, a rare and incurable disease, which would later take

Flannery's life as well.

O'Connor was educated at Georgia State College for Women, and graduated in 1945. The following year, she published her first short story, "The Geranium." She then went on to study creative writing at the University of Iowa, where she received her MFA in 1947.

In 1950, she finished the novel *Wise Blood*, which tells the tale of Hazel Motes, a man who tries to start the Church Without Christ. Later that year, she began suffering from lupus, and returned home to the family farm in Milledgeville, where she raised peacocks and wrote. She was given cortisone injections, which managed to stop the disease, but weakened her bones to such an extent that she had to walk on crutches from 1955 until the end of her life.

Wise Blood was published in 1952 (John Huston turned it into a film in 1979). Her second novel, *The Violent Bear It Away* (1960) was also religious in nature. Though a devout Roman Catholic, the characters she portrayed in her work were Protestant. She explained this by saying that Protestants are more likely to express their faith through dramatic action.

In 1955, she published her first book of short stories, *A Good Man Is Hard to Find*. It contained titles such as "The Life You Save May Be Your Own" and "Good Country People." Her short stories are darkly comic, featuring the rhythms of everyday Southern life and Southern speech patterns. Critics referred to her as a writer of the grotesque, as she often focused her tales on the darkness of human nature.

Flannery O'Connor died from lupus in 1964 at the age of 39, leaving behind 31 short stories, various letters and speeches, and two novels. Posthumous collections include *Everything That Rises Must Converge* (1965), *Mystery and Manners: Occasional Prose* (1969), *The Complete Short Stories of Flannery O'Connor* (1971, National Book Award Winner), *The Habit of Being: Letters* (1979), *The Presence of Grace and Other Book Reviews* (1983), *The Correspondence of Flannery O'Connor and the Brainars Cheneys* (1986), and *Complete Works* (1988).

O'Connor's fiction frequently addresses the theme of violence in modern life, questioning the efficacy of religion as a way of overcoming evil.

A Good Man Is Hard to Find

The Grandmother didn't want to go to Florida. She wanted to visit some of her connections in east Tennessee and she was seizing at every chance to change Bailey's mind. Bailey was the son she lived with, her only boy. He was sitting on the edge of his chair at the table, bent over the orange sports section of the Journal. "Now look here, Bailey," she said, "see here, read this," and she stood with one hand on her thin hip and the other rattling the newspaper at his bald head. "Here this fellow that calls himself The Misfit is aloose from the Federal Pen and headed toward Florida and you read here what it says he did to these people. Just you read it. I wouldn't take my children in any direction with a criminal like that aloose in it. I couldn't answer to my conscience if I did."

Bailey didn't look up from his reading so she wheeled around then and faced the children's mother, a young woman in slacks, whose face was as broad and innocent as a cabbage and was tied around with a green head-kerchief that had two points on the top like rabbit's ears. She was sitting on the sofa, feeding the baby his apricots out of a jar. "The children have been to Florida before," the old lady said. "You all ought to take them somewhere else for a change so they would see different parts of the world and be broad. They never have been to east Tennessee."

The children's mother didn't seem to hear her but the eight-year-old boy, John Wesley, a stocky child with glasses, said, "If you don't want to go to Florida, why dontcha stay at home?" He and the little girl, June Star, were reading the funny papers on the floor.

"She wouldn't stay at home to be queen for a day," June Star said without raising her yellow head.

"Yes and what would you do if this fellow, The Misfit, caught you?" the grandmother asked.

"I'd smack his face," John Wesley said.

"She wouldn't stay at home for a million bucks," June Star said. "Afraid she'd miss something. She has to go everywhere we go."

"All right, Miss," the grandmother said. "Just remember that the next time you want me to curl your hair."

June Star said her hair was naturally curly.

The next morning the grandmother was the first one in the car, ready to go. She had her big black valise that looked like the head of a hippopotamus in one corner, and underneath it she was hiding a basket with Pitty Sing, the cat, in it. She didn't intend for the cat to be left alone in the house for three days because he would miss her too much and she was afraid he might brush against one of the gas burners and accidentally asphyxiate himself. Her son, Bailey, didn't like to arrive at a motel with a cat.

She sat in the middle of the back seat with John Wesley and June Star on either side of her. Bailey and the children's mother and the baby sat in front and they left Atlanta at eight forty-five with the mileage on the car at 55890. The grandmother wrote this down because she thought it would be interesting to say how many miles they had been when they got back. It took them twenty minutes to reach the outskirts of the city.

The old lady settled herself comfortably, removing her white cotton gloves and putting them up with her purse on the shelf in front of the back window. The children's mother still had on slacks and still had her head tied up in a green kerchief, but the grandmother had on a navy blue straw sailor hat with a bunch of white violets on the brim and a navy blue dress with a small white dot in the print. Her collars and cuffs were white organdy trimmed with lace and at her neckline she had pinned a purple spray of cloth violets containing a sachet. In case of an accident, anyone seeing her dead on the highway would know at once that she was a lady.

She said she thought it was going to be a good day for driving, neither too hot nor too cold, and she cautioned Bailey that the speed limit was fifty-five miles an hour and that the patrolmen hid themselves behind billboards and small clumps of trees and sped out after you before you had a chance to slow down. She pointed out interesting details of the scenery: Stone Mountain; the blue granite that in some places came up to both sides of the highway; the brilliant red clay banks slightly streaked with purple; and the various crops that made rows of green lace-work on the ground. The trees were full of silver-white sunlight and the meanest of them sparkled. The children were reading comic magazines and their mother had gone back to sleep.

"Let's go through Georgia fast so we won't have to look at it much," John Wesley said.

"If I were a little boy," said the grandmother, "I wouldn't talk about my native state that way. Tennessee has the mountains and Georgia has the hills."

"Tennessee is just a hillbilly dumping ground," John Wesley said, "and Georgia is a lousy state too."

"You said it," June Star said.

"In my time," said the grandmother, folding her thin veined fingers, "children were more respectful of their native states and their parents and everything else. People did right then. Oh, look at the cute little pickaninny①!" she said and pointed to a Negro child standing in the door of a shack. "Wouldn't that make a picture, now?" she asked and they all turned and looked at the little Negro out of the back window. He waved.

"He didn't have any britches on," June Star said.

"He probably didn't have any," the grandmother explained. "Little niggers in the country don't have things like we do. If I could paint, I'd paint that picture," she said.

The children exchanged comic books.

The grandmother offered to hold the baby and the children's mother passed him over the front seat to her. She set him on her knee and bounced him and told him about the things they were passing. She rolled her eyes and screwed up her mouth and stuck her leathery thin face into his smooth bland one. Occasionally he gave her a faraway smile. They passed a large cotton field with five or six graves fenced in the middle of it, like a small island. "Look at the graveyard!" the grandmother said, pointing it out. "That was the old family burying ground. That belonged to the plantation."

"Where's the plantation?" John Wesley asked.

"Gone With the Wind," said the grandmother. "Ha. Ha."

---

① pickaninny: an offensive term that means a small black child.

When the children finished all the comic books they had brought, they opened the lunch and ate it. The grandmother ate a peanut butter sandwich and an olive and would not let the children throw the box and the paper napkins out the window. When there was nothing else to do they played a game by choosing a cloud and making the other two guess what shape it suggested. John Wesley took one the shape of a cow and June Star guessed a cow and John Wesley said, no, an automobile, and June Star said he didn't play fair, and they began to slap each other over the grandmother.

The grandmother said she would tell them a story if they would keep quiet. When she told a story, she rolled her eyes and waved her head and was very dramatic. She said once when she was a maiden lady she had been courted by a Mr. Edgar Atkins Teagarden from Jasper, Georgia. She said he was a very good-looking man and a gentleman and that he brought her a watermelon every Saturday afternoon with his initials cut in it, E. A. T. Well, one Saturday, she said, Mr. Teagarden brought the watermelon and there was nobody at home and he left it on the front porch and returned in his buggy to Jasper, but she never got the watermelon, she said, because a nigger boy ate it when he saw the initials, E. A. T. ! This story tickled John Wesley's funny bone and he giggled and giggled but June Star didn't think it was any good. She said she wouldn't marry a man that just brought her a watermelon on Saturday. The grandmother said she would have done well to marry Mr. Teagarden because he was a gentleman and had bought Coca-Cola stock when it first came out and that he had died only a few years ago, a very wealthy man.

They stopped at The Tower for barbecued sandwiches. The Tower was a part stucco and part wood filling station and dance hall set in a clearing outside of Timothy. A fat man named Red Sammy Butts ran it and there were signs stuck here and there on the building and for miles up and down the highway saying, TRY RED SAMMY'S FAMOUS BARBECUE. NONE LIKE FAMOUS RED SAMMY'S! RED SAM! THE FAT BOY WITH THE HAPPY LAUGH. A VETERAN! RED SAMMY'S YOUR MAN!

Red Sammy was lying on the bare ground outside The Tower with his head under a truck while a gray monkey about a foot high, chained to a small chinaberry tree, chattered nearby. The monkey sprang back into the tree and got on the highest limb as soon as he saw the children jump out of the car and run toward him.

Inside, The Tower was a long dark room with a counter at one end and tables at the other and dancing space in the middle. They all sat down at a board table next to the nickelodeon and Red Sam's wife, a tall burnt-brown woman with hair and eyes lighter than her skin, came and took their order. The children's mother put a dime in the machine and played "The Tennessee Waltz," and the grandmother said that tune always made her want to dance. She asked Bailey if he would like to dance but he only glared at her. He didn't have a naturally sunny disposition like she did and trips made him nervous. The grandmother's brown eyes were very bright. She swayed her head from side to side and pretended she was dancing in her chair. June Star said play something she could tap to so the children's mother put in another dime and played a fast number and June Star stepped out onto the dance floor and did her tap routine.

"Ain't she cute?" Red Sam's wife said, leaning over the counter. "Would you like to come be my little girl?"

"No I certainly wouldn't," June Star said. "I wouldn't live in a broken-down place like this for a million bucks!" and she ran back to the table.

"Ain't she cute?" the woman repeated, stretching her mouth politely.

"Aren't you ashamed?" hissed the grandmother.

Red Sam came in and told his wife to quit lounging on the counter and hurry up with these people's order. His khaki trousers reached just to his hip bones and his stomach hung over them like a sack of meal swaying under his shirt. He came over and sat down at a table nearby and let out a combination sigh and yodel. "You can't win," he said. "You can't win," and he wiped his sweating red face off with a gray handkerchief. "These days you don't know who to trust," he said. "Ain't that the truth?"

"People are certainly not nice like they used to be," said the grandmother.

"Two fellers come in here last week," Red Sammy said, "driving a Chrysler. It was a old beat-up car but it was a good one and these boys looked all right to me. Said they worked at the mill and you know I let them fellers charge the gas they bought? Now why did I do that?"

"Because you're a good man!" the grandmother said at once.

"Yes'm, I suppose so," Red Sam said as if he were struck with this answer.

His wife brought the orders, carrying the five plates all at once without a tray, two in each hand and one balanced on her arm. "It isn't a soul in this green world of God's that you can trust," she said. "And I don't count nobody out of that, not nobody," she repeated, looking at Red Sammy.

"Did you read about that criminal, The Misfit, that's escaped?" asked the grandmother.

"I wouldn't be a bit surprised if he didn't attack this place right here," said the woman. "If he hears about it being here, I wouldn't be none surprised to see him. If he hears it's two cent in the cash register, I wouldn't be a tall surprised if he..."

"That'll do," Red Sam said. "Go bring these people their Co'-Colas," and the woman went off to get the rest of the order.

"A good man is hard to find," Red Sammy said. "Every-thing is getting terrible. I remember the day you could go off and leave your screen door unlatched. Not no more."

He and the grandmother discussed better times. The old lady said that in her opinion Europe was entirely to blame for the way things were now. She said the way Europe acted you would think we were made of money and Red Sam said it was no use talking about it, she was exactly right. The children ran outside into the white sunlight and looked at the monkey in the lacy chinaberry tree. He was busy catching fleas on himself and biting each one carefully between his teeth as if it were a delicacy.

They drove off again into the hot afternoon. The grandmother took cat naps and woke up every few minutes with her own snoring. Outside of Toombsboro she woke up and recalled an old plantation that she had visited in this neighborhood once when she was a young lady.

She said the house had six white columns across the front and that there was an avenue of oaks leading up to it and two little wooden trellis arbors on either side in front where you sat down with your suitor after a stroll in the garden. She recalled exactly which road to turn off to get to it. She knew that Bailey would not be willing to lose any time looking at an old house, but the more she talked about it, the more she wanted to see it once again and find out if the little twin arbors were still standing. "There was a secret panel in this house," she said craftily, not telling the truth but wishing that she were, "and the story went that all the family silver was hidden in it when Sherman came through but it was never found..."

"Hey!" John Wesley said. "Let's go see it! We'll find it! We'll poke all the woodwork and find it! Who lives there? Where do you turn off at? Hey Pop, can't we turn off there?"

"We never have seen a house with a secret panel!" June Star shrieked. "Let's go to the house with the secret panel! Hey Pop, can't we go see the house with the secret panel!"

"It's not far from here, I know," the grandmother said. "It wouldn't take over twenty minutes."

Bailey was looking straight ahead. His jaw was as rigid as a horseshoe. "No," he said.

The children began to yell and scream that they wanted to see the house with the secret panel. John Wesley kicked the back of the front seat and June Star hung over her mother's shoulder and whined desperately into her ear that they never had any fun even on their vacation, that they could never do what THEY wanted to do. The baby began to scream and John Wesley kicked the back of the seat so hard that his father could feel the blows in his kidney.

"All right!" he shouted and drew the car to a stop at the side of the road. "Will you all shut up? Will you all just shut up for one second? If you don't shut up, we won't go anywhere."

"It would be very educational for them," the grandmother murmured.

"All right," Bailey said, "but get this: this is the only time we're going to stop for anything like this. This is the one and only time."

"The dirt road that you have to turn down is about a mile back," the grandmother directed. "I marked it when we passed."

"A dirt road," Bailey groaned.

After they had turned around and were headed toward the dirt road, the grandmother recalled other points about the house, the beautiful glass over the front doorway and the candle-lamp in the hall. John Wesley said that the secret panel was probably in the fireplace.

"You can't go inside this house," Bailey said. "You don't know who lives there."

"While you all talk to the people in front, I'll run around behind and get in a window," John Wesley suggested.

"We'll all stay in the car," his mother said.

They turned onto the dirt road and the car raced roughly along in a swirl of pink dust. The grandmother recalled the times when there were no paved roads and thirty miles was a day's journey. The dirt road was hilly and there were sudden washes in it and sharp curves on dangerous embankments. All at once they would be on a hill, looking down over the blue tops of trees for miles around, then the next minute, they would be in a red depression with the dust-coated trees looking down on them.

"This place had better turn up in a minute," Bailey said, "or I'm going to turn around."

The road looked as if no one had traveled on it in months.

"It's not much farther," the grandmother said and just as she said it, a horrible thought came to her. The thought was so embarrassing that she turned red in the face and her eyes dilated and her feet jumped up, upsetting her valise in the corner. The instant the valise moved, the newspaper top she had over the basket under it rose with a snarl and Pitty Sing, the cat, sprang onto Bailey's shoulder.

The children were thrown to the floor and their mother, clutching the baby, was thrown out the door onto the ground; the old lady was thrown into the front seat. The car turned over once and landed right-side-up in a gulch off the side of the road. Bailey remained in the driver's seat with the cat — gray-striped with a broad white face and an orange nose — clinging to his neck like a caterpillar.

As soon as the children saw they could move their arms and legs, they scrambled out of the car, shouting, "We've had an ACCIDENT!" The grandmother was curled up under the dashboard, hoping she was injured so that Bailey's wrath would not come down on her all at once. The horrible thought she had had before the accident was that the house she had remembered so vividly was not in Georgia but in Tennessee.

Bailey removed the cat from his neck with both hands and flung it out the window against the side of a pine tree. Then he got out of the car and started looking for the children's mother. She was sitting against the side of the red gutted ditch, holding the screaming baby, but she only had a cut down her face and a broken shoulder. "We've had an ACCIDENT!" the children screamed in a frenzy of delight.

"But nobody's killed," June Star said with disappointment as the grandmother limped out of the car, her hat still pinned to her head but the broken front brim standing up at a jaunty angle and the violet spray hanging off the side. They all sat down in the ditch, except the children, to recover from the shock. They were all shaking.

"Maybe a car will come along," said the children's mother hoarsely.

"I believe I have injured an organ," said the grandmother, pressing her side, but no one answered her. Bailey's teeth were clattering. He had on a yellow sport shirt with bright blue parrots designed in it and his face was as yellow as the shirt. The grandmother decided that she would not mention that the house was in Tennessee.

The road was about ten feet above and they could see only the tops of the trees on the other side of it. Behind the ditch they were sitting in there were more woods, tall and dark and deep. In a few minutes they saw a car some distance away on top of a hill, coming slowly as if the occupants were watching them. The grandmother stood up and waved both arms dramatically to attract their attention. The car continued to come on slowly, disappeared around a bend and appeared again, moving even slower, on top of the hill they had gone over. It was a big black battered hearse-like automobile. There were three men in it.

It came to a stop just over them and for some minutes, the driver looked down with a steady expressionless gaze to where they were sitting, and didn't speak. Then he turned his head and muttered something to the other two and they got out. One was a fat boy in black trousers and a red sweat shirt with a silver stallion embossed on the front of it. He moved around on the right side of them and stood staring, his mouth partly open in a kind of loose grin. The other had on khaki pants and a blue striped coat and a gray hat pulled down very low, hiding most of his face. He came around slowly on the left side. Neither spoke.

The driver got out of the car and stood by the side of it, looking down at them. He was an older man than the other two. His hair was just beginning to gray and he wore silver-rimmed spectacles that gave him a scholarly look. He had a long creased face and didn't have on any shirt or undershirt. He had on blue jeans that were too tight for him and was holding a black hat and a gun. The two boys also had guns.

"We've had an ACCIDENT!" the children screamed.

The grandmother had the peculiar feeling that the bespectacled man was someone she knew. His face was as familiar to her as if she had known him all her life but she could not recall who he was. He moved away from the car and began to come down the embankment, placing his feet carefully so that he wouldn't slip. He had on tan and white shoes and no socks, and his ankles were red and thin. "Good afternoon," he said. "I see you all had you a little spill."

"We turned over twice!" said the grandmother.

"Oncet," he corrected. "We seen it happen. Try their car and see will it run, Hiram," he said quietly to the boy with the gray hat.

"What you got that gun for?" John Wesley asked. "Whatcha gonna do with that gun?"

"Lady," the man said to the children's mother, "would you mind calling them children to sit down by you? Children make me nervous. I want all you all to sit down right together there where you're at."

"What are you telling US what to do for?" June Star asked.

Behind them the line of woods gaped like a dark open mouth. "Come here," said their mother.

"Look here now," Bailey began suddenly, "we're in a predicament! We're in..."

The grandmother shrieked. She scrambled to her feet and stood staring. "You're The Misfit!" she said. "I recognized you at once!"

"Yes'm," the man said, smiling slightly as if he were pleased in spite of himself to be known, "but it would have been better for all of you, lady, if you hadn't of reckernized me."

Bailey turned his head sharply and said something to his mother that shocked even the children. The old lady began to cry and The Misfit reddened.

"Lady," he said, "don't you get upset. Sometimes a man says things he don't mean. I don't reckon he meant to talk to you thataway."

"You wouldn't shoot a lady, would you?" the grandmother said and removed a clean handkerchief from her cuff and began to slap at her eyes with it.

The Misfit pointed the toe of his shoe into the ground and made a little hole and then covered it up again. "I would hate to have to," he said.

"Listen," the grandmother almost screamed, "I know you're a good man. You don't look a bit like you have common blood. I know you must come from nice people!"

"Yes mam," he said, "finest people in the world." When he smiled he showed a row of strong white teeth. "God never made a finer woman than my mother and my daddy's heart was pure gold," he said. The boy with the red sweat shirt had come around behind them and was standing with his gun at his hip. The Misfit squatted down on the ground. "Watch them children, Bobby Lee," he said. "You know they make me nervous." He looked at the six of them huddled together in front of him and he seemed to be embarrassed as if he couldn't think of anything to say. "Ain't a cloud in the sky," he remarked, looking up at it. "Don't see no sun but don't see no cloud neither."

"Yes, it's a beautiful day," said the grandmother. "Listen," she said, "you shouldn't call yourself The Misfit because I know you're a good man at heart. I can just look at you and tell."

"Hush!" Bailey yelled. "Hush! Everybody shut up and let me handle this!" He was squatting in the position of a runner about to sprint forward but he didn't move.

"I prechate that, lady," The Misfit said and drew a little circle in the ground with the butt of his gun.

"It'll take a half a hour to fix this here car," Hiram called, looking over the raised hood of it.

"Well, first you and Bobby Lee get him and that little boy to step over yonder with you," The Misfit said, pointing to Bailey and John Wesley. "The boys want to ast you something," he said to Bailey. "Would you mind stepping back in them woods there with them?"

"Listen," Bailey began, "we're in a terrible predicament! Nobody realizes what this is," and his voice cracked. His eyes were as blue and intense as the parrots in his shirt and he remained perfectly still.

The grandmother reached up to adjust her hat brim as if she were going to the woods with him but it came off in her hand. She stood staring at it and after a second she let it fall on the ground. Hiram pulled Bailey up by the arm as if he were assisting an old man. John Wesley caught hold of his father's hand and Bobby Lee followed. They went off toward the woods and just as they reached the dark edge, Bailey turned and supporting himself against a gray naked pine trunk, he shouted, "I'll be back in a minute, Mamma, wait on me!"

"Come back this instant!" his mother shrilled but they all disappeared into the woods.

"Bailey Boy!" the grandmother called in a tragic voice but she found she was looking at The Misfit squatting on the ground in front of her. "I just know you're a good man," she said desperately. "You're not a bit common!"

"Nome, I ain't a good man," The Misfit said after a second as if he had considered her statement carefully, "but I ain't the worst in the world neither. My daddy said I was a different breed of dog from my brothers and sisters. 'You know,' Daddy said, 'it's some that can live their whole life out without asking about it and it's others has to know why it is, and this boy is one of the latters. He's going to be into everything!'" He put on his black hat and looked up suddenly and then away deep into the woods as if he were embarrassed again. "I'm sorry I don't have on a shirt before you ladies," he said, hunching his shoulders slightly. "We buried our clothes that we had on when we escaped and we're just making do until we can get better. We borrowed these from some folks we met," he explained.

"That's perfectly all right," the grandmother said. "Maybe Bailey has an extra shirt in his suitcase."

"I'll look and see terrectly," The Misfit said.

"Where are they taking him?" the children's mother screamed.

"Daddy was a card himself," The Misfit said. "You couldn't put anything over on him. He never got in trouble with the Authorities though. Just had the knack of handling them."

"You could be honest too if you'd only try," said the grandmother. "Think how wonderful it would be to settle down and live a comfortable life and not have to think about somebody chasing you all the time."

The Misfit kept scratching in the ground with the butt of his gun as if he were thinking about it. "Yes'm, somebody is always after you," he murmured.

The grandmother noticed how thin his shoulder blades were just behind his hat because she was standing up looking down on him. "Do you ever pray?" she asked.

He shook his head. All she saw was the black hat wiggle between his shoulder blades. "Nome," he said.

There was a pistol shot from the woods, followed closely by another. Then silence. The old lady's head jerked around. She could hear the wind move through the tree tops like a long satisfied insuck of breath. "Bailey Boy!" she called.

"I was a gospel singer for a while," The Misfit said. "I been most everything. Been in the arm service, both land and sea, at home and abroad, been twice married, been an undertaker, been with the railroads, plowed Mother Earth, been in a tornado, seen a man burnt alive oncet," and he looked up at the children's mother and the little girl who were sitting close together, their faces white and their eyes glassy; "I even seen a woman flogged," he said.

"Pray, pray," the grandmother began, "pray, pray..."

"I never was a bad boy that I remember of," The Misfit said in an almost dreamy voice, "but somewheres along the line I done something wrong and got sent to the penitentiary. I was buried alive," and he looked up and held her attention to him by a steady stare.

"That's when you should have started to pray," she said. "What did you do to get sent to the penitentiary that first time?"

"Turn to the right, it was a wall," The Misfit said, looking up again at the cloudless sky. "Turn to the left, it was a wall. Look up it was a ceiling, look down it was a floor. I forget what I done, lady. I set there and set there, trying to remember what it was I done and I ain't recalled it to this day. Oncet in a while, I would think it was coming to me, but it never come."

"Maybe they put you in by mistake," the old lady said vaguely.

"Nome," he said. "It wasn't no mistake. They had the papers on me. "

"You must have stolen something," she said.

The Misfit sneered slightly. "Nobody had nothing I wanted," he said. "It was a head-doctor at the penitentiary said what I had done was kill my daddy but I known that for a lie. My daddy died in nineteen ought nineteen of the epidemic flu and I never had a thing to do with it. He was buried in the Mount Hopewell Baptist churchyard and you can go there and see for yourself. "

"If you would pray," the old lady said, "Jesus would help you. "

"That's right," The Misfit said.

"Well then, why don't you pray?" she asked trembling with delight suddenly.

"I don't want no hep," he said. "I'm doing all right by myself. "

Bobby Lee and Hiram came ambling back from the woods. Bobby Lee was dragging a yellow shirt with bright blue parrots in it.

"Thow me that shirt, Bobby Lee," The Misfit said. The shirt came flying at him and landed on his shoulder and he put it on. The grandmother couldn't name what the shirt reminded her of. "No, lady," The Misfit said while he was buttoning it up, "I found out the crime don't matter. You can do one thing or you can do another, kill a man or take a tire off his car, because sooner or later you're going to forget what it was you done and just be punished for it. "

The children's mother had begun to make heaving noises as if she couldn't get her breath. "Lady," he asked, "would you and that little girl like to step off yonder with Bobby Lee and Hiram and join your husband?"

"Yes, thank you," the mother said faintly. Her left arm dangled helplessly and she was holding the baby, who had gone to sleep, in the other. "Hep that lady up, Hiram," The Misfit said as she struggled to climb out of the ditch, "and Bobby Lee, you hold onto that little girl's hand. "

"I don't want to hold hands with him," June Star said. "He reminds me of a pig. "

The fat boy blushed and laughed and caught her by the arm and pulled her off into the woods after Hiram and her mother.

Alone with The Misfit, the grandmother found that she had lost her voice. There was not a cloud in the sky nor any sun. There was nothing around her but woods. She wanted to tell him that he must pray. She opened and closed her mouth several times before anything came out. Finally she found herself saying, "Jesus. Jesus," meaning, Jesus will help you, but the way she was saying it, it sounded as if she might be cursing.

"Yes'm," The Misfit said as if he agreed. "Jesus shown everything off balance. It was the same case with Him as with me except He hadn't committed any crime and they could prove I had committed one because they had the papers on me. Of course," he said, "they never shown me my papers. That's why I sign myself now. I said long ago, you get you a signature and sign everything you do and keep a copy of it. Then you'll know what you done and you can hold up the crime to the punishment and see do they match and in the end you'll have something to prove you ain't been treated right. I call myself The Misfit," he said, "because I can't make what all I done wrong fit what all I gone through in punishment."

There was a piercing scream from the woods, followed closely by a pistol report. "Does it seem right to you, lady, that one is punished a heap and another ain't punished at all?"

"Jesus!" the old lady cried. "You've got good blood! I know you wouldn't shoot a lady! I know you come from nice people! Pray! Jesus, you ought not to shoot a lady. I'll give you all the money I've got!"

"Lady," The Misfit said, looking beyond her far into the woods, "there never was a body that give the undertaker a tip."

There were two more pistol reports and the grandmother raised her head like a parched old turkey hen crying for water and called, "Bailey Boy, Bailey Boy!" as if her heart would break.

"Jesus was the only One that ever raised the dead," The Misfit continued, "and He shouldn't have done it. He shown everything off balance. If He did what He said, then it's nothing for you to do but thow away everything and follow Him, and if He didn't, then it's nothing for you to do but enjoy the few minutes you got left the best way you can — by killing somebody or burning down his house or doing some other meanness to him. No pleasure but meanness," he said and his voice had become almost a snarl.

"Maybe He didn't raise the dead," the old lady mumbled, not knowing what she was saying and feeling so dizzy that she sank down in the ditch with her legs twisted under her.

"I wasn't there so I can't say He didn't," The Misfit said. "I wisht I had of been there," he said, hitting the ground with his fist. "It ain't right I wasn't there because if I had of been there I would of known. Listen lady," he said in a high voice, "if I had of been there I would of known and I wouldn't be like I am now." His voice seemed about to crack and the grandmother's head cleared for an instant. She saw the man's face twisted close to her own as if he were going to cry and she murmured, "Why you're one of my babies. You're one of my own children!" She reached out and touched him on the shoulder. The Misfit sprang back as if a snake had bitten him and shot her three times through the chest. Then he put his gun down on the ground and took off his glasses and began to clean them.

Hiram and Bobby Lee returned from the woods and stood over the ditch, looking down at the grandmother who half sat and half lay in a puddle of blood with her legs crossed under her like a child's and her face smiling up at the cloudless sky.

Without his glasses, The Misfit's eyes were red-rimmed and pale and defenseless-looking. "Take her off and throw her where you thrown the others," he said, picking up the cat that was rubbing itself against his leg.

"She was a talker, wasn't she?" Bobby Lee said, sliding down the ditch with a yodel.

"She would of been a good woman," The Misfit said, "if it had been somebody there to shoot her every minute of her life."

"Some fun!" Bobby Lee said.

"Shut up, Bobby Lee!" The Misfit said. "It's no real pleasure in life."

> ## Questions for Consideration and Discussion

1. What's your immediate reaction when seeing the title " A Good Man Is Hard to Find?" What do you think it means to be good?

2. Discuss the role of coincidence in the story. How are the later events adequately foreshadowed?

3. Paraphrase The Misfit's philosophy. In what sense could Jesus be said to throw "everything off balance"? Gu Hongming (辜鸿铭), in *The Spirit of the Chinese People*, claims that "in modern Europe, the people have a religion which satisfies their heart, but not their head, and a philosophy which satisfies their head but not their heart. " What's your opinion?

4. A recurring theme in O'Connor is that redemption can be achieved through catastrophe or sanctity through great sinfulness. Do you agree or disagree? Please explain.

Allen Ginsberg (1926 – 1997)

Allen Ginsberg, a central figure and a guru of American "beat generation," is best known for his long poem *Howl* (1956), which combined criticism of the dull, prosperous Eisenhower years with celebration of an emerging counterculture.

The "beat generation" refers to a group of American poets and artists in the late 1950s, with the core figures being Allen Ginsberg, Jack Kerouac, and William S. Burroughs. It has been widely believed that the word "beat" has punning overtones of "beaten down" and "beatific," with the latter layer of meaning directing to a spiritual connotation as in " beatitude," meaning blissfulness or happiness. Living in the climate of post-World War II , the "beat generation" writers rebelled against American mainstream cultural values and middle-class tastes in poetry. They rejected materialism, militarism, consumerism, and conformity of the 1950s in search of "beatific" ecstasy through drugs, sex, and Zen Buddhism. Their loose styles favor spontaneous self-expression and recitation to jazz accompaniment. The principal works of the group are Ginsberg's *Howl* (1956), Kerouac's *On the Road* (1957), and William S. Burroughs' *The Naked Lunch* (1959). The Beats had a strong influence on the "counterculture" of the 1960s.

Ginsberg was born in New Jersey in 1926. His father was a schoolteacher and a poet. His mother was a Russian emigrant, whose madness and eventual death Ginsberg memorialized in *Kaddish* (1959).

Ginsberg graduated from Columbia University in 1948 with high grades but under a legal cloud. Because a colorful but irresponsible addict friend had been using Ginsberg's apartment as a storage depot for the goods he stole to support his drug habit, to avoid prosecution as an accomplice, Ginsberg had to plead insanity and spend eight months in the Columbia Psychiatric Institute. Later, attracted by San Francisco's long honorable tradition of Bohemian, Buddhist, mystical, and anarchist social involvement, he moved there. In the years after 1954 he met San Francisco poets, including Lawrence Ferlinghetti, whose City Lights Bookshop became the publisher of *Howl*.

Howl consists of three parts. The first part is about the poet's going through hell, showing the reader that any eccentricity and unconventionality characterizing the Beat Generation are natural and understandable in the nightmarish surrounding. The second part offers an opportunity for the poet to launch his fierce attack on the mechanical civilization of America, which is named "Moloch[①]." The third is about the poet's experience influenced by Carl Solomon while they were in the mental institute. The title of the long poem was suggested by Jack Kerouac, to whom the poem's outpouring of pent-up rage resembled the rising and falling cry of wolves or dogs in pain or distress.

Ginsberg writes in a style of free verse more free than Whitman's. He experiments with long lines, which might be called "breath lines." At his best he gives a sense of both doom and beauty.

During the 1960s, Ginsberg served as a kind of guru himself for many young people disoriented by the Vietnam War. He was a gentle and persuasive presence at hearings for many kinds of reforms: revision of severe drug laws and laws against homosexuality.

Howl
For Carl Solomon
(Excerpt)
I

I saw the best minds of my generation destroyed by madness, starving hysterical naked,
    dragging themselves through the negro streets at dawn looking for an angry fix,

---

① Moloch: Also spelled Molech. It is the biblical name (in 2 Kings 23:10) of a Canaanite god whose worship was marked by child sacrifice, with a parent throwing his or her own child alive into fire within a bronze statue.

angelheaded hipsters burning for the ancient heavenly connection to the starry dynamo in
the machinery of night,

who poverty and tatters and hollow-eyed and high sat up smoking in the supernatural
darkness of cold-water flats floating across the tops of cities contemplating jazz,

5   who bared their brains to Heaven under the El and saw Mohammedan angels staggering
on tenement roofs illuminated,

who passed through universities with radiant cool eyes hallucinating Arkansas and Blake-
light tragedy among the scholars of war,

who were expelled from the academies for crazy & publishing obscene odes on the
windows of the skull,

who cowered in unshaven rooms in underwear, burning their money in wastebaskets and
listening to the Terror through the wall,

who got busted in their pubic beards returning through Laredo with a belt of marijuana
for New York,

10   who ate fire in paint hotels or drank turpentine in Paradise Alley, death, or purgatoried
their torsos night after night,

with dreams, with drugs, with waking nightmares, alcohol and cock and endless balls,

incomparable blind streets of shuddering cloud and lightning in the mind leaping toward
poles of Canada & Paterson, illuminating all the motionless world of Time
between,

…

▶ Questions for Consideration and Discussion

1. Read the excerpt aloud and see if you like it or not. Please explain.
2. How did you view the unconventionalities, say, people with homosexual tendency or
   with mental problems? Would you view them differently after reading Ginsberg and
   his associates? Why or why not?

Robert Lowell (1917 –1977)

Robert Lowell is best remembered for his initiative role in the confessional poetry
movement and for his confessional poems. He was a two-time Pulitzer Prize winner, in
1947 and 1974 respectively, but for poems of different styles.

Lowell was born into one of the oldest and most distinguished of Boston families:
Two well-known American poets, James Russell Lowell and Amy Lowell, were among
his ancestors. Lowell both embraced and rebelled against his aristocratic background.

In 1935, Lowell entered the family's alma mater, Harvard College. But two years later, he dropped out and left the East to enroll in Kenyon College in Ohio, where he studied under the poet John Crowe Ransom. Immensely talented and thoughtful, Lowell achieved early success as a poet, winning the Pulitzer Prize for *Lord Weary's Castle* (1946) in 1947. In this book and in *The Mills of Kavanaughs* (1951), he examined his own world-weariness in verse that is highly crafted, heavy, and dense with symbols. In this style, he seemed to have achieved a permanent reputation.

In mid-life, when finding that some young American poets, in particular Allen Ginsberg, were writing in a much more open and direct style, Lowell was no longer pleased with his early poetry, though it had brought him much fame. He described his early poetry as being " willfully difficult," with a " stiff, humorless and even impenetrable surface. " So he began working on a new kind of poetry that has come to be called confessional poetry. In his new poems, he began to speak with a sometimes embarrassing openness and frankness about his own life (though more controlled and severe than Beat writers), such as about his mental breakdown and about his marital difficulties. Apart from domestic and personal things, in his confessional poems he also explores public and historical subjects. His best confessional poems are in his books *Life Studies* (1959) and *For the Union Dead* (1964).

Lowell was also a political activist. He was imprisoned during World War II for refusing to join the Army, and in the 1960s he openly opposed United States involvement in Vietnam.

Katherine's Dream
from *Lord Weary's Castle*

It must have been a Friday. I could hear
The top-floor typist's thunder and the beer
That you had brought in cases hurt my head;
I'd sent the pillows flying from my bed,
5   I hugged my knees together and I gasped.
The dangling telephone receiver rasped
Like someone in a dream who cannot stop
For breath or logic till his victim drop

To darkness and the sheets. I must have slept,

10 But still could hear my father who had kept

Your guilty presents but cut off my hair.

He whispers that he really doesn't care

If I am your kept woman all my life,

Or ruin your two children and your wife;

15 But my dishonor makes him drink. Of course

I'll tell the court the truth for his divorce.

I walk through snow into St. Patrick's yard.

Black nuns with glasses smile and stand on guard

Before a bulkhead in a bank of snow,

20 Whose charred doors open, as good people go

Inside by twos to the confessor. One

Must have a friend to enter there, but none

Is friendless in this crowd, and the nuns smile.

I stand aside and marvel; for a while

25 The winter sun is pleasant and it warms

My heart with love for others, but the swarms

Of penitents have dwindled. I begin

To cry and ask God's pardon for our sin.

Where are you? You were with me and are gone.

30 All the forgiven couples hurry on

To dinner and their nights, and none will stop.

I run about in circles till I drop

Against a padlocked bulkhead in a yard

Where faces redden and the snow is hard.

Epilogue

from *Day by Day*

Those blessed structure, plot and rhyme —

Why are they no help to me now

I want to make

something imagined, not recalled?

5 I hear the noise of my own voice:

The painter's vision is not a lens,

It trembles to caress the light.

But sometimes everything I write

with the threadbare art of my eye
10   seems a snapshot,
lurid, rapid, garish, grouped,
heightened from life,
yet paralyzed by fact.
All's misalliance.
15   Yet why not say what happened?
Pray for the grace of accuracy
Vermeer① gave to the sun's illumination
stealing like the tide across a map
to his girl solid with yearning.
20   We are poor passing facts,
warned by that to give
each figure in the photograph
his living name.

▶▶ Questions for Consideration and Discussion

1. In the poem "Katherine's Dream," who is the "I" and who is the "you?" What do we learn about Katherine? What troubled her mind?

2. What was Katherine's dream? Are you sympathetic with her? What would you advise Katherine to do to escape from her plight?

3. In "Epilogue," what complaint does the speaker make? Does the speaker come to terms with his work? Please explain.

4. Let's take a minute to consider fact and fiction (imagination). What do you think is the relationship between them? What does the speaker strive to do?

▌ Toni Morrison (1931 – 2019)

    Toni Morrison, the first African American recipient of the Nobel Prize for Literature (1993), plays a central role in putting fiction by and about African American women at the forefront of the late-twentieth-century literary canon.

    Morrison was born to a working-class family in Ohio. She received her B. A. in English from Howard University in 1953, and then her M. A. in English from Cornell University in 1955. Since then, she has been an educator and editor, in addition to

---

①   Vermeer: Jan Vermeer (1632 – 1675), Dutch painter noted for his subtle handling of the effects of light.

being a writer.

Her first novel is *The Bluest Eye* (1970). Set in Lorain, Ohio, it tells the tragic life of the black girl Pecola, who was born to a poor, dysfunctional African American family and grows up during the years following the Great Depression. Due to her mannerisms and dark skin, she is consistently regarded as "ugly." As a result, she longs to have blue eyes, which she equates with "whiteness," so that she'll be as beautiful and as beloved as those blue-eyed, blonde children.

Morrison's other most outstanding novels are as follows. *Sula* (1973) portrays two black women — Sula and Nel — who choose different paths in life. *Song of Solomon* (1977), winner of two national awards, relates Milkman Dead, a northern black young man's search for the southern sources of his identity. Here he discovers a strengthening legacy in communal tales about Grandmother and Great-Grandfather, each long dead but infusing the local culture with emotionally sustaining lore. His search is, in a sense, a cultural-mythological pursuit. *Tar Baby* (1981) portrays a love affair between Jadine and Son, two Black Americans from very different worlds. It is considered an allegory of colonialism. *Beloved* (1987), the winner of her first major award, the Pulitzer Prize, is perhaps Morrison's best novel. Set in the middle of 1870s, *Beloved* shows a mother (Sethe) being haunted and eventually destroyed by the ghost of a daughter (Beloved) whom she had killed eighteen years earlier rather than let her be taken by a vicious slave-master. Told in a style of magical realism, this novel is central to Morrison's canon because it involves so many important themes and techniques, such as love and guilt, a rebuilding of history and history's role in clarifying the past's influence on the present.

Morrison's other works include *Jazz* (1992), *Paradise* (1997), *Love* (2003), *A Mercy* (2008), *Home* (2012), *God Help the Child* (2015) and her essays collected in *Playing in the Dark: Whiteness and the Literary Imagination* (1992).

"Sweetness" is a short story by Morrison published in *The New Yorker* in 2015.

Sweetness

It's not my fault. So you can't blame me. I didn't do it and have no idea how it happened. It didn't take more than an hour after they pulled her out from between my legs for me to realize something was wrong. Really wrong. She was so black she scared me. Midnight black, Sudanese black. I'm light-skinned, with good hair, what we call high yellow, and so is Lula Ann's father. Ain't nobody in my family anywhere near that color. Tar is the closest I can think of, yet her hair don't go with the skin. It's different — straight but curly, like the hair on those naked tribes in Australia. You might think she's a throwback, but a throwback to what? You should've seen my grandmother; she passed for white, married a white man, and never said another word to any one of her children. Any letter she got from my mother or my aunts she sent right back, unopened. Finally they got the message of no message and let her be. Almost all mulatto types and quadroons did that back in the day — if they had the right kind of hair, that is. Can you imagine how many white folks have Negro blood hiding in their veins? Guess. Twenty per cent, I heard. My own mother, Lula Mae, could have passed easy, but she chose not to. She told me the price she paid for that decision. When she and my father went to the courthouse to get married, there were two Bibles, and they had to put their hands on the one reserved for Negroes. The other one was for white people's hands. The Bible! Can you beat it? My mother was a housekeeper for a rich white couple. They ate every meal she cooked and insisted she scrub their backs while they sat in the tub, and God knows what other intimate things they made her do, but no touching of the same Bible.

Some of you probably think it's a bad thing to group ourselves according to skin color — the lighter the better — in social clubs, neighborhoods, churches, sororities, even colored schools. But how else can we hold on to a little dignity? How else can we avoid being spit on in a drugstore, elbowed at the bus stop, having to walk in the gutter to let whites have the whole sidewalk, being charged a nickel at the grocer's for a paper bag that's free to white shoppers? Let alone all the name-calling. I heard about all of that and much, much more. But because of my mother's skin color she wasn't stopped from trying on hats or using the ladies' room in the department stores. And my father could try on shoes in the front part of the shoe store, not in a back room. Neither one of them would let themselves drink from a "Colored Only" fountain, even if they were dying of thirst.

I hate to say it, but from the very beginning in the maternity ward the baby, Lula Ann, embarrassed me. Her birth skin was pale like all babies', even African ones, but it changed fast. I thought I was going crazy when she turned blue-black right before my eyes. I know I went crazy for a minute, because — just for a few seconds — I held a blanket over her face and pressed. But I couldn't do that, no matter how much I wished she hadn't been born with that terrible color. I even thought of giving her away to an orphanage someplace. But I was scared to be one of those mothers who leave their babies on church steps. Recently, I heard about a couple in Germany, white as snow, who had a dark-skinned baby nobody could explain. Twins, I believe — one white, one colored. But I don't know if it's true. All I know is that, for me, nursing her was like having a pickaninny sucking my teat. I went to bottle-feeding soon as I got home.

My husband, Louis, is a porter, and when he got back off the rails he looked at me like I really was crazy and looked at the baby like she was from the planet Jupiter. He wasn't a cussing man, so when he cussed me and said, "What is this?" I knew we were in trouble. That was what did it — what caused the fights between me and him. It broke our marriage to pieces. We had three good years together, but when she was born he blamed me and treated Lula Ann like she was a stranger — more than that, an enemy. He never touched her.

I never did convince him that I ain't never, ever fooled around with another man. He was dead sure I was lying. We argued and argued till I told him her blackness had to be from his own family — not mine. That was when it got worse, so bad he just up and left and I had to look for another, cheaper place to live. I did the best I could. I knew enough not to take her with me when I applied to landlords, so I left her with a teenage cousin to babysit. I didn't take her outside much, anyway, because, when I pushed her in the baby carriage, people would lean down and peek in to say something nice and then give a start or jump back before frowning. That hurt. I could have been the babysitter if our skin colors were reversed. It was hard enough just being a colored woman — even a high-yellow one — trying to rent in a decent part of the city. Back in the nineties, when Lula Ann was born, the law was against discriminating in who you could rent to, but not many landlords paid attention to it. They made up reasons to keep you out. But I got lucky with Mr. Leigh, though I know he upped the rent seven dollars from what he'd advertised, and he had a fit if you were a minute late with the money.

I told her to call me "Sweetness" instead of "Mother" or "Mama." It was safer. Her being that black and having what I think are too thick lips and calling me "Mama" would've confused people. Besides, she has funny-colored eyes, crow black with a blue tint — something witchy about them, too.

So it was just us two for a long while, and I don't have to tell you how hard it is being an abandoned wife. I guess Louis felt a little bit bad after leaving us like that, because a few months later on he found out where I'd moved to and started sending me money once a month, though I never asked him to and didn't go to court to get it. His fifty-dollar money orders and my night job at the hospital got me and Lula Ann off welfare. Which was a good thing. I wish they would stop calling it welfare and go back to the word they used when my mother was a girl. Then it was called "relief." Sounds much better, like it's just a short-term breather while you get yourself together. Besides, those welfare clerks are mean as spit. When finally I got work and didn't need them anymore, I was making more money than they ever did. I guess meanness filled out their skimpy paychecks, which was why they treated us like beggars. Especially when they looked at Lula Ann and then back at me — like I was trying to cheat or something. Things got better but I still had to be careful. Very careful in how I raised her. I had to be strict, very strict. Lula Ann needed to learn how to behave, how to keep her head down and not to make trouble. I don't care how many times she changes her name. Her color is a cross she will always carry. But it's not my fault. It's not my fault. It's not.

Oh, yeah, I feel bad sometimes about how I treated Lula Ann when she was little. But you have to understand: I had to protect her. She didn't know the world. With that skin, there was no point in being tough or sassy, even when you were right. Not in a world where you could be sent to a juvenile lockup for talking back or fighting in school, a world where you'd be the last one hired and the first one fired. She didn't know any of that or how her black skin would scare white people or make them laugh and try to trick her. I once saw a girl nowhere near as dark as Lula Ann who couldn't have been more than ten years old tripped by one of a group of white boys and when she tried to scramble up another one put his foot on her behind and knocked her flat again. Those boys held their stomachs and bent over with laughter. Long after she got away, they were still giggling, so proud of themselves. If I hadn't been watching through the bus window I would have helped her, pulled her away from that white trash. See, if I hadn't trained Lula Ann properly she wouldn't have known to always cross the street and avoid white boys. But the lessons I taught her paid off, and in the end she made me proud as a peacock.

I wasn't a bad mother, you have to know that, but I may have done some hurtful things to my only child because I had to protect her. Had to. All because of skin privileges. At first I couldn't see past all that black to know who she was and just plain love her. But I do. I really do. I think she understands now. I think so.

Last two times I saw her she was, well, striking. Kind of bold and confident. Each time she came to see me, I forgot just how black she really was because she was using it to her advantage in beautiful white clothes.

Taught me a lesson I should have known all along. What you do to children matters. And they might never forget. As soon as she could, she left me all alone in that awful apartment. She got as far away from me as she could; dolled herself up and got a big-time job in California. She don't call or visit anymore. She sends me money and stuff every now and then, but I ain't seen her in I don't know how long.

I prefer this place — Winston House — to those big, expensive nursing homes outside the city. Mine is small, homey, cheaper, with twenty-four-hour nurses and a doctor who comes twice a week. I'm only sixty-three — too young for pasture — but I came down with some creeping bone disease, so good care is vital. The boredom is worse than the weakness or the pain, but the nurses are lovely. One just kissed me on the cheek when I told her I was going to be a grandmother. Her smile and her compliments were fit for someone about to be crowned. I showed her the note on blue paper that I got from Lula Ann — well, she signed it "Bride," but I never pay that any attention. Her words sounded giddy. "Guess what, S. I am so, so happy to pass along this news. I am going to have a baby. I'm too, too thrilled and hope you are, too." I reckon the thrill is about the baby, not its father, because she doesn't mention him at all. I wonder if he is as black as she is. If so, she needn't worry like I did. Things have changed a mite from when I was young. Blue-blacks are all over TV, in fashion magazines, commercials, even starring in movies.

There is no return address on the envelope. So I guess I'm still the bad parent being punished forever till the day I die for the well-intended and, in fact, necessary way I brought her up. I know she hates me. Our relationship is down to her sending me money. I have to say I'm grateful for the cash, because I don't have to beg for extras, like some of the other patients. If I want my own fresh deck of cards for solitaire, I can get it and not need to play with the dirty, worn one in the lounge. And I can buy my special face cream. But I'm not fooled. I know the money she sends is a way to stay away and quiet down the little bit of conscience she's got left.

If I sound irritable, ungrateful, part of it is because underneath is regret. All the little things I didn't do or did wrong. I remember when she had her first period and how I reacted. Or the times I shouted when she stumbled or dropped something. True. I was really upset, even repelled by her black skin when she was born and at first I thought of... No. I have to push those memories away — fast. No point. I know I did the best for her under the circumstances. When my husband ran out on us, Lula Ann was a burden. A heavy one, but I bore it well.

Yes, I was tough on her. You bet I was. By the time she turned twelve going on thirteen, I had to be even tougher. She was talking back, refusing to eat what I cooked, primping her hair. When I braided it, she'd go to school and unbraid it. I couldn't let her go bad. I slammed the lid and warned her about the names she'd be called. Still, some of my schooling must have rubbed off. See how she turned out? A rich career girl. Can you beat it?

Now she's pregnant. Good move, Lula Ann. If you think mothering is all cooing, booties, and diapers you're in for a big shock. Big. You and your nameless boyfriend, husband, pickup — whoever — imagine, *Oooh! A baby! Kitchee kitchee koo*!

Listen to me. You are about to find out what it takes, how the world is, how it works, and how it changes when you are a parent.

Good luck, and God help the child.

▷▷ Questions for Consideration and Discussion

1. Who is the narrator of the story? What's the advantage of the first-person point of view in relating this story?
2. Who is Lula Ann? If you could write a short message to her, what would you say? Why?
3. What does this story say about race, colorism, and motherhood?

▌ Alice Walker(1944 –)

As a feminist black writer, Alice Walker achieved fame in novels, short stories, poetry, and literary-political essays. But she is best known for *The Color Purple* (1982), a novel which won both the American Book Award and the Pulitzer Prize in 1983.

Born in the South in a sharecropper's home in rural Georgia, Alice Walker was the youngest of eight children. Her mother, Minnie Grant Walker, "labored beside — not behind" her husband when she was not caring for her eight children. "As I remember it," Alice Walker has reminisced, "we were really not allowed to be discouraged. Discouragement couldn't hold out against her faith."

Walker lost the sight of one eye in a domestic accident at eight years old. She was first educated at Spelman College, and then at prestigious Sara Lawrence College on a scholarship. During her university years, she actively participated in the Civil Rights movement of the 1960s, which profoundly influenced her subsequent writing.

Like Toni Morrison, she has been an educator and editor, in addition to being a writer. Her other novels are *The Third Life of Grange Copeland* (1970), *Meridian* (1976), *The Temple of My Familiar* (1989), and *Possessing the Secret of Joy* (1992).

The Color Purple is an epistolary novel. It focuses on the story of Celie, a black woman in the South. Celie is a poor, uneducated, fourteen-year-old black girl living in rural Georgia. She starts writing letters to God to relate her miseries and sufferings on account of her father's physical and sexual abuses. Her father (who turns out to be her stepfather) impregnates her twice and sends away her baby boy and baby girl. Later on, Celie is married to a black widower known only as Mr. _, who takes Celie into a difficult and joyless married life, using her as a tool for sex and as a coolie. But eventually, influenced and encouraged by the black women around her, Celie rises to an independent and confident woman. The black women who help to shape her life include: her bright and beautiful younger sister Nettie, who becomes a missionary teacher in Africa; Shug Avery, the Blues singer her husband Mr. _ is in love with; Sofia, her husband's oldest son Harpo's strong-willed wife; and Squeak, Harpo's girlfriend.

It is characteristic of Walker to be proud of her origins, which is demonstrated in her works.

Walker's short story "Everyday Use" originally appeared in her 1973 collection, *In Love & Trouble: Stories of Black Women*. It has been widely anthologized since. In it and in her autobiographical essay *In Search of Our Mother's Gardens*, Walker explores the dynamics of the empowerment she gained through her own matrilineage.

Everyday Use

I will wait for her in the yard that Maggie and I made so clean and wavy yesterday afternoon. A yard like this is more comfortable than most people know. It is not just a yard. It is like an extended living room. When the hard clay is swept clean as a floor and the fine sand around the edges lined with tiny, irregular grooves, anyone can come and sit and look up into the elm tree and wait for the breezes that never come inside the house.

Maggie will be nervous until after her sister goes: she will stand hopelessly in corners, homely and ashamed of the burn scars down her arms and legs, eying her sister with a mixture of envy and awe. She thinks her sister has held life always in the palm of one hand, that "no" is a word the world never learned to say to her.

You've no doubt seen those TV shows where the child who has "made it" is confronted, as a surprise, by her own mother and father, tottering in weakly from backstage. (A pleasant surprise, of course: What would they do if parent and child came on the show only to curse out and insult each other?) On TV mother and child embrace and smile into each other's faces. Sometimes the mother and father weep, the child wraps them in her arms and leans across the table to tell how she would not have made it without their help. I have seen these programs.

Sometimes I dream a dream in which Dee and I are suddenly brought together on a TV program of this sort. Out of a dark and soft-seated limousine I am ushered into a bright room filled with many people. There I meet a smiling, gray, sporty man like Johnny Carson who shakes my hand and tells me what a fine girl I have. Then we are on the stage and Dee is embracing me with tears in her eyes. She pins on my dress a large orchid, even though she has told me once that she thinks orchids are tacky flowers.

In real life I am a large, big-boned woman with rough, man-working hands. In the winter I wear flannel nightgowns to bed and overalls during the day. I can kill and clean a hog as mercilessly as a man. My fat keeps me hot in zero weather. I can work outside all day, breaking ice to get water for washing; I can eat pork liver cooked over the open fire minutes after it comes steaming from the hog. One winter I knocked a bull calf straight in the brain between the eyes with a sledge hammer and had the meat hung up to chill before nightfall. But of course all this does not show on television. I am the way my daughter would want me to be: a hundred pounds lighter, my skin like an uncooked barley pancake. My hair glistens in the hot bright lights. Johnny Carson has much to do to keep up with my quick and witty tongue.

But that is a mistake. I know even before I wake up. Who ever knew a Johnson with a quick tongue? Who can even imagine me looking a strange white man in the eye? It seems to me I have talked to them always with one foot raised in flight, with my head fumed in whichever way is farthest from them. Dee, though. She would always look anyone in the eye. Hesitation was no part of her nature.

"How do I look, Mama?" Maggie says, showing just enough of her thin body enveloped in pink skirt and red blouse for me to know she's there, almost hidden by the door.

"Come out into the yard," I say.

Have you ever seen a lame animal, perhaps a dog run over by some careless person rich enough to own a car, sidle up to someone who is ignorant enough to be kind to him? That is the way my Maggie walks. She has been like this, chin on chest, eyes on ground, feet in shuffle, ever since the fire that burned the other house to the ground.

Dee is lighter than Maggie, with nicer hair and a fuller figure. She's a woman now, though sometimes I forget. How long ago was it that the other house burned? Ten, twelve years? Sometimes I can still hear the flames and feel Maggie's arms sticking to me, her hair smoking and her dress falling off her in little black papery flakes. Her eyes seemed stretched open, blazed open by the flames reflected in them. And Dee. I see her standing off under the sweet gum tree she used to dig gum out of; a look of concentration on her face as she watched the last dingy gray board of the house fall in toward the red-hot brick chimney. Why don't you do a dance around the ashes? I'd wanted to ask her. She had hated the house that much.

I used to think she hated Maggie, too. But that was before we raised money, the church and me, to send her to Augusta to school. She used to read to us without pity; forcing words, lies, other folks' habits, whole lives upon us two, sitting trapped and ignorant underneath her voice. She washed us in a river of make-believe, burned us with a lot of knowledge we didn't necessarily need to know. Pressed us to her with the serious way she read, to shove us away at just the moment, like dimwits, we seemed about to understand.

Dee wanted nice things. A yellow organdy dress to wear to her graduation from high school; black pumps to match a green suit she'd made from an old suit somebody gave me. She was determined to stare down any disaster in her efforts. Her eyelids would not flicker for minutes at a time. Often I fought off the temptation to shake her. At sixteen she had a style of her own; and knew what style was.

I never had an education myself. After second grade the school was closed down. Don't ask me why: in 1927 colored asked fewer questions than they do now. Sometimes Maggie reads to me. She stumbles along good-naturedly but can't see well. She knows she is not bright. Like good looks and money, quickness passes her by. She will marry John Thomas (who has mossy teeth in an earnest face) and then I'll be free to sit here and I guess just sing church songs to myself. Although I never was a good singer. Never could carry a tune. I was always better at a man's job. I used to love to milk till I was hooked in the side in '49. Cows are soothing and slow and don't bother you, unless you try to milk them the wrong way.

I have deliberately turned my back on the house. It is three rooms, just like the one that burned, except the roof is tin; they don't make shingle roofs any more. There are no real windows, just some holes cut in the sides, like the portholes in a ship, but not round and not square, with rawhide holding the shutters up on the outside. This house is in a pasture, too, like the other one. No doubt when Dee sees it she will want to tear it down. She wrote me once that no matter where we "choose" to live, she will manage to come see us. But she will never bring her friends. Maggie and I thought about this and Maggie asked me, "Mama, when did Dee ever have any friends?"

She had a few. Furtive boys in pink shirts hanging about on washday after school. Nervous girls who never laughed. Impressed with her they worshiped the well-turned phrase, the cute shape, the scalding humor that erupted like bubbles in lye. She read to them.

When she was courting Jimmy T she didn't have much time to pay to us, but turned all her faultfinding power on him. He *flew* to marry a cheap city girl from a family of ignorant flashy people. She hardly had time to recompose herself.

When she comes I will meet — but there they are!

Maggie attempts to make a dash for the house, in her shuffling way, but I stay her with my hand. "Come back here," I say. And she stops and tries to dig a well in the sand with her toe.

It is hard to see them clearly through the strong sun. But even the first glimpse of leg out of the car tells me it is Dee. Her feet were always neat-looking, as if God himself had shaped them with a certain style. From the other side of the car comes a short, stocky man. Hair is all over his head a foot long and hanging from his chin like a kinky mule tail. I hear Maggie suck in her breath. "Uhnnnh, " is what it sounds like. Like when you see the wriggling end of a snake just in front of your foot on the road. "Uhnnnh. "

Dee next. A dress down to the ground, in this hot weather. A dress so loud it hurts my eyes. There are yellows and oranges enough to throw back the light of the sun. I feel my whole face warming from the heat waves it throws out. Earrings gold, too, and hanging down to her shoulders. Bracelets dangling and making noises when she moves her arm up to shake the folds of the dress out of her armpits. The dress is loose and flows, and as she walks closer, I like it. I hear Maggie go "Uhnnnh" again. It is her sister's hair. It stands straight up like the wool on a sheep. It is black as night and around the edges are two long pigtails that rope about like small lizards disappearing behind her ears.

"Wa-su-zo-Tean-o①!" she says, coming on in that gliding way the dress makes her move. The short stocky fellow with the hair to his navel is all grinning and he follows up with "Asalamalakim, my mother and sister!" He moves to hug Maggie but she falls back, right up against the back of my chair. I feel her trembling there and when I look up I see the perspiration falling off her chin.

"Don't get up," says Dee. Since I am stout it takes something of a push. You can see me trying to move a second or two before I make it. She turns, showing white heels through her sandals, and goes back to the car. Out she peeks next with a Polaroid. She stoops down quickly and lines up picture after picture of me sitting there in front of the house with Maggie cowering behind me. She never takes a shot without making sure the house is included. When a cow comes nibbling around the edge of the yard she snaps it and me and Maggie and the house. Then she puts the Polaroid in the back seat of the car, and comes up and kisses me on the forehead.

Meanwhile Asalamalakim is going through motions with Maggie's hand. Maggie's hand is as limp as a fish, and probably as cold, despite the sweat, and she keeps trying to pull it back. It looks like Asalamalakim wants to shake hands but wants to do it fancy. Or maybe he don't know how people shake hands. Anyhow, he soon gives up on Maggie.

---

① Wa-su-zo-Tean-o: some sort of African dialect greeting.

"Well," I say. "Dee. "

"No, Mama," she says. "Not 'Dee,' Wangero Leewanika Kemanjo!"

"What happened to 'Dee'?" I wanted to know.

"She's dead," Wangero said. "I couldn't bear it any longer, being named after the people who oppress me. "

"You know as well as me you was named after your aunt Dicie,"I said. Dicie is my sister. She named Dee. We called her "Big Dee" after Dee was born.

"But who was she named after?" asked Wangero.

"I guess after Grandma Dee," I said.

"And who was *she* named after?" asked Wangero.

"Her mother," I said, and saw Wangero was getting tired. "That's about as far back as I can trace it," I said. Though, in fact, I probably could have carried it back beyond the Civil War through the branches.

"Well," said Asalamalakim, "there you are. "

"Uhnnnh," I heard Maggie say.

"There I was not," I said, "before 'Dicie' cropped up in our family, so why should I try to trace it that far back?"

He just stood there grinning, looking down on me like somebody inspecting a Model A car①. Every once in a while he and Wangero sent eye signals over my head.

"How do you pronounce this name?" I asked.

"You don't have to call me by it if you don't want to," said Wangero.

"Why shouldn't 1?" I asked. "If that's what you want us to call you, we'll call you. "

"I know it might sound awkward at first," said Wangero.

"I'll get used to it," I said. "Ream it out again. "

Well, soon we got the name out of the way. Asalamalakim had a name twice as long and three times as hard. After I tripped over it two or three times he told me to just call him Hakim-a-barber. I wanted to ask him was he a barber, but I didn't really think he was, so I didn't ask.

"You must belong to those beef-cattle peoples down the road," I said. They said "Asalamalakim" when they met you, too, but they didn't shake hands. Always too busy: feeding the cattle, fixing the fences, putting up salt-lick shelters, throwing down hay. When the white folks poisoned some of the herd the men stayed up all night with rifles in their hands. I walked a mile and a half just to see the sight.

Hakim-a-barber said, "I accept some of their doctrines, but farming and raising cattle is not my style. " [They didn't tell me, and I didn't ask, whether Wangero (Dee) had really gone and married him.]

We sat down to eat and right away he said he didn't eat collards and pork was unclean.

---

① Model A car: Very old automobile designed by Henry Ford.

Wangero, though, went on through the chitlins and corn bread, the greens and everything else. She talked a blue streak over the sweet potatoes. Everything delighted her. Even the fact that we still used the benches her daddy made for the table when we couldn't afford to buy chairs.

"Oh, Mama!" she cried. Then turned to Hakim-a-barber. "I never knew how lovely these benches are. You can feel the rump prints," she said, running her hands underneath her and along the bench. Then she gave a sigh and her hand closed over Grandma Dee's butter dish. "That's it!" she said. "I knew there was something I wanted to ask you if I could have." She jumped up from the table and went over in the corner where the churn stood, the milk in it clabber by now. She looked at the churn and looked at it.

"This churn top is what I need," she said. "Didn't Uncle Buddy whittle it out of a tree you all used to have?"

"Yes," I said.

"Un huh," she said happily. "And I want the dasher, too."

"Uncle Buddy whittle that, too?" asked the barber.

Dee (Wangero) looked up at me.

"Aunt Dee's first husband whittled the dash," said Maggie so low you almost couldn't hear her. "His name was Henry, but they called him Stash."

"Maggie's brain is like an elephant's," Wangero said, laughing. "I can use the churn top as a centerpiece for the alcove table," she said, sliding a plate over the churn, "and I'll think of something artistic to do with the dasher."

When she finished wrapping the dasher the handle stuck out. I took it for a moment in my hands. You didn't even have to look close to see where hands pushing the dasher up and down to make butter had left a kind of sink in the wood. In fact, there were a lot of small sinks; you could see where thumbs and fingers had sunk into the wood. It was beautiful light yellow wood, from a tree that grew in the yard where Big Dee and Stash had lived.

After dinner Dee (Wangero) went to the trunk at the foot of my bed and started rifling through it. Maggie hung back in the kitchen over the dishpan. Out came Wangero with two quilts. They had been pieced by Grandma Dee and then Big Dee and me had hung them on the quilt frames on the front porch and quilted them. One was in the Lone Star pattern. The other was Walk Around the Mountain. In both of them were scraps of dresses Grandma Dee had worn fifty and more years ago. Bits and pieces of Grandpa Jattell's Paisley shirts. And one teeny faded blue piece, about the size of a penny matchbox, that was from Great Grandpa Ezra's uniform that he wore in the Civil War.

"Mama," Wangro said sweet as a bird. "Can I have these old quilts?"

I heard something fall in the kitchen, and a minute later the kitchen door slammed.

"Why don't you take one or two of the others?" I asked. "These old things was just done by me and Big Dee from some tops your grandma pieced before she died."

"No," said Wangero. "I don't want those. They are stitched around the borders by machine. ”

“That'll make them last better,” I said.

“That's not the point,” said Wangero. “These are all pieces of dresses Grandma used to wear. She did all this stitching by hand. Imagine!” She held the quilts securely in her arms, stroking them.

“Some of the pieces, like those lavender ones, come from old clothes her mother handed down to her,” I said, moving up to touch the quilts. Dee (Wangero) moved back just enough so that I couldn't reach the quilts. They already belonged to her.

“Imagine!” she breathed again, clutching them closely to her bosom.

“The truth is,” I said, “I promised to give them quilts to Maggie, for when she marries John Thomas. ”

She gasped like a bee had stung her.

“Maggie can't appreciate these quilts!” she said. “She'd probably be backward enough to put them to everyday use. ”

“I reckon she would,” I said. “God knows I been saving 'em for long enough with nobody using 'em. I hope she will!” I didn't want to bring up how I had offered Dee (Wangero) a quilt when she went away to college. Then she had told they were old-fashioned, out of style.

“But they're *priceless*!” she was saying now, furiously; for she has a temper. “Maggie would put them on the bed and in five years they'd be in rags. Less than that!”

“She can always make some more,” I said. “Maggie knows how to quilt. ”

Dee (Wangero) looked at me with hatred. “You just will not understand. The point is these quilts, *these* quilts!”

“Well,” I said, stumped. “What would you do with them?”

“Hang them,” she said. As if that was the only thing you could do with quilts.

Maggie by now was standing in the door. I could almost hear the sound her feet made as they scraped over each other.

“She can have them, Mama,” she said, like somebody used to never winning anything, or having anything reserved for her. “I can 'member Grandma Dee without the quilts. ”

I looked at her hard. She had filled her bottom lip with checkerberry snuff and gave her face a kind of dopey, hangdog look. It was Grandma Dee and Big Dee who taught her how to quilt herself. She stood there with her scarred hands hidden in the folds of her skirt. She looked at her sister with something like fear but she wasn't mad at her. This was Maggie's portion. This was the way she knew God to work.

When I looked at her like that something hit me in the top of my head and ran down to the soles of my feet. Just like when I'm in church and the spirit of God touches me and I get happy and shout. I did something I never done before: hugged Maggie to me, then dragged her on into the room, snatched the quilts out of Miss Wangero's hands and dumped them into Maggie's lap. Maggie just sat there on my bed with her mouth open.

“Take one or two of the others,” I said to Dee.

But she turned without a word and went out to Hakim-a-barber.

"You just don't understand," she said, as Maggie and I came out to the car.

"What don't I understand?" I wanted to know.

"Your heritage," she said. And then she turned to Maggie, kissed her, and said, "You ought to try to make something of yourself, too, Maggie. It's really a new day for us. But from the way you and Mama still live you'd never know it. "

She put on some sunglasses that hid everything above the tip of her nose and chin.

Maggie smiled; maybe at the sunglasses. But a real smile, not scared. After we watched the car dust settle I asked Maggie to bring me a dip of snuff. And then the two of us sat there just enjoying, until it was time to go in the house and go to bed.

▶▶ Questions for Consideration and Discussion

1. From whose point of view is "Everyday Use" told? What does the story gain from this point of view — instead of, say, from the point of view of Dee (Wangero)?

2. What in particular is valuable about the quilts for Dee and Maggie? Whose love for the quilts never changes?

3. Why does Dee (Wangero) want those old quilts she once refused to accept before she went to college?

4. Contrast Dee's attitude toward her heritage with the attitudes of her mother and sister. How much truth is there in Dee's accusation that her mother and sister don't understand their heritage?

▌ Maxine Hong Kingston (1940 –)

Maxine Hong Kingston is a distinguished Chinese American writer. She is best known for her debut work *The Woman Warrior*: *Memoirs of a Girlhood Among Ghosts* (1976), which received the National Book Critics' Circle Award for general nonfiction.

Born in Stockton, California, to parents who emigrated from China, Kingston is the eldest of six children of the couple. She grew up helping in the family-run laundry and listening to her mother telling stories about China before her emigration. Maxine adopted the last name of her husband, Earl Kingston.

Kingston graduated from the University of California at Berkeley. She studied there in the turbulent middle sixties.

Before publishing her debut in 1976, Kingston was an unknown. *The Woman Warrior* became an immediate success and has entered the American mainstream. Though it draws on Kingston's autobiographical facts, it is by no means an autobiography. Rather, it is a fictionalized autobiography, freely mixing memories, stories, Chinese legends, and psychological fantasies to present the difficulties Kingston has gone through in her upbringing as an ethnic-minority female, and how she has become a woman warrior like Hua Mulan (spelled as Fa Mu Lan in the book). Different from conventional autobiography, the book tells, in its five chapters, the stories of her female antecedents including her paternal aunt "no-name woman," her mother Brave Orchid, her maternal aunt Moon Orchid, as well as the legendary Chinese heroine Mulan and the Chinese poetess Cai Yan (spelled as Ts'ai Yen in the book). All these women affect her in one way or another.

Kingston's second success came from *China Men* (1981), a recipient of National Book Award for nonfiction. Kingston had originally conceived of *The Woman Warrior* and *China Men as* one long book, but decided to preserve an overall division by gender. *China Men* depicts the stories of her male family people, especially her father and the earlier male forebears who came to America and worked on building the railroads. In a final section, she writes about her brother who served in the U. S. Navy during the Vietnam War.

Tripmaster Monkey: His Fake Book (1989) is presented more deliberately as a novel. Its hero is a Chinese American young man named Wittman Ah Sing. It is an extended, picaresque account of Wittman's adventures as an aspiring playwright who imagines himself to be an incarnation of the legendary Monkey King Sun Wukong. Combining magic, realism, and black humor, *Tripmaster Monkey* is about a young male's search for a community in America.

The Woman Warrior
(Excerpt)
White Tigers

When we Chinese girls listened to the adults talk-story, we learned that we failed if we grew up to be but wives or slaves. We could be heroines, swordswomen. Even if she had to rage across all China, a swordswoman got even with anybody who hurt her family. Perhaps women were once so dangerous that they had to have their feet bound. It was a woman who invented white crane boxing only two hundred years ago. She was already an expert pole fighter, daughter of a teacher trained at the Shao-lin temple, where there lived an order of fighting monks. She was combing her hair one morning when a white crane alighted outside her window. She teased it with her pole, which it pushed aside with a soft brush of its wing. Amazed, she dashed outside and tried to knock the crane off its perch. It snapped her pole in two. Recognizing the presence of great power, she asked the spirit of the white cane if it would teach her to fight. It answered with a cry that white crane boxers imitate today. Later the bird returned as an old man, and he guided her boxing for many years. Thus she gave the world a new martial art.

This was one of the tamer, more modern stories, mere introduction. My mother told others that followed swordswomen through woods and palaces for years. Night after night my mother would talk-story until we fell asleep. I couldn't tell where the stories left off and the dreams began, her voice the voice of the heroines in my sleep. And on Sundays, from noon to midnight, we went to the movies at the Confucius Church. We saw swordswomen jump over houses from a standstill; they didn't even need a running start.

At last I saw that I too had been in the presence of great power, my mother talking-story. After I grew up, I heard the chant of Fa Mu Lan, the girl who took her father's place in battle. Instantly I remembered that as a child I had followed my mother about the house, the two of us singing about how Fa Mu Lan fought gloriously and returned alive from war to settle in the village. I had forgotten this chant that was once mine, given me by my mother, who may not have known its power to remind. She said I would grow up a wife and a slave, but she taught me the song of the warrior woman, Fa Mu Lan. I would have to grow up a warrior woman.

The call would come from a bird that flew over our roof. In the brush drawings it looks like the ideograph for "human," two black wings. The bird would cross the sun and lift into the mountains (which look like the ideograph "mountain"), there parting the mist briefly that swirled opaque again. I would be a little girl of seven the day I followed the bird away into the mountains. The brambles would tear off my shoes and the rocks cut my feet and fingers, but I would keep climbing, eyes upward to follow the bird. We would go around and around the tallest mountain, climbing ever upward. I would drink from the river, which I would meet again and again. We would go so high the plants would change, and the river that flows past the village would become a waterfall. At the height where the bird used to disappear, the clouds would gray the world like an ink wash.

Even when I got used to that gray, I would only see peaks as if shaded in pencil, rocks like charcoal rubbings, everything so murky. There would be just two black strokes — the bird. Inside the clouds — inside the dragon's breath — I would not know how many hours or days passed. Suddenly, without noise, I would break clear into a yellow, warm world. New trees would lean toward me at mountain angles, but when I looked for the village, it would have vanished under the clouds.

The bird, now gold so close to the sun, would come to rest on the thatch of a hut which, until the bird's two feet touched it, was camouflaged as part of the mountainside.

The door opened, and an old man and an old woman came out carrying bowls of rice and soup and a leafy branch of peaches.

"Have you eaten rice today, little girl?" they greeted me.

"Yes, I have," I said out of politeness. "Thank you."

("No, I haven't," I would have said in real life, mad at the Chinese for lying so much. "I'm starved. Do you have any cookies? I like chocolate chip cookies. ")

...

After I returned from my survival test, the two old people trained me in dragon ways, which took another eight years. Copying the tigers, their stalking kill and their anger, had been a wild, bloodthirsty joy. Tigers are easy to find, but I needed adult wisdom to know dragons. "You have to infer the whole dragon from the parts you can see and touch," the old people would say. Unlike tigers, dragons are so immense, I would never see one in its entirety. But I could explore the mountains, which are the top of its head. "These mountains are also *like* the tops of *other* dragons' heads," the old people would tell me. When climbing the slopes, I could understand that I was a bug riding on a dragon's forehead as it roams through space, its speed so different from my speed that I feel the dragon solid and immobile. In quarries I could see its strata, the dragons' veins and muscles; the minerals, its teeth and bones. I could touch the stones the old woman wore — its bone marrow. I had worked the soil, which is its flesh, and harvested the plants and climbed the trees, which are its hairs. I could listen to its voice in the thunder and feel its breathing in the winds, see its breathing in the clouds. Its tongue is the lightning. And the red that the lightning gives to the world is strong and lucky — in blood, poppies, roses, rubies, the red feathers of birds, the red carp, the cherry tree, the peony, the line alongside the turtle's eyes and the mallard's. In the spring when the dragon awakes, I watched its turnings in the rivers.

The closest I came to seeing a dragon whole was when the old people cut away a small strip of bark on a pine that was over three thousand years old. The resin underneath flows in the swirling shapes of dragons. "If you should decide during your old age that you would like to live another five hundred years, come here and drink ten pounds of this sap," they told me. "But don't do it now. You're too young to decide to live forever." The old people sent me out into thunderstorms to pick the red-cloud herb, which grows only then, a product of dragon's fire and dragon's rain. I brought the leaves to the old man and old woman, and they ate them for immortality.

I learned to make my mind large, as the universe is large, so that there is room for paradoxes. Pearls are bone marrow; pearls come from oysters. The dragon lives in the sky, ocean, marshes, and mountains; and the mountains are also its cranium. Its voice thunders and jingles like copper pans. It breathes fire and water; and sometimes the dragon is one, sometimes many.

I worked every day. When it rained, I exercised in the downpour...

...

Menstrual days did not interrupt my training; I was as strong as on any other day. "You're now an adult," explained the old woman on the first one, which happened halfway through my stay on the mountain. "You can have children." I had thought I had cut myself when jumping over my swords, one made of steel and the other carved out of a single block of jade. "However," she added, "we are asking you to put off children for a few more years."

"Then can I use the control you taught me and stop this bleeding."

"No. You don't stop shitting and pissing," she said. "It's the same with the blood. Let it run. " ("Let it walk" in Chinese.)

To console me for being without family on this day, they let me look inside the gourd. My whole family was visiting friends on the other side of the river. Everybody had on good clothes and was exchanging cakes. It was a wedding. My mother was talking to the hosts: "Thank you for taking our daughter. Wherever she is, she must be happy now. She will certainly come back if she is alive, and if she is a spirit, you have given her a descent line. We are so grateful. "

Yes, I would be happy. How full I would be with all their love for me. I would have for a new husband my own playmate, dear since childhood, who loved me so much he was to become a spirit bridegroom for my sake. We will be so happy when I come back to the valley, healthy and strong and not a ghost.

The water gave me a close-up of my husband's wonderful face — and I was watching when it went white at the sudden approach of armored men on horseback, thudding and jangling. My people grabbed iron skillets, boiling soup, knives, hammers, scissors, whatever weapons came to hand, but my father said, "There are too many of them," and they put down the weapons and waited quietly at the door, open as if for guests. An army of horse-men stopped at our house; the foot soldiers in the distance were coming closer. A horse-man with silver scales afire in the sun shouted from the scroll in his hands, his words opening a red gap in his black beard. "Your baron has pledged fifty men from this district, one from each family," he said, and then named the family names.

"No!" I screamed into the gourd.

"I'll go," my new husband and my youngest brother said to their fathers.

"No," my father said, "I myself will go," but the women held him back until the foot soldiers passed by, my husband and my brother leaving with them.

As if disturbed by the marching feet, the water churned; and when it stilled again ("Wait!" I yelled. "Wait!"), there were strangers. The baron and his family — all of his family — were knocking their heads on the floor in front of their ancestors and thanking the gods out loud for protecting them from conscription. I watched the baron's piggish face chew open-mouthed on the sacrificial pig. I plunged my hand into the gourd, making a grab for his thick throat, and he broke into pieces, splashing water all over my face and clothes. I turned the gourd upside-down to empty it, but no little people came tumbling out.

"Why can't I go down there now and help them?" I cried. "I'll run away with the two boys and we'll hide in the caves. "

"No," the old man said. "You're not ready. You are only fourteen years old. You'd get hurt for nothing. "

"Wait until you are twenty-two," the old woman said. "You'll be big then and more skillful. No army will be able to stop you from doing whatever you want. If you go now, you will be killed, and you'll have wasted seven and a half years of our time. You will deprive your people of a champion. "

"I'm good enough now to save the boys. "

"We didn't work this hard to save just two boys, but whole families. "

...

When I could point at the sky and make a sword appear, a silver bolt in the sunlight, and control its slashing with my mind, the old people said I was ready to leave. The old man opened the gourd for the last time. I saw the baron's messengers leave our house, and my father was saying, "This time I must go and fight. " I would hurry down the mountain and take his place. The old people gave me the fifteen beads, which I was to use if I got into terrible danger. They gave me men's clothes and armor. We bowed to one another. The bird flew above me down the mountain, and for some miles, whenever I turned to look for them, there would be the two old people waving. I saw them through the mist; I saw them on the clouds; I saw them big on the mountain top when distance had shrunk the pines. They had probably left images of themselves for me to wave at and gone about their other business.

When I reached my village, my father and mother had grown as old as the two whose shapes I could at last no longer see. I helped my parents carry their tools, and they walked ahead so straight, each carrying a basket or a hoe not to overburden me, their tears falling privately. My family surrounded me with so much love that I almost forgot the ones not there. I praised the new infants.

"Some of the people are saying the Eight Sages took away to teach you magic," said a little girl cousin. "They say they changed you into a bird, and you flew to them. "

"Some say you went to the city and became a prostitute," another cousin giggled.

"You might tell them that I met some teachers who were willing to teach me science," I said.

"I have been drafted," my father said.

"No, Father," I said. "I will take your place. "

My parents killed a chicken and steamed it whole, as if they were welcoming home a son, but I had gotten out of the habit of meat. After eating rice and vegetables, I slept for a long time, preparation for the work ahead.

In the morning my parents woke me and asked that I come with them to the family hall. "Stay in your night clothes," my mother said. "Don't change yet. " She was holding a basin, a towel, and a kettle of hot water. My father had a bottle of wine, and ink block and pens, and knives of various sizes. "Come with us," he said. They had stopped the tears with which they had greeted me. Forebodingly I caught a smell — metallic, the iron smell of blood, as when a woman gives birth, as at the sacrifice of a large animal, as when I menstruated and dreamed red dreams.

My mother put a pillow on the floor before the ancestors. "Kneel here," she said. "Now take off your shirt. " I kneeled with my back to my parents so none of us felt embarrassed. My mother washed my back as if I had left for only a day and were her baby yet. "We are going to carve revenge on your back," my father said. "We'll write out oaths and names. "

"Wherever you go, whatever happens to you, people will know our sacrifice," my mother said. "And you'll never forget either. " She meant that even if I got killed, the people could use my dead body for a weapon, but we do not like to talk out loud about dying.

My father first brushed the words in ink, and they fluttered down my back row after row. Then he began cutting; to make fine lines and points he used thin blades, for the stem, large blades.

My mother caught the blood and wiped the cuts with a cold towel soaked in wine. It hurt terribly — the cuts sharp; the air burning; the alcohol cold, then hot — pain so various. I gripped my knees. I released them. Neither tension nor relaxation helped. I wanted to cry. If not for the fifteen years of train, I would have writhed on the floor; I would have had to be held down. The list of grievances went on and on. If an enemy should flay me, the light would shine through my skin like lace.

At the end of the last word, I fell forward. Together my parents sang what they had written, then let me rest. My mother fanned my back. "We'll have you with us until your back heals," she said.

When I could sit up again, my mother brought two mirrors, and I saw my back covered entirely with words in red and black files, like an army, like my army. My parents nursed me just as if I had fallen in battle after many victories. Soon I was strong again.

...

I led my army northward, rarely having to sidetrack; the emperor himself sent the enemies I was hunting chasing after me. Sometimes they attacked us on two or three sides; sometimes they ambushed me when I rode ahead. We would always win, Kuan Kung, the god of war and literature riding before me. I would be told of in fairy tales myself. I overheard some soldiers — and now there weremany who had not met me — say that whenever we had been in danger of losing, I made a throwing gesture and the opposing army would fall, hurled across the battlefield. Hailstones as big as heads would shoot out of the sky and the lightning would stab like swords, but never at those on my side. "On *his* side," they said. I never told them the truth. Chinese executed women who disguised themselves as soldiers or students, no matter how bravely they fought or how high they scored on the examinations.

...

I stood on top of the last hill before Peiping and saw the roads below me flow like living rivers. Between roads the woods and plains moved too; the land was peopled—the Han people, the People of One Hundred Surnames, marching with one heart, our tatters flying. The depth and width of Joy were exactly known to me: the Chinese population. After much hardship a few of our millions had arrived together at the capital. We faced our emperor personally. We beheaded him, cleaned out the palace, and inaugurated the peasant who would begin the new order. In his rags he sat on the throne facing south, and we, a great red crowd, bowed to him three times. He commended some of us who were his first generals.

I told the people who had come with me that they were free to go home now, but since the Long Wall was so close, I would go see it. They could come along if they liked. So, loath to disband after such high adventures, we reached the northern boundary of the world, chasing Mongols en route.

I touched the Long Wall with my own fingers, running the edge of my hand between the stones, tracing the grooves the builders' hands had made. We lay our foreheads and our cheeks against the Long Wall and cried like the women who had come here looking for their men so long building the wall. In my travels north, I had not found my brother.

Carrying the news about new emperor, I went home, where one more battle awaited me. The baron who had drafted my brother would still be bearing sway over our village. Having dropped my soldiers off at crossroads and bridges, I attacked the baron's stronghold alone. I jumped over the double walls and landed with swords drawn and knees bent, ready to spring. When no one accosted me, I sheathed the swords and walked about like a guest until I found the baron. He was counting his money, his fat ringed fingers playing over the abacus.

"Who are you? What do you want?" he said, encircling his profits with his arms. He sat square and fat like a god.

"I want your life in payment for your crimes against the villagers."

"I haven't done anything to you. All this is mine. I earned it. I didn't steal it from you. I've never seen you before in my life. Who are you?"

"I am a female avenger."

Then — heaven help him — he tried to be charming, to appeal to me man to man. "Oh, come now. Everyone takes the girls when he can. The families are glad to be rid of them. 'Girls are maggots in the rice.' 'It is more profitable to raise gees than daughters.'" He quoted to me the sayings I hated.

"Regret what you've done before I kill you," I said.

"I haven't done anything other men — even you — wouldn't have done in my place."

"You took away my brother."

"He was not an apprentice."

"I free my apprentices."

"China needs soldiers in wartime."

"You took away my childhood."

"I don't know what you're talking about. We've never met before. I've done nothing to you."

"You've done this," I said, and ripped off my shirt to show him my back. "You are responsible for this." When I saw his startled eyes at my breasts, I slashed him across the face and on the second stroke cut off his head.

...

The swordswoman and I are not so dissimilar. May my people understand the resemblance soon so that I can return to them. What we have in common are the words at our backs. The idioms for *revenge* are "report a crime" and "report to five families." The reporting is the vengeance — not the beheading, not the gutting, but the words. And I have so many words — "chink" words and "gook" works too — that they do not fit on my skin.

▶▶ Questions for Consideration and Discussion

1. From whom did the narrator learn the story of Fa Mu Lan? In what way is her Fa Mu Lan different from the Chinese legendary heroine Hua Mulan?
2. The narrator was trained first in tiger ways then in dragon ways. What different feelings did she have with regard to the two ways? What might these two creatures symbolize? Please explain.
3. How is Kingston's Mulan different from the Chinese legendary Mulan? What do you make of these changes? Should Kingston be criticized for misrepresenting Chinese history and legends? Why or why not?

N. Scott Momaday (1934 –)

N. Scott Momaday, the only Native American who has been awarded the Pulitzer Prize for Literature, is one of the most distinguished Native American writers and a pioneer in Native American Studies.

Momaday, a Native American of Kiowa and Cherokee descent, was born in Oklahoma, a state renowned for the large number of Native Americans who live there. When Momaday was only one year old, his family moved to Arizona, where his parents served as teachers on a reservation. Momaday spent most of his childhood in Arizona where he encountered not only his father's Kiowa traditions but also those of other southwest Native Americans, such as the Navajo, Apache, and Pueblo. He spent his teenage years in New Mexico, and subsequently attended the University, of New Mexico, graduating with a Bachelor of Arts degree in English. He then went on to earn a Ph. D. in English from Stanford University.

Momaday has earned tenure at a number of American universities, such as the University of Santa Barbara, the University of California at Berkeley, Stanford University, and the University of Arizona. Also he has been a visiting professor at Columbia University, Princeton University, and the University of New Mexico. He was also the first professor to teach American Literature in Moscow, Russia, at Moscow State University.

Momaday has written novels, memoirs, short stories, essays, and poetry. In 1969, his novel *House Made of Dawn* was awarded the Pulitzer Prize for Fiction and is considered the first major work of the Native American Renaissance, a term coined by literary critic Kenneth Lincoln. His subsequent book, *The Way to Rainy Mountain* (1969), combines Kiowa folklore with memoirs of his childhood and family.

The excerpt below is the introduction to his memoir, *The Way to Rainy Mountain*, his personal favorite selection from his life's work.

The Way to Rainy Mountain
Introduction

A single knoll rises out of the plain in Oklahoma, north and west of the Wichita Range. For my people, the Kiowas, it is an old landmark, and they gave it the name Rainy Mountain. The hardest weather in the world is there. Winter brings blizzards, hot tornadic winds arise in the spring, and in summer the prairie is an anvil's edge. The grass turns brittle and brown, and it cracks beneath your feet. There are green belts along the rivers and creeks, linear groves of hickory and pecan, willow and witch hazel. At a distance in July or August the steaming foliage seems almost to writhe in fire. Great green and yellow grasshoppers are everywhere in the tall grass, popping up like corn to sting the flesh, and tortoises crawl about on the red earth, going nowhere in the plenty of time. Loneliness is an aspect of the land. All things in the plain are isolate; there is no confusion of objects in the eye, but one hill or one tree or one man. To look upon that landscape in the early morning, with the sun at your back, is to lose the sense of proportion. Your imagination comes to life, and this, you think, is where Creation was begun.

I returned to Rainy Mountain in July. My grandmother had died in the spring, and I wanted to be at her grave. She had lived to be very old and at last infirm. Her only living daughter was with her when she died, and I was told that in death her face was that of a child.

I like to think of her as a child. When she was born, the Kiowas were living the last great moment of their history. For more than a hundred years they had controlled the open range from the Smoky Hill River to the Red, from the headwaters of the Canadian to the fork of the Arkansas and Cimarron. In alliance with the Comanches, they had ruled the whole of the southern Plains. War was their sacred business, and they were among the finest horsemen the world has ever known. But warfare for the Kiowas was preeminently a matter of disposition rather than of survival, and they never understood the grim, unrelenting advance of the U. S. Cavalry. When at last, divided and ill provisioned, they were driven onto the Staked Plains in the cold rains of autumn, they fell into panic. In Palo Duro Canyon they abandoned their crucial stores to pillage and had nothing then but their lives. In order to save themselves, they surrendered to the soldiers at Fort Sill and were imprisoned in the old stone corral that now stands as a military museum. My grandmother was spared the humiliation of those high gray walls by eight or ten years, but she must have known from birth the affliction of defeat, the dark brooding of old warriors.

Her name was Aho, and she belonged to the last culture to evolve in North America. Her forebears came down from the high country in western Montana nearly three centuries ago.

Part V   American Literature since World War II (1945 –)

They were a mountain people, a mysterious tribe of hunters whose language has never been positively classified in any major group. In the late seventeenth century, they began a long migration to the south and east. It was a journey toward the dawn, and it led to a golden age. Along the way the Kiowas were befriended by the Crows, who gave them the culture and religion of the Plains. They acquired horses, and their ancient nomadic spirit was suddenly free of the ground. They acquired Tai-me, the sacred Sun Dance doll, from that moment the object and symbol of their worship, and so shared in the divinity of the sun. Not least, they acquired the sense of destiny, therefore courage and pride. When they entered upon the southern Plains they had been transformed. No longer were they slaves to the simple necessity of survival; they were a lordly and dangerous society of fighters and thieves, hunters and priests of the sun. According to their origin myth, they entered the world through a hollow log. From one point of view, their migration was the fruit of an old prophecy, for indeed they emerged from a sunless world.

Although my grandmother lived out her long life in the shadow of Rainy Mountain, the immense landscape of the continental interior lay like memory in her blood. She could tell of the Crows, whom she had never seen, and of the Black Hills, where she had never been. I wanted to see in reality what she had seen more perfectly in the mind's eye, and traveled fifteen hundred miles to begin my pilgrimage.

Yellowstone, it seemed to me, was the top of the world, a region of deep lakes and dark timber, canyons and waterfalls. But, beautiful as it is, one might have the sense of confinement there. The skyline in all directions is close at hand, the high wall of the woods and deep cleavages of shade. There is a perfect freedom in the mountains, but it belongs to the eagle and the elk, the badger and the bear. The Kiowas reckoned their stature by the distance they could see, and they were bent and blind in the wilderness.

Descending eastward, the highland meadows are a stairway to the plain. In July the inland slope of the Rockies is luxuriant with flax and buckwheat, stonecrop and larkspur. The earth unfolds and the limit of the land recedes. Clusters of trees, and animals grazing far in the distance, cause the vision to reach away and wonder to build upon the mind. The sun follows a longer course in the day, and the sky is immense beyond all comparison. The great billowing clouds that sail upon it are shadows that move upon the grain like water, dividing light. Farther down, in the land of the Crows and Blackfeet, the plain is yellow. Sweet clover takes hold of the hills and bends upon itself to cover and seal the soil. There the Kiowas paused on their way; they had come to the place where they must change their lives. The sun is at home on the plains. Precisely there does it have the certain character of a god. When the Kiowas came to the land of the Crows, they could see the dark lees① of the hills at dawn across the Bighorn River, the profusion of light on the grain shelves, the oldest deity ranging after the solstices. Not yet would they veer southward to the caldron of the land that lay below; they must wean

---

①   the dark lees: figuratively, the remains.

· 359 ·

their blood from the northern winter and hold the mountains a while longer in their view. They bore Tai-me in procession to the east.

A dark mist lay over the Black Hills, and the land was like iron. At the top of a ridge I caught sight of Devil's Tower upthrust against the gray sky as if in the birth of time the core of the earth had broken through its crust and the motion of the world was begun. There are things in nature that engender an awful quiet in the heart of man; Devil's Tower is one of them. Two centuries ago, because they could not do otherwise, the Kiowas made a legend at the base of the rock. My grandmother said:

> *Eight children were there at play, seven sisters and their brother. Suddenly the boy was struck dumb; he trembled and began to run upon his hands and feet. His fingers became claws, and his body was covered with fur. Directly there was a bear where the boy had been. The sisters were terrified; they ran, and the bear after them. They came to the stump of a great tree, and the tree spoke to them. It bade them climb upon it, and as they did so it began to rise into the air. The bear came to kill them, but they were just beyond its reach. It reared against the tree and scored the bark all around with its claws. The seven sisters were borne into the sky, and they became the stars of the Big Dipper.*

From that moment, and so long as the legend lives, the Kiowas have kinsmen in the night sky. Whatever they were in the mountains, they could be no more. However tenuous their well-being, however much they had suffered and would suffer again, they had found a way out of the wilderness.

My grandmother had a reverence for the sun, a holy regard that now is all but gone out of mankind. There was a wariness in her, and an ancient awe. She was a Christian in her later years, but she had come a long way about, and she never forgot her birthright. As a child she had been to the Sun Dances; she had taken part in those annual rites, and by them she had learned the restoration of her people in the presence of Tai-me. She was about seven when the last Kiowa Sun Dance was held in 1887 on the Washita River above Rainy Mountain Creek. The buffalo were gone. In order to consummate the ancient sacrifice — to impale the head of a buffalo bull upon the medicine tree — a delegation of old men journeyed into Texas, there to beg and barter for an animal from the Goodnight herd. She was ten when the Kiowas came together for the last time as a living Sun Dance culture. They could find no buffalo; they had to hang an old hide from the sacred tree. Before the dance could begin, a company of soldiers rode out from Fort Sill under orders to disperse the tribe. Forbidden without cause the essential act of their faith, having seen the wild herds slaughtered and left to rot upon the ground, the Kiowas backed away forever from the medicine tree. That was July 20, 1890, at the great bend of the Washita. My grandmother was there. Without bitterness, and for as long as she lived, she bore a vision of deicide.

Now that I can have her only in memory, I see my grandmother in the several postures that were peculiar to her: standing at the wood stove on a winter morning and turning meat in a great iron skillet; sitting at the south window, bent above her beadwork, and afterwards, when her vision failed, looking down for a long time into the fold of her hands; going out upon a cane, very slowly as she did when the weight of age came upon her; praying. I remember her most often at prayer. She made long, rambling prayers out of suffering and hope, having seen many things. I was never sure that I had the right to hear, so exclusive were they of all mere custom and company. The last time I saw her she prayed standing by the side of her bed at night, naked to the waist, the light of a kerosene lamp moving upon her dark skin. Her long, black hair, always drawn and braided in the day, lay upon her shoulders and against her breasts like a shawl. I do not speak Kiowa, and I never understood her prayers, but there was something inherently sad in the sound, some merest hesitation upon the syllables of sorrow. She began in a high and descending pitch, exhausting her breath to silence; then again and again — and always the same intensity of effort, of something that is, and is not, like urgency in the human voice. Transported so in the dancing light among the shadows of her room, she seemed beyond the reach of time. But that was illusion; I think I knew then that I should not see her again.

Houses are like sentinels in the plain, old keepers of the weather watch. There, in a very little while, wood takes on the appearance of great age. All colors wear soon away in the wind and rain, and then the wood is burned gray and the grain appears and the nails turn red with rust. The windowpanes are black and opaque; you imagine there is nothing within, and indeed there are many ghosts, bones given up to the land. They stand here and there against the sky, and you approach them for a longer time than you expect. They belong in the distance; it is their domain.

Once there was a lot of sound in my grandmother's house, a lot of coming and going, feasting and talk. The summers there were full of excitement and reunion. The Kiowas are a summer people; they abide the cold and keep to themselves, but when the season turns and the land becomes warm and vital they cannot hold still; an old love of going returns upon them. The aged visitors who came to my grandmother's house when I was a child were made of lean and leather, and they bore themselves upright. They wore great black hats and bright ample shirts that shook in the wind. They rubbed fat upon their hair and wound their braids with strips of colored cloth. Some of them painted their faces and carried the scars of old and cherished enmities. They were an old council of warlords, come to remind and be reminded of who they were. Their wives and daughters served them well. The women might indulge themselves; gossip was at once the mark and compensation of their servitude. They made loud and elaborate talk among themselves, full of jest and gesture, fright and false alarm. They went abroad in fringed and flowered shawls, bright beadwork and German silver. They were at home in the kitchen, and they prepared meals that were banquets.

There were frequent prayer meetings, and great nocturnal feasts. When I was a child I played with my cousins outside, where the lamplight fell upon the ground and the singing of the old people rose up around us and carried away into the darkness. There were a lot of good things to eat, a lot of laughter and surprise. And afterwards, when the quiet returned, I lay down with my grandmother and could hear the frogs away by the river and feel the motion of the air.

Now there is a funeral silence in the rooms, the endless wake of some final word. The walls have closed in upon my grandmother's house. When I returned to it in mourning, I saw for the first time in my life how small it was. It was late at night, and there was a white moon, nearly full. I sat for a long time on the stone steps by the kitchen door. From there I could see out across the land; I could see the long row of trees by the creek, the low light upon the rolling plains, and the stars of the Big Dipper. Once I looked at the moon and caught sight of a strange thing. A cricket had perched upon the handrail, only a few inches away from me. My line of vision was such that the creature filled the moon like a fossil. It had gone there, I thought, to live and die, for there, of all places, was its small definition made whole and eternal. A warm wind rose up and purled like the longing within me.

The next morning I awoke at dawn and went out on the dirt road to Rainy Mountain. It was already hot, and the grasshoppers began to fill the air. Still, it was early in the morning, and the birds sang out of the shadows. The long yellow grass on the mountain shone in the bright light, and a scissortail hied① above the land. There, where it ought to be, at the end of a long and legendary way, was my grandmother's grave. Here and there on the dark stones were ancestral names. Looking back once, I saw the mountain and came away.

▶▶ Questions for Consideration and Discussion

1. How does the author combine the telling of his grandmother's story with his exploration of the history of his Kiowa ancestors? In what ways, do you think, does the narrator capture the culture of the Kiowas? Give details from the selection to support your opinion.

2. According to their origin myth, how did the Kiowa enter the world? Why does the author say that from one point of view, their migration was the fruit of an old prophecy?

3. How does the author feel about his Kiowa identity? Is it important for a person to seek his/her roots to understand his/her identity? What do you find exciting about the Kiowa heritage?

4. How did the author's grandmother regard the sun? Did she forget her birthright after becoming a Christian in her later years?

5. How does this modern Native story compare to the historical chants from the beginning of the literature course?

---

① hied: went quickly.